Lecture Notes in Computer Science   11112

Commenced Publication in 1973
Founding and Former Series Editors:
Gerhard Goos, Juris Hartmanis, and Jan van Leeuwen

More information about this series at http://www.springer.com/series/7409

Esteban Clua · Licinio Roque
Artur Lugmayr · Pauliina Tuomi (Eds.)

Entertainment Computing – ICEC 2018

17th IFIP TC 14 International Conference
Held at the 24th IFIP World Computer Congress, WCC 2018
Poznan, Poland, September 17–20, 2018
Proceedings

 Springer

Editors
Esteban Clua (iD)
Fluminense Federal University
Niteroi, Rio de Janeiro
Brazil

Licinio Roque (iD)
University of Coimbra
Coimbra
Portugal

Artur Lugmayr (iD)
Curtin University
Perth, WA
Australia

Pauliina Tuomi (iD)
Tampere University of Technology
Pori
Finland

ISSN 0302-9743   ISSN 1611-3349 (electronic)
Lecture Notes in Computer Science
ISBN 978-3-319-99425-3   ISBN 978-3-319-99426-0 (eBook)
https://doi.org/10.1007/978-3-319-99426-0

Library of Congress Control Number: 2018952237

LNCS Sublibrary: SL3 – Information Systems and Applications, incl. Internet/Web, and HCI

This Springer imprint is published by the registered company Springer Nature Switzerland AG
The registered company address is: Gewerbestrasse 11, 6330 Cham, Switzerland

Preface

This LNCS volume collects all contributions that were accepted for the 17th edition of the International Conference on Entertainment Computation 2018 (IFIP-ICEC 2018). IFIP-ICEC is the longest lasting conference on entertainment computation, with a series of successful conferences held in São Paulo, Brazil (2013), Sydney, Australia (2014), Trondheim, Norway (2015), Vienna, Austria (2016), and Tsukuba, Japan (2017). This year's event was held in Poznan, Poland, during September 17–20, 2018, and was co-located with the IFIP World Computer Congress (WCC 2018).

Overall, we received 66 submissions by authors from several countries across Europe, North and South America, Asia, and Australia. Each submission underwent a rigorous review process and received at least three reviewers by members of the entertainment computation community. Eventually, we accepted 14 full papers, 14 short papers, nine posters, one demo, four workshop proposals, and two art and exhibition entries. Furthermore, the workshop on "Designing Entertainment for the Aging Population" (DEAP 2018; five papers), and the workshop on "Entertainment Computing – A Key for Improving Inclusion and Reducing Gender Gap?" (four papers) also provided their papers for this conference proceedings volume. Several workshop submissions included in the proceedings were reviewed double-blind. The conference also hosted two other workshops, entitled "Bio-Sensing Platforms for Wellness Entertainment System Design," and the workshop on "Robot Competitions."

IFIP-ICEC 2018 innovated several aspects of the conference: an emerging topics paper track was added to provide a forum for emerging new topics; art exhibition and interactive sessions enriched the conference with more creative types of contributions; the IFIP-ICEC award was introduced to promote best contributions; and thematic areas were introduced to broaden the thematic cover of the conference. The areas added in 2018 covered the topics of human–computer interaction; entertainment systems and technology; digital games; and entertainment business, information systems and media studies. Besides these novelties, the conference called for full papers, short papers, posters, demonstrations, and doctoral consortium papers. The conference program was enriched by two keynote speakers – Prof. Ellen Yi-Luen Do from the University of Colorado Boulder (USA) and Prof. Aisling Kelliher from the Institute for Creativity, Arts, and Technology (USA), contributing with their views on the latest developments in entertainment computing.

We would like to thank all Program Committee members for their hard work, and as a surprise to us as organizers, all reviews were conducted on time. Therefore, we would truly like to thank them for their hard work. We also would like to thank Poznan University of Technology, Poland, which organized the WCC 2018 event, for their help and support. We especially would like to express our gratitude to all the Organizing Committee members, especially our area chairs. Many thanks also go to our

sponsors, the International Federation for Information Processing (IFIP), and the IFIP
World Computer Congress (IFIP-WCC 2018) for supporting this year's conference.

July 2018

Esteban Clua
Licinio Roque
Pauliina Tuomi
Artur Lugmayr

Organization

Program Committee

Alexander Hofmann	University of Applied Sciences FH Technikum Wien, Austria
Anton Nijholt	University of Twente, The Netherlands
Antonio J. Fernández Leiva	Universidad de Málaga, Spain
Artur Lugmayr	Curtin University, Australia
Benedikt Berger	Ludwig Maximilian University of Munich, Germany
Chris Geiger	University of Applied Sciences Düsseldorf, Germany
Elpida Tzafestas	National Technical University of Athens, Greece
Esteban Clua	Universidade Federal Fluminense, Brazil
Flavio S. Correa Da Silva	University of São Paulo, Brazil
Guenter Wallner	University of Applied Arts Vienna, Austria
Haruhiro Katayose	Kwansei Gakuin University, Japan
Helmut Hlavacs	University of Vienna, Austria
Hyun Seung Yang	Korea Advanced Institute of Science and Technology, South Korea
Ines Di Loreto	UTT - Université de Technologie de Troyes, France
Irene Mavrommati	Hellenic Open University, School of Applied Arts, Greece
Jannicke Baalsrud Hauge	Bremer Institut für Produktion und Logistik/University of Bremen, Germany
Javier Gomez	Universidad Autónoma de Madrid, Spain
Joaquim Madeira	University of Aveiro, Portugal
Johanna Pirker	Graz University of Technology, Austria
Junghyun Han	Korea University, South Korea
Junichi Hoshino	University of Tsukuba, Japan
Jussi Holopainen	University of Lincoln, USA
Kathrin Maria Gerling	Katholieke Universiteit Leuven, Belgium
Kendra Cooper	Independent
Licinio Roque	University of Coimbra, Portugal
Luca Chittaro	HCI Lab, University of Udine, Italy
Maic Masuch	University of Duisburg-Essen, Germany
Marc Cavazza	University of Greenwich, UK
Marc Herrlich	University of Kaiserslautern (TUK), Germany
Maria Letizia Jaccheri	Norwegian University of Science and Technology, Norway
Matthias Rauterberg	Eindhoven University of Technology, The Netherlands
Monica Divitini	Norwegian University of Science and Technology, Norway

Nikitas Sgouros   University of Piraeus, Greece
Owen Noel Newton   Nanyang Technological University, Singapore
  Fernandon
Paolo Ciancarini   University of Bologna, Italy
Pauliina Tuomi   Tampere University of Technology, Finland
Pedro González Calero   Universidad Politécnica de Madrid, Spain
Radu Daniel Vatavu   Universitatea Stefan cel Mare Suceava, Romania
Rafael Bidarra   Delft University of Technology, The Netherlands
Rainer Malaka   University of Bremen, Germany
Rui Craveirinha   University of Coimbra, Portugal
Ryohei Nakatsu   Kyoto University, Japan
Simone Kriglstein   Vienna University of Technology, Austria
Sobah Abbas Petersen   Norwegian University of Science and Technology,
                                         Norway
Staffan Björk   University of Gothenburg, Sweden
Sung-Bae Cho   Yonsei University, Japan
Teresa Romão   Universidade NOVA de Lisboa, Portugal
Tim Marsh   Griffith University, Australia
Valentina Nisi   Carnegie Mellon|Portugal, University of Madeira,
                                         Portugal
Valter Alves   Polytechnical Institute of Viseu, Portugal
Walt Scacchi   University of California, Irvine, USA
Werner Gaisbauer   University of Vienna, Austria
Zlatogor Minchev   IICT-BAS, Bulgaria
Zvezdan Vukanovic   Abu Dhabi University, UAE

Contents

Short Papers

Posters

Demonstration

Art Exhibition

Workshops

Full Papers

Dynamic Projection Mapping on Multiple Non-rigid Moving Objects for Stage Performance Applications

Ryohei Nakatsu[1](✉), Ningfeng Yang[1], Hirokazu Takata[2],
Takashi Nakanishi[2], Makoto Kitaguchi[3], and Naoko Tosa[4]

[1] NT & Associates, Kyoto, Japan
nakatsu.ryohei@gmail.com, yangnf@gmail.com
[2] TakumiVision, Kyoto, Japan
{takata,nakanishi}@takumivision.co.jp
[3] TECHMAC, Kyoto, Japan
makoto.kitaguchi@techne-magic.co.jp
[4] Graduate School of Advanced Integrated Studies in Human Survivability,
Kyoto University, Kyoto, Japan
tosa.naoko.5c@kyoto-u.ac.jp

Abstract. In this paper we have proposed and developed a projection mapping system that can project 3D images on multiple moving objects that change their positions and shapes. Although projection mapping has become a new type of image projection method, so far most of the projection mappings have focused on the projection of 3D images on objects such as buildings that stay static without changing their shapes. If projection mapping on non-rigid moving objects such as human performers is realized, application area of projection mapping will become far wider.

To demonstrate this, a simple test of integrating projection mapping and Noh performance was carried out. Although Noh performance has been considered difficult to understand for beginners and foreigners because of its minimalism, by projecting 2D images that suggest inner emotion of a main character and also ongoing story, the evaluation result show that this new type of Noh performance could make it easier to be understood. This means that the integration of projection mapping and various stage performances could open-up new possibilities for various kinds of performing arts to add their values.

To realize this, we have proposed a projection mapping system consisting of multiple depth sensors and multiple projectors. In the first step, using multiple depth sensors the position and shape of multiple objects are detected in real time and the obtained 3D models of the multiple objects are sent to the projection phase. In the projection phase, the images to be projected on the objects are rendered on the obtained 3D model of the object. Then using multiple projectors real-time 3D projection mapping is carried out on the multiple moving objects. The system is now under development and demonstration of actual Noh performance using this technology will be achieved.

Keywords: Projection mapping · Depth sensor · Moving object
Performing arts · Noh performance · Japanese culture · Inner emotion
Media art

© IFIP International Federation for Information Processing 2018
Published by Springer Nature Switzerland AG 2018. All Rights Reserved
E. Clua et al. (Eds.): ICEC 2018, LNCS 11112, pp. 3–15, 2018.
https://doi.org/10.1007/978-3-319-99426-0_1

1 Introduction

Projection mapping is a technology to project 3D images/videos on 3D objects such as buildings [1, 2]. As this is one area of Augmented Reality, sometimes projection mapping has been called Spatial Augmented Reality [3]. Conventional projection has been done onto a rectangular flat screen. Once a projection onto a 3D object such as a building is realized by adopting the projection to the shape of the object, it is possible to give the impression that the building has changed into something different.

So far, it seems that the aims of projection mapping have been limited only to entertainment such as a show at a theme park [4] or ceremonial event [5]. In most of these cases images used for the event are made of computer graphics and include entertaining contents. If art contents would be used for projection mapping, however, such projection mapping would create new possibility by changing art exhibition spaces from closed space such as museums and galleries to open public spaces such as city centers, parks, etc. Two of the authors of this paper, Naoko Tosa and Ryohei Nakatsu, have noticed the possibility of projection mapping for such new applications, and have been working on the projection mapping events using Naoko Tosa's media artworks as the contents. Below are two of such events carried out the by them.

(1) Projection mapping at ArtScience Museum in Singapore
    Naoko Tosa has been working on the creation of media art based on the concept of integrating Japanese tradition and her modern media art, and based on this she has been working on various projects of letting Japanese traditional/modern art to be understood by people not only in Japan but also in overseas. As one of such activities she has created a new media art called "Sound of Ikebana: Four Seasons," in which she let liquid such as color paint jumping up by giving it sound vibration, and then by shooting the generated form using high-speed camera she succeeded in merging her Japanese sensitivity with technologies [6] [7]. Funded by METI (Ministry of Economy, Trade and Industry), the projection mapping using this media art as the content was carried out in 2014 at ArtScience Museum in Singapore (Fig. 1). As in Singapore there is no clear difference among each season, this projection mapping focusing the clear transition from one season to

Fig. 1. A scene of the projection mapping of "Sound of Ikebana" carried out at ArtScience Museum in Singapore.

another in Japan gave a strong impression about Japan and Japanese culture to the people in Singapore and nearby countries. The event gathered lots of audience and various media in Singapore treated this event.

(2) Projection mapping at Kyoto National Museum

Year 2015 was the 400 anniversary of famous Japanese art school called RIMPA [8] and in Kyoto there were many events celebrating the anniversary. As one of those events Kyoto Prefectural Government called for a projection mapping event. Submitting our proposal responding to this call for event and being accepted by the local government, Naoko Tosa and Ryohei Nakatsu have created a media art called "Thunder God and Wind God in 21st Century." Using this media art as the content, they carried out the projection mapping in March 2015 at Kyoto National Museum [9].

When a RIMPA exhibition is carried out, the usual way is to exhibit one or several of famous RIMPA paintings as the core of the event. However, RIMPA is not a simple heritage that existed long time ago. On the other hand, RIMPA is an art concept that has to be handed to the present and even to the future [8]. Therefore, they tried to create new RIMPA-style content. Also to appeal the modernity of RIMPA, it is adequate to connect technology and content. Therefore they introduced several cutting-edge technologies in the content creation process. For the projection, twenty most recent high-end projectors with more than 20,000 lm were used to project the created video content onto the two buildings of Kyoto National Museum. The event gathered almost 20,000 people during the four-day event and was successful. Figure 2 shows a scene of the projection mapping.

Fig. 2. A scene of projection mapping of "21 Centuries Wind God and Thunder God in 21st Century" at Kyoto National Museum

Through these event, we came to the belief that art contents very well fits the new image expression method such as projection mapping. In Kyoto, because of its long-time history and tradition, traditional performing art such as "Noh" is frequently performed. Therefore, we came to an idea of integrating Noh performance and projection mapping using art content. Also, this idea could be applied to other traditional performance such as Kabuki, dance performance, etc. and could open a new possibility for new type of traditional performance and performing arts. Unfortunately, so far most of the projection mapping events have been limited to those where objects for the projection mapping do not move and do not change their shapes. If the above idea is to be realized, it is necessary to develop projection mapping technologies that can realize projection mapping on moving non-rigid object. This idea led us to the development of the new technology described in this paper.

The structure of this paper is the following. In Sect. 2, a simple experiment where integration of Noh performance and 2D projection mapping is realized is described. Based on the evaluation of this experiment, the basic concept of projection mapping on non-rigid moving object is introduced. In Sect. 3, Related works on projection mapping is described. In Sect. 4, overview of the whole system, technologies for tracking 3D objects and extracting 3D model of the objects, and technologies for 3D projection mapping on the moving non-rigid objects using the obtained 3D models are described. And Sect. 5 concludes the paper.

2   Integration of Noh Performance and Projection Mapping: Projection Mapping on Non-rigid Moving Objects

As is described in the introduction, we, based on the belief that the integration of projection mapping and art would give a new value to traditional performing art such as Noh, carried out the trial of achieving projection mapping onto Noh performers and Noh background.

"Noh" is globally well known because of its condensed and abstracted body movement and speech, which can be called "minimalism" [10]. Because of this minimalism, however, it is very difficult for foreigners and even for Japanese Noh beginners to understand the story development of Noh play. It is a key issue for Noh, if Japan wants to appeal globally the charm of Noh, to be understood by foreigners and Japanese beginners keeping its sophistication and aesthetics. For this difficult challenge, we think that integration of Noh and projection mapping would be able to create a new style of Noh performance in which Noh would be more easily understood and appreciated. Our idea is to project images onto a Noh performer and background. For example, one idea is to project images that would indicate the inner emotion of the main character acted by the Noh performer. Also, it would be interesting to project images that indicate the story development on the background wall.

Based on such concept we have developed a simple system in which 2D projection is carried out on a Noh performer and background wall. In this case it is necessary for the system to trace the position and posture of the Noh performer and to carry out the projection. Figure 3 illustrates the system setting on the Noh stage and Fig. 4 illustrates how the trial of the Noh performance was carried out. Although this was a closed performance carried out at Kyoto University, the main character of the Noh performance was acted by a very famous Noh player in Kyoto. Therefore, the aesthetics the original Noh performance had was maintained and the viewers could judge whether projection of two types of images really increased the value of the original Noh performance or not.

In this trial, Microsoft Kinect was used as a position sensor. Microsoft Kinect has the capability of detecting a position and a posture of a person using infrared depth sensor and we have used this function. Based on this trial it was revealed that, as the major application area of Kinect is gaming, the preciseness of the function of detecting person's position and posture is not satisfactory. Also we recognized that in artistic performance such as Noh, such precision is the key to add values to such performance. At the same time we understood that the angle range of the Kinect for the human detection is narrow and it is difficult for it to trace the movement of a Noh player who moves around a wide Noh stage.

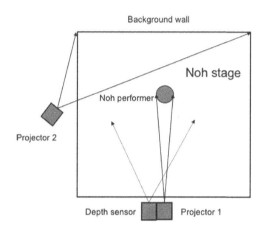

Fig. 3. Stage setting of projection on Noh performance.

Fig. 4. A scene of traial experiement of projection on Noh performance

At the same time, however, we found that this new trial of integrating projection mapping, although it was a simple 2D projection mapping, and Noh performance was highly appreciated by viewers as a new Noh performing style. Especially international students who joined this experimental trial expressed that, although beforehand they thought Noh is difficult to understand because of slow and subtle movements of Noh performers, this new Noh style was easier for them to understand both the ongoing story and also the inner emotion of a Noh character. Also they expressed thatand, this new trial could create new Noh performance style.

This means that, if we could develop a system that can trace the position and posture of a Noh performer who moves around a Noh stage and carry out projection mapping on the moving Noh performer, we could expand the possibility of not only traditional performance such as Noh but also other stage performances including art and entertainment. Also, when we showed this results to the organizer and director of various events, they told us that this system could be applied not only to stage performances but also to other areas such as fashion shows, live events, wedding ceremonies, etc. and could add new value and charm to these events/shows. Therefore, we believe that the development of dynamic projection mapping on moving non-rigid objects has the possibility of creating new market for projection mapping.

3   Related Works

Shader Lamps [11] is a pioneering research showing the possibility of projection mapping by making it possible to project images on objects with complicated shapes. Since then various types of projection mapping has been proposed, but most of them have been limited to static and/or rigid objects [12, 13].

To overcome these restrictions, recently various studies focusing dynamic projection mapping on moving objects have been reported. The key technology for dynamic projection mapping is how to detect/trace the position and shape of moving objects. There are several ways to approach this key issue.

One is to utilize the texture on the object and by using image processing technologies to trace the position and also the shape of the target object [14, 15]. Although these texture-based methods have the advantage that they don't need any additional equipment for the detection of the position and shape of the object, these methods have several problems. For example, the tracking performance depends on the texture itself and its density. Also, the lighting, especially the lighting of projection mapping itself, would influence the accuracy of the tracing very much.

Another method to precisely trace the object is the usage of markers. Compared with texture-based methods, the usage of markers can achieve more robust tracking, as the markers could be designed optimally depending on the type of the object, its movement, etc. [16, 17]. Probably one of the most notable research among them is by Narita et al. [18] that presents a projection mapping system that is able to dynamically project onto moving objects. They use a 1000 fps camera and galvanometer mirrors to track and illuminate the object with a single projector. The resulting tracking is extremely fast and impressive results are achieved. However, this research needs special equipment such as high-speed camera and high-speed projector, and is limited only to experimental environment.

Recently by the emergence of depth camera that, by using infra-red beamer and detector, can detect the distance between the sensor and many points on the target object. Especially by the introduction of Microsoft Kinect that has this capability and that could be purchased by reasonable price, many researcher have used this sensor for the detection of moving object [19, 20]. However, Kinect has been developed mainly aiming the gaming situation in which gamers would do physical actions just in front of the sensor, and therefore its effective range including distance to the object and the angle between the object and the sensor is narrowly limited. Because of this, the usage of Kinect has restricted the trial of dynamic projection mapping to only experimental use.

Compared with these previous achievements, the system we propose and are developing has the below originality.

(1) Most of the previous works have stayed only at research stage. Some used markers that is cumbersome in actual applications. Others used special hardware such as a high-speed projector that is expensive and is not adequate for actual applications. On the other hand, we aim to develop dynamic projection mapping system focusing actual application such as Noh performance, dance performance, etc. by using off-the-shelf equipment.

(2) In actual stage performances, it is natural that multiple performers achieve the performances. By preparing multiple depth-sensors and by merging the obtained results, we try to detect and trace the position and shapes of multiple performers. Also by using multiple projectors, we try to achieve 3D projection mapping on multiple performers avoiding the problem of occlusion.

4 Structure of the System

4.1 Basic Structure of the System

The basic concept of our dynamic projection mapping system on non-rigid moving objects is illustrated by Fig. 5. As the dynamic projection mapping on non-rigid moving objects is the target of the topic, we neglect the projection mapping on background wall and focus on the projection mapping on multiple moving performers.

It is hypothesized that the width of the stage would be 6 m × 6 m (the size of Nor stage is 6 m × 6 m). Two depth sensors and two projectors are set at the two edge positions of the front side of the stage (position 1 and position 2). In our first trial we tried to set a projector and a sensor at the same place as much as possible so that the calibration between the sensor and the projector is not necessary. However, in our setting we have decided that there should be freedom for the position of depth sensors and projectors as we have introduced calibration process. It is considered that this is the basic unit system and when the stage is wider than 6 m, multiple basic unit system will be used to cover the whole stage.

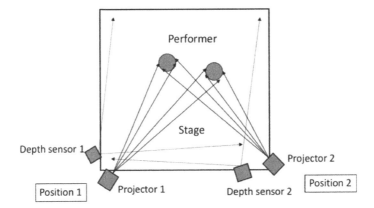

Fig. 5. Conceptual illustration of projection mapping system on non-rigid moving objects.

The sensors 1 and 2 detect and trace the positions and shapes of multiple performers and by merging the detection results the 3D models of multiple performers are constructed. Then the images to be projected on the performers are rendered on the 3D models and using multiple projectors the projection mapping is to be carried out. By using a single sensor, the obtained model is not complete 3D model. Also, as there are multiple performers, the problem of occlusion frequently occurs. The usage of multiple sensors will solve these problems to satisfactory extent. Also, in the projection stage, although the projection on a performer by the projector 1 is achieved only on the front side of the performer, projector 2 can do the supplementary role by projecting on the performer on different side of it, providing satisfactory projection result to the viewers. Figure 6 illustrates the structure of the software of the system.

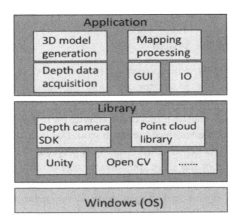

Fig. 6. Construction of the software of the projection mapping system

4.2   Tracking of Moving Objects Using Depth Sensors

The process flow of the detection and tracking of moving objects using depth sensors is illustrated in Fig. 7. Below are several explanation of the each process.

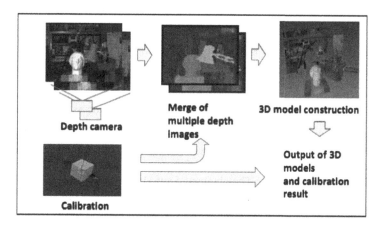

Fig. 7. Process flow of the detection and tracking of moving objects

Calibration

As the positions of two depth sensors and two projectors are different, calibration among these devices is necessary to be carried out. As a first step, calibration among the projector 1 and the depth sensors 1, 2 is carried out. The calibration is carried out by projecting several grid patterns on some object by the projector 1 and by detecting the patterns by the cameras mounted on each of the depth sensors 1, 2. Also the calibration among the projector 2 and the depth sensors 1, 2 is carried out by the projector 2 projecting grid patterns and by the cameras of the depth sensors 1, 2 detecting the patterns. These processes realize the calibration among each of the four devices, the depth sensors 1, 2 and the projectors 1, 2.

Depth Image Acquisition by Multiple Depth Sensors

Then two depth images, depth image 1 and depth image 2, of the moving objects in front of the depth sensors are obtained by the depth sensor 1 and depth sensor 2.

For the depth sensor we used Kinect. However, instead of using the software development kit provided by Microsoft, we developed the necessary software by ourselves. By doing so we found that the limitations of Kinect, distance limitation and angle range limitation, is largely reduced. Now the device can detect object within 8 m distance instead of original 3 m capability. Also for angle range, objects within 90° range can be detected instead of original 60° range.

Merge of Multiple Depth Images

Then these two depth images are merged. For the depth image 2, based on the result of the calibration, it is converted the depth image 2', which is the depth image obtained at the position of the depth sensor 1, and then the two images are merged. As the depth image obtained by the depth sensor 2 covers the area that cannot been seen by the depth sensor 1, this merge will make the obtained depth image more precise.

3D Image Construction
The depth data, which is a set of points data with its position in the world coordinate system and distance from the depth sensors, is considered to construct the 3D image of the surroundings. The obtained 3D image is sent to the next stage for the 3D projection mapping.

4.3   Projection Mapping on Moving Objects

The process flow of the projection mapping on moving objects and tracking is illustrated in Fig. 8. Below are several explanation of the each process.

Object Detection and Conversion
From the set of depth data, depth data set corresponding to the moving objects to be tracked are detected. For the detection the distance between each depth data and the depth sensor is used for the key. The obtained depth data set is considered as 3D model data of the objects to be tracked and to be projected. Then this 3D model is converted into two models; 3D model 1 is the model of the object seen from the position of the projector 1 and 3D model 2 is the model from the position of the projector 2.

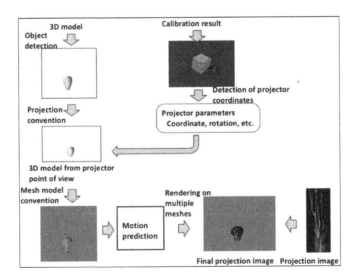

Fig. 8. The flow of the 3D projection mapping on moving objects.

Mesh Model Conversion
Still at this stage each model is a set of depth point data. From these point data relevant mesh data that construct the surface the objects are determined. As the number of the meshes greatly influences the calculation time of the rendering described below, the number of the meshes is to be determined carefully taking the PC's calculation

capability into consideration. As the model 1 and model 2 provide supplementary 3D model for the objects, the meshes for the projection 1 should focus on the planes situated in front of the projector 1 and for projector 2 vice versa.

Motion Prediction
While our system should run at real-time frame rates, the object tracking suffers from delays introduced by the round trip time through our computation pipeline for tracking. This is noticeable as a lag between the actual position and shape of a performer and the projected image. Since this effect impairs the immersion for the user, motion prediction is to be implemented in our system. We use a statistically based predictor to fit a spline into the past N frames that is extrapolated to predict the tracking trajectory. An additional weighted low-pass filter over new frames improves the robustness against outliers.

Rendering of Projection Images and Output
Finally, the image to be projected on the object are rendered on each of the detected meshes both for the projector 1 and the projector 2. Then the final projection is carried out using the projectors 1 and 2.

5 Conclusion

In this paper we have proposed the projection mapping system that can project 3D images onto multiple non-rigid moving objects. Although projection mapping has become a new image/video projection method for entertainment and other applications, most of the projection mapping so far proposed have the function of projecting 3D images on objects such as buildings that do not move and do not change their shapes. On the other hand, if projection mapping on non-rigid moving objects such as Noh performers or dancers is realized, the application area of projection mapping will become far wider.

To confirm this assumption, as a first step we have carried out a simple experiment in which the integration of projection mapping and Noh performance, one of the most well known Japanese traditional stage performance, was carried out. In the experiment two types of video images were projected while Noh performance was carrying out. Video images that suggest the Noh story development was projected on the back wall of the stage. In addition to this, 2D video images that suggest inner emotion of a Noh main character was projected on the Noh performer. Based on the interview-based evaluation of the system, viewers of the performance, especially most of the international students who viewed the performance, replied that, although the projected images were only 2D the produced effect was very immersive and also the Noh performance became easier to understand. Based on this experiment, we came to the belief that the integration of stage performance such as Noh and projection mapping has the possibility of creating new types of performing arts.

Based on this, we have proposed the concept of a projection mapping system that can trace the positions and shapes of moving object and can achieve 3D projection mapping on the moving objects, and developed the first prototype of the system. From hardware aspect, the system consists of multiple depth sensors and also multiple projectors and PCs. From software aspect the system consists of two parts; the objects detection part and the 3D projection part. In the object detection part, multiple depth sensors detect and trace the positions and shapes of multiple moving non-rigid objects such as dancers or performers, compose 3D models for each of the objects and give them to the projection part. Because of the usage of multiple depth sensors, even if multiple objects are moving around such as in dance performances, precise detection of positions and postures of the multiple moving objects became possible. Then in the projection mapping part, using the obtained 3D model of the objects, the object is represented as a mesh model, in which each mesh is a plane, and the images to be projected on these moving objects are rendered on these meshes and then projected on the moving objects.

The system is now being brushed up and will be used for a Noh performance as a first application of the system. The demonstration video will be shown at the time of the paper presentation.

References

1. Murayama, S., Torii, I., Ishii, N.: Development of projection mapping with utility of digital signage. In: IIAI 3rd International Conference on Advanced Applied Informatics, pp. 895–900 (2014)
2. Rowe, A.: Designing for engagement in mixed reality experiences that combine projection mapping and camera-based interaction. Digit. Creat. **25**(2), 155–168 (2013)
3. Bimber, O., Raskar, R.: Spatial Augmented Reality; Merging Real and Virtual Worlds. CRC Press, Boca Raton (2005)
4. Mine, M., Rose, D., Yang, B., van Baar, J., Grundhofer, A.: Projection-based augmented reality in Disney theme parks. Computer **45**(7), 32–40 (2012)
5. Maniello, D.: Augmented Reality in Public Spaces Basic Techniques for Video Mapping, vol. 1. Paperback (2015)
6. Tosa, N., Nakatsu, R., Yunian, P.: Creation of media art utilizing fluid dynamics. In: 2017 International Conference on Culture and Computing, pp. 130–135 (2017)
7. Yunian, P, Liang, Z., Nakatsu, R., Tosa, N.: A study of variable control of Sound Vibration Form (SVF) for media art creation. In: 2017 International Conference on Culture and Computing, pp. 137–142 (2017)
8. Yasumura, T.: Rimpa: Decorative Japanese Painting. PIE Books (2011)
9. Tosa, N., Nakatsu, R., Yunian, P.: Projection mapping celebrating RIMPA 400th Anniversary. In: 2015 International Conference on Culture and Computing (2015)
10. Sadler, A.L.: Japanese Plays: Classic Noh, Kyogen and Kabuki Works. Tuttle Publishing, Clarendon (2011)
11. Raskar, R., Welch, G., Low, K.L., Bandyopadhyay, D.: Shader lamps: animating real objects with image-based illumination. In: Gortler, S.J., Myszkowski, K. (eds.) Rendering Techniques 2001. Eurographics. Springer, Vienna (2001)
12. Bimber, O., Iwai, D., Wetzstein, G., Grundhofer, A.: The visual computing of projector-camera systems. Comput. Graph. Forum **27**(8), 2219–2245 (2008)
13. Fua, P., Leclerc, Y.G.: Object-centered surface reconstruction: combining multi-image stereo and shading. Int. J. Comput. Vis. **16**(1), 35–56 (1995)

14. Gay-Bellile, V., Bartoli, A., Sayd, P.: Deformable surface augmentation in spite of self-occlusions. In: Proceedings of 6th IEEE ACM International Symposium on Mixed Augmented Reality, pp. 235–238 (2007)

15. Uchiyama, H., Marchand, E.: Object detection and pose tracking for augmented reality: recent approaches. In: Proceedings of 18th Korea-Japan Joint Workshop Frontiers Computer Vision, pp. 1–8 (2012)

16. Park, H., Park, J.-I.: Invisible marker based augmented reality system. In: Proceedings of SPIE Visual Communication Image Processing, Art. No. 59601 (2006)

17. Guskov, I.: Efficient tracking of regular patterns on non-ridig geometry. In: Proceedings of 16th International Conference on Pattern Recognition, vol. 2, pp. 1057–1060 (2002)

18. Narita, G., Watanabe, Y., Ishikawa, M.: Dynamic projctin mapping onto deforming non-ridig surface using deformable dot cluster marker. IEEE Trans. Visual. Comput. Graph. **23** (3), 1235–1248 (2017)

19. Jones, B.R., Benko, H., Ofek, E., Wilson, A.D.: Illumiroom: peripheral projected illusions for interactive experiences. In: ACM SIGGRAPH 2013 Emerging Technologies, SIGGRAPH 2013, p. 7:1. ACM, New York (2013)

20. Siegl, C., et al.: Real-time pixel luminance optimization for dynamic multi-projection mapping. ACM Trans. Graph. **34**(6), 237:1–237:11 (2015)

Applying Design Thinking
for Prototyping a Game Controller

Gabriel Ferreira Alves[✉], Emerson Vitor Souza, Daniela Gorski Trevisan,
Anselmo Antunes Montenegro, Luciana Cardoso de Castro Salgado,
and Esteban Walter Gonzalez Clua

Universidade Federal Fluminense, Instituto de Computação,
Niterói, RJ 24210-310, Brazil
{gabrielferreiraalves,esouza}@id.uff.br,
{daniela,anselmo,luciana,esteban}@ic.uff.br

Abstract. Game controllers design is undergoing a major shift due to
the disruptive forces of new paradigms of interaction and a wide set of
game genres. With so many approaches involving this device, in this work
we want to address the challenge of generating ideas for a totally new and
innovative game controller that pleases its players. In order to achieve
this objective, we applied a set of Design Thinking techiques such as one
day in life, empathy map, persona, ideation workshop, paper prototyping and experimental tests. The results have shown that the techniques
were useful in informing and guiding idea generation and were perceived
as appealing. Drawing on observations and participants feedbacks, we
reflect on the strengths of using this methodology to develop games controllers and discuss some of the needs that they still have.

Keywords: Gamepad · Design Thinking · Games · Controllers

1 Introduction

Digital games have become a major technological force, given the evolution
in computational power employed in it. Such area has exceeded the limits of
entertainment and have become educational, simulation and even sports tools.
Many innovations have been proposed for new game interfaces, mostly focused
in gesture and body movement interpretation and motion based sensors, such
as accelerometers and gyroscopes [15]. However, the paradigm of the traditional
gamepad has proved to be irreplaceable, with most console games still relying
on it.

With all this evolution going on in digital gaming environments, gameplay
controllers also go through evolution, though not as drastic: controllers, also
known as joysticks or gamepads, have undergone some changes over the years,
receiving more buttons, features, components and devices. Thanks to its dynamics (like touchscreen, Wi-Fi/Bluetooth connection, sensors, etc.), smartphones

E. Clua et al. (Eds.): ICEC 2018, LNCS 11112, pp. 16–27, 2018.
https://doi.org/10.1007/978-3-319-99426-0_2

have become universal controllers. Among the various types, video game controls are included. Although they have the potential to control games due to the various components present in their hardware and software, smartphones have a major disadvantage: the lack of tactile feedback. Due to the lack of physical buttons where the user can feel a return of the action being performed, the number of times he needs to look at the screen is greater than when a joystick is used, which can directly result in his performance during a game [1].

This work seeks to use a design technique that allows generating a great amount of ideas in a short period, making designers to immerse themselves in the proposed subject and thus develop solutions to the problem. Therefore, we chose Design Thinking as method because it meets these requirements and it allows to understand user needs and understand their principle problems in daily life [8]. Based on studies and researches on the various types of controllers for video games in the market and in the literature [1,2,9,16], this work seeks, through applying Design Thinking techniques, to discover the strengths and weaknesses of existent controllers and propose one or more controllers that can be used by lovers of digital games, casual gamers and even people who do not play at all.

This paper is organized in four sections, including the introduction. In Sect. 2 we present the works that relate to this. In Sect. 3 we describe the methodology and results. Finally, in Sect. 4, we conclude, summarizing our contributions and sharing new research questions and future work.

2   Related Work

When searching for images using the word "joysticks", you can find various game controllers with different formats, sizes, number of buttons and connection systems with devices that are controlled. These devices began their career by being just a little box with a button and a lever, then getting added action buttons, directional buttons, until they have wireless connections, motion sensors, and tactile screens [2]. Nintendo's latest innovative invention relies on cardboard and user creativity to build its controllers, called the Nintendo Labo™ for Nintendo Switch™ [12].

Some solutions for virtual controllers have been developed to help the player deal with the lack of tactile feedback, as can be seen in Fig. 1. Companies have developed controllers that communicate with smartphones via Wi-Fi or USB connections so that the player is able to perform action on games for mobile devices with greater excellence.

In his work, Baldauf et al. [1] did a comparative laboratory study where four gamepad designs were developed using a framework created by the authors for touchscreen smartphones, which are equivalent of existing controllers and have been tested in two popular games: the arcade game Pac-Man and the platform game Super Mario Bros. This comparative study was done seeking to make evident what the main characteristics that users would realize that physical and virtual controls have different and in common with each other.

After the application of tests with users, several participants related the gamepad with the respective physical controllers and mentioned the negative

Fig. 1. Some models of mobile controllers: (1) Grayhaus Brick Joystick [3]; (2) Ipega 9021 [7]; (3) Moga Hero Power [10].

lack of tactile feedback. The post-test comments included that the buttons were difficult to reach precisely, that the especially opposite directions were difficult to press, and thus, the looks at the device were necessary. This is the main point raised in surveys that consider the use of virtual controls. On the other hand, it was said that the control that had movement sensor and device rotation can be interesting in games that require the player to perform such movement, as in racing games, for example.

Meanwhile, Merdenyan et al. [9] review the gamepads of four video games (Logitech Gamepad F310, Microsoft Xbox 360 Controller for Windows, Dual-Shock 4 Wireless Controller for PlayStation 4 and Wii Classic Controller Pro) by users to investigate which improvements are required in their designs. The content was taken from user ratings posted on 'Amazon.com' through December 15, 2014. The sampling policy for reviews was: twenty comments for each of the four gamepads were sampled using Amazon.com's "Most Helpful First" review criteria and only the 50–500 word evaluations were sampled. The collected data revealed that the main characteristics raised on the controllers were: battery life, comfort, compatibility, durability, ease of use, functionality, layout (button positioning), quality of the material, recognition, responsiveness and user manual.

Through research carried out in academic search libraries such as Google Scholar and the ACM library, we sought to find design techniques focused on solutions for game controllers interaction. Although we could find works using Design Thinking techniques in the area of Game Design [4,6], there were no studies related to the use of Design Thinking process applied to the design of game controllers. In this direction our work describes the experience obtained and the lessons learned in using the Design Thinking process to create a unique game controller.

3   Design Thinking Application and Results

In order to find out a game controller solution that is capable to fit all kind of games interaction and still pleases its players, a study was conducted using Design Thinking as a methodology. The Design Thinking refers to the designer's way of thinking, which uses abductive thinking. In this type of thinking, it is sought to formulate questions through the apprehension or understanding of the phenomena, that is, questions are formulated to be answered from the information collected during the observation of the universe that permeates the problem [14].

Over the years, several models and pipeline proposals of Design Thinking have emerged, where each one seeks to better suit the profile and the research environment. To perform this work we used the model proposed by the Stanford d.school [14], chosen for its level of detail of processes and ease of understanding. The pipeline proposed by d.school consists of a few steps, where each step is composed of one or more techniques. Figure 2 shows the pipeline used in the design of the gaming controller. It is important to say that though we have presented this pipeline as a sequence of activities, this is not mandatory and the activities can be combined according to each project needs.

Fig. 2. The pipeline used in the design of the gaming controller.

3.1   Empathy and Immersion

The first step is called "Empathy and Immersion". At this point the project team approaches the context of the problem, both from the point of view of the designer and the end user. In order to empathize with the subject and immerse it in it, three techniques of this first stage of Design Thinking process were used: the DESK Research, where it is sought to find general knowledge about the subject matter; the Empathy Map, an artifact constructed with the purpose of knowing better the aspects related to the interaction between the user and the research environment; and the "One Day in Life", which consists of living a day in the skin of the player, seeking to understand their feelings and thoughts.

When performing the DESK Research, mainly using the material described in the related work section, some relevant data were collected. Joysticks are important tools in the world of virtual games, responsible for giving the player control of actions within games. It is this tool that integrates and separates, at the same time, the player from the virtual world. The first joysticks consisted of two boxes with two switches (for rotation and acceleration) and a firing button. Over time, the controllers have grown and evolved, gaining directional buttons, motion sensors, touchscreen contact areas and several other features [2].

After that, we considered an Empathy Map workshop with stakeholders (researchers engineers, designers, gamers and non gamers participants). Empathy maps focus on identifying what other people are thinking, feeling, doing, seeing, and hearing as they engage with a product or service. Findings obtained when creating the map are found in Fig. 3. However, while we felt like this tool was helpful in isolating their interaction with a product, we thought it lacked the context of 'real-life' or real observation on the activity of playing. Because of this, the second technique, called One Day In Life, was applied.

PLAYERS		
Positive points:	What do users hear about it?	Negative points:
• Have weight control; • Have tactile screens; • Have standardization (within the same company).	• "The control is of quality"; • "There are controls for professional players"; • "X control is better than Y control."	• They do not have accessibility; • High costs; • Low durability; • Amount of buttons • (many buttons can scare); Lack of standardization between controls.
What do users feel?	What do users say about it?	What do users see about it?
• Envy of other controls; • Happiness when using a new control; • Comfort / Discomfort; • Difficulty / ease when using a control; • Good quality/poor quality.	• "X control is better than Y control"; • "The control is of quality"; • "I like playing with this control."	• Friends playing; • YouTubers playing; • Number of buttons; • Aesthetics of control; • Professional players playing.

Fig. 3. Empathy map.

Seeking to immerse in the lives of players using multiple controllers, four models of joysticks were used to control games: Nintendo 3DS controller, Steam controller, DualShock 4 for PlayStation 4 and Xbox One controller. Some random games were played, like Portal 2, Pokemon X and Super Mario Bros using the controllers that can be seen in Fig. 4.

Fig. 4. Game controllers observed. From left to right: Nintendo 3DS, Steam, PlayStation 4 and Xbox One.

Given the variation between the number of functionalities, the layout of buttons, shape and size of the controller, some evaluations were carried out. Two of the researchers owned video games. Seeking a way to make the search valid, gamers have played games with controllers they are unfamiliar with. Researcher 1 (R1) owns a Nintendo 3DS, while Researcher 2 (R2) owns a PlayStation 4. Thus, R1 used the Steam, Xbox One and PlayStation 4 controllers to play, while R2 used the Steam, Xbox One and Nintendo 3DS controllers. A volunteer (V1), who owns the Steam and XboX One controllers, also participated in the research, running games using the Nintendo 3DS and PlayStation 4 controllers. After being tested with all controllers, the researchers and the volunteer responded to a questionnaire which was assessed using the Likert 7-point scale.

The following aspects were analyzed:

Q1: Did you feel comfortable using the controller?
Q2: Did you find the button layout pleasant?
Q3: Did you find the size of the buttons reasonable?
Q4: Would you use this controller regularly while playing?
Q5: Did you find that the controller is ergonomic?

The results can be found in the table below (Fig. 5).

	R1				R2				V1			
	N3DS	Steam	Xone	PS4	N3DS	Steam	Xone	PS4	N3DS	Steam	Xone	PS4
Q1		2	6	7	5	3	7		3			6
Q2		3	6	7	5	1	6		5			6
Q3		5	7	7	3	3	7		2			5
Q4		1	6	7	2	1	6		1			6
Q5		6	7	7	3	5	7		1			4

Fig. 5. One day in life results.

Each controller received a note from two different evaluators who did not have contact with that type of controller previously, avoiding the introduction of bias in the evaluation. The Nintendo 3DS and Steam controllers achieved lower scores when compared to the Xbox One and PlayStation 4 controllers: on ergonomic issues, button size, and hence comfort, the Nintendo 3DS is rated with low scores. The Steam controller achieved a good ergonomics rating but was unable to please players over the good response in-game. The Xbox One and PlayStation 4 controllers had high ratings and almost all the requirements, pleasing the evaluators.

3.2 Definition

The second stage of Design Thinking is called Definition. It consists of synthesizing the findings of the empathy process into compelling needs and insights. It is a mode of "focus" rather than "flaring". The purpose of the definition is to develop a deep understanding of users and the design space and, based on this understanding, present a statement of the problem - the Point of View (PoV). The Point of View defined for our research was created following the findings in the Empathy and Immersion stage, and consists of the following sentence: *"A player needs good controller because he seeks to achieve good performance, overcome obstacles in games, achieve goals and feel comfortable while playing with his/her friends".*

With the PoV in mind, together with the insights gained from the Empathy and Imersion techniques, a Persona was defined so that it became possible to study in more detail the needs of the player. This persona-player had experience

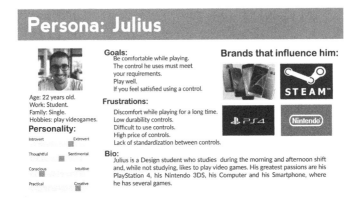

Fig. 6. The persona developed in the definition phase.

in several different platforms of video games, being they PlayStation 4, Xbox One, Nintendo DS and Computer. More details can be found in Fig. 6.

In addition to the persona, a Conceptual Map (the Mental Map) was also defined, in which the characteristics related to the research environment were listed. The Conceptual Map is a graphical view, built to simplify and visually organize data at different levels of depth and abstraction. Its purpose is to illustrate the links between the data and produce new meanings that are extracted from the information raised in the initial stages of the Immersion phase. It can be found in Fig. 7.

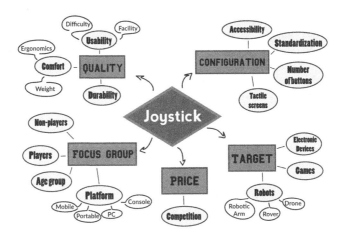

Fig. 7. The mental map used in the definition phase.

3.3   Ideation Workshop

After all the constructions in the topic of Definition, we move on to the next step of Design Thinking: Ideation. At this stage a workshop was developed with engineers researches, designers, players and non players participants. This workshop was a way to make all participants feel more integrated with the subject and also to state their opinions and develop solutions in creative ways.

At the beginning of the Workshop participants were presented with what was the subject of the research and what was the purpose of that activity. The Point of View developed in the Definition stage along with the Persona that they should be basing to develop the desired solution were presented. Both are important to make participants assiduous of the research theme. Next, some existing game scenarios were presented. These scenarios allowed participants to know that the controllers developed by them should work perfectly in all types of games, such as action games, adventure games, sports games and other.

To begin the practical part of the Workshop, participants were grouped into two groups. There were eight participants, among them, six men and two women, with ages between 20 and 30 years. Of the participants, only two did not have contact with digital games.

The first activity developed was Brainwriting [13]. Brainwriting is a variation of Brainstorming that allows a group to be able to generate a lot of ideas in a short period of time. In this activity only one sheet of paper, pencil and eraser is used, and the participants' creativity is stimulated. For this activity, each of the groups with four members of each group was responsible for writing, on a blank sheet, the requirements that they believed a controller must possess in order to be able to perform all the necessary activities within a game. After two minutes of thinking and writing a requirement, the members switched the sheets clockwise. Each member of the group who received a sheet from his colleague had to examine the requirement that the colleague had written, comment below whether or not he agreed with him and why, and then add another requirement to the paper. After completing the cycle, the Brainwriting stage was completed and the group was able to discuss the results written on each sheet.

The next step was Braindrawing [13]. Braindrawing is also a variation of Brainstorming, where participants had to draw what they believed a video game controller should possess. As in Brainwriting, the members of each group had a limited time to design components of a video game controller, and after the time ended, the participant at their side had the task of supplementing the controller that he started. At the end of the cycle, a totally new controller was generated.

After the Braindrawing, each group met to discuss the results of their texts and drawings, pick up pertinent points, and perform a Brainstorming. The idea here was for each group to unite their findings and generate a single result that encompasses all or a large part of the results they found during Branwriting and Braindrawing. After Brainstorming, the groups presented the results to the rest of the classmates: each one exemplified his solution to the problem, where a controller could adapt to the varied contexts of the games. Figure 8 shows their solutions.

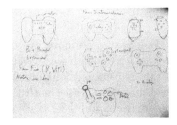

Fig. 8. Group 1 and Group 2 solutions.

3.4 Prototyping

Based on the results generated in the Workshop, we analyzed and selected interesting components of each idea generated. It was possible to notice that participants prefer physical controllers to virtual ones, given the lack of tactile feedback from the second, but the participants were tempted to integrate both controller models to form a single component. The first one was called "Modular Controller", which makes it possible to create your own physical controller while a smartphone runs a virtual controller application. The second solution was named "Gamer Case". Both of them are shown in Fig. 9.

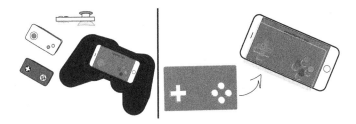

Fig. 9. The "Modular Controller" and the "Gamer Case".

The Modular Controller is summarized in a physical base of joystick as already known, but empty. In its central region there is a space where you can deposit your smartphone, running software that simulates a gamepad virtually. The innovation of this controller comes in modules that can be plugged into your controller, which can be developed into a three-dimensional modeling software and printed on a 3D printer, fully functional for the controller you need to use. This module has buttons with suction cups that, when they fit in the space that contains the smartphone, touch the screen of the device and perform the actions that it should do individually. This solution is versatile, since you can assemble your own controller and also solves the problem of the lack of tactile feedback that the virtual controller has. It is important to note that the joystick casing does not work separate from the smartphone: it is only a support for the phone, being the true game controller.

The solution that the Gamer Case provides is to try to solve the lack of tactile feedback that digital controls have, as mentioned in Baldauf et al. [1], that is, the user can not realize that he is actually pressing a button on the virtual control. Thus, using a 3D printer, for instance, it is possible to print punched transparent films with the format that suits the virtual controller software (cross, d-pad, buttons, etc.) and place it on top of the device, leaving only exposed areas which must be clicked by the player (see Fig. 10). In this way, the user can feel if he is actually touching the correct area of the controller, increasing his performance when performing the actions within the game.

3.5   Experimental Tests

In the testing phase, as follows the Design Thinking pipeline chosen by d.school, the Gamer Case solution was implemented so that some informal tests could be performed. Before starting the tests, participants were given a User Profile questionnaire to fill out. At the end of this questionnaire the tests were started.

For the experiment, 12 people with age group between 18 and 60 years of age participated. Among them, 67% were male and 33% were female, 11 had smartphones for more than 2 years and 42% of the participants have a habit of playing. To perform the tests was used a smartphone Zenfone 3 Zoom with 4 GB of RAM and 64 GB of internal storage. In it was run a software that simulates a virtual controller called PC Remote [11], which connects via Wi-Fi with a computer that, in turn, runs the game. Players could choose between playing Sonic The Hedgehog (Master System) or Super Mario Bros (NES). Figure 10 shows both the virtual controller and the Gamer Case.

Fig. 10. The Gamer Case and the virtual gamepad.

In the first phase of the tests, the player was responsible for playing, for five minutes, the game of his preference using the smartphone without the Gamer Case. In the second phase, the Case was placed on the smartphone and it resumed the game for another five minutes. After completing the tests, an informal questionnaire was made available so that users could evaluate the two ways to use the controller. Figure 11 shows two users playing Super Mario Bros using the controller with and without the Gamer Case solution.

Given the participants' responses about controller without the Gamer Case, 83% stated that they felt uncomfortable using it, 58% stated that the controller

Fig. 11. Player using the virtual gamepad without (left) and with (right) the Gamer Case.

is user-friendly but could be better, and only 8.3% gave a grade 4 (on a scale of 1 to 5, where 1 is too bad and 5 is too good) for the controller, 33.3% gave a grade 3, 50% gave a grade 2 and 8.3% gave a grade 1. Meanwhile, when using the controller with the Gamer Case, 58.3% felt very comfortable using it, 91.7% managed to perform the tasks properly and 50% evaluated it with the maximum score.

4 Final Considerations

The main contributions of this work are the use of the Design Thinking methodology for the development of new ideas and solutions for game controllers that can help the player to have a better experience when playing.

Existing controllers have great similarities but also diverge on some points that can leave the user a little confused when using them after getting used to another. Virtual controllers, despite using innovative technologies such as the gyroscope and the accelerometer, have one major disadvantage: the lack of tactile feedback. With this work, as already observed in previous works [5,16] we realized that the participants prefer a physical controller to a virtual one. However they did not fail to integrate the two solutions.

By using the techniques of Design Thinking, it was possible for a group of people to develop a solution that would unite both the physical and virtual approaches that a video game controller can have. All the steps: Empathy and Immersion, Definition, Ideation Workshop and Prototyping were followed seeking to develop an interesting and innovative result. Based on this, the Modular Controller - a modular physical controller that can be integrated and built with the help of mobile devices and customizable modules - and the Gamer Case - a case for smartphones that suits the screen leaving only touchable where the user has to touch - were created, making the experience that the player can have something totally new.

By understanding how to design innovative game controllers, the Design Thinking techniques used in this process shown to be efficients to alternate between moments of focusing and spreading ideas. Therefore, with this study we find in the techniques of Design Thinking support to develop two innovative solutions in a short period of time and in a simple and inexpensive way.

References

1. Baldauf, M., Fröhlich, P., Adegeye, F., Suette, S.: Investigating on-screen gamepad designs for smartphone-controlled video games. ACM Trans. Multimed. Comput. Commun. Appl. (TOMM) **12**(1s), 22 (2015)
2. Cornish, D.: History of the video game controller (2018). https://www.shortlist. com/tech/gaming/history-of-the-video-game-controller/3231. Accessed 26 Apr 2018
3. DesignBoom: Grayhaus brick joystick (2018). https://www.designboom.com/ readers/grayhaus-brick/. Accessed 27 Apr 2018
4. Games, I.A., Squire, K.: Design thinking in gamestar mechanic: the role of gamer experience on the appropriation of the discourse practices of game designers. In: Proceedings of the 8th International Conference on Learning Sciences, vol. 1, pp. 257–264. International Society of the Learning Sciences (2008)
5. Gonçalves, G., Mourão, É., Torok, L., Trevisan, D., Clua, E., Montenegro, A.: Understanding user experience with game controllers: a case study with an adaptive smart controller and a traditional gamepad. In: Munekata, N., Kunita, I., Hoshino, J. (eds.) ICEC 2017. LNCS, vol. 10507, pp. 59–71. Springer, Cham (2017). https:// doi.org/10.1007/978-3-319-66715-7_7
6. Hayes, E.R., Games, I.A.: Making computer games and design thinking: a review of current software and strategies. Games Cult. **3**(3–4), 309–332 (2008)
7. Ipega: Pg-9021 (2018). http://www.ipega.hk/. Accessed 27 Apr 2018
8. Lugmayr, A., Stockleben, B., Zou, Y., Anzenhofer, S., Jalonen, M.: Applying "design thinking" in the context of media management education. Multimed. Tools Appl. **71**(1), 119–157 (2014)
9. Merdenyan, B., Petrie, H.: User reviews of gamepad controllers: a source of user requirements and user experience. In: Proceedings of the 2015 Annual Symposium on Computer-Human Interaction in Play, pp. 643–648. ACM (2015)
10. Moga: Moga Hero Power (2018). http://www.mogaanywhere.com/controllers/ heropower. Accessed 27 Apr 2018
11. Monect: PC Remote (2018). https://www.monect.com/pc-remote/. Accessed 02 May 2018
12. Nintendo^{TM}: Nintendo labo^{TM} for the nintendo switch^{TM} (2018). https://labo. nintendo.com/. Accessed 26 Apr 2018
13. Paulus, P.B., Brown, V.R.: Enhancing ideational creativity in groups. Group creativity: innovation through collaboration, pp. 110–136 (2003)
14. Plattner, H.: Bootcamp Bootleg. Design School Stanford, Palo Alto (2010)
15. Tara, R.Y., Teng, W.C.: A suitability evaluation of controlling 3D map viewpoint by gamepad orientation for remote navigation. IEEE Access **5**, 10686–10693 (2017)
16. Torok, L., Pelegrino, M., Trevisan, D., Montenegro, A., Clua, E.: Smart controller: introducing a dynamic interface adapted to the gameplay. Entertain. Comput. **27**, 32–46 (2018)

Diminishing Reality

Andreas Hackl and Helmut Hlavacs[✉]

Entertainment Computing Research Group, University of Vienna, Vienna, Austria
a1308402@unet.univie.ac.at, helmut.hlavacs@univie.ac.at
http://entertain.univie.ac.at/~hlavacs/

Abstract. We explore ways of removing objects from live video feeds in augmented reality-like use cases, using a method for inpainting unwanted objects using previously captured visuals of the surrounding environment. In contrast to related previous work, this approach can completely retain and reproduce hidden objects in all their detail. We describe the approach and detail results from our evaluation.

1 Introduction

Augmented reality (AR), the "augmentation" of a view of the physical world, has found its way into normal peoples' everyday lives, with smartphones becoming ubiquitous devices in the developed world. For entertainment purposes it found widespread use in humorous overlays over peoples' faces, or even real-time alteration of their physical appearances [16], in social networking applications like Snapchat or SNOW, and in video games that use real environments as backdrops to render in-game graphics onto.

On a different front, technologies and applications for the removal of unwanted objects from still images and even video, generally described as "inpainting", have existed for some time, mainly for the improvement of pre-recorded media. They allow removal of a person from a scenic photograph, the seamless stitching panoramas, or removal of strings from a video that should not be visible to viewers. These technologies have also found their way into software available to standard consumer software, most notably in Adobe Photoshop with its "content-aware fill" feature, based on the PatchMatch [1,7] algorithm.

By combining both of these technologies, objects could be made to vanish from a user's view in real-time. In doing so, reality would not be augmented with additional information, but real information would be reduced, resulting in *diminished reality* (DR). The goal of this work is to devise and implement an efficient and lightweight DR approach to this on the Android platform.

2 Related Work

While the subject of inpainting is well researched and continues to be subject of new research, there have not been many applications so far with the aim

© IFIP International Federation for Information Processing 2018
Published by Springer Nature Switzerland AG 2018. All Rights Reserved
E. Clua et al. (Eds.): ICEC 2018, LNCS 11112, pp. 28–39, 2018.
https://doi.org/10.1007/978-3-319-99426-0_3

of, or any functionality similar to, the concept of diminished or reduced reality proposed in this work.

A single application has been developed as part of very promising research into exactly this topic in 2010, with viable results, on even then-current hardware, named "Diminished Reality" [12]. The rendering pipeline proposed by Broll et al. is very similar to the one chosen by us, but differs in that it uses a patch-based approach, similar to PatchMatch, that operates entirely on a frame-by-frame basis, without considering any earlier input. The visual fidelity and accuracy of its inpainting is therefore largely dependent on the input image and surroundings of the object to be inpainted.

Research into the broader topic of general video inpainting by Newson et al. [14] utilises a sort of memory, while still being patch-based, by considering patches from multiple frames of a video to inpaint objects. It manages to produce very convincing results, but is not efficient enough for real-time use.

Other approaches to improve accuracy and fidelity in real-time inpainting, compared to the traditional patch-based ones, have originally been considered, but turned out to not be quite applicable to this task.

Neural networks in particular have in recent years become sophisticated enough, and consumer hardware powerful and cheap enough, to make the implementation and use of powerful networks for various image generation and alteration tasks viable.

An application of Generative Adversarial Networks (GAN) to the problem of texture synthesis and style transfer by Ulyanov et al. [17] provides an entirely feed-forward way of generating images, once a model has been trained. Because of its promises of very fast image generation, it has been tested in consideration of its viability as a base for real-time inpainting.

Using a relatively inexpensive GPU (Nvidia GTX 960 with 2 GB VRAM) generation of images was possible at an average of 20 frames per second with a resolution of 512×512 pixels, which makes it fast enough for real-time use. It can however only generate textures that were trained into a model beforehand. Although one model can be trained for multiple textures at once, without much increase in needed computation time or loss in image quality, is a very limiting factor. Training one such model on the same hardware limits the maximum input size to 256×256 pixels (although not necessarily the output size), due to the high VRAM requirements of the training process, and takes more than 20 min. In real-world environments, where any kind of texture could appear in a user's surroundings, this training process would therefore need to be on an as-needed basis, for which this time frame is still far too long. It also does unfortunately not provide any consistency between generated inputs, or any facility to blend generated textures into an existing background texture (cf. Fig. 1).

Another promising project based on Convolutional Neural Networks (CNN) by Yang et al. [20], with the explicit purpose of high-quality inpainting of images, similar to PatchMatch but with better results, has recently managed to reduce processing time to only half a minute per image [20]. That means it might soon be usable even for real-time purposes, but at this time it is not.

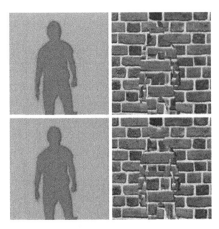

Fig. 1. Two frames, foreground (red) generated by [17] over a static image of the image the model was trained. (Color figure online)

Since this kind of method poses a great challenge in making it fit the purpose of real-time inpainting, in either some kind of extensive pre- or post-processing being necessary or being simply too slow overall, while still offering behaviour, strengths and drawbacks very similar to patch-based ones, it has been discarded in favour of the method described here.

3   Our Inpainting Approach

The image processing pipeline for inpainting relies on a simple in-memory structure that can be used to store the visual appearance of the environment around a point in space and later retrieve parts of it to fill in regions in images. It consists of five core parts:

1. **Input:** Capturing of frames from the camera. Every captured frame potentially needs to be put into a spacial relation to other frames and/or the positioning of the capturing device in space. For this purpose, at the time of frame capture, the orientation of the device is queried and stored alongside it, adding other metadata, such as a measurement of time (e.g. timestamp or frame number).
2. **Object detection:** Detection of objects and generation of regions inside of a frame that are to be inpainted. An object detection algorithm is applied to the newly captured frame, identifying one or more regions inside it that contain objects which the user might want to vanish. To make description of arbitrary regions easy, and because later stitching of frames requires it anyway, they are stored as monochrome bitmaps.
3. **Frame storage:** Input frames in which no objects of interest have been detected are candidates for use in inpainting to fill in objects and as such need to be stored in a *frame store* for later use. Frames are stored uncompressed

in a 2D array-like structure with each cell representing a few degrees of yaw and pitch, essentially subdividing the range of possible device orientations (disregarding roll) into a grid. Each cell can hold one frame at most at any given time, limiting the maximum amount of frames to be stored in a given range of orientation, therefore preventing the storage of too many too similar frames.

4. **Frame search:** For input frames in which objects have been detected that are to be inpainted, a frame that is potentially suitable to fill in the region(s) generated by the object detection step needs to be found. As comparison of actual frame content, of potentially many pairs of frames, is computationally too expensive to do for each input frame in real-time, a frame is searched inside the frame store by the most similar orientation to that of the input frame.

5. **Stitching:** If a frame suitable for inpainting has been found in the frame store, a single frame is stitched together using the newly captured frame, the frame found in the frame store, and an object mask. The stored frame needs to be aligned to the input frame as precisely as possible and then blended together according to the object mask.

Other than simple, direct storage of input frames into memory during runtime, there is no need for any lengthy preprocessing (e.g. pre-generating a sphere map) in order to work in any given environment, as frames are stored and accessed independently of each other.

4 Implementation

An application implementing the proposed method has been developed for Android using OpenCv4Android [2], which provides Java bindings for OpenCV's C++-based API. It is largely based on the desktop OpenCV Java API, with several Android-specific convenience features added.

OpenCV provides basic functions for image manipulation (e.g. translation, colour manipulation, conversion), as well as more advanced features typical for computer vision (e.g. feature extraction), both of which this project heavily relies on. Because it is a thin wrapper around natively compiled C++ code, it avoids many potential performance problems caused by the JVM and its garbage collection. It being a standard API available on many platforms also makes porting applications using it easy.

The architecture is kept largely modular, with the main roles in the program separated out into their own classes/interfaces.

4.1 Input

The camera provides the image as both 4-channel RGBA (red, green, blue and alpha channels) and 1-channel monochrome data. A sensor manager class provides a combined 3-component orientation vector, computed from the "gravity" (virtual device based on accelerometer and gyroscope) and "magnetic field" (uncalibrated magnetometer data) sensors. Data provided by the magnetometer, by nature of the hardware built into smartphones, reflects changes in orientation nearly instantly but is very noisy, sometimes jumping rapidly between up to 10° above/below the expected value. To get more stable readings, for every input value, the average of the last 100 values (including the new one) is calculated using a moving window approach.

4.2   Object Detection and Mask Generation

Video frames are passed to a mask generator class that creates a monochrome mask for detected objects, which are masked white. All other pixels are masked black.

There are two approaches for object detection implemented. Colour keying computes a mask by converting the RGB colour image to HSV (hue, saturation and value) and generates a greyscale image, setting all pixels in it to white if their corresponding pixels' HSV values are within a given range. HSV is used because RGB makes it difficult to define a range of similar looking colours.

Because this is prone to create very holey masks and include undesirable single pixels, the resulting mask is blurred using a simple box blur with a kernel size of 10 pixels and then all pixels above a value of 50 (in the range of 0–255) are set to pure white, all below to pure black (cf. Fig. 2). This produces more coherent, hole-less areas and discards single stray pixels.

For performance reasons, input is (optionally) downscaled before processing and the result upscaled afterwards.

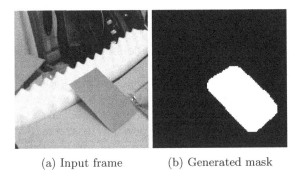

(a) Input frame   (b) Generated mask

Fig. 2. Generating a mask using colour keying, with downscaling. (Color figure online)

The second detector is a face detector and uses OpenCV's `Cascade Classifier` and its `detectMultiScale` method, which uses Haar feature [18] or LBP-based (local binary pattern [13]) cascade classifiers to detect objects in a greyscale image. LBP cascade descriptors were chosen because the detection process is computationally less intensive than the Haar feature-based one, even if slightly more inaccurate.

For each detected object, the function returns a rectangle describing its position inside the image and its size. Because these rectangles often do not completely cover the object, instead of simply filling them with pure white to create a mask, a circle is drawn over each one, with the centre being that of the rectangle and the radius the average of its sides' lengths. This results in circles with approximately double the diameter of the rectangles (cf. Fig. 3).

(a) `detectMultiScale` output   (b) Generated mask

Fig. 3. Generating a mask from a rectangle describing a face detected using an LBP cascade.

4.3   Frame Storage and Search

The `FrameStore` utilises a basic fixed-size 2D array of `VideoFrame`s, with each element representing a certain amount of degrees of yaw and pitch. Unoccupied elements are initialised to `null` to conserve memory.

To store a frame input to the frame store via its `replace` method, the X and Y indices in the array are computed using the frame's orientation. The new frame and the frame previously stored there, if there is one, are passed to the `shouldReplace` method of an `IReplacementPolicy` provided to the frame store, to determine if the old frame should really be replaced (hence the method name `replace`). A copy of the new frame is then stored in the array.

The replacement policy implemented compares the two frames' `frameNumbers` (a value incremented every frame) and indicates to replace an old frame, only if their difference is large enough. This prevents frames from being copied and discarded many times per second, for a similar device orientation, which can lead to large memory consumption and even crashing of the application, depending on available memory and garbage collection frequency of the JVM. To search for the nearest frame to a given orientation, the `getNearest` method again calculates the corresponding array indices, and then searches from there outwards until a frame is found.

4.4 Stitching

If a suitable frame has been found in the frame store, the input frame and stored frame need to be *stitched* together, to fill regions marked in the generated mask and produce a single, coherent image.

Since orientation is recorded alongside every captured frame, and changes in orientation of the input device are reflected in captured frames as mainly translation and rotation, using these data an approximate translation of the `fill` frame to match the `base` frame can be computed.

A simple translation matrix is computed, with X and Y components' pixel values approximated using the difference in yaw and pitch angles of both frames and the number of pixels per degree of field of view of the camera. The exact formula being (for the X component, FOV being the field of view in degrees along the X axis):

$$\frac{frame\_size}{FOV} \cdot (fill\_yaw - base\_yaw) \cdot (1 + \frac{|fill\_yaw - base\_yaw|}{FOV})$$

As this is only a simple translation based on angles and percentages, it does not correct for difference in roll (image rotation) or any distortion, like the distortion caused by the camera lens. It is further hindered from reliably overlaying the frames accurately by the inaccuracy and lag in recorded orientation data and the possibility of the capturing device having moved, other than simple orientation change.

Translating the `fill` frame in this manner before further processing has still proven beneficial, as it is not a very computationally expensive operation and in most cases provides a better overlap of both frames (cf. Fig. 4).

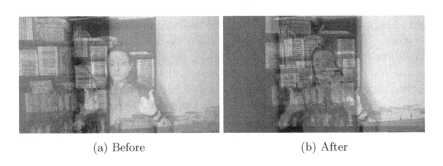

(a) Before   (b) After

Fig. 4. Overlap of `base` and `fill` before and after orientation-based translation.

Transformation by Features. After the `fill` frame has been translated once, key features from both it and the `base` frame are extracted from their greyscale variants using OpenCV's `FeatureDetector` and `DescriptorExtractor` classes and their implementation of ORB (Oriented FAST and rotated BRIEF) [8]. Although OpenCV does implement other algorithms for feature detection, ORB proved to be the most efficient while still producing good features. Features of both frames are then correlated using OpenCV's `DescriptorMatcher` class and its "Bruteforce Hamming" algorithm, which is a brute-force search based on the Hamming distance of extracted feature descriptors.

Found matches are then filtered by the distance (in pixels) between the features matched of each match, discarding all matches with distances greater than two times the smallest matched distance (cf. Fig. 5). This serves to exclude disproportionately far matches, which are likely to be wrong. Including only relatively very short distances proved to often produce very accurate overlap in the final image, at the expense of sometimes not producing a match at all.

Filtering this way has purely empirically turned out to work well; other factors or for example basing the calculation on the mean distance also leads to usable results.

A translation matrix is then computed using OpenCV's `estimateRigid Transform` function, the filtered matches and the `fill` frame translated by it.

Fig. 5. Extracted ORB features in both frames and selected matches.

Final Blending. To blend the now aligned frames together into one complete frame, the `fill` frame is multiplied by the `base` frame's mask and the `base` frame by the inverse of its own mask, leaving holes in the `base` frame and only the content to fill them in the `fill` frame, which are then added together (cf. Fig. 6, an app screen shot is shown in Fig. 9).

5 Evaluation

Although conceptionally relatively simple, our DR application manages to produce visually coherent and realistic looking results. Through the use of a simple visual memory, structures and objects entirely hidden behind an inpainted area of a frame can be successfully retained with all their details. This amount of detail is impossible to produce using inpainting methods that operate exclusively on the content of one frame (cf. Fig. 7).

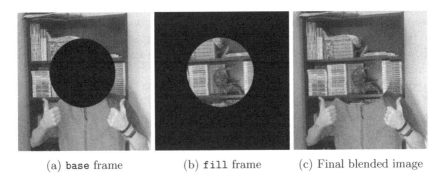

(a) `base` frame   (b) `fill` frame   (c) Final blended image

Fig. 6. Blending of `base` and `fill` frames into the final complete image.

(a) Content aware fill   (b) Our DR app

Fig. 7. Comparison of inpainted frames using Adobe Photoshop's PatchMatch-based content-aware fill and output of our DR application.

Fig. 8. Half of an envelope in front of the detected face being wrongly inpainted.

5.1 Foreground and Background

Because the only concept of separation between fore- and background is that of inpainted objects being "in front of" the stored frames' content, other things moving in the camera's view cannot really be distinguished or separately reacted to. This leads to moving backgrounds leaving out of date data in the frame store and (partly) view-obstructing things being wrongly inpainted (cf. Fig. 8). Largely static surroundings produce the best results for this reason.

A more sophisticated object detection algorithm may solve at least the foreground problem (e.g. the colour key method does not suffer from this problem), the background problem however is somewhat inherent to the use of a frame store and may not be easily solvable.

5.2 Blending

In addition to non-static surroundings possibly leaving wrong data in the frame store, even mostly static environments can change slightly over time, through lighting changes, moving shadows or the often not software-controllable adjustments made by Android and camera hardware in smartphones to parameters like exposure and white balance.

The naive blending approach of only masking areas in both frames does not correct for these differences and can lead to visible seams, sometimes even very obvious ones (cf. Fig. 10).

Fig. 9. Split view containing (from top left to bottom right): camera input, fill frame, (inpainted) output frame, frame store array

Fig. 10. Obvious seam after the exposure auto-adjusted.

Correcting for colour shift and blurring the edges between the two blended frames could drastically reduce these effects. Less uniform changes, like shadows cast by an inpainted object, may not be as easily corrected for.

If objects are detected in a frame, but no usable frame is found in the frame store, the frame is shown to the user unaltered. Instead of doing so, in a kind of best-effort way, another inpainting method that is independent of the frame store could be used to hide the objects. Using such a fallback method may then be less accurate, but would hide objects in these circumstances, which is better than not doing so at all.

5.3   Runtime Performance

During runtime, various timings are taken of different parts of the program to provide an overview over their performance. Running the application on different devices and comparing them reveals a relatively clear bottleneck in need of improvement (cf. Table 1).

Stitching is responsible for the majority of the processing time of one frame, taking around 150 ms even on a relatively recent high-performance mobile processor, limiting the overall frame rate to below 6 frames per second. While not extremely slow and especially in hand-held situations still very usable and good enough to prove the concept, for users to better enjoy using the application, the highest possible frame-rate should be pursued.

Since the application runs all image manipulation sequentially in a single thread, performance could be dramatically improved by parallelising these operations and possibly offloading them to the GPU. Although OpenCV implements

Table 1. Average performance on three different Android devices at a resolution of 1280×720 pixels.

Device/CPU	Stitching	Colour mask	Face detection	Frame search
Galaxy Nexus Arm Cortex A-9 (1.2 GHz)	433.7 ms	9.8 ms	65.4 ms	0.8 ms
Google Nexus 7 (2013) Krait 300 (1.51 GHz)	253.2 ms	4.7 ms	32.7 ms	1.5 ms
Oneplus One Krait 400 (2.5 GHz)	147.5 ms	1.6 ms	22.3 ms	0.7 ms

acceleration using OpenCL for most of the functionality used by our DR application [4], which would enable exactly this kind of parallelisation, OpenCL is not officially supported on Android. Some devices nonetheless support it [3,5] and tests have in the past shown very good performance using it [15], but getting OpenCL support for OpenCV working on Android turned out to be non-trivial and it was therefore not used in our DR application.

Reimplementing key parts of the application using RenderScript would likely yield similar performance improvements, but be equally non-trivial and specific to the Android platform.

6   Conclusion

This project explored not only a way of utilising AR technology that has not been subject of much research so far, but also an approach to it that has not yet been described. The proposed approach to removing objects from the live view of a camera has in practice turned out to work quite well within its inherent limitations and even produce more accurate images than prior approaches. Performance of the implementation is not on-par with them yet, but the potential for optimisation is still great, depending mainly on the support of OpenCL on the chosen platform. On other, less restricted platforms these improvements may even be implemented easily.

Although users are restricted to orientation and otherwise only very limited movement of the device, since users of smartphones and similar devices are often very stationary (i.e. sat at a desk), this may not be a big problem in many cases. It is not unthinkable that an application like this could in the future be used, if AR technology has matured enough to be widely used in work environments, to filter out unwanted visual distractions, much like noise cancelling headphones are used to filter out unwanted distracting sounds.

Overall this was an interesting foray into a niche topic, which maybe in the future, as AR technology improves and new use-cases thereof emerge, could even become a basis for solving real needs.

References

1. Adobe research. https://research.adobe.com/project/content-aware-fill/. Accessed 10 Feb 2018
2. Android - OpenCV library. https://opencv.org/platforms/android/. Accessed 13 Feb 2018
3. Android devices with OpenCL support. https://docs.google.com/spreadsheets/d/1Mpzfl2NmLUVSAjIph77-FOsJeuyD9Xjha89r5iHw1hI/edit. Accessed 14 Feb 2018
4. OpenCL - OpenCV library. https://docs.opencv.org/2.4/modules/ocl/doc/object_detection.html. Accessed 28 Feb 2018
5. OpenCL overview. https://www.khronos.org/opencl/resources. Accessed 14 Feb 2018
6. opencv/data/lbpcascades at master. https://github.com/opencv/opencv/tree/master/data/lbpcascades. Accessed 20 Feb 2018
7. Barnes, C., Shechtman, E., Finkelstein, A., Goldman, D.B.: PatchMatch: a randomized correspondence algorithm for structural image editing. TOG **28**(3), 1 (2009)
8. Bartolini, I., Patella, M.: WINDSURF: the best way to SURF. Multimed. Syst. **24**, 459–476 (2017)
9. Bruno Patrão, S.P., Menezes, P.: How to deal with motion sickness in virtual reality. Sci. Technol. Interact. (2015)
10. Daly, S.: Google translate App. Nurs. Stand. **28**(29), 33 (2014). Accessed 10 Feb 2018
11. Guihot, H.: RenderScript. In: Guihot, H. (ed.) Pro Android Apps Performance Optimization, pp. 231–263. Apress, New York (2012). https://doi.org/10.1007/978-1-4302-4000-6_9. Accessed 13 Feb 2018
12. Herling, J., Broll, W.: Advanced self-contained object removal for realizing real-time diminished reality in unconstrained environments. In: 2010 IEEE International Symposium on Mixed and Augmented Reality, pp. 207–212. IEEE, October 2010
13. Liao, S., Zhu, X., Lei, Z., Zhang, L., Li, S.Z.: Learning multi-scale block local binary patterns for face recognition. In: Lee, S.-W., Li, S.Z. (eds.) ICB 2007. LNCS, vol. 4642, pp. 828–837. Springer, Heidelberg (2007). https://doi.org/10.1007/978-3-540-74549-5_87
14. Newson, A., Almansa, A., Fradet, M., Gousseau, Y., Pérez, P.: Video inpainting of complex scenes. SIAM J. Imaging Sci. **7**(4), 1993–2019 (2014)
15. Ross, J.A., Richie, D.A., Park, S.J., Shires, D.R., Pollock, L.L.: A case study of OpenCL on an android mobile GPU. In: 2014 IEEE High Performance Extreme Computing Conference (HPEC), pp. 1–6. IEEE, September 2014
16. Shaburova, E.: Method for real time video processing for changing proportions of an object in the video (2014)
17. Ulyanov, D., Lebedev, V., Vedaldi, A., Lempitsky, V.S.: Texture networks: feedforward synthesis of textures and stylized images. CoRR abs/1603.03417 (2016)
18. Viola, P., Jones, M.: Rapid object detection using a boosted cascade of simple features
19. Ware, C., Balakrishnan, R.: Reaching for objects in VR displays: lag and frame rate. ACM Trans. Comput.-Hum. Interact. **1**(4), 331–356 (1994)
20. Yang, C., Lu, X., Lin, Z., Shechtman, E., Wang, O., Li, H.: High-resolution image inpainting using multi-scale neural patch synthesis. In: 2017 IEEE Conference on Computer Vision and Pattern Recognition (CVPR). IEEE, July 2017

Live Probabilistic Editing for Virtual Cinematography

Luiz Velho$^{(\boxtimes)}$, Leonardo Carvalho, and Djama Lucio

IMPA, Rio de Janeiro, Brazil
lvelho@impa.br

Abstract. This paper introduces Probabilistic Editing for Virtual Cinematography. It is part of the VR Kino+Theater platform and provides high level authoring tools for cinematic presentations. The director acts as a DJ controlling in real-time an A/V switcher interface that selects the camera views of a theatrical performance in a virtual reality experience.

Keywords: Virtual reality · Real-time cinema · Immersive theatre
Storytelling · Montage

1 Introduction

Entertainment is presently going through radical transformations as a consequence of technological developments, advances in the state of the art, and social changes. This will shape the way cultural audio-visual products will be delivered and consumed.

A direct consequence of the above scenario is that new creative possibilities become available for content producers. Here we explore one of these avenues, related to live editing and virtual cinematography.

2 Related Work

A seminal work in the area of interest is "Live Cinema", an initiative of the film director Coppola [2]. His proposal is an attempt to combine theater, film and television as an experimental form of storytelling.

In this setting, performances are acted live and viewed by an audience in real time on a movie screen. The goal is to achieve a more cinematic *look and feel* than what is typically employed for dramatic broadcasts. It employs professional television technology borrowed from TV sports.

In order to demonstrate the concept, Coppola promoted a workshop with American Zoetrope at the UCLA School of Theater, Film and Television in 2016. During an one-month period, 75 UCLA students and faculty produced a 27 min piece called "Distant Vision" for a live broadcast to a limited audience. The production involved operating over 40 cameras, acting and working on sound, set design and construction, costume, props, editing, and stage management.

© IFIP International Federation for Information Processing 2018
Published by Springer Nature Switzerland AG 2018. All Rights Reserved
E. Clua et al. (Eds.): ICEC 2018, LNCS 11112, pp. 40–51, 2018.
https://doi.org/10.1007/978-3-319-99426-0_4

The main issue of the project is the coordination of all these practical aspects restricted by the traditional video technology. In that respect, we can arguably say that Live Cinema was a vision 'ahead of its time', impaired in many ways by the *physicality* of the medium.

Another related work is [4], where probabilistic editing is used for video in a post-production phase, consequently it cannot be applied to a live show.

3 VR Kino+Theater

VR Kino+Theater [6] is a new platform for storytelling that shares various aspects of Coppola's vision of Live Cinema. The main difference is that it is based on 3D Computer Graphics and Digital Network Communications.

The platform we propose integrates traditional forms of entertainment, such as Theater and Cinema, with advanced technology, more specifically Virtual Reality and Gaming.

The main components of VR Kino+Theater exploits the concepts of *Situated Participatory Virtual Reality* and also *Live 3D Digital Cinema*. We believe this initiative points to the directions for the future of media.

3.1 Situated Participatory VR

Situated Participatory Virtual Reality [7] is a modality of VR that allows the creation of *Shared Multi-User Virtual Environments*. For this purpose, it combines real and virtual objects in tangible spaces, where the participants, represented by digital avatars, are completely immersed in a simulated world. They use VR headsets and markers for full body motion capture.

The above setting implements the *Theater* component of the platform. As such, the actors perform in a VR stage that is mapped into a virtual set. Figure 1 shows the real actors performing in the VR stage and the corresponding action of their avatars in the CG virtual set.

Fig. 1. VR theater - VR stage and CG Virtual set.

3.2   Live 3D Cinema

Live 3D Digital Cinema is the technology behind the non-immersive Audio-Visual presentation format of VR Kino+Theater. It consists of the Computer Graphics infra-structure for Animation, Real-Time Simulation and Rendering of the experience.

The virtual cinematography framework includes *Pre-Programmed Cameras* and *Interactive Editing* for generating the cinematic content.

The above setting implements the *Kino* component of the platform. In this context, the director selects in real-time the views that are shown on the live movie projection screen.

Figure 2 shows the director operating a multi-camera switcher during a live presentation.

Fig. 2. Director operating the camera switcher and detail of the interface.

Figure 3 shows the image selected by the director at a moment of the presentation (the lower right camera in the interface).

Fig. 3. Image of the selected camera exhibited on the movie screen.

4   VR Kino+Theater Cinematography

In this section we give an overview of the VR Kino+Theater Cinematography. It is composed of a camera specification infrastructure and an interface for the camera selection by the director in real-time.

The camera specification infrastructure is implemented through a layered architecture with three levels: Unity CG Cameras; Cinemachine Camera Operators; and K+T Virtual Cameras. The director interface consists of a live camera switcher.

4.1   Unity Camera

The Unity Camera Layer corresponds to the low level of the camera specification infrastructure. It consists of a standard Computer Graphics Camera of the Unity Game Engine [5]. The camera is defined by the usual parameters, such as position, orientation, field of view, etc.

4.2   Cinemachine Operators

The Cinemachine camera operators constitute the intermediate level of the camera specification infrastructure. These camera operators embody a framework for smart, programmable cameras. In that respect the operator knows about the entities in a Unity scene and controls the camera specification based on visual composition rules.

The two main control mechanisms are the Composer and the Transposer, they allow to specify the camera in screen and scene space respectively.

4.3   Kino+Theater Cameras

The VR Kino+Theater Camera layer forms the higher level of the camera specification infrastructure. It consists of an object based abstraction for creating the entity of a *Virtual Cameraman* and allowing to instantiate these objects for specific purposes.

In that respect, the Kino+Theater Cameras are designed for Cinematography Storytelling and allow the director to compose shots for each scene of the narrative.

There are two classes of camera objects: General; and Timeline. General cameras refer to shot types that can be used freely during a scene, while Timeline cameras are meant to be used at certain times along the scene and are choreographed for specific events of the action.

4.4   Kino+Theater Camera Switcher

The Director's Interface allows the control a live image on the movie screen by selecting the active view using an special-purpose multi-camera switcher.

This interface contains the views of 12 pre-programmed cameras showing in real-time the CG simulation. A view is activated by a simple click. The director interface also contains additional controls for triggering simulation events. The cameras are divided in two blocks: one block with 8 general multi-purpose cameras, such as close ups, medium shots and characters points of view; and another block with a sequential list of timeline cameras which are custom designed for specific parts of the action. Figure 4 shows the Kino+Theater Camera Switcher interface.

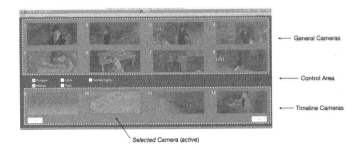

Fig. 4. Multi-camera switcher interface.

5   Reaching to a Higher Level

The VR Kino+Theater Cinematography infrastructure implements a power-ful mechanism for live editing of cinematic experiences. Nonetheless, the image director operates the camera switcher interface using a rather explicit control. He/she has to exercise every single cut of the visual piece (at precise moments in real-time).

The scenario described above motivates us to reach to a higher level of control that could provide more expressive power. In that sense, the goal is to allow the director to act as a DJ, using an interface designed for stylistic control and live improvisation.

Such an interface has to expose the "right parameters" in a concise and intuitive way. It should be pre-configured based on the scene content and the desired cinematic style variations. The key for creating this device is to exploit the concept of generative interfaces.

Another important point is that the proposed functionality should be built on top of the VR Kino+Theater Application Framework and rely on the layered architecture of its Cinematography infrastructure.

5.1   Stylistic Control

The Stylistic Control is based on Shot Classes and Timeline Events.

The Shot Classes are related to visual characteristics of the movie image. For example: Close-Ups; Middle; and Wide shots. The Timeline Events are related to specific moments when an action occurs.

These two style elements are combined using Cinematic Rules that are part of the Cinematographic language. Together they deal with aspects such as pacing of cuts, etc.

5.2   Architecture

The Cinematography Infrastructure of VR Kino+Theater is implemented using a layered architecture. It consists of several layers for the camera entities.

As presented in Sect. 4 the first three layers correspond respectively to the levels of abstraction for: the Unity Camera; Cinemachine Operator; and K+T Cameraman.

In order to incorporate style control, we extend this hierarchy to include a higher order level: the K+T AutoShot. Figure 5 shows the complete camera abstraction hierarchy.

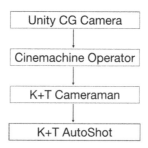

Fig. 5. Camera abstraction hierarchy.

The K+T AutoShot embodies a high level cinematic style control that is the basis of probabilistic editing, as will be discussed in the next section.

6   Probabilistic Editing

Probabilistic Editing is a framework for the design of cinematic style in live audio/visual performance presentations. The framework is based on Film Grammar, Stylistic Edit Patterns and Flow of Action in order to create a *Live High-Level Control* mechanism.

In this framework the Film Grammar maps to the concept of Camera Groups, the Stylistic Patterns are represented by a Cut Graph and the Flow of Action follows mark-up sequences in the Timeline.

The result is a generative edit interface that extends the VR Kino+Theater camera switcher.

6.1   Camera Groups

Camera Groups embody the main conceptual entity that is manipulated in the probabilistic setting of our framework. They form the building blocks of Cut Graphs (see next subsection) that are used to represent a cinematic style design.

Typically, camera groups are created by the image director following classification principles that are based on shot classes. Furthermore, they are defined per scene, i.e., they depend on the narrative content and the staging of specific scenes.

For example, Fig. 6 illustrates a camera group for the CloseUps in the Cell Scene of the experiment "The Tempest". This group includes the close-up shots of the characters Miranda and Prospera.

Fig. 6. Camera Group for CloseUp Shots of the Cell Scene in The Tempest.

6.2   Cut Graph

Cut Graphs are the probabilistic representation of a cinematic style in our framework. They are mathematically a Probabilistic Graphical Model [3], in which the nodes are random variables and the links are statistical dependencies among these variables.

The nodes describe in probability terms the particular cinematic style rules for a given sequence that is part of the narrative. For example, Table 1 shows a rule for the Camera Group "CloseUp of Cell Scene" mentioned above. Essentially, it specifies that close-ups of Miranda have a 20% chance of being selected, while close-ups of Prospera have 80% chance.

Table 1. Node R1

Close Miranda	Close Prospera
0.2	0.8

As a whole, the cut graph models a probability distribution that characterizes a particular cinematic style. Intuitively, this density distribution is a way to decide which shots to select for a cut in a probabilistic sense.

Figure 7 shows an example of a Cut Graph. The top nodes (R1 to R3) are associated with parametric input decisions, and the bottom node (Rn) is associated with the final cut selection.

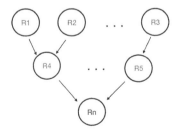

Fig. 7. Example of a Cut Graph.

6.3   Modeling the Distributions

In order to model the probability distributions in the Cut Graph we can use either *parametric* or *non-parametric* models.

In the parametric setting we have the following characterization of distribution functions $\mathcal{P} = \{P_\Theta \in \mathcal{P} : \theta \in \Theta\}$, where Θ is the set of parameters. While in the non-parametric setting the distribution is given by a table, for instance, in the form of a histogram (as in the example of Table 1).

6.4   Timeline

One important aspect that remains to be considered is related to the Timeline. That is, to answer the question: "When to perform a Cut"? In order to model this temporal aspect we resort to Track Markers. They are associated with Camera Groups and defined by a list of time-stamped annotations indicating the moments to evaluate the cut graph for a decision of which cut to make.

In other words, the several layers of track markers collectively specify how often to perform a Cut. In that sense, the image director can determine the Granularity of Markers, which could also have a Nesting structure. Figure 8 illustrate the Timeline and Track Marker layers.

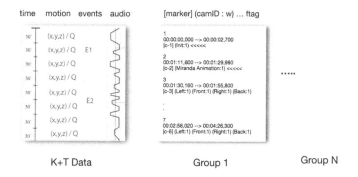

Fig. 8. Timeline and Track Marker Layers.

6.5   Style Design

The Style Design is accomplished by combining the nodes in a cut graph to set the conditional probabilities. Each node is associated with a track marker layer that specifies both the camera groups involved and type of probabilistic model, as well as, the timeline events for potential cut evaluation using the graph.

The general format of the track mark entries is as follows (Fig. 9):

For non-parametric models the specification is the list of cameras of a camera group and their associated weights. This allows a computation of the histogram description (See below Fig. 10).

```
index 1
start time --> end time
[camera group id] {optional list of camera / weight pairs}

   .
   .
index N
start time --> end time
[camera group id] {optional list of camera / weight pairs}
```

Fig. 9. Track Marker File.

```
(camera 1 name : weight) .... (camera N name : weight)
```

Fig. 10. Camera/Weigth list for non-parametric model.

Parametric models are associated with camera groups and a procedural layer that has controls for their parameters, which can be exposed in the live editing interface as we will see in the next subsection.

Figure 11 shows an example of a style design using both non-parametric and parametric models.

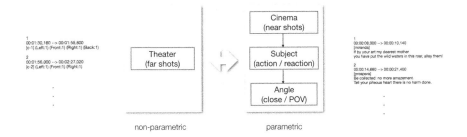

Fig. 11. Cinematic Style Design using parametric and non-parametric models.

6.6   Editing Interface

The editing Interface extends the live image switcher to provide high levels controls. It is programmable with the style parameters for each scene and is meant to be used in Live Cinema.

The interface operates either in an auto or manual mode. The auto mode selects automatically the cuts based on the probabilistic style graph, without the interference of the director. However, the director can also change the style parameters using the interface controls and these modifications will be reflected in real-time on the cut decisions by the machine. Furthermore, the director can override the probabilistic style machine to select individual cameras at any moment—virtually operating the switcher in manual mode.

Figure 12 shows the Editing interface. Note the highlighted area indicating the style controls.

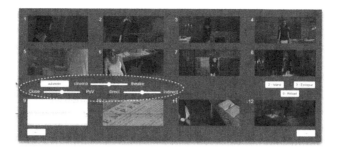

Fig. 12. Probabilistic Editing interface.

7   Case Study: The Tempest

In this section we present a case study of using the high level live edting functionality on an actual A/V experiment.

We used the tool for the Cinema presentation of the Shakespeare's play, "The Tempest" [8].

7.1   Cameras

The production of the experiment consisted of three scenes: the Cell; the Clearing and the Epilogue.

The cinematic style design is the one depicted in Fig. 11. At the top node of the cut graph, the random variables control the decision between a theatrical and film styles – in this case, that means respectively wide shots of longer duration versus near shots with fast paced cuts.

In the Cell scene the camera groups are close-ups and points-of-view for the track of film style and mid shots from fixed angles (front, back, left, right) for the track of theatrical style.

In the Clearing scene the camera groups are also close-ups and points-of-view for the track of film style but for the track of theatrical style we included both wide and mid shots.

The Epilogue scene does not have a probabilistic editing setting, only a deterministic zoom shot.

7.2   Results

In order to verify the effectiveness of the high level cinematic style control of our framework, we performed several laboratory tests and also produced a live presentation with participation of the audience.

The first test was a comparison between Film and Theatrical styles. In that case, we generated two different montages of the experiment "The Tempest", featuring these two extremes, i.e., respectively 100% of Film style and 100% of Theatrical style. In the Film style montage, only near shots have been used and the cuts performed when each characters started a new line of the dialogue. In the Theatrical style montage, only mid and wide hots have been used and the cuts selected when the action caused a change in relative position of the characters.

Also, the Film style was controlled by a parametric probability distribution that would decide between action or reaction shots (i.e., showing the character speaking or listening) and between close-up or point-of-view shots of the selected character. In contrast, the Theatrical style was controlled by a non-parametric probability distribution, created by the director to maximize the visibility of the characters in the frame during their action.

The second test was a montage that combined Film and Theatrical styles with equal probability (i.e., a 50%/50% chance).

7.3 Evaluation

The evaluation of our tests revealed that the proposed probabilistic cinematic style designed for the experiment "The Tempest" provided a simple and intuitive control of the style variables involved.

The extreme cases: Film and Theatrical montages showed what was expected, in terms of framing coverage and pace of cuts.

The intermediate case: combination of 50% Film and 50% Theatrical montage produced a result very close to a realistic editing setting, with a well balanced combination of wide and near shots and a good cut dynamics.

8   Conclusions and Future Work

In this paper we described a new expressive tool for Audio/Visual Presentations in the context of Live Cinema. It extends the VR Kino+Theater image switcher to provide high level style controls that allows the director to act as a DJ.

Future work goes into two directions: investigate the inverse approach to generate a Cut Graph, and experiment with an editing interface controlled by the viewer.

Our current work proposes a generative interface for high-level probabilistic live editing with virtual cinematography. In that sense, the probability distributions in the cut graph, as well as the parametric controls in the interface, are created by the director. This is the direct approach to solve the problem.

The other side of the coin is the inverse approach to automatically generate the solution. The problem, then, is to generate the editing machinery from examples, using machine learning techniques, such as *Deep Learning* with Neural Networks. In this setting, we can have two possible scenarios: the first scenario would be to estimate only the editing style from montages of an author, using supervised learning; the second scenario would entail a full understanding of the editing style structure manifold, including the style, the parametrization and the AIA interface controls.

It is worth noting that this inverse approach to the problem has many potential applications, for example in Live presentations of Sports and Music Shows.

Finally, another way to explore the ideas discussed in this paper is in a live non-linear editing setting where the montage of the story would be controlled by viewer through an interactive interface for selecting the relevant shots and show them on the screen. This kind of interface has been proposed by the Eko group in the context of interactive storytelling [1]. They recently released the series "War Games" using this approach.

References

1. Company, E.: Eko studio (2017). https://studio.helloeko.com/
2. Coppola, F.: Live Cinema and Its Techniques. Liveright, New York (2017)
3. Jordan, M.I.: Graphical models. Statist. Sci. **19**(1), 140–155 (2004)
4. Leake, M., Davis, A., Truong, A., Agrawala, M.: Computational video editing for dialogue-driven scenes. ACM Trans. Graph. **36**(4), 130:1–130:14 (2017)
5. Technologies, U.: Web portal (2017). https://unity3d.com/
6. Velho, L., Carvalho, L., Lucio, D.: VR Kino+Theater: a platform for the future digital media. Technical report TR-01-2018, VISGRAF Lab - IMPA (2018)
7. Velho, L., Lucio, D., Carvalho, L.: Situated participatory virtual reality. In: Proceedings of XVI Simposio Brasileiro de Jogos e Entretenimento Digital (2017)
8. Velho, L., et al.: Making the tempest. Technical report TR-02-2018, VISGRAF Lab - IMPA (2018). https://www.visgraf.impa.br/tempest/

Virtual and Real Body Experience Comparison Using Mixed Reality Cycling Environment

Wesley Oliveira[1]([✉]), Werner Gaisbauer[2], Michelle Tizuka[1],
Esteban Clua[1], and Helmut Hlavacs[2]

[1] Computer Science Institute, Universidade Federal Fluminense, Niterói, Brazil
{wesleyoliveira,mmtizuka}@id.uff.br, esteban@ic.uff.br
[2] University of Vienna, Universitätsring 1, 1010 Vienna, Austria
werner.gaisbauer@gmail.com,
helmut.hlavacs@univie.ac.at

Abstract. Different solutions present the usage of bicycles with Head Mounted Display (HMD) in which virtual scenarios are visualized as background for athletes training or as cardiac patient rehabilitation systems. However, assessments on presence, degrees of immersion and user involvement with real bicycles in those virtual scenarios still are rare. In this paper we present a haptic interface of a real bicycle using HMDs as a mixed reality display using a procedural city as a background scenario. To measure and evaluate presence, two experiments had been conducted. One that simulates a virtual reality mode and a second that corresponds to a mixed reality mode. By think aloud method, it was possible to analyze the degree of presence, through control, focus, immersion and involvement factors. Six of the seven participants described that immersion is augmented as well as the feeling of presence in the mixed reality interface, feeling a better experience with the improvement of movements. Issues related to comfort and the visual graphic were also evaluated with some results on the stimulus that also opens new possibilities for future works in different areas.

Keywords: Mixed reality · Haptic interface · VR bicycle
Procedural content generation (PCG)

1 Introduction

Several researches in VR environments have been developed in the past decade in different areas and scenarios. Some solutions already present the usage of bicycles with Head Mounted Display (HMD) in which virtual scenarios are visualized as background for athletes training or as cardiac patient rehabilitation systems [1]. In the case of user's body perception, there are still few in development, leaving those focused on the perception only of the hands by the users [2, 3]. However, assessments on the interactivity and appropriation of the user's real body itself with the bicycle are still rare or unknown.

In this paper we present a haptic interface of a real bicycle using HMDs as Mixed Reality (MR) display and programmable controller boards with Arduino to capture user

E. Clua et al. (Eds.): ICEC 2018, LNCS 11112, pp. 52–63, 2018.
https://doi.org/10.1007/978-3-319-99426-0_5

interaction with the bicycle. This system can be defined as a "proxy object" [4, 5], where the rotational movement from the handlebar is possible within the virtual environment, allowing a closer approximation of reality and better communication capacity between users' hands. We introduce the concept of real hands, forearms and legs appearance, capturing images from the HMD camera and showing real interfaces for the user.

To measure and evaluate the MR interface, two experiments had been conducted: one that simulates a virtual reality (VR) mode and the other that corresponds to a MR simulation mode, where the user's real body and the front part of the real bicycle are visualized inside the virtual environment. We conducted experiments with seven gamers users. Some of them don't usually ride a bicycle. However, six from the seven participants described that immersion is augmented as well as the feeling of presence in the MR simulation environment, feeling a better experience with the improvement of movements (speed, pedals and rotation of the handlebars).

On Sect. 2 of this paper we discuss related works that influenced and lead to the development of this experiment. After that, on Sect. 3 is shown the methodology used to develop the interactive bicycle and virtual environment. Following Sect. 4 describes the design technique chosen to guide the experiment and the results obtained. Finally, on Sect. 5, the conclusion achieved based on the results is presented.

2   Related Works

2.1   Presence in Mixed and Virtual Reality

The ability to permeate between virtuality and the real world is one of the main characteristics of Mixed Reality [6]. Currently, the usage of MR is the most varied, from tools to development of collaborative projects [5, 7] that allow teams to interact with telepresence projects, educational projects [8–10], medical fields [11], games [12] or "pervasive games" [13, 14].

A new MR paradigm that has emerged recently and still is not well understood by both industry and academia is the "pervasive virtuality" [4, 15–17], which comprises a MR environment that is constructed and enriched using real-world information sources that causes extremely intense and immersive feeling. It is also known that to make the user experience immersive, with environments generated through sensorial elements, usually visual, auditory and tactile stimuli and also by the continuous tracking of the surrounding environment it is crucial to track and switch between real and virtual world, maintaining their correct positioning during interaction. [5, 18] present several variables that influences on the feeling of presence, such as: user's head rotation, path curvature, scaling of translational movements, and scaling of objects (and/or the entire environment). Some works about situations experienced by the user and the position of the objects in a way that has connection with the context and interaction through the perception or manipulation of their own hands had been developed [4, 19–21], but the concern on measuring presence in virtual environments are still rare. [22] defines presence as a normal awareness phenomenon that requires directed attention and is based in the interaction between sensory stimulation, environmental factors that encourage involvement and enable immersion, in addition to internal tendencies to become involved but few had taken those questions through a real virtual environment evaluation [23], in order to mitigate the effects of interruption to measure presence. Most of the works continues on measuring presence in the formal way as presence questionnaires or interviews after the experience on the virtual environment [24].

2.2   Procedural City Generation

Procedural city generation can be achieved by multiple means, and the basic idea is to apply procedural content generation (PCG) algorithms [25] to generate a whole city at the push of a button [26]. As an example, L-systems have been successfully used to generate realistic cities with complex street networks and a very high number of buildings [27]. Furthermore, shape grammars have been utilized to generate realistic buildings [28] like in our procedural city scenario. A newer development in PCG is Maxim Gumin's WaveFunctionCollapse (WFC) algorithm that was first published in 2016 [29, 30] and became very popular on the internet in a short time frame with many developers running experiments and reimplementing the source code for other environments like the Unity game engine. It has been successfully used before in the wild for different interesting scenarios like ours [31]. Infinitown is a procedurally generated city [32] that is related to our idea of an endless city, but our version does not use a finite grid of random city blocks but WFC to achieve variation and generation of city blocks. The present work uses methods of procedural city generation for creating endless environments.

3   Methodology

3.1   Implementation

The bicycle apparatus consists of a standard commercial bicycle, a stand to hold the bicycle stable, an Arduino board connected to the sensors, a Hall sensor and magnets attached to the rear rims used to measure the RPM of the rear wheel of the bicycle and a 10 KΩ potentiometer connected through 3D printed gears to the handlebars allowing to capture the turning angle of the bicycle (see Fig. 1).

The MR build is composed of an HTC Vive HMD, the HTC Vive camera, a Leap Motion sensor mounted on the front of the HMD using a 3D-printed frame and a Chroma key background. The project is composed of two experiments, one that uses the Leap Motion to track the user hands position to interact with a virtual bicycle while the user real hand touches the real bicycle, serving as a haptic interface; and other that uses the HMD camera and the Chroma key to create the MR environment where the user sees his own body and the real bicycle.

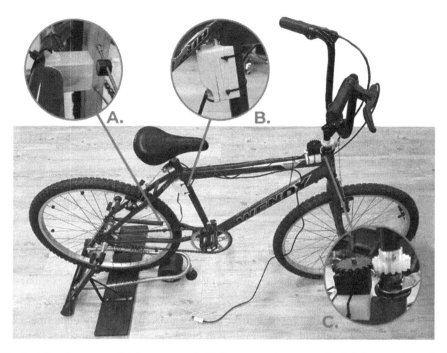

Fig. 1. Bicycle system with the sensors. A: Hall sensor and magnets. B: Arduino board attached to a case. C: Potentiometer and 3d printed gears

The Chroma key effect was achieved using a custom Chroma key shader created communicate with a Stencil shader. This set allowed the Chroma key background to be placed only in front of the bicycle in the room. If the participant look towards the handle to see his hands or the bicycle the Chroma key shader would come in effect removing the green background and if the participant look on others directions, for ex.: up or to the sides, the Stencil shader erase the camera image allowing the visualization of the real bicycle and hands overlayed on the virtual environment without an extensive Chroma key background. A scheme with the main controllers can be seen in Fig. 2. The software was developed in Unity3D (2017.1.0f3) using Leap Motion Orion (3.2.1) and SteamVR (1.2.3) plugins and using the arduino sensors data as input on the application. Our experiment was running on a Windows PC with an Intel i7 3, 10 GHz, 8 GB RAM and a Nvidia GTX 1050.

3.2   Scenario

As a background scenario, we use a procedural virtual city [26], which we call "Endless City". We use Maxim Gumin's WaveFunctionCollapse (WFC) algorithm [30], an example-driven image generation algorithm (but applying it to 3D Unity game objects rather than colored pixels using Joseph Parker's WFC version [34]) to bootstrap the procedural generation and achieve variation by generating city blocks and streets on a 20 by 20 grid which we call a city superblock [33]. Each element of the grid can

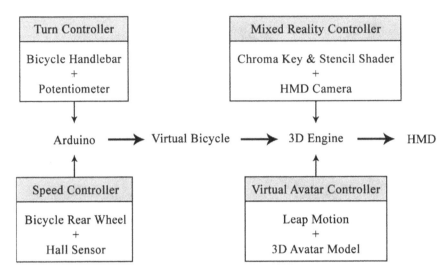

Fig. 2. Scheme showing the controllers responsible for each key element of the experiment

either be occupied by a building or a street and has a size of 30 Unity units (meters). Each building has a single sidewalk around it to make the city more plausible. The city is procedurally generated on the fly and continues quasi-endless in all directions including the ground.

The seeds from the random number generator are stored for already visited areas (city superblocks) and restored if the user visits that area again. Only a three by three grid of city superblocks are procedurally generated and held in memory simultaneously. The bicycle is always located in the center superblock, and if, for example it moves into the superblock located to the north, three new superblocks are generated (to the north of the already existing ones), and the redundant three superblocks (to the south) are removed from memory. The same is true for the other compass directions. In the space between the superblocks there is always a street present to make it possible to connect them easily (Fig. 3).

Each building texture is generated using a tiny software library (TinyCgaShape) written by one of the authors of this paper in Unity C# and based on CGA shape, a grammar for the procedural modeling of computer graphics architecture [28, 35]. Although the buildings are not yet photorealistic, we plan to add more realistic building textures using Unity assets or procedural methods (e.g., using Perlin noise [36] to create a tiling brick texture) as future work. We were aiming to create a small sized Unity asset (which is clearly possible using PCG): TinyCgaShape is just 5-kilobytes in size and the code for generating a building including sidewalks is just 17-kilobytes, and finally, the WFC code (for the generation part) is just 24-kilobytes. The buildings are made of cubes that can vary in height to give them the look of skyscrapers and the building textures are fully parametric (they can vary in the number of floors, floor height, window width and height, and building color).

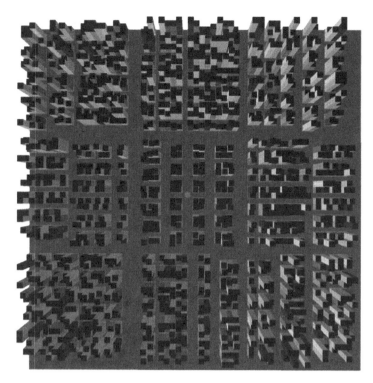

Fig. 3. Endless City as seen from above consisting of a three by three grid of superblocks. The bicycle, represented as the red dot, is always located in the center superblock and the city extends in all directions quasi-infinitely. (Color figure online)

3.3   Participants, Stimuli, Tasks and Measures

Seven gamers were invited to participate on the experiments. Our sample was drawn from students of our University, all male, between 22 and 38 years performed the two experiments. After signing the consent, image and voice forms, each participant was asked to go up on the real bicycle and received the explanation about the devices and the procedure of the study. After setting up the HMD and being familiarized with the virtual handlebar, the participant started the first experiment. On the first task, the participant was asked to drive through the cones circuit inside "Endless City". On the second task, the participant only needed to free pedal to any part of the city like a simulation tour. In the second experiment, the user was asked to repeat both tasks (see Fig. 4).

Through thinking aloud method the users were encouraged to describe their feelings on immersion and controls of the system answering questions about focus, immersion and interaction, that could later be analysed to measure the degree of presence (see Table 1). All the experiments were recorded through video and photographs inside the laboratory of the University.

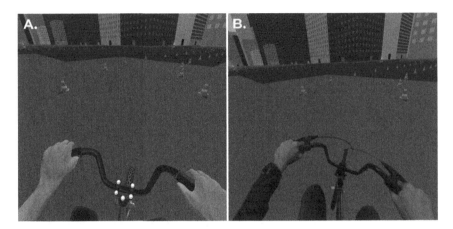

Fig. 4. User's body, handlebars and scenario on the two experiments. A: 3d avatar mode and B: real user's body in the virtual environment.

Table 1. Questions made by the facilitators to the participants.

Before the experiments	Experiment 1	Experiment 2	After the experiments
How often do you ride a bike?	How do you feel about this experiment?	How do you feel about this experiment?	How much did the control devices interfere with the performance of assigned tasks or other activities?
	Are you having any difficulty during this experiment?	How is the merge of virtual and real worlds?	
How do you feel today	Are you feeling immersed now?	Are you having any difficulty during this experiment	Were you involved in the experimental task as you lost track of time?
	How do you feel about the bike?	Are you feeling immersed now?	
How well can you move or handle the handlebars?	How convincing was your feeling of moving inside the virtual environment?	How do you feel about the bike?	Which experiment is more comfortable to ride a bike?
		Which is more immersive?	
		How convincing was your feeling of moving inside the virtual environment?	If there was a simulator like that, would it encourage you to ride a bike?

Virtual Reality Experiment   Mixed Reality Experiment

4 Results and Data Analyses

The initial step was to listen, see and take notes on the video recordings of all feedback. Even in a still exploratory way and as "simulation stage" [4], the physical environment (city) equipped with the infrastructure allowed the creation of a mixed reality environment and with it was possible to analyse the degree of presence, through control, focus, immersion and involvement factors (see Table 2).

All users were feeling well before performing the tests and were able to complete the tasks without any immediate physical or dexterity difficulties even though five of the seven participants didn't use a bicycle frequently. However, it was noticed that the two participants who were used to ride bicycles had problems with balance in the VR experiment, while they felt no problems with our proposed MR solution.

All seven participants felt immersed in the first experiment (VR), but one mentioned that the virtual hand was not like his real hands. Also, three of the seven participants felt a difference between the actual handlebar angle to the virtual handlebar angle. However, none of the participants had difficulty with the sensors or changes made in the actual bicycle to allow the experiments.

It is known by now, that rendering the user's body in VR increases presence and consequently immersion and involvement, which enable the illusion of "being there" in various situations, whether in games, sports training, medical rehabilitation or even in the form of simulations and exploration of the environment. What this study could demonstrate is that not only rendering, but the real images of the user's body and the "proxy object" could transpose the feeling of immersion for a better experience, as six participants felt more comfortable and immersed in the MR experiment. One fact that could have influenced is that a direct tracking was not applied to the legs of the user. In VR their leg position was estimated by the speed captured from the wheel, while in MR they could see their real legs without the need of programming or tracking, having an increased feeling of body presence in MR.

About realism factors, it can be said that all participants found the first experiment (VR) convincing, although two have mentioned changes that could improve the immersion in the procedural scenario, as applying a texture on the floor and reduce the sizes of buildings and sidewalks, for example. Either way, on both experiments, all participants felt so immersed that they felt losing track of time within the VR and MR during the whole test, which took about 10 to 15 min in total.

Table 2. Participants answers divided by experiments and presence factors.

Focus	Control	Immersion	Involvement
The bike is very realistic and faithful, only the amount of turning the handlebar is off		The city seems to be bigger than a real one, maybe make the bike ride faster	
I was a little dizzy with the curves and the floor could have a texture on it for better view	The virtual bike seems to turn less than the real one	At first I found it strange but it is quick to get used to the feeling and adapt that does not need to turn too much the handlebars. But I found it very convincing	
I feel a little uncomfortable because it looks like the image is late	The movement is close to the real	I am immersed, but I'm not looking at my hand because I'm looking forward.	It's a bit strange, that I move and it happens in the virtual. It's a different / new thing
I felt lack of sensation of tilting and g-force when turning in the curves, it gives a little dizziness but in the straight lines it is better		Yes I'm feeling immersed although a bit unbalanced	I prefer this one because I can see my leg pedaling
The only difficulty is to keep balanced on the bike in VR and the floor because it is one color only I don't have a sense of movement.	No difficulty to use the bicycle	I'm feeling immersed	It is more convincing than the first because the bike seems to move better in the second experiment
	I feel good, I feel immersed in the environment, but I find strange that the virtual handlebar does not turn the same amount as the actual handlebars		
It seems that I feel the same way of the first experiment, but I can see the hand and the bike more easily.	Concerning the movement of the bike it seems that it has not changed, but I think the feedback of turning the handlebars is better in this experiment.	I think the immersion in the first experiment was better, because the virtual hand matches the city.	The first thing I realize is that the movement seems more fluid than in the virtual model, it's cooler
I liked it as I can see the bike moving along with my legs moving too		See the real bicycle in the environment did not help at all for the immersion.	
I found it better to see the real bike because the movements are real, they are mine.	I think because I'm seeing myself and the feedback seems faster, it seems I can control it better.	The second is more immersive because I can see my arms instead of a 3D model	The fact that I can see my feet and the real bicycle moving makes me move better
In a matter of aesthetics, I prefer the first but for the interaction and fidelity of movement I prefer the second		The merge of the virtual with the real gets a bit strange because it is a cartoon style environment and my hand does not match	
In the movement I prefer this (MR) in the visual aspect I prefer the other (VR)		I found interesting to have the real interaction, I liked being able to see my hand	

Virtual Reality Experiment   Mixed Reality Experiment

5 Conclusions

Even with only seven participants, this study could demonstrate that not only rendering, but seen your own body and the "proxy object" in a mixed reality haptic interface could transpose the feeling of immersion for a better experience. It was able to comprove the illusion of "being there" by rendering user's real body in MR. For all the participants it can be said that they found the first experiment (VR) convincing, but it was clear by the users answers and reactions that the MR experiment had a greater degree of presence. The comparison of experiments by the users showed capability of seeing your real body in the MR experiment allowed them to have a better handling and balance of the haptic interface being tested, some of the users linked that improvement to the fact that they were able to see their real body.

With the think aloud method it was possible to analyse the degree of presence, through control, focus, immersion and involvement factors, though an integrated VR/MR questionnaire inside the virtual environment could also have been developed to achieve quantitative results. This probably will be one of the future works that the researchers aim to improve. This can demonstrate a still open world ahead to be taken, not only to measure presence and evaluate immersion and involvement in mixed reality systems, but also different applications, for instance changing scenarios and adding tasks to enable possibilities of future works in this new pervasive virtuality mixed reality paradigm with a real and not so expensive nor rare object as a bicycle.

Acknowledgments. We thank the Medialab from the Computer Science Institute – Universidade Federal Fluminense for providing the bicycle and infrastructure required to develop the haptic system and the University of Vienna for supporting this work through a doctoral promotion stipend.

References

1. Ranky, R., Mark Sivak, M., Lewis, J., Gade, V., Deutsch, J.E., Mavroidis, C.: VRACK - virtual reality augmented cycling kit: design and validation. In: Virtual Reality. IEEE, Waltham (2010)
2. Argelaguet, F., Hoyet, L., Trico, M., Lécuyer, A.: The role of interaction in virtual embodiment: effects of the virtual hand representation. In: Virtual Reality (VR), pp. 3–10. IEEE (2016)
3. Schwind, V., Knierim, P., Tasci, C., Franczak, P., Haas, N., Henze, N.: These are not my hands!: effect of gender on the perception of avatar hands in virtual reality. In: Proceedings of the 2017 CHI Conference on Human Factors in Computing Systems, CHI 2017, pp. 1577–1582. ACM, Denver (2017)
4. Valente, L., Feijó, B., Ribeiro, A., Clua, E.: The concept of pervasive virtuality and its application in digital entertainment systems. In: Wallner, G., Kriglstein, S., Hlavacs, H., Malaka, R., Lugmayr, A., Yang, H.-S. (eds.) ICEC 2016. LNCS, vol. 9926, pp. 187–198. Springer, Cham (2016). https://doi.org/10.1007/978-3-319-46100-7_16
5. Steinicke, F., Ropinski, T., Bruder, G., Hinrichs, K.: The holodeck construction manual. In: ACM SIGGRAPH 2008 Posters, pp. 97:1–97:3. ACM, New York (2008)
6. Milgran, P., Kishino, F.: A taxonomy of mixed reality visual displays. IEICE Trans. Inf. Syst. **77**(12), 1321–1329 (1994)

7. Lee, J.Y., Rhee, G.: Context-aware 3D visualization and collaboration services for ubiquitous cars using augmented reality. Int. J. Adv. Manuf. Technol. **37**(5), 431–442 (2008)
8. Billinghurst, M., Kato, H., Poupyrev, I.: The MagicBook: a transitional AR interface. Comput. Graph. **25**(5), 745–753 (2001)
9. Mateu, J., Lasala, M.J., Alamán, X.: Developing mixed reality educational applications: the virtual touch toolkit. Sensors **15**(9), 21760–21784 (2015)
10. Hoffmann, M., Meisen, T., Jeschke, S.: Shifting virtual reality education to the next level – experiencing remote laboratories through mixed reality. In: Jeschke, S., Isenhardt, I., Hees, F., Henning, K. (eds.) Automation, Communication and Cybernetics in Science and Engineering 2015/2016, pp. 293–307. Springer, Cham (2016). https://doi.org/10.1007/978-3-319-42620-4_23
11. Tepper, O.M., et al.: Mixed Reality with HoloLens: where virtual reality meets augmented reality in the operating room. Plast. Reconstr. Surg. **140**(5), 1066–1070 (2017)
12. Valente, L., Clua, E., Silva, A.R., Feijó, B.: Live-action virtual reality games. arXiv preprint arXiv:1601.01645 (2016)
13. Valente, L., Feijó, B., do Prado Leite, J.C.S.: Mapping quality requirements for pervasive mobile games. Requirements Eng. **22**(1), 137–165 (2017)
14. Montola, M.: A ludological view on the pervasive mixed-reality game research paradigm. Pers. Ubiquitous Comput. **15**(1), 3–12 (2011)
15. Artanim: Real Virtuality. http://artaniminteractive.com/real-virtuality. Accessed 21 Apr 2018
16. Silva, A.R., Clua, E., Valente, L., Feijó, B.: An indoor navigation system for live-action virtual reality games. In: Proceedings of SBGames 2015, pp. 84–93. SBC, Teresina (2015)
17. The VOID: The vision of infinite dimensions. https://thevoid.com. Accessed 21 Mar 2018
18. Abrash, M.: What VR could, should, and almost certainly will be within two years. Steam Dev Days, Seattle (2014). 4. Accessed 09 Dec 2017
19. Hettiarachchi, A., Wigdor, D.: Annexing reality: enabling opportunistic use of everyday objects as tangible proxies in augmented reality. In: Proceedings of the 2016 CHI Conference on Human Factors in Computing Systems, pp. 1957–1967. ACM, San Jose (2016)
20. Valente, L., Feijó, B., Silva, A.R., Clua, E.: Notes on pervasive virtuality. arXiv preprint arXiv:1605.08035 (2016)
21. Oliveira, T.: Imersão ectodigética em jogos pervasivos: a inclusão de elementos externos na experiência narrativa. Comunicação Sociedade **37**(3) (2015)
22. Witmer, B.G., Singer, M.J.: Measuring presence in virtual environments: a presence questionnaire. Presence **7**(3), 225–240 (1998)
23. Frommel, J., et al.: Integrated questionnaires: maintaining presence in game environments for self-reported data acquisition. In: Proceedings of the 2015 Annual Symposium on Computer-Human Interaction in Play (CHI PLAY 2015), pp. 359–368. ACM Press, London (2015)
24. Schubert, T., Friedmann, F., Regenbrecht, H.: The experience of presence: factor analytic insights. Presence **10**(3), 266–281 (2001)
25. Shaker, N., Togelius, J., Nelson, M.J.: Procedural Content Generation in Games: A Textbook and an Overview of Current Research. Springer, Heidelberg (2015). https://doi.org/10.1007/978-3-319-42716-4
26. Gaisbauer, W., Hlavacs, H.: Procedural attack! procedural generation for populated virtual cities: a survey. Int. J. Serious Games **4**, 19–29 (2017)
27. Parish, Y.I.H., Müller, P.: Procedural modeling of cities. Presented at the Proceedings of the 28th Annual Conference on Computer Graphics and Interactive Techniques, New York, NY, USA (2001)

28. Müller, P., Wonka, P., Haegler, S., Ulmer, A., Van Gool, L.: Procedural modeling of buildings. Presented at the ACM SIGGRAPH 2006 Papers, New York, NY, USA (2006)
29. Gumin, M.: WaveFunctionCollapse. https://github.com/mxgmn/WaveFunctionCollapse. Accessed 15 Mar 2018
30. Karth, I., Smith, A.M.: WaveFunctionCollapse is constraint solving in the wild. Presented at the Proceedings of the 12th International Conference on the Foundations of Digital Games, New York, NY, USA (2017)
31. Parker, J.: New Tool: Unity Wave Function Collapse - procedural generation from sample patterns!. https://twitter.com/jplur_/status/792440594845032448
32. Frauenfelder, M.: Infinitown is a procedurally generated city that seems to go on forever. https://boingboing.net/2017/11/28/infinitown-is-a-procedurally-g.html
33. Wikipedia contributors: City block — Wikipedia, The Free Encyclopedia (2017)
34. Parker, J.: unity-wave-function-collapse. https://selfsame.itch.io/unitywfc
35. Esri R&D Center Zurich: CityEngine Help. http://cehelp.esri.com/help/index.jsp?topic=/com.procedural.cityengine.help/html/manual/cga/basics/toc.html. Accessed 02 Apr 2018
36. Perlin, K.: An image synthesizer. SIGGRAPH Comput. Graph. **19**, 287–296 (1985)

Aspects that Need to Be Addressed During the Development of Location-Based Games

Jacques Barnard, Magda Huisman, and Günther Drevin[✉]

School of Computer Science and Information Systems, North-West University,
Potchefstroom, South Africa
jacques.barnard1984@gmail.com, {magda.huisman,gunther.drevin}@nwu.ac.za

Abstract. To determine the suitability of a software development methodology (SDM) to aid in the development of location-based games, it is necessary to determine to what degree SDMs address certain aspects that need to be addressed in the process of developing location-based games.

These aspects will be identified based on information gathered in a literature review focused on aspects needed for a successful mobile application development process, game development process, as well as a mobile game development process. This is done to ensure that these aspects will better represent the needs of developing location-based games.

These aspects will be evaluated by using a survey to measure their importance in the development process and also to determine whether any aspects were overlooked.

Keywords: Software development methodologies
Location-based games · Game development

1 Introduction

The gaming industry is a rapidly expanding industry and is expected to reach 100 billion dollars worldwide by the year 2018. Furthermore, it is expected that the mobile gaming market will grow from 10 billion dollars in 2013 to 29 billion dollars in 2018 [1,2].

The complexity of the development of games has increased exponentially [3] with one of the elements that contribute to this complexity being the multidisciplinary development process [4]. Different specialist areas, such as art, gameplay, sound, control systems, and human factors interacting with traditional software development all indicate that a specialised software engineering methodology is needed for this domain. Elements that lead to the complexity of game development are the technical challenges for the developers as well as tools, project size, workflow and other technical aspects [5].

This paper focuses on location-based games which is defined as a type of ubigame that focuses on the player's location and incorporates it in the game

© IFIP International Federation for Information Processing 2018
Published by Springer Nature Switzerland AG 2018. All Rights Reserved
E. Clua et al. (Eds.): ICEC 2018, LNCS 11112, pp. 64–75, 2018.
https://doi.org/10.1007/978-3-319-99426-0_6

play [6]. This is to allow the player to be more immersed in the game world were the magic happens. Furthermore, location-based games are a type of mobile game and it is important to mention that the development of mobile games is just as complicated as console or on-line games [7]. This is due to the fact that the development of mobile games entails different aspects that are not included in the development of the other two previously mentioned game genres.

In this paper unique aspects that need to be addressed during the development process of location-based games are identified from the literature. These aspects are discussed in Sect. 2.

A survey is used to gather information from the gaming industry to determine the importance of each aspect and to determine whether the study has failed to identify any aspects. The survey process is discussed in Sect. 3 while the results are described in Sect. 4

2 Aspects Identified from the Literature

A list of 15 aspects, which are needed in the development process of location-based games, were identified from literature that focuses on the development process of mobile applications, games and mobile games. Most of the identified aspects applies to game development projects in general, however some of the aspects are more applicable to location-based games. Each aspect will now be described in detail.

2.1 Playability

Playability can be defined as the property of an activity that has the ability to yield enjoyment [8]. This binary measure indicates whether or not a game can be enjoyed. This is one of the factors that determines the success of a game release. This is very important, as the main objective of any game is to provide the player with an enjoyable experience when playing the game. Playability leads to player experience, which is another aspect that will be discussed next [9]. Based on this it can be said that playability is a prerequisite for player experience. Playability is regarded to be very important to the game development process. The importance of playability can be further emphasised by indicating that there is a dedicated research area that focuses on playability heuristics [9–12]. This research focuses on determining issues with playability, as well as how to improve the playability of games. Furthermore, the research also mentions that usability alone is not enough in a game and that playability is also needed.

2.2 Player Experience

As mentioned previously, playability is a prerequisite for player experience. This prerequisite emphasises the tightly connected nature of these two aspects. The difference between the two aspects is that playability is the evaluative process of the player in respect of the game, whereas player experience is the evaluation of the players [9]. Player experience describes all sensorial experiences that a player experiences when playing a game [13]. Player experience can be compared with user experience in traditional information systems. The difference is that games are interactive systems with the main objective of exploiting the feelings of the player and ensuring fun and entertainment [13,14]. This difference enhances the complexity of player experience in a game compared to that of information systems [13,15]. However, it is insufficient to analyse the player experience by only using usability [12,15]. Usability, as well as playability are needed for the player experience to be fully incorporated in the game development. In the game design process player experience is an important focus and needs to be incorporated in the development of games [15].

2.3 Usability

Usability can be defined as the effectiveness, efficiency and user satisfaction in a specific context of use. Player experience benefits from incorporating usability in the game design process [15]. Furthermore, usability also affects playability [9]. By considering these two facts, it is clear that usability is important for game development. Another measure of the importance of usability is that the gaming industry is adopting formal techniques from human computer interaction [16]. These techniques are known as usability heuristics. Different usability heuristics to evaluate the usability of the game exist [9,11,14,16]. However, only applying usability to the analysis of player experience is not sufficient due to the fact that games are more complex [11,12] and applying these usability heuristics improves the design of games [16].

2.4 Value to the Player

Value to the player is also known as value to the user in the case of mobile applications. In this study, the term value to the player will be used. There are many mobile games that compete to be downloaded and played by players. An application or game is worthless if it does not add value to the player [17]. In other words, what makes a person choose a mobile game or application is the value that the game or application has for the person. This is done by utilising the functionality of the platform on which the mobile game or application is deployed, in this case a mobile device [7,18]. This functionality is valuable to the player if there is no other mobile game or application that can utilise the mobile device as the specific mobile game or application, thereby ensuring a unique gaming experience. Mobile applications or mobile games must also share their time with other activities conducted on the player's device, such as listening to music and instant messaging [7]. Another aspect that contributes to the value of the mobile game or application is incorporating the game or application into everyday life. Mobile games or applications that can increase productivity, help players perform day-to-day tasks, save time and relax players are some of the factors that can increase the value for the player [19,20]. Based on this, it is clear that value to the player is important and should be taken into account when developing a game.

2.5   User Interface Design

Location-based games are usually deployed on mobile devices as a location-based game is a mobile application. Knowledge about mobile applications with regard to user interface design is therefore also relevant for location-based games. The fact that location-based games are developed for hand-held devices allows the interface to be divided into three user interfaces (UIs), namely graphical user interface (GUI) [21,22], logical user interface (LUI) [21,23] and physical user interface (PUI). The GUI includes components that render the gaming world on the screen of the device. The LUI represents the logical flow of the mobile game. This can be navigation, player controls, menus and the use of gesture in the gaming world. The PUI is the physical medium that the player uses as input for the mobile game. This can be keyboard, touchscreen and different sensors, such as GPS, camera, accelerometer, etc. During the development of a location-based game, these UI elements need to be incorporated to improve the satisfaction of playing the game.

2.6   Development Team

The development team in a game company consists of different specialists [24–26]. This adds complexity in managing the development process of games. Management needs to be able to create a balance between the needs of the different specialists, as well as the managerial tasks of the development team. The development process needs to take into account that different specialists need to work together on the same project. By addressing this aspect, the complexity of managing the development process can be reduced.

2.7   Re-playability

Re-playability can be defined as the quantifiable measure for the enjoyment that a player experiences while playing the game [8,27]. Re-playability also refers to the number of times a person can enjoy playing the specific game [8]. Re-playability can also be divided into different aspects, namely difficulty, completion, social aspects, randomisation and the experience [28]. The re-playability of games keeps players interested in the game until the release of either the next instalment of the game, or a game that is similar [27]. Due to the fact that most location-based games are restricted to a specific area in which they can be played, players can quickly become bored with the same game [28]. This is why it is important that the development process takes re-playability into account to allow players to replay the game as many times as possible without getting bored.

2.8 Learnability

Learnability can be defined as a player's ability to understand and master the game [29,30]. Aspects that need to be understood and mastered can include the game's mechanics, objectives, rules and how to interact with the game. Learnability should also offer the player satisfaction in learning the game. It should also expand the player's knowledge and techniques to resolve challenges presented by new games. Learnability is one of the aspects that also influences the playability, as well as usability of a game. To focus on learnability as one of the aspects in the development process of games could enhance the playability and the usability of the game.

2.9 Efficiency

Efficiency is one of the measures that directly impacts usability. By this it can be said that usability incorporates efficiency [31]. Efficiency can be described as the player using the least amount of resources to achieve the goal of the game. This is also known as efficiency in user interaction. Furthermore, the efficiency of utilising hardware is also a crucial factor for mobile games, as resources on hand-held devices are limited [32]. For example, mobile games need graphics, sound and location-based services. For all these services the efficiency needs to be taken into account in the development of the game.

2.10 Security and Privacy

Security and privacy, although two very different concepts, are usually utilised in combination, as they are interdependent. Location-based games or services need to ensure that the location privacy of the players is secure [33]. If this is not done, the location or location history of the player can be made known to certain people [33,34]. When the players start to share, it does not mean that the players want to share all the information with everybody [33]. This is why it is important when developing a location-based game that privacy is kept in mind. The challenge of location-based games is in securing the privacy of the player without sacrificing the accuracy of the game [34]. This is why it is important that security aspects need to be included in the development process of a location-based game.

2.11 Availability and Accessibility

Mobile games, such as location-based games do not serve a purpose if they cannot be distributed to and utilised by players. Due to the rapid development and the shift that mobile technology has made to Android, Apple and Blackberry, the distribution and utilisation of mobile games have been simplified [35]. By creating centralised application or game portals, updates can be readily available, helping to reduce the management and support of these applications and games [20,36,37]. The effect that availability and accessibility have on developers, are that they need to incorporate and work towards publishing games and applications onto various markets to make it accessible to the public. These application markets make it possible for developers, with a level of ease, to make sure that applications and games are more available to the public [19]. For these reasons it is important to ensure that the development process of a location-based game incorporates availability and accessibility.

2.12   Cognitive Support

This aspect focuses on structuring the game's controls or input logically so that the player can play the game without uncertainty or excess effort [21]. It is important that players be able to predict the flow of operations when planning to perform a task on the game or application [19]. If the cognitive flow of an application or game is designed effectively, the user or player's chance of making a mistake decrease [21,38]. In addition, the cognitive process is the process a player carries out when executing a mobile phone task namely: planning, execution, translation and assessment [21]. A mobile game should also support these steps to decrease the effort of playing the game.

2.13   Compatibility

The rapid development in the mobile market has led to an increased in the different mobile devices and platforms [39,40]. This can result in complications for the development of location-based games, such as screen size, input device, control structures for sensor, etc. Because of these constraints, the development of any mobile application or game can be time consuming if a new project has to be developed for all platforms. Therefore, it is important that different techniques should be utilised for cross-platform development [40,41]. The techniques that could aid in the development for different platforms are: using web application and application programming interfaces (APIs) that allow cross-platform development [39].

2.14   Adaptability

Adaptability can be described in two dimensions. The first is that the game should be adaptable to the context within which it is being used [19,20,41]. This can include making use of data, such as time, day, weather, GPS location and Internet connectivity. Secondly, the game should be able to adapt to the players' specifications, such as configuring display options, sounds, different sensor settings, difficulty settings, vibrations, etc. Lastly, location-based games usually focus on only one location for the game to be played [28]. If adaptability is incorporated in the development process, it may allow the location of the location-based game to be adaptable to the player's surroundings, adding another dimension to the location-based game.

2.15   Organisational Structure

The organisational structure of a gaming company does not reflect the traditional structure of functional departments [25, 42]. Gaming companies resemble project-based firms. Furthermore, if a gaming company is to be classified as a project-based firm, the nature of the company exhibits specific aspects that are different from more traditional project-based firms. The complexity of managing a game project lies in the ability to maintain a balance between different specialists. Another complexity that is added to the development of game projects is that there needs to be a balance between artistic flexibility and strict managerial devices [42]. The development process needs to take this into account when a game is being developed.

3   Survey

The survey was in the form of a questionnaire with 15 questions, each of which was in the format "Rank the importance of ...". The responses were on a Likert scale from 1 to 10 where 1 was least important and 10 most important. The 15 questions were used to determine the rank of each of the 15 aspects identified from the literature, and discussed in Sect. 2.

In addition, the survey also had an open-ended question that allowed the respondents to add additional aspects if any were overlooked.

The survey was targeted at gaming companies, indie gamers and game development research labs and researchers. The response rate of the survey cannot be calculated accurately, as different forms of media were used to reach the respondents. The different types of media that were used to gather information via the survey were: email, an on-line survey, email groups and social media.

The first attempt at gathering information was done by attaching the questionnaire to an email that was then mailed to gaming companies and research labs. Using this approach, 15 completed questionnaires were gathered. However, the respondents indicated that it would be better to develop an online survey. This was done in Google Docs and emails were once again sent with the link to the questionnaire attached. The emails were sent to the developers that did not respond in the previous round. This resulted in a further 19 completed questionnaires. Next, the game research group gamesnetwork@listserv.uta.fi. was approached and a further 17 completed questionnaires were gathered.

After this the questionnaire was posted on gaming community groups on LinkedIn. These groups specifically cater for games developers and include: Android Game Development, design3, Games Developers, Games Developers Group, Game Development & Design, Game Development Business, Gaming Passion and Profession, Mobile Game Development, The Online Game Group, Video Game Professionals and iPhone Android Mobile App Design, Development & Promotion.

The last 27 responses to the questionnaires were gathered in this attempt. Through this iterative process, 78 completed questionnaires were collected during the survey.

The results of the questionnaire will now be used to determine the importance of addressing each of the aspects during the development of location-based games.

4   Results

The results of the 78 completed questionnaires are shown in Table 1. Frequency analysis was also carried out on the data to show the frequency distribution of each question and the number of times each ranking occurs. This is shown in Table 2. In Table 1 the aspects have been arranged according to the average that each aspect scored in the survey. It is not surprising that playability ranked the highest amongst all the aspects according to mobile games developers and location-based games developers, as this is one of the most important aspects in games [9]. It is also interesting to see that the three aspects that are closely related, namely playability, user experience and usability scored the highest out of all the aspects. These results confirmed the findings in the literature that playability was more important than player experience, as playability is a prerequisite for player experience.

Table 1. Results of ranking aspects

	Average	Median	Minimum	Maximum	Standard deviation
Playability	8.81	10	3	10	1.77
Player experience	8.70	10	1	10	1.91
Usability	7.93	8	3	10	1.90
Value to the player	7.67	8	1	10	2.44
User interface design	7.47	8	2	10	2.12
Development team	7.37	8	1	10	2.32
Re-playability	7.34	8	1	10	2.47
Learnability	7.15	7	1	10	2.31
Efficiency	7.14	8	1	10	2.46
Security and privacy	7.11	8	1	10	2.69
Availability and accessibility	7.07	7	1	10	2.56
Cognitive support	6.90	7	1	10	2.20
Compatibility	6.62	7	1	10	2.73
Adaptability	6.40	7	1	10	2.53
Organisational structure	6.23	6	1	10	2.57
Average	7.33*	8.00	1.33	10.00	2.44*

*(Total value for entire dataset)

The security and privacy aspect scored an average of 7.11, which is lower than the average of 7.33 for all the aspects. From this it would seem that although security and privacy is important to the developers it is not as important as one would expect in the light of security concerns regarding online activity [43,44]. To ensure the development of secure location-based games, there should be more emphasis on security and privacy in the development process.

The aspect that scored the lowest was organisational structure. This might be due to the fact that games developers still try to be solo developers or lone wolf developers, as was the case at the inception of game development [45].

The average score of 73.3% (7.33 out of 10) for all the aspects indicates that the games developers on average agreed that the aspects identified were important for the development of location-based games.

In addition to the average, the median, minimum, maximum and standard deviation were also calculated to demonstrate the grouping of the data. Most of the aspects' standard deviations were between 1.77 and 2.73 with a total standard deviation for the entire dataset of 2.44. The ranking of the aspects seems to indicate that the games developers agree with the identified aspects.

Table 2. Frequency analysis

	Ranking									
	1	2	3	4	5	6	7	8	9	10
Playability	0	0	1	4	3	0	2	9	17	42
Player experience	1	0	0	3	4	2	3	10	12	43
Usability	0	0	3	3	2	6	10	21	10	23
Value to the player	1	3	3	3	5	6	5	17	9	26
User interface design	0	2	2	4	6	7	16	13	10	18
Development team	2	1	2	4	6	7	14	13	8	21
Re-playability	2	2	4	3	6	10	6	12	15	18
Learnability	1	3	2	3	8	9	14	12	8	18
Efficiency	1	2	6	4	6	11	6	14	10	18
Security and privacy	3	2	3	7	7	5	8	9	11	23
Availability and accessibility	1	4	3	4	9	11	12	4	7	23
Cognitive support	1	1	3	7	8	9	15	15	5	14
Compatibility	3	5	4	5	14	4	8	12	7	16
Adaptability	3	2	6	7	11	7	16	8	4	14
Organisational structure	5	2	4	5	15	10	12	7	6	12

The distribution of the rankings across the different aspects is shown in Table 2. The frequency indicates the number of times that a rank was assigned by the participants for that aspect. Ranking 10 with a frequency of 42 for playability shows that 42 of the 78 participants ranked playability's importance as 10 out of 10.

The aspects that have been identified were matched to the responses given to the open-ended question to determine whether any aspects were overlooked in the literature search and to add any such aspects, however, all of the suggestions that the games developers made were either included in the list or was not deemed to be an aspect of location-based games.

5   Conclusions and Future Work

In this study aspects that need to be addressed during the development of location-based games were identified from the literature. The aspects were then validated using an online survey to gather information from the gaming industry to determine how important each aspect is. Furthermore, this survey also gave the participants the ability to add aspects if any were neglected.

It was also noted that security and privacy was not regarded as one of the most important aspects needed in the development process of location-bases games. This is troubling as it leaves the players with a big security gap.

The results of this study can now be used to develop a framework that can be used to evaluate the suitability of different SDMs for the development of location-based games [46].

References

1. gamesindustry.biz: Game software market to hit $100 billion by 2018, June 2014. http://www.dfcint.com/wp/worldwide-market-forecasts-for-the-video-game-and-interactive-entertainment-industry/
2. Intelligence, D.: Worldwide market forecasts for the video game and interactive entertainment industry (2014). http://www.dfcint.com/wp/?p=48
3. Reyno, E.M., Carsí Cubel, J.A.: Model-driven game development: 2D platform game prototyping. In: Proceedings of the 13th IEEE International Conference on Requirements Engineering, GAMEON 2008, pp. 5–7 (2008)
4. Callele, D., Neufeld, E., Schneider, K.: Requirements engineering and the creative process in the video game industry. In: Proceedings of the 13th IEEE International Conference on Requirements Engineering, RE 2005, pp. 240–252 (2005)
5. Blow, J.: Game development: harder than you think. Queue 1(10), 28–37 (2004)
6. Buzeto, F.N., e Silva, T.B.P., Castanho, C.D., Jacobi, R.P.: Reconfigurable games: games that change with the environment. In: 2014 Brazilian Symposium on Computer Games and Digital Entertainment, pp. 61–70, November 2014
7. Feijoo, C., Gómez-Barroso, J.L., Aguado, J.M., Ramos, S.: Mobile gaming: industry challenges and policy implications. Telecommun. Policy 36(3), 212–221 (2012)
8. Krall, J., Menzies, T.: Aspects of replayability and software engineering: towards a methodology of developing games. J. Softw. Eng. Appl. 5(7), 459–466 (2012)
9. Nacke, L.E., et al.: Playability and player experience research [panel abstracts]. In: Proceedings of the 2009 DiGRA International Conference: Breaking New Ground: Innovation in Games, Play, Practice and Theory. Brunel University, DiGRA 2009, September 2009
10. Desurvire, H., Caplan, M., Toth, J.A.: Using heuristics to evaluate the playability of games. In: CHI 2004 Extended Abstracts on Human Factors in Computing Systems, CHI EA 2004, pp. 1509–1512 (2004)

11. Korhonen, H., Koivisto, E.M.I.: Playability heuristics for mobile games. In: Proceedings of the 8th Conference on Human-Computer Interaction with Mobile Devices and Services, MobileHCI 2006, pp. 9–16 (2006)
12. Korhonen, H., Koivisto, E.M.I.: Playability heuristics for mobile multi-player games. In: Proceedings of the 2nd International Conference on Digital Interactive Media in Entertainment and Arts, DIMEA 2007, pp. 28–35 (2007)
13. González-Sánchez, J.L., Gutiérrez-Vela, F.L., Simarro, F.M., Padilla-Zea, N.: Playability: analysing user experience in video games. Behav. Inf. Technol. **31**(10), 1033–1054 (2012)
14. Hagen, U.: Designing for player experience: how professional game developers communicate design visions. J. Gaming Virtual Worlds **3**(3), 259–275 (2011)
15. Nacke, L., Drachen, A.: Towards a framework of player experience research. In: Proceedings of the Second International Workshop on Evaluating Player Experience in Games at FDG, vol. 11 (2011)
16. Nacke, L.E., Drachen, A., Göbel, S.: Methods for evaluating gameplay experience in a serious gaming context. Int. J. Comput. Sci. Sport **9**(2), 1–12 (2010)
17. Verkasalo, H.: From intentions to active usage: a study on mobile services in Finland. In: 19th European Regional ITS Conference, Rome, pp. 18–20 (2008)
18. Rice, R.E., Katz, J.E.: Assessing new cell phone text and video services. Telecommun. Policy **32**(7), 455–467 (2008)
19. Kao, Y.W., Lin, C., Yang, K.A., Yuan, S.M.: A web-based, offline-able, and personalized runtime environment for executing applications on mobile devices. Comput. Stan. Interfaces **34**(1), 212–224 (2012)
20. Verkasalo, H., López-Nicolás, C., Molina-Castillo, F.J., Bouwman, H.: Analysis of users and non-users of smartphone applications. Telematics Inform. **27**(3), 242–255 (2010)
21. Heo, J., Ham, D.H., Park, S., Song, C., Yoon, W.C.: A framework for evaluating the usability of mobile phones based on multi-level, hierarchical model of usability factors. Interact. Comput. **21**(4), 263–275 (2009)
22. Plaza, I., Martín, L., Martin, S., Medrano, C.: Mobile applications in an aging society: status and trends. J. Syst. Softw. **84**(11), 1977–1988 (2011)
23. Unhelkar, B., Murugesan, S.: The enterprise mobile applications development framework. IT Prof. **12**(3), 33–39 (2010)
24. Bach, L., Cohendet, P., Pénin, J., Simon, L.: Creative industries and the IPR dilemma between appropriation and creation: some insights from the videogame and music industries. Manag. Int. **14**(3), 59–72 (2010)
25. Cohendet, P., Simon, L.: Playing across the playground: paradoxes of knowledge creation in the videogame firm. J. Organ. Behav. **28**(5), 587–605 (2007)
26. Novak, J.: Game Development Essentials: An Introduction. Cengage Learning, Boston (2011)
27. Frattesi, T., Griesbach, D., Leith, J., Shaffer, T., DeWinter, J.: Replayability of video games. IQP, Worcester Polytechnic Institute, Worcester (2011)
28. Hansen, D., Bonsignore, E., Ruppel, M., Visconti, A., Kraus, K.: Designing reusable alternate reality games. In: Proceedings of the SIGCHI Conference on Human Factors in Computing Systems, CHI 2013, pp. 1529–1538 (2013)
29. Padilla-Zea, N., López-Arcos, J.R., Sánchez, J.L.G., Vela, F.L.G., Abad-Arranz, A.: A method to evaluate emotions in educational video games for children. J. Univers. Comput. Sci. **19**(8), 1066–1085 (2013)
30. Ryan, W., Siegel, M.A.: Evaluating interactive entertainment using breakdown: understanding embodied learning in video games. In: Proceedings of DiGRA (2009)

31. Federoff, M.A.: Heuristics and usability guidelines for the creation and evaluation of fun in video games. Master's thesis, Indiana University (2002)
32. Lukashev, D., Puresev, A., Makhlushev, I.: 3D applications for 3G mobile phones: design, development, resource utilization. In: 2006 IEEE International Symposium on Consumer Electronics, pp. 1–4 (2006)
33. Scipioni, M.P., Langheinrich, M.: I'm here! privacy challenges in mobile location sharing. In: Second International Workshop on Security and Privacy in Spontaneous Interaction and Mobile Phone Use (IWSSI/SPMU) (2010)
34. Puttaswamy, K.P.N., et al.: Preserving location privacy in geosocial applications. IEEE Trans. Mob. Comput. **13**(1), 159–173 (2014)
35. Holzer, A., Ondrus, J.: Mobile application market: a developer's perspective. Telematics Inform. **28**(1), 22–31 (2011)
36. Al Bar, A., Mohamed, E., Akhtar, M.K., Abuhashish, F.: A preliminary review of implementing enterprise mobile application in ERP environment. Int. J. Eng. Technol. **11**(4), 77–82 (2011)
37. Kim, H., Choi, B., Wong, W.E.: Performance testing of mobile applications at the unit test level. In: 2009 Third IEEE International Conference on Secure Software Integration and Reliability Improvement, pp. 171–180, July 2009
38. Benbunan-Fich, R., Benbunan, A.: Understanding user behavior with new mobile applications. J. Strateg. Inf. Syst. **16**(4), 393–412 (2007)
39. Duarte, C., Afonso, A.P.: Developing once, deploying everywhere: a case study using JIL. Procedia Comput. Sci. **5**, 641–644 (2011)
40. Viana, W., Andrade, R.M.: XMobile: a MB-UID environment for semi-automatic generation of adaptive applications for mobile devices. J. Syst. Softw. **81**(3), 382–394 (2008)
41. Ali, N., Ramos, I., Sols, C.: Ambient-PRISMA: ambients in mobile aspect-oriented software architecture. J. Syst. Softw. **83**(6), 937–958 (2010)
42. Tschang, F.T.: Balancing the tensions between rationalization and creativity in the video games industry. Organ. Sci. **18**(6), 989–1005 (2007)
43. Jain, A.K., Shanbhag, D.: Addressing security and privacy risks in mobile applications. IT Prof. **14**, 28–33 (2012)
44. Zhu, H., Xiong, H., Ge, Y., Chen, E.: Mobile app recommendations with security and privacy awareness. In: Proceedings of the 20th ACM SIGKDD International Conference on Knowledge Discovery and Data Mining, KDD 2014, pp. 951–960 (2014)
45. Keith, C.: Agile Game Development with Scrum. Pearson Education, Turin (2010)
46. Barnard, J., Drevin, G., Huisman, M.: A framework to determine the suitability of software development methodologies for the development of location-based games. In: Munekata, N., Kunita, I., Hoshino, J. (eds.) ICEC 2017. LNCS, vol. 10507, pp. 335–342. Springer, Cham (2017). https://doi.org/10.1007/978-3-319-66715-7_36

Games that Make Curious: An Exploratory Survey into Digital Games that Invoke Curiosity

Marcello A. Gómez Maureira[1]([⊠]) and Isabelle Kniestedt[2]

[1] Leiden Institute of Advanced Computer Science,
Niels Bohrweg 1, Leiden, The Netherlands
`m.a.gomez.maureira@liacs.leidenuniv.nl`
[2] Delft University of Technology, Jaffalaan 5, Delft, The Netherlands
`i.kniestedt@tudelft.nl`

Abstract. Curiosity is an important aspect of life, but studying it is challenging without reliable stimuli. Digital games provide an ideal stimulus to investigate the circumstances that trigger curiosity and how it is expressed. A survey was conducted with the goal of assessing what game titles and game genres should be analysed to further the study of curiosity. To consider different types of curiosity, we included the Five-Dimensional Curiosity Scale (5DC) questionnaire. The survey was completed by 113 participants, and resulted in 301 game suggestions that warrant further analysis. Exploration, social simulation, and collecting tasks within games were found to rank high in triggering curiosity. We further found that social curiosity in individuals correlates with having curiosity triggered by social simulations.

Keywords: Game user research · Curiosity research · Game analysis

1 Introduction

Curiosity plays a crucial role in many aspects of human life. It is a sign for intrinsic motivation to learn and explore. In education and research, curiosity is frequently credited as one of the most important factors for progress. It is equally high regarded as motivator for creative endeavours, ingredient for stimulating communication, and sign for personal well-being. As a concept that involves both behavioural and emotional components, studying curiosity is challenging. However, recent work has made progress in establishing definitions of curiosity and psychometric instruments to measure it. As a result, there is growing interest in the applied use of what has been learned about curiosity, such as to improve teaching methods [11,24] and the design of video games [26,31]. Games, here understood as systems for structured play, provide multi-faceted environments for stimulating curious behaviour. At the same time, there is a lack of specific knowledge on which games or game genres stand out in their ability to invoke

E. Clua et al. (Eds.): ICEC 2018, LNCS 11112, pp. 76–89, 2018.
https://doi.org/10.1007/978-3-319-99426-0_7

curiosity. Knowing this would allow for more in-depth analysis of the methods that existing games use to make players curious.

In this study we thus aim to lay the groundwork for filling this gap with an exploratory survey involving 113 participants. In the survey, we asked players to rank well-known games according to how curious they felt while playing them. We further inquired which game titles made them curious in the past, using established dimensions of curiosity as prompts (see Sect. 3.3). The individual dimensions, described in detail in Sect. 3.1, give a more nuanced account of an individual's curiosity than assessing it on a single scale. A total of 301 games were mentioned by participants and were then categorized according to a list of pre-defined game genres. This categorization allowed us to analyse patterns within the varied selection. With this, we examine **what games and game genres are successful in invoking curiosity.** As final part of the survey, participants filled in the 5DC questionnaire [13]. This empirically validated questionnaire establishes a score for each participant according to five dimensions of curiosity (see Sect. 3.1). With this data, we examined **whether there is a connection between an individual's tendency to become curious and the game genres that invoke curiosity.**

The primary contribution of this study takes the form of an informed *selection of games and game genres* that warrant closer analysis in regards to how the elicitation of curiosity may be designed for within a game. We also looked for results that would help inform the starting point of this analysis and impacts of personality dimensions on the games that invoke an individual's curiosity. Due to its exploratory nature, this work does not provide sufficient data to formulate a generalizable theory. Nonetheless, we believe that it is an important step in exploring curiosity within different games and a basis for further work in this direction.

2   Related Work

Most research efforts regarding curiosity have taken place in the fields of philosophy [9, 27] and psychology [1, 6]. Inherent in this past is the fact that definitions of curiosity vary, ranging from accounts of human aspirations to describing it as instigating stimulant for interaction with the environment.

In this study we understand curiosity as an intrinsic motivation for pursuing new knowledge and experiences that is accompanied by pleasure and excitement. This understanding of curiosity is based on a meta review of academic articles which aimed to find commonalities in prior research [7]. In the review, the author discusses different research lenses through which curiosity has been studied. These lenses do not necessarily contradict each other, but focus on different aspects of curiosity. One view of curiosity, for example, is to consider it a primal drive that requires satisfaction [1, 2], not unlike satisfying hunger [27]. Another view is to see curiosity as a need to fill gaps in knowledge [21], requiring both existing knowledge to be aware of such a gap, as well as the evaluation that the gap is neither too large nor too insignificant to be filled [30]. Important for our study is the differentiation between curiosity as a state and curiosity as a trait. The former is the 'in-the-moment' drive for exploratory behaviour and its emotional impact [21]. Trait curiosity, on the other hand, is an individual's tendency or disposition to become curious and is considered a relatively stable personality trait [20]. It should be noted that studies have shown an influential relationship between trait and state curiosity [12,18,25].

Most of the existing work in quantifying curiosity is concerned with measuring trait curiosity [17,19] or related personality traits, such as intrinsic motivation [5,22] or sensation seeking [33]. To quantify curiosity in our study, we follow the curiosity model proposed by Kashdan et al. which suggests the involvement of five dimensions to describe an individual's disposition to become curious [13]. The individual dimensions were selected based on preceding work and validated through three surveys. The result of their study is the 'Five-Dimensional Curiosity Scale' (5DC) which quantifies trait curiosity through a validated questionnaire. We describe the individual dimensions of the 5DC in Sect. 3.1.

Games are an interesting area for researching curiosity, as they introduce further related concepts that can help to gain a better understanding. Costikyan's work regarding the role of uncertainty in games, for example, involves curiosity and describes it as an important motivator to engage in gameplay [4]. For Klimmt [14], curiosity is part of a conceptual model for player engagement, i.e. the reason for why people choose to play games. Studies into player profiling seek to establish player archetypes that involve personality traits and motivations, including curiosity [26]. In these cases, curiosity is not studied on its own but mentioned as a contributing factor. Games have also been proposed as instruments for measuring curiosity, as was done in a study from 2012 to measure scientific curiosity in children [10]. In this experiment, the performance of players within an exploration game was used as a behavioural measure instead of relying on self-report through a questionnaire.

An improved understanding of curiosity also benefits efforts in understanding player experience and can inform game development. Research by To et al. [31] investigated how game designers can elicit the curiosity of players. In their study, they follow a model of curiosity [15] that distinguishes between different triggers of curiosity. This approach is particularly useful for creating generalizable design guidelines, as it gives game designers a range of possible design interventions for invoking curiosity. Overall, existing research shows that games are able to elicit curiosity, and that this ability is useful for both research and development. We are not aware of work that investigates which games stand out as being particularly capable of invoking curiosity, and thus aim to provide such insights with this study.

3   Research Design

To gather data from a large number of participants we used an online survey aimed at people playing video games. The survey link was distributed on Facebook groups connected to gaming and game research, and included the following modules: Demographics, shared selection of games, suggestions by curiosity dimensions, and the 5DC questionnaire. We describe each of the modules below, as well as the formulation of genres to categorize games suggested by participants.

3.1 5DC Questionnaire

We used the 5DC questionnaire [13] to explore if the individual dimensions of trait curiosity predict the game genres that invoke curiosity in a player. It involves 25 questions, rated on a 5-point Likert scale, and results in scores on five dimensions: *Joyous Exploration* (JE) - being motivated by novelty, *Deprivation Sensitivity* (DS) - need of resolving, *Stress Tolerance* (ST) - ability to cope with uncertainty, *Social Curiosity* (SC) - wanting to know about others, and *Thrill Seeking* (TS) - enjoyment of anxiety.

The questionnaire has been developed by selecting items of existing measures that evaluate interest and curiosity, openness to experience, need for cognition, boredom proneness, and sensation seeking. The individual items were evaluated through three studies with a combined sample size of 3911 participants. The resulting questionnaire is not limited to a specific demographic, but has been evaluated with a representative sample of the U.S. population. Finally, the questionnaire was examined in regards to test-retest reliability through a 4-month follow-up, with results being within the range of stable personality traits.

3.2 Shared Selection of Games

Players were asked to rank games they had played out of a selection of 15 acclaimed game titles, in order to explore which of the games invoked curiosity while playing (see Fig. 1). It should be noted that this study is not about how curious people are to play a specific game (e.g. not played yet, but curious to do so), but how curious they felt as part of the gameplay. Any question regarding curiosity was phrased to reflect this focus. By presenting a predefined list we could collect data on specific game titles that can be considered of solid quality in terms of design. The measure for quality is provided by a game's Metacritic score [23], which itself is comprised of the evaluation of several game critics. While this measure is based on subjective evaluations, it is a productive approximation for choosing games of comparable quality. We took the top 15 games listed on Metacritic, after restricting our selection to games that were released in the last 10 years and combining games of the same series that met that criteria. The resulting selection involved games with a Metacritic score of 94 or higher (out of 100).

3.3 Suggestions by Curiosity Dimensions

Given that we are interested in exploring what game titles should be analysed in regards to their ability to invoke curiosity, we asked participants to suggest game titles. In order to consider different dimensions of curiosity, we used five categories for which suggestions could be added (up to two games per category). These were described as "Games that ...": "let me explore or find out new things" (GEXP), "let me solve something" (GSOL), "let me feel safe and stress-free" (GSAF), "let me understand people or let me connect to people" (GCON), and "make me feel excited and alive" (GALI).

We based the category descriptions on the *questions* that make up the dimensions of the 5DC questionnaire, rather than the descriptions of the categories themselves as defined by the researchers. As a result, the categories should match the five curiosity dimensions: GEXP matching JE, GSOL = DS, GSAF = ST, GCON = SC, and GALI = TS. In addition to suggesting game titles, participants ranked the games they provided in order of how curious they felt while playing them.

3.4 Ranking

At this point we should note how the ranking of game titles is evaluated, and why we chose to let participants rank rather than rate them on a scale. Reporting about affective constructs is challenging, especially if it has to be mapped to a numerical expression. Likert scales that measure such constructs often use short phrases against which a scale number can be compared. It can, however, be difficult to consistently apply such a mapping [32]. Ranking alleviates this problem as it allows participants to use the individual items as points of reference. The challenge is then how to evaluate such rankings across participants. While some participants play the same game titles, a lot more do not. Likewise, while some rank a large number of items, others only rank a few, either because they have not played as many games or do not consider them as invoking curiosity. To address this challenge, we implemented the TrueSkill rating system, developed by Microsoft for ranking and match-making on their Xbox LIVE online platform [8]. Available as a Python package [16], TrueSkill uses a Bayesian inference algorithm that updates the score of individual match items (usually representing the skill of players) every time a match is played. Since score-points can be lost, participating in a high number of matches (i.e. having been played by many participants) does not necessarily result in a higher ranking. As such, we can use this algorithm to compare items (the individual games) that vary in regards to how often they were mentioned. To use TrueSkill, we paired up all combinations within a ranking to create 'match-ups', taking the rank as deciding factor on which item 'wins' the match. After matching up all possible combinations, we used the resulting score as a measure for both the rank of an item, as well as the relative distance to other items. While the score is an arbitrary number, it can be used in relation to other scores. Items that have relatively similar scores can then be considered closer to equal, while those that differ by wide margins are likely to have 'won' a large number of comparisons. While using the TrueSkill algorithm provides a useful model for ranking items, we cannot evaluate how significant the resulting rank is. To our knowledge there is no statistical test that could be consulted to estimate how representative the overall rankings are for a larger population. While a different survey design would have remedied this, it would mean to either only include participants that have played the same games, or resort to rating games on a scale.

3.5 Formulation of Game Genres

When asking participants to suggest game titles, we can expect a wide range of games. This makes it difficult to explore general patterns, as the number of participants that will have played the same games will be limited. In order to capture the most defining aspects of a game instead, we assigned two game genres to each of the suggested games. The challenge of involving genres is the lack of a shared definition. Genre classifications can originate from multiple motivations, such as easing retrieval of titles, academic efforts of building a taxonomy, or marketing considerations [3]. For this reason we devised a list of 11 game genres based on commercially used genres, but qualified by a statement that defines the genre in our study. Some of the more commonly used genres have been omitted or modified to suit the goals of this study. As an example, "Action" can be a problematic genre, as a large number of games involve fast-paced sequences but may be based on vastly different game mechanics. An additional challenge is that games frequently involve a wide range of game genres. *Grand Theft Auto V* lets players shoot virtual characters, race cars, but also allows them to ride a roller-coaster, perform yoga, and solve a murder mystery. By attributing the genres *Reflex* and *Exploration*, some nuance is undoubtedly lost. While imperfect, this approach still provides a tentative measure for evaluating which actions performed in a game can be conductive to invoking curiosity. We assigned the following genres:

- *Reflex* - requires fast reflexes to perform well.
- *Exploration* - provides spatial or conceptual discovery that is not automatically brought to the attention of the player.
- *Puzzle* - presents tasks that must be solved through predefined processes.
- *Strategy* - requires players to plan their actions in advance, taking into consideration available resources.
- *RPG* - defined by assuming the role of one or more characters and making choices that impact game progression.
- *Story* - progresses as part of a structured narrative.
- *Task Sim* - asks players to perform tasks that are associated with professions, emphasizing the nature of the task.
- *Social Sim* - asks players to perform tasks associated with social interactions and everyday tasks.
- *Collecting* - is structured around gathering items for the purpose of having gathered all or as many items as possible.
- *Frantic* - uses aesthetic elements and/or concurrent game mechanics to saturate the cognitive capabilities of players.
- *Chance* - progress in the game is largely independent from the actions taken by the player, but differs between game sessions.

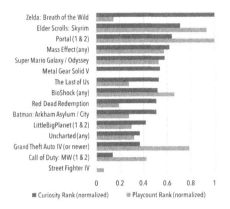

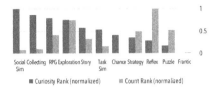

Fig. 2. Game genres ranked by participants' curiosity and how often it was mentioned.

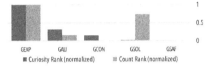

Fig. 1. Shared selection of games ranked by how curious participants felt and how many participants had played them. Values are normalized to 0–1 for comparison (0 = lowest rank, 1 = highest rank).

Fig. 3. Curiosity categories participants' curiosity and how many games were mentioned.

4 Procedure

The survey was conducted over a period of one month during which 117 participants completed the survey. Participants were recruited through convenience sampling and referral sampling. The target demographic included everyone who does or has played video games at some point in their lives. While we did not track the nationality of participants, the most likely audience was English-speaking people in Western Europe and the U.S. The first part of the survey asked questions about demographics. Items for playing frequency were: Every day, Every week, Occasionally, Rarely, and Never – the survey ended for those who chose 'Never'. The second part asked which of 15 games they had played. If two or more games were selected, the next page asked participants to rank the games they had played in terms of how much they had triggered their curiosity while playing. The third part asked participants to provide up to two games (entered as free text) for each of the five curiosity dimensions (see Sect. 3.3). If participants provided two or more items overall, they were asked to rank those games. Participants were free to rank any number of items in both rankings, including none. The final part of the survey included the 25 questions of the 5DC questionnaire. Each game provided by participants was assigned two game genres in order of importance. To determine which game genres should be assigned, the authors individually assigned game genres in accordance to the definitions (see Sect. 3.5). Assigned game genres were then compared for each game, and disagreements were resolved through discussion.

4.1   Data Processing

A text matching algorithm [28] was used to sort game titles that were entered as free text. The resulting list was checked for misspellings and corrected if necessary. Abbreviations were adjusted manually, and entries that could not be resolved were removed from the dataset. Entries belonging to the same game series, or referring to the same game by another name, were combined into a single entry (e.g. *Oblivion* becomes *Elder Scrolls*), with the exception of *Zelda: Breath of the Wild* (separate from *Zelda*) and *World of Warcraft* (separate from *Warcraft*). While this makes it impossible to consider elements of the individual games, games in a series tend to share many of the same general mechanics. This decision allowed us to examine the games over a larger sample size, in service of our exploration of general patterns in game design. Since *Zelda: BotW* and *WoW* show significant departures from their predecessors, these titles were retained. To identify correlations between the rankings and dimensions on the 5DC questionnaire, three ranks were created for each participant: Shared selection ranking, game genre ranking, and curiosity category ranking. Shared selection ranking ranged from 1 to 15, as a maximum of 15 games could be ranked. A game that was ranked as most curiosity invoking was given rank 1, followed by 2, continuing to rank 15. Games that a participant had not played, or had not ranked, were given the lowest possible rank of 15.

To create ranks by genre, every ranked game title was assigned two genre labels. With 11 genres, the ranking for each ranged from 1 to 11. Since game titles at different ranks could involve the same genres, a TrueSkill rating was calculated for every genre that was part of a participant's ranking. The rating was calculated by comparing all possible genre combinations within a participant's ranking, using both the rank and whether the genre was the primary or secondary label. The genre with the highest rating was ranked 1, followed by lower rated genres. Genres that were not used received the lowest possible rank of 11. In addition to creating this ranking for each participant, an overall ranking across all participants was created as well.

Curiosity category ranking closely followed the procedure for game genre ranking, with the difference that each game title represented a single category: the category under which the game title was entered. Possible ranks ranged from 1 to 5, reflecting the number of curiosity categories used to represent the five curiosity dimensions of the 5DC questionnaire. Again, an overall ranking was created in addition to per-participant rankings. Finally, 5DC questionnaire scores were created for each participant by calculating the mean of Likert scale ratings of questions contributing to one of the five dimensions. Likert scale ratings were reverse scored for the *Stress Tolerance* (ST) dimension, as required by the questionnaire.

Table 1. Game titles mentioned for each of the five curiosity categories (showing titled with at least 5 mentions). Titles in bold appear in multiple categories.

Game category	Game titles (number of mentions)
GEXP *(Explore, find out)* 92 unique titles	**Elder Scrolls (17)**, Fallout (14), Minecraft (11), Zelda: BotW (9), Dark Souls (8), **Horizon: Zero Dawn (8)**, The Witcher (8), Subnautica (7), **World of Warcraft (7)**, **Final Fantasy (5)**, Assassin's Creed (5), Zelda (5)
GSOL *(Solve)* 113 unique titles	Portal (29), The Witness (8), **Elder Scrolls (7)**, Myst (5), The Talos Principle (5)
GSAF *(Safe, stress-free)* 100 unique titles	Sims (8), Stardew Valley (7), **Elder Scrolls (6)**, Cities: Skylines (5)
GCON *(Connect to people)* 84 unique titles	**World of Warcraft (13)**, **Final Fantasy (7)**, Journey (5), **Sims (5)**
GALI *(Excited, feeling alive)* 108 unique titles	GTA (7), PlayerUnknown's Battlegrounds (6), **World of Warcraft (5)**, **Horizon: Zero Dawn (5)**, **Elder Scrolls (5)**

Table 2. Two-tailed Spearman's rank correlations between 5DC dimensions and other measures. VS-MPR shows maximum possible odds in favour of H_1 [29].

5DC dimension	—	Measure	rho	p	VS-MPR
JE Joysy Exploration	—	RPG	0.2	0.037	3.019
	—	GCON	0.234	0.016	5.617
DS - Deprivation Sensitivity	—	Collecting	−0.193	0.045	2.655
ST Stress Tolerance	—	GTA (IV+)	0.252	0.007	10.607
	—	Zelda: BotW	−0.239	0.011	7.499
	—	Call of Duty	0.214	0.023	4.295
	—	RPG	0.293	0.002	29.545
	—	Puzzle	−0.226	0.018	5.037
	—	GSOL	−0.222	0.022	4.310
SC Social Curiosity	—	Social Sim	0.220	0.022	4.414
	—	Frantic	−0.212	0.03	3.535
TS Thrill Seeking	—	GTA (IV+)	0.279	0.003	22.456
	—	RPG	0.230	0.016	5.515

5   Results

Out of 117 participants, 113 played video games at least 'Rarely', and thus completed the survey (38.9% female, mean age $M = 27.64$, $SD = 5.8$). The mean playing frequency was $M = 2.0$ ($SD = 0.94$), which corresponds to 'Every week'.

The overall ranking of the shared game selection is shown in Fig. 1, with TrueSkill ratings normalized to a 0–1 range. The count ranged from 19 for *Metal Gear Solid V* (normalized to 0) to 66 for *Portal* (normalized to 1). To evaluate the quality of the ranking, all 105 possible combinations of pair-wise rank comparisons (involving only participants who had played both games) were checked. Out of these, 7 combinations (6.7%) did not confirm the ranking, while the rest did. For the game suggestions per category module, a total of 301 unique game titles were mentioned. Table 1 shows which game titles were mentioned most frequently for each of the five game categories. Figure 3 shows the TrueSkill ranking of the five categories with measures normalized to a 0–1 range. In terms of counts, GSAF had the fewest game suggestions (103, normalized to 0), and GEXP had the most (180, normalized to 1). The overall TrueSkill ranking of game genres associated with games provided by participants is shown in Fig. 2. The frequency of game genres used ranged from 10 for *Chance* (normalized to 0), to 318 for *Reflex* (normalized to 1).

The aggregated results of the 5DC questionnaire were: JE (M = 5.38, SD = 0.86), DS (M = 4.98, SD = 1.15), ST (M = 4.36, SD = 1.42), SC (M = 5.11, SD = 1.14), TS (M = 4.20, SD = 1.34) – each based on Likert scale ratings from 1 to 7. We note that we use a significance level of 0.05 for all statistical tests in this study. Significant correlations between 5DC dimensions and rankings are shown in Table 2. For the purpose of clarity, rho was inverted to match the meaning of an increase in score in the individual 5DC dimensions (that is, a rating of 1 in a ranking is 'higher' than a 2, but 1 is lower than 2 in the 5DC questionnaire).

In terms of demographics, playing frequency differed between genders (Mann-Whitney U = 1987, p = 0.004, two-tailed), with male participants playing more frequently. Further differences were found in the ranking of the game genres *Strategy* (U = 1911, p = 0.002, two-tailed, lower ranking in females) and *Task Sim* (U = 1714, p = 0.036, two-tailed, lower ranking in females). Looking at differences in scores of curiosity dimensions, ST was significantly higher in males (U = 978, p = 0.001, two-tailed), while SC was significantly higher in females (U = 1988, p = 0.006, two-tailed). Participants' age was found to be correlated with a lower score of the 5DC dimension *Social Curiosity* (rho = −0.297, p = 0.001), a lower ranking of the game category GSAF (rho = −0.231, p = 0.018), and with a higher ranking of the *Puzzle* genre (rho = 0.226, p = 0.019).

6 Discussion

In the following section we discuss the implications of our results. First, we identify the game titles and genres that warrant further attention. We then look at correlations between the games, game genres, and the curiosity dimensions. Finally, we examine the connection between the curiosity-based categories of suggested games and the 5DC curiosity dimensions.

6.1 Games and Genres for Analysis

Participants offered a wide range of games when asked to suggest titles for each of the five curiosity categories. As shown in Table 1, several titles were mentioned by more than one person. Most of these games gravitated towards one of the five categories (e.g. *Minecraft* in GEXP). For these games, further analysis towards curiosity invoking design should focus on the theme of the category. Some games (shown in bold) span multiple categories and, for this reason, should be examined in regards to how multiple kinds of curiosity can be motivated in harmony. From the shared selection of games, we decided to specifically focus on those that ranked 0.6 or higher: *Zelda: Breath of the Wild* (*Z:BotW*), *The Elder Scrolls: Skyrim*, *Portal 1 & 2*, and the *Mass Effect* series. Of these games, the defining game genres are *Exploration*, *Puzzle*, *RPG*, and *Reflex*. Another interesting pattern to consider is games that have not been played by many participants, but ended up high in the ranking. This includes *Z:BotW*, *Metal Gear Solid V*, *The Last of Us*, *Red Dead Redemption*, and *Batman: Arkham Asylum/City*. The game genres of these games consist of *Exploration*, *Reflex*, *Strategy*, *Puzzle*, and *Story*.

In both patterns we can see that *Exploration* and *Reflex* seem to be involved in games that rank high in curiosity elicitation. For *Exploration* this is also reflected in the ranking of game categories derived from the 5DC dimensions (see Fig. 3). When asking participants to rank the games they provided, the GEXP category ranked far above other categories, suggesting that exploration and "finding out new things" are considered dominant aspects of what elicits curiosity in a game. Next, we examined potential correlations between the participants' scores on trait curiosity and the shared selection of games. *GTA* was ranked higher by participants with increased *Stress Tolerance* and *Thrill Seeking*, while *Call of Duty (CoD)* was ranked higher with increased *Stress Tolerance*. Given that both *GTA* and *CoD* were ranked low overall, this could mean that players do not consider these dimensions as defining of what elicits their curiosity. *Z:BotW* was ranked higher with decreasing ST. Here as well, given the high rating of *Z:BotW*, stress tolerance does not seem to be a predictor of overall curiosity. We speculate that, despite having combat and potentially stressful elements, *Z:BotW* allows players that are easily stressed to still express their curiosity. On the other hand, to express curiosity in *GTA* or *CoD*, players need a higher stress tolerance.

Turning to the game labels, we note several interesting results. *Social Sim* and *Collecting* stand out as genres that were part of only a few games, but ended up at the top of the ranking. These genres, and the suggested games that had this genre assigned to them, should be analysed more closely to see how games can benefit from such elements in terms of increasing their potential to invoke curiosity. *Reflex* and *Puzzle* are the opposite of these categories, as they ranked low in curiosity despite being present often. This is interesting as *Deprivation Sensitivity* specifically deals with puzzle-like stimuli. Games suggested under the corresponding category (GSOL) are mentioned frequently, but ranked low in curiosity (see Fig. 3). It could be that this dimension of curiosity does not strike players as an important component of curiosity. Interestingly, both *Z:BotW* and *Portal* rank high in the shared game list, despite carrying the *Puzzle* genre. For these games, it may not be the fact that they include puzzles that invokes curiosity in players. Instead, we hypothesise that exploration is a more defining component in *Z:BotW*, whereas *Portal* stands out through an unusual base mechanic and surprising narrative components. Overall, we speculate that game genres that strike a balance between uncertainty and structure tend to rank high, while genres that are highly deterministic (requiring cognitive or physical aptitude) or highly random tend to rank lower in curiosity.

Looking at correlations between game labels and trait curiosity dimensions, *RPG* stands out as the only genre that correlates positively with several dimensions: *Joyous Exploration*, *Stress Tolerance*, and *Thrill Seeking*. It should be noted that these dimensions have been found to correlate with each other. However, given that other game genres correlate with only one of these dimensions, it is likely that *RPG* invokes curiosity across several dimensions through its gameplay. As a genre, *RPG* is less defined by a specific sort of gameplay and rather by how game actions are carried out and contextualized by the player. It can be argued that *RPG* is a game genre that reflects a sense of going on an adventure, encapsulating both elements of discovery and physical excitement.

Another interesting finding is *Social Curiosity*, which correlates with high ranking of *Social Sim*, as well as low ranking of *Frantic* games. The associated game category (GCON) was not ranked high, and did not correlate with *Social Curiosity*. While we expected to find a positive correlation, the actual finding does makes sense. The phrasing of the category ("Games that let me understand people or let me connect to people") can be interpreted as a physical affordance, instead of a more conceptual social connection to, for instance, in-game characters. Given that *Social Sim* ranked highly among game genres, social simulation games and socially oriented curiosity should be analysed closely for their ability to make players curious. This is especially important given that *Social Curiosity* was the only dimension not correlated to another dimension, which suggests a certain uniqueness.

6.2   Impact of Curiosity Dimensions

Few correlations were found between the created game genres and the corresponding dimensions of the 5DC. A possible explanation for this could be that participants have strong associations with the terms that were used (e.g. "explore or find out") that do not match the definitions of the curiosity dimensions. 'Exploration', for example, is often understood within games to be spatial in nature, i.e. exploring an environment. The 5DC questions on the other hand are more focused on the exploration of knowledge and (challenging) stimuli. Similarly, the GCON category asked participants to list games related to connectedness and understanding people. Being connected in games, however, might not necessitate social curiosity. At present, the only curiosity dimension that corresponded with a directly similar game genre was *Social Curiosity* (with *Social Sim*). Besides this, while we did not find the direct correlations between game categories and trait dimensions that we would expect to see, we do see plausible connections between dimensions, game genres and individual games. It could therefore be that connections exist, but were not detected due to decisions in our research design. Despite our efforts in basing the game categories on the 5DC questions, a rephrasing might elicit game suggestions more in line with the curiosity dimensions. Another possibility is that trait curiosity is not (fully) predictive of what makes a person curious within a game.

7   Conclusion

The aim of this study was to provide a starting point for the consideration of what game titles and genres should be analysed in regards to their potential to invoke curiosity. Through the suggestions of survey participants, we have gathered such a collection and established a ranking of critically acclaimed games for further study. We further investigated what game genres were likely to be ranked high in triggering curiosity, and have looked at how they correspond to individual dimensions of trait curiosity. We found that games involving exploration, collecting, and social simulations were ranked above other game genres.

These genres should be explored in regards to how they promote curiosity and whether they remain effective when introduced into games that emphasise other, lower ranked game genres.

The results of our study suggest that what makes players curious in a game does not necessarily correspond to their scores on the Five-Dimensional Curiosity Scale (5DC), although we caution that this finding is not conclusive. The closest connection was found in social curiosity, which corresponded to higher ranking of social simulation games. We also note that role-playing games were found to correlate with several dimensions of curiosity, suggesting that this game genre is able to invoke curiosity in different ways.

Through this study we have gathered valuable data for further research into how digital games invoke curiosity in players. We will expand on this work through an analysis of individual games to identify design patterns and related choices that are conductive to eliciting curiosity. This investigation should aid in the formulation of guidelines to design for curiosity. Ultimately, by fostering the development of games that intentionally invoke curiosity, we may be able to increase an individual's disposition to become curious. Such games would also provide interactive environments through which curiosity and related behaviour can be studied in the laboratory. Whether this potential can be fulfilled remains to be seen, but we hope that our work inspires continued exploration of this topic.

Acknowledgements. We would like to thank Max van Duijn and Stefano Gualeni for their insight and support in carrying out this research. We further want to thank all of our participants for their time and effort.

References

1. Berlyne, D.E.: A theory of human curiosity. Br. J. Psychol. **45**(3), 180–191 (1954)
2. Berlyne, D.E.: Conflict, Arousal, and Curiosity. McGraw-Hill Book Company, New York (1960)
3. Clarke, R.I., Lee, J.H., Clark, N.: Why video game genres fail: a classificatory analysis. Games Cult. **12**(5), 445–465 (2017)
4. Costikyan, G.: Uncertainty in Games. MIT Press, Cambridge (2013)
5. Day, H.I., et al.: Intrinsic Motivation: A New Direction in Education (1971)
6. Dewey, J.: How We Think. Heath & Co., Lexington (1910)
7. Grossnickle, E.M.: Disentangling curiosity: dimensionality, definitions, and distinctions from interest in educational contexts. Educ. Psychol. Rev. **28**(1), 23–60 (2016)
8. Herbrich, R., Minka, T., Graepel, T.: TrueSkill(TM): a Bayesian skill rating system, pp. 569–576. MIT Press, January 2007. https://www.microsoft.com/en-us/research/publication/trueskilltm-a-bayesian-skill-rating-system/
9. Inan, I.: The Philosophy of Curiosity. Routledge, Abingdon (2013)
10. Jirout, J., Klahr, D.: Childrens scientific curiosity: in search of an operational definition of an elusive concept. Dev. Rev. **32**(2), 125–160 (2012)
11. Kang, M.J., et al.: The wick in the candle of learning: epistemic curiosity activates reward circuitry and enhances memory. Psychol. Sci. **20**(8), 963–973 (2009)
12. Kashdan, T.B., Roberts, J.E.: Trait and state curiosity in the genesis of intimacy: differentiation from related constructs. J. Soc. Clin. Psychol. **23**(6), 792 (2004)

13. Kashdan, T.B., et al.: The five-dimensional curiosity scale: capturing the bandwidth of curiosity and identifying four unique subgroups of curious people. J. Res. Pers. **73**, 130–149 (2018)
14. Klimmt, C.: Dimensions and determinants of the enjoyment of playing digital games: a three-level model. In: Level Up: Digital Games Research Conference, pp. 246–257 (2003)
15. Kreitler, S., Zigler, E., Kreitler, H.: The nature of curiosity in children. J. Sch. Psychol. **13**(3), 185–200 (1975)
16. Lee, H.: Trueskill 0.4.4 python package (2015). http://trueskill.org/
17. Litman, J.A.: Interest and deprivation factors of epistemic curiosity. Pers. Individ. Differ. **44**(7), 1585–1595 (2008)
18. Litman, J.A., Collins, R.P., Spielberger, C.D.: The nature and measurement of sensory curiosity. Pers. Individ. Differ. **39**(6), 1123–1133 (2005)
19. Litman, J.A., Jimerson, T.L.: The measurement of curiosity as a feeling of deprivation. J. Pers. Assess. **82**(2), 147–157 (2004)
20. Litman, J.A., Silvia, P.J.: The latent structure of trait curiosity: evidence for interest and deprivation curiosity dimensions. J. Pers. Assess. **86**(3), 318–328 (2006)
21. Loewenstein, G.: The psychology of curiosity: a review and reinterpretation. Psychol. Bull. **116**(1), 75 (1994)
22. McAuley, E., Duncan, T., Tammen, V.V.: Psychometric properties of the intrinsic motivation inventory in a competitive sport setting: a confirmatory factor analysis. Res. Q. Exerc. Sport **60**(1), 48–58 (1989)
23. Metacritic.com: Page: Best video games of all time (2018). http://www.metacritic.com/browse/games/score/metascore/all/all/filtered. Accessed 31 Jan 2018
24. Pluck, G., Johnson, H.: Stimulating curiosity to enhance learning. GESJ: Educ. Sci. Psychol. **2** (2011)
25. Reio, T.G., Callahan, J.L.: Affect, curiosity, and socialization-related learning: a path analysis of antecedents to job performance. J. Bus. Psychol. **19**(1), 3–22 (2004)
26. Schaekermann, M., et al.: Curiously motivated: profiling curiosity with self-reports and behaviour metrics in the game destiny. In: Proceedings of the Annual Symposium on Computer-Human Interaction in Play, pp. 143–156. ACM (2017)
27. Schmitt, F.F., Lahroodi, R.: The epistemic value of curiosity. Educ. Theory **58**(2), 125–148 (2008)
28. SeatGeek: Fuzzywuzzy (2017). https://github.com/seatgeek/fuzzywuzzy
29. Sellke, T., Bayarri, M., Berger, J.O.: Calibration of ρ values for testing precise null hypotheses. Am. Stat. **55**(1), 62–71 (2001)
30. Spielberger, C.D., Starr, L.M.: Curiosity and exploratory behavior. In: Motivation: Theory and Research, pp. 221–243 (1994)
31. To, A., Safinah, A., Kaufman, G.F., Hammer, J.: Integrating curiosity and uncertainty in game design. In: Proceedings of 1st International Joint Conference of DiGRA and FDG, pp. 1–16 (2016)
32. Yannakakis, G.N., Martínez, H.P.: Ratings are overrated!. Front. ICT **2**, 13 (2015)
33. Zuckerman, M.: The sensation seeking scale V (SSS-V): still reliable and valid. Pers. Individ. Differ. **43**(5), 1303–1305 (2007)

Learning to Identify Rush Strategies in StarCraft

Teguh Budianto[1], Hyunwoo Oh[2], and Takehito Utsuro[1(✉)]

[1] Graduate School of Systems and Information Engineering,
University of Tsukuba, Tsukuba, Japan
utsuro@iit.tsukuba.ac.jp
[2] Graduate School of Interdisciplinary Information Studies,
The University of Tokyo, Tokyo, Japan

Abstract. This paper examines strategies used in StarCraft II, a real-time strategy (RTS) game in which two opponents compete in a battlefield context. The RTS genre requires players to make effective strategic decisions. How players execute the selected strategies affects the game result. We propose a method to automatically classify strategies as rush or non-rush strategies using support vector machines (SVMs). We collected game replay data from an online StarCraft II community and focused on high-level players to design the proposed classifier by evaluating four feature functions: (i) the upper bound of variance in time series for the numbers of workers, (ii) the upper bound of the numbers of workers at a specific time, (iii) the lower bound of the start time to build a second base, and (iv) the upper bound of the start time to build a specific building. By evaluating these features, we obtained the parameters combinations required to design and construct the proposed SVM-based rush identifier. Then we implemented our findings into a StarCraft: Brood War (StarCraft I) agent to demonstrate the effectiveness of the proposed method in a real-time game environment.

Keywords: Real-time strategy game · StarCraft · Rush strategy
Support vector machine · Game log

1 Introduction

Real-time strategy (RTS) games are popular online computer games in which two opponents compete on a battlefield. RTS game players must gather resources to develop combat strength by obtaining advanced buildings, technologies, and armies. Unlike other strategy games, such as Go and Chess, RTS game information is more complex and partially limited to the players which only can be seen by carefully observing through scouting. The complexity in RTS games covers both the number of available actions and locations to choose which contributes to the wide decisions among all possibilities [11]. Such information changes rapidly as players respond to various actions [4,6,12]. Therefore, players must perform multiple tasks simultaneously within a short period [17]. These characteristics

ⓒ IFIP International Federation for Information Processing 2018
Published by Springer Nature Switzerland AG 2018. All Rights Reserved
E. Clua et al. (Eds.): ICEC 2018, LNCS 11112, pp. 90–102, 2018.
https://doi.org/10.1007/978-3-319-99426-0_8

contribute to an RTS game's level of difficulty [3]. In addition, such characteristics make developing artificial intelligence (AI) or bots for such games difficult [2].

RTS games can be considered a simplification of real-life environments [11]. An RTS game environment is constructed from complex [11,14,19] and dynamic information [20] simultaneously. In an RTS game, such information changes frequently depending on the players' actions. Dealing with this type of environment is a significant challenge for AI developers. The quality of RTS game AI has been improved due to various competitions [16], such as the Student StarCraft AI Tournament,[1] the AIIDE StarCraft AI Competition,[2] and the CIG StarCraft RTS AI Competition.[3]

In RTS games, selecting effective and timely strategies is extremely important to counter an opponent's play style. Making ineffective and poorly timed decisions can lead to a strategy that hinders the player. Note that this can happen even to high-level players. With professional gamers, human players perform various strategies with good decision making and control skills based on the information they receive. How human players determine their strategy develops their own play style and results in a high win rate. In addition, it is important to learn and analyze effective human player strategies when developing RTS game AI. In consideration of these factors, we investigate the classification of StarCraft strategies as rush and non-rush strategies. A rush strategy aims to destroy the opponent early before the enemy has prepared an effective defense while a non-rush strategy is generally the opposite of rush strategy that more focus on the development (e.g., building and technology advancement). To examine player strategies, we design a support vector machine (SVM)-based model that automatically classifies strategies from StarCraft II game logs into rush and non-rush strategies. We then evaluated our findings by implementing a rush detection manager into a StarCraft: Brood War (StarCraft I) agent to examine the effectiveness of the proposed model in a real-time game environment.

2 Related Work

Many studies have investigated game prediction and analysis in StarCraft. Avontuur, Spronck, and Van Zanen [1] focused on player model prediction to distinguish the level of a player. Accordingly, Liu et al. [9] investigated a player's game style in StarCraft II using several machine learning techniques to predict player actions. Predicting player actions can help human players to determine the strategies used by other players.

Studies into the prediction of strategies have also been conducted [13,18]. Weber and Mateas [18] used data mining techniques to create data about an opponent's constructed buildings to predict their strategy. They indicated that analyzing information about an opponent's buildings can help discriminate different strategies. Park et al. [13] used a scouting algorithm and several

---

[1] https://sscaitournament.com/.

[2] http://www.cs.mun.ca/~dchurchill/starcraftaicomp/.

[3] http://cilab.sejong.ac.kr/sc_competition/.

Table 1. Game log data of StarCraft II (with T = Terran, Z = Zerg, and P = Protoss)

Game type	T vs. T	Z vs. Z	P vs. P	T vs. Z	T vs. P	Z vs. P	Total
Number of game logs	65	102	28	240	177	141	753

machine learning approaches to predict an opponent's strategy. They applied this approaches to an AI bot that recognizes an opponent's constructed building (the build order) by sending a scout. Ruíz-Granados [15] developed a model that can predict the winner of a StarCraft match at a specific time using replay information. In addition, Justesen and Risi [7] trained a deep neural network to learn build orders from StarCraft replays. They focused on game macromanagement to enhance a bot's competitiveness against other bots. Another study of StarCraft rush games is presented in [10] introducing features for identifying the rush games, but it does not implement any machine learning technique which examines their proposed features by using AND and OR logic feature combinations. We extend the accomplishments of these studies by exploring strategy in RTS games by focusing on rush matches. Our goal is to develop a method to collect data and identify a human player's strategies using an SVM. Furthermore, we integrated the proposed rush identification method in an agent to play real games to evaluate the correctness of the proposed rush identification method.

3   StarCraft

3.1   Overview

StarCraft is a well-known RTS game series developed by Blizzard Entertainment™. The most common match in StarCraft is the one-versus-one game [18], where the purpose is to destroy another player's units. Its game expansion, StarCraft: Brood War, turns into the version that is played competitively and becomes a subject of AI development through bot competition [8]. StarCraft series was followed by the release of StarCraft II: Wings of Liberty with two expansions, Heart of the Swarm and Legacy of the Void. Both in StarCraft and StarCraft II, there are three races that can be chosen in the game environment, i.e., the Terran, Zerg, and Protoss, and each race has unique but comparable strengths and weaknesses [11]. In these games, players must collect resources, build structures, and train armies to compete in battle. Moreover, to perform competitively, the games demand good decision making and control skills.

3.2   Rush Strategy

Rush strategies are used to initiate a quick attack against the opponent. The goal of a rush strategy is to destroy the opponent in the early stages of the games, i.e., before the opponent has prepared an effective defense. Note that players who engage rush strategies often sacrifice the ability to improve their base

Table 2. Dataset for evaluation

Logs	Rush strategy	Non-rush strategy	Total
Number of game logs	137	616	753

and upgrade to advance technology because they quickly spend many resources preparing an army and constructing buildings. Rush strategies can be used in any type of RTS game to defeat an opponent as quickly as possible.

4   Resources and Datasets

We collected game replays of one-versus-one StarCraft II games from a website, namely ***spawningtool.com***[4]. To standardize our examination, we only used game replays from *StarCraft II: Legacy of the Void* because other game versions have different building and army characteristics. All replay files were extracted as human-readable log files using a library that obtains StarCraft II replay information, i.e., *SC2Reader*[5]. A game log contains the list of time and actions performed by the players in the game such as training a unit, and creating a building shown as following sample *[04.13][PlayerName][Unit born UnitName]*.

　　To examine the rush strategy, we received an assistance from a StarCraft player in Diamond league to manually classified each game as a rush or non-rush game. Note that we focused on only high-level league games i.e., Diamond, Master, and Grandmaster leagues, because it was necessary to collect data for successful strategies from high-level players. From the collected total 5,150 data, we obtained 753 game logs under this condition which the distribution of all race matches of this data is shown in Table 1. Each sample consists of a single player's game log that could be categorized as a game with a rush or non-rush strategy (Table 2).

5   Time Series Changes in Number of Workers

We propose several features closely related to the number of workers of each player. These features are based on the observation of rush games. Rush strategy players do not consume a lot of resources on infrastructure, such as workers, building upgrades, technologies, and resource extractors. Figure 1 compares typical average time series changes in the numbers of workers between the rush and non-rush strategies. As can be seen, there is a significant difference in the number of workers in these different strategies. Here, rush strategy players train a moderate number of workers and do not train additional workers in the next phase of the game; thus, there is no change in time series of the number of workers. In contrast, non-rush strategy players continue producing a significantly greater

---

[4] http://www.spawningtool.com.
[5] https://github.com/GraylinKim/sc2reader.

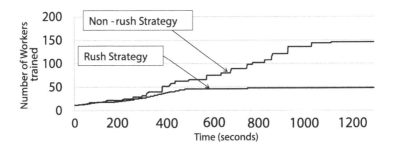

Fig. 1. Time series changes in the numbers of workers of rush/non-rush strategies

number of workers compared to rush strategy players. By considering typical situations in rush and non-rush strategies, we designed features based on the variance of the time series of the number of workers and the number of workers at a specific time. Note that we consider only the number of workers a player has trained up to a given time rather than the number of workers a player has at a certain time. This means the number of workers a player has at a certain time is always affected by how many workers survive in the battle. Thus, we only consider the number of workers the player has direct control over.

6   Game Log Features

Here, let g be a game replay comprising the game logs g_1 and g_2 of players 1 and 2, respectively, and let x be either game log g_1 or g_2:

$$g = \langle g_1, g_2 \rangle, \ x = g_1 \text{ or } g_2$$

Table 3 defines the four types of features, i.e., the upper bound of variance of the time series of the number of workers (vw), the upper bound of the number of workers at a specific time (nw), the lower bound of the start time of building a second base (b), and the upper bound of the start time to build a specific building (sp).

6.1   Upper Bound of Variance of Time Series of Number of Workers

The feature function $f_{vw}(x; u_0, d_0, e_0)$ of game log x examines whether the variance of the time series of the number of workers (vw) for time duration d_0 at end time e_0 of the variance calculation satisfies the upper bound u_0 as follows.

$$f_{vw}(x; u_0, d_0, e_0) = (x.f_{vw}^v \leq u_0) \wedge (x.f_{vw}^d = d_0) \wedge (x.f_{vw}^e = e_0)$$

The variance of the time series in the numbers of workers is measured at a time interval of one minute.

6.2 Upper Bound of Number of Workers at a Specific Time

The feature function $f_{nw}(x; n_0, t_0)$ of game log x examines whether the number of workers (nw) at time t_0 satisfies the upper bound n_0 as follows.

$$f_{nw}(x; t_0, n_0) = (x.f_{nw}^t = t_0) \wedge (x.f_{nw}^n \leq n_0)$$

6.3 Lower Bound of Start Time to Build Second Base

In addition to the feature functions discussed in the previous sections, which are related to the number of workers of each player, we also propose a third feature that is related to the start time of building a second base. The existence of a base (a building for collecting resources) in the field is important in the game. To collect more resources, the players should expand their base by building a second base as quickly as possible at a location that potentially provides more resources. In the case of non-rush strategies, resources are more important compared to rush strategies because such resources are required to build a second base immediately and safely. Players who use the rush strategy do not necessarily build a second base as early as possible. Accordingly, it is expected that a rush strategy player will build a second base over a certain time. Based on this observation, this section introduces the lower bound of the start time of building a second base. The feature function $f_b(x; t_0)$ of the lower bound of the second base build start time (b) of game log x examines whether the start time satisfies the lower bound t_0 as follows.

$$f_b(x; t_0) = (x.f_b^t \geq t_0)$$

6.4 Upper Bound of Start Time to Build a Specific Building

The fourth feature is also related to building information. Each race in a rush game must prioritize specific buildings as early as possible to enable a rush attack. Those buildings differ based on the build start time for each race. In the case of Zerg, the starting time to build first *Spawning Pool* is used, and the starting time to build second *Barracks* and second *Gateway* for Terran and Protoss respectively are used to examine this feature function. We observed the timing of these specific buildings (sp), and each player tended to build them before reaching a particular time. In the rush attack, the timing to build these buildings for each race is observed in the beginning of the game. The feature function $f_{sp}(x; t_0)$ of the upper bound of the start time to build the specific building (sp) satisfies the upper bound t_0 as follows.

$$f_{sp}(x; t_0) = (x.f_{sp}^t \leq t_0)$$

Table 3. Features of game log x

Features	Variables of x	
Upper bound of variance of time series of numbers of workers $f_{vw}(x; u_0, d_0, e_0) = (x.f_{vw}^v \leq u_0) \wedge (x.f_{vw}^d = d_0) \wedge (x.f_{vw}^e = e_0)$	$x.f_{vw}^v$	Variance of x
	$x.f_{vw}^d$	Time duration of calculating variance [s]
	$x.f_{vw}^e$	End time of calculating [s]
Upper bound of number of workers at a specific time $f_{nw}(x; t_0, n_0) = (x.f_{nw}^t = t_0) \wedge (x.f_{nw}^n \leq n_0)$	$x.f_{nw}^t$	Specific time [s]
	$x.f_{nw}^n$	Number of workers
Lower bound of start time of building a second base $f_b(x; t_0) = (x.f_b^t \geq t_0)$	$x.f_b^t$	Start time of building the second base [s]
Upper bound of start time to build a specific building $f_{sp}(x; t_0) = (x.f_{sp}^t \leq t_0)$	$x.f_{sp}^t$	Start time of building a specific building [s]

7   Overall Design

Parameter combinations of the feature functions f_{vw}, f_{nw}, f_b, and f_{sp} were examined to determine the parameter combinations which possess the maximum recall, precision and f-measure. For f_{vw}, combinations of parameters were examined by changing v_0 from 0 to 2, d_0 from 60 to 300, and e_0 from 240 to 360. For f_{nw}, combinations of parameters were examined by changing t_0 from 300 to 600 and n_0 from 25 to 40. For f_b, the parameter was examined by changing t_0 from 60 to 360. Finally, for f_{sp}, the parameter was examined by changing t_0 from 20 to 360. The number we selected for each parameter of the feature functions is based on our observation to the logs of the rush games.

We first divided our dataset into 10 subsets of equal size to perform 10-fold cross validation. Each subset was used sequentially as test data, where the remaining 90% was used as training data. From the training data of each fold, the parameter combinations of each feature functions f_{vw}, f_{nw}, f_b and f_{sp} were identified from the combinations that yielded the maximum recall, precision, and f-measure values as shown in Fig. 2. Moreover, Table 4 shows the parameter combinations of each fold with maximum recall, precision, and f-measure. Note that variables depicted in the tuples in Table 4 follow the order of Table 3. Using this procedure, each feature function generated three parameters combinations, resulting in a total of 12 parameter combinations for each fold. Formally, those 12 parameters are as follows.

$$F = \{f_{vw}^r, f_{vw}^p, f_{vw}^f, f_{nw}^r, f_{nw}^p, f_{nw}^f, f_b^r, f_b^p, f_b^f, f_{sp}^r, f_{sp}^p, f_{sp}^f\}$$

Here, F is a set of parameters combinations generally constructed of a set of feature functions f_{vw}, f_{nw}, f_b, and f_{sp}, where r, p, and f are maximum recall, precision, and f-measure respectively. We created and used a feature vector constructed of these 12 features. Eventually, our design had 10 different sets of parameter combinations, which were used to train the SVM classifier.

Table 4. Parameter combinations with maximum recall, precision, and f-measure

Fold	$f_{vw}^r, f_{vw}^p, f_{vw}^f$	$f_{nw}^r, f_{nw}^p, f_{nw}^f$	f_b^r, f_b^p, f_b^r	$f_{sp}^r, f_{sp}^p, f_{sp}^f$
1	$(2, 120, 300),$ $(0, 220, 240),$ $(2, 195, 300)$	$(300, 40),$ $(520, 25),$ $(390, 31)$	$(60), (293), (118)$	$(96), (24), (37)$
2	$(2, 120, 300),$ $(0, 220, 240),$ $(2, 165, 300)$	$(300, 40),$ $(520, 25),$ $(390, 31)$	$(60), (293), (139)$	$(96), (24), (37)$
3	$(2, 120, 340),$ $(0, 290, 340),$ $(2, 150, 260)$	$(310, 40),$ $(520, 25),$ $(390, 31)$	$(60), (293), (118)$	$(90), (24), (37)$
4	$(2, 120, 340),$ $(0, 290, 340),$ $(0.5, 150, 300)$	$(300, 40),$ $(530, 25),$ $(390, 31)$	$(60), (293), (118)$	$(96), (24), (46)$
5	$(2, 120, 340),$ $(0, 285, 340),$ $(1, 135, 320)$	$(300, 40),$ $(520, 25),$ $(390, 31)$	$(60), (291), (118)$	$(96), (24), (37)$
6	$(2, 120, 340),$ $(0, 290, 340),$ $(1, 135, 320)$	$(300, 40),$ $(410, 25),$ $(390, 31)$	$(62), (293), (139)$	$(96), (25), (37)$
7	$(2, 120, 320),$ $(0, 290, 240),$ $(2, 165, 300)$	$(300, 40),$ $(520, 25),$ $(420, 32)$	$(60), (293), (118)$	$(96), (24), (37)$
8	$(2, 120, 340),$ $(0, 240, 260),$ $(2, 165, 300)$	$(300, 40),$ $(410, 25),$ $(390, 31)$	$(70), (293), (119)$	$(96), (24), (37)$
9	$(2, 120, 360),$ $(0, 285, 340),$ $(2, 155, 300)$	$(300, 40),$ $(520, 25),$ $(390, 31)$	$(60), (293), (118)$	$(96), (31), (37)$
10	$(2, 120, 300),$ $(0, 285, 340),$ $(2, 155, 300)$	$(300, 40),$ $(520, 28),$ $(390, 31)$	$(60), (293), (118)$	$(96), (24), (37)$

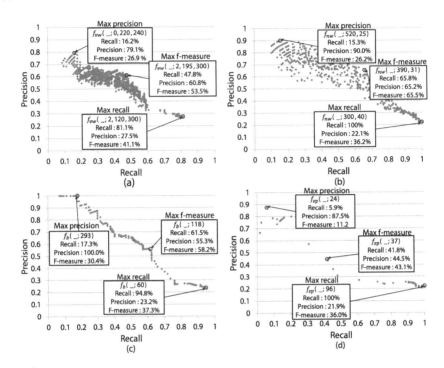

Fig. 2. Parameters combinations of the first fold of 10-fold cross-validation of feature functions (a)f_{vw}, (b)f_{nw}, (c)f_b, and (d)f_{sp}

8   Evaluation

8.1   Experimental Setup

We attempted to design a model for rush game classification from the game logs using an SVM. We applied an SVM technique to identify whether a game log includes a rush strategy, and we used an SVM library provided by LIBSVM[6]. The number of instances in this experiment is shown in Table 2. Using only the training data in each iteration, we found the parameter combinations with maximum recall, precision and f-measure, which we applied as SVM features to both the training and test sets. These procedures were replicated 10 times.

8.2   Results

We used confidence to calculate the performance of each fold of the proposed approach using recall and precision. We then plotted the average performance curve based on this calculation (Fig. 3). The curve in Fig. 3 shows 11 plot points (from 0 to 100) that represent the average performance of all folds. We generalized the recall value of each fold to the closest position among these 11

---

[6] https://www.csie.ntu.edu.tw/~cjlin/libsvm/.

points. Figure 3 also shows the recall-precision curves of the proposed design compared to four alternatives. Each alternative curve was produced by removing each set of parameter combinations of feature functions f_{vw}, f_{nw}, f_b, and f_{sp} from the evaluation. By comparing the proposed design to its alternatives, it was found that the proposed design was outperformed slightly by an alternative design constructed without feature functions f_{vw}. This result indicates that a design using parameter combinations of $f_{nw}^r, f_{nw}^p, f_{nw}^f, f_b^r, f_b^p, f_b^f, f_{sp}^r, f_{sp}^p, f_{sp}^f$ demonstrates better performance than the proposed design with all four feature functions. We selected this alternative's feature as the optimal feature function (Fig. 3).

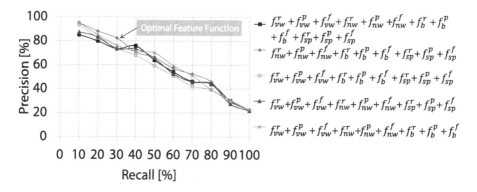

Fig. 3. Recall and precision curve of the combinations of f_{vw}, f_{nw}, f_b, and f_{sp}.

Based on these results, we further examined the optimal feature function of $f_{nw}^r, f_{nw}^p, f_{nw}^f, f_b^r, f_b^p, f_b^f, f_{sp}^r, f_{sp}^p, f_{sp}^f$ by comparing this design by removing each remaining parameter combinations f_{nw}, f_b and f_{sp} from the evaluation. The results are shown in Table 4. The overall recall-precision performance shows that the proposed design using combinations of $f_{nw}^r, f_{nw}^p, f_{nw}^f, f_b^r, f_b^p, f_b^f, f_{sp}^r, f_{sp}^p, f_{sp}^f$ demonstrates the highest recall and precision among all alternatives. We received worse performance when evaluating alternative design without including feature function f_{nw}. This may be because the difference in the number of workers at a specific time in a rush game provides meaningful information to classify the rush game. Moreover, the build time and feature function f_{nw} information contributes to the performance of the proposed method. The results (Fig. 4) indicates that there was a significant correlation to the parameter combinations with maximum recall, precision and f-measure of the features functions f_{nw}, f_b, and f_{sp}. The result indicate that the proposed design with these three parameter combinations worked better than using all four feature functions. Therefore, the proposed design could possibly be effective at identifying rush games in collections of RTS game logs.

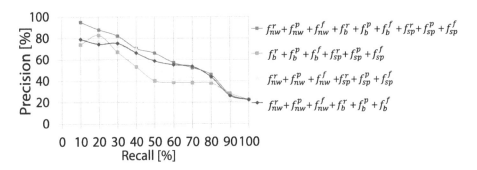

Fig. 4. Recall and precision curve of the combinations of f_{nw}, f_b, and f_{sp}.

8.3   Incorporating Rush Identifier to StarCraft: Brood War Agent

We further evaluated the proposed method by developing an agent called *RushIdentifierBot* in StarCraft: Brood War based on the UAlbertaBot[7] architecture as the seed bot. The UAlbertaBot was implemented using a build order planning system that focuses on optimizing build order problems in StarCraft [3] and unit combat scenarios that result in unit actions as the outcome [4,5]. There also exists a StarCraft II bot which is based on the architecture of UAlbertaBot, CommandCenter[8]. We could possibly do the same things on StarCraft II since the source of our bot architecture is the same. Note that we selected using StarCraft: Brood War rather than StarCraft II due to the availability of opponent bots. We selected an existing bot framework because it has been integrated using the basic functions required to run the game. Thus, we could focus on our purpose, i.e., improving rush strategy identification in RTS games. The RushIdentifierBot has a strategy changing ability integrated into a module call the Rush Detection Manager. This module detects the opponent's rush action in the early of the game state using scouting information to identify rush or non-rush strategies.

The feature functions f_{nw}, f_b, and f_{sp} of the proposed model were integrated into the rush detection manager. Here, we used these three feature functions and removed feature function f_{vw} from the development of the rush detection manager because feature function f_{vw} reduced performance. Moreover, due to computational complexity, we did not implement the SVM model in our agent; however, we did implement a rule-based system for the rush detection manager using the optimum result obtained by the SVM. We tuned the parameters combinations of the three features f_{nw}, f_b, and f_{sp} by trial and error using held-out data, the additional data used for trial error, to determine the number of wins and loses of our bot. The data were based on the information obtained in a real-time game played by our agent against several bots that participated in the 2017 AIIDE StarCraft AI Competition. Note that the trial and error game data are not included in the evaluation results.

---

[7] https://github.com/davechurchill/ualbertabot.
[8] https://github.com/davechurchill/commandcenter.

Table 5. Judgment correctness

Bot's judgment		Correct judgment		Incorrect Judgment		Total	
Win or loss		Win	Loss	Win	Loss	Win	Loss
Bot's Judgment	Rush	19	12	0	0	19	12
	Non-rush	31	26	0	3	31	29
	No judgment	0	0	0	9	0	9
Total		50	38	0	12	50	50

Furthermore, we evaluated the correctness of our bot's rush identification by playing 400 games against 15 well-known bots from the 2017 AIIDE StarCraft AI Competition: *Arrakhammer, cpac, IceBot, Iron, Juno, KillAll, LetaBot, McRave, MegaBot, Microwave, Overkill, Sling, Steamhammer, AIUR,* and *Tyr.* Note that these bots use different races. We randomly selected 50 games for each win and loss sample from the 400 games played by our bot in this evaluation. Table 5 shows the correctness of the rush identification function in our agent. The judgment of rush or non-rush by our bot was made during the game in the range from minute 2 until 6. The majority of the sample in Table 5 shows that our bot could, for the most part, judge opponent rush actions correctly. However, there were only three samples our bot judged incorrectly. All winning cases were observed when our bot could make correct judgments in the real-time game. Note that, even though our bot could judge rush or non-rush actions correctly, there were still games in which our bot lost. This could have occurred because our bot did not appropriately adapt to the opponent's late-game strategy. In addition, when our bot could not make a judgment, we categorized this situation as an incorrect judgment. Such cases occurred because our bot did not have any information about the opponent's state such as failure to find the location of the opponent's base.

9   Conclusion

This study has proposed a method to identify rush strategies in an RTS game using replay log data. We collected game replays from a StarCraft II community website to identify rush and non-rush strategies. Note that we primarily focused on rush games played by high-level StarCraft II players. We examined 12 parameter combinations of our four feature functions, i.e., f_{vw}, f_{nw}, f_b, and f_{sp}. We found that using f_{nw}, f_b, and f_{sp} features showed better performance than using all four features. Therefore, we used these features to design the SVM used to identify rush strategies. Further evaluation were performed by implementing our rush strategy identification in a StarCraft I agent. We evaluated the correctness of our bot identification function in games against 15 well-known bots. Even though our bot could identify rush or non-rush actions, it could not defeat all of the opponent bots, which may have been due to lack of appropriate late-game strategy decisions. Note that rush strategies are only employed in the early stage of a game, and in longer games, do not provide any advantages to the overall strength of bots. Thus, it would be beneficial to further evaluate late-game strategies to improve bots performance.

References

1. Avontuur, T., et al.: Player skill modeling in StarCraft II. In: Proceedings of the 9th AIIDE, pp. 2–8 (2013)
2. Buro, M., Furtak, T.M.: RTS games and real-time AI research. In: Proceedings of BRIMS, vol. 6370 (2004)
3. Churchill, D., Buro, M.: Build order optimization in StarCraft. In: AIIDE, pp. 14–19 (2011)
4. Churchill, D., Buro, M.: Incorporating search algorithms into RTS game agents. In: AIIDE (2012)
5. Churchill, D., et al.: Fast heuristic search for RTS game combat scenarios. In: AIIDE, pp. 112–117 (2012)
6. Gaudl, S.E., et al.: Behaviour oriented design for real-time-strategy games. In: FDG, pp. 198–205 (2013)
7. Justesen, N., Risi, S.: Learning macromanagement in Starcraft from replays using deep learning. In: CIG, pp. 162–169 (2017)
8. Lewis, J., et al.: A corpus analysis of strategy video game play in StarCraft: Brood War. In: CogSci, vol. 33 (2011)
9. Liu, S., et al.: Player identification from RTS game replays. In: Proceedings of the 28th CATA, pp. 313–317 (2013)
10. Oh, H., et al.: Identifying the rush strategies in the game logs of the real-time strategy game StarCraft-II. In: Proceedings of the 31st Annual Conference on JSAI (2017)
11. Ontanón, S.: A survey of real-time strategy game AI research and competition in StarCraft. IEEE T-CIAIG **5**(4), 293–311 (2013)
12. Ontanón, S.: RTS AI problems and techniques. In: Lee, N. (ed.) Encyclopedia of Computer Graphics and Games, pp. 1–12. Springer, Cham (2015). https://doi.org/10.1007/978-3-319-08234-9
13. Park, H., et al.: Prediction of early stage opponents strategy for StarCraft AI using scouting and machine learning. In: Proceedings of WASA, pp. 7–12 (2012)
14. Robertson, G., Watson, I.: A review of real-time strategy game AI. AI Mag. **35**(4), 75–104 (2014)
15. Ruíz-Granados, A.S.: Predicting the winner in two player StarCraft games. In: Proceeedings of the 2nd CoSECiVi, pp. 24–35 (2015)
16. Čertický, M., Churchill, D.: The current state of StarCraft AI competitions and bots. In: AIIDE (2017)
17. Usunier, N., et al.: Episodic exploration for deep deterministic policies: an application to starcraft micromanagement tasks. arXiv preprint arXiv:1609.02993 (2016)
18. Weber, B.G., Mateas, M.: A data mining approach to strategy prediction. In: Proceedings of the 5th CIG, pp. 140–147 (2009)
19. Weber, B.G., et al.: Building human-level AI for real-time strategy games. In: AAAI Fall Symposium: Advances in Cognitive Systems, vol. 11, p. 1 (2011)
20. Wintermute, S.: SORTS: a human-level approach to real-time strategy AI. Ann Arbor **1001**(48), 109–2121 (2007)

Design and Evaluation of a Fall Prevention Multiplayer Game for Senior Care Centres

Joana Silva[1(✉)], Elsa Oliveira[1], Dinis Moreira[1], Francisco Nunes[1],
Martina Caic[1,2], João Madureira[1], and Eduardo Pereira[1]

[1] Fraunhofer Portugal AICOS, Porto, Portugal
`joana.silva@fraunhofer.pt`
[2] Maastricht University, Maastricht, Netherlands

Abstract. Preventing falls is extremely important today as people live long sedentary lives. Fall prevention platforms can help, by stimulating seniors to perform exercises that improve balance and muscular strength. However, existing platforms for fall prevention mostly target individual users exercising at home. This paper describes the design and evaluation of a multi-player fall prevention game platform, FallSensing Games, to be used in senior care centers. The game design was inspired by the Otago Exercise Programme and the evaluation focused on biomechanical parameters, game experience, and technology acceptance. Results showed that the game was easy to follow, that seniors performed exercises correctly, and that the game integrated well with the activities of the senior care centers. Lessons learned from this project may inspire the development of similar platforms, and, in this way, support group exercise practices at senior care centers.

Keywords: Serious games · Exergames · Multiplayer games
Fall prevention · Older adults · Wearable devices

1 Introduction

Falling is normal and can happen to everyone, but, as people age, falls can become dangerous. One often hears about seniors who fall and need to be admitted to the hospital or become unable to pursue their everyday activities. Falls have a multi-factorial origin being mostly related to biological, behavioural, and environmental factors. Biological factors include characteristics of an individual such as age, gender, functional ability, gait disturbances, and co-morbidity associated with chronic conditions. Environmental and behavioural factors include indoor and outdoor hazards like loose rugs, stairs, uneven pavements, or insufficient lightning, inappropriate footwear, excess of medication, lack of exercise, and sedentary lifestyle [1,6,13]. Most risk factors can be amendable, with the implementation of alternative daily choices and physical exercise. Specially for

© IFIP International Federation for Information Processing 2018
Published by Springer Nature Switzerland AG 2018. All Rights Reserved
E. Clua et al. (Eds.): ICEC 2018, LNCS 11112, pp. 103–114, 2018.
https://doi.org/10.1007/978-3-319-99426-0_9

seniors, promoting physical activity and an active lifestyle is essential to postpone frailty and physical vulnerability [1,13].

Several solutions have been proposed to prevent falls using serious games [11,12,17,18,23]. However, the majority of existing solutions were designed to be used individually by a senior at home. Solutions to be used at home may work in some situations, but they disregard the social component of exercising practices, often present in senior care centres. Moreover, designing technologies for promoting and supporting exercise in senior care centres may contribute to the active and healthy ageing of the seniors in those institutions.

This paper describes a fall prevention technological solution based on an interactive (exer)game. Players have a TV screen in front of them displaying a game and wear a strap on the lower limbs which contains an inertial measurement unit (IMU). This wearable device enables movement identification and characterization in real time, triggering actions in the game, and, ultimately, allowing an analysis of each participant's performance. The included exercises are a subset of a validated fall prevention exercise plan - the Otago Exercise Programme (OEP) [4] - used to promote mobility, muscular strength, and balance. The exercises are presented through a series of interactive mini-games[1] specially designed for groups (up to 6 persons) playing in senior care centres.

The developed solution was tested in three field trials in senior care centres. Our field work draws on interviews, questionnaires, and observation in senior care centres, where a total of 37 seniors used the system. The analysis focused on the usability, acceptance, and appropriation of the system in the centre. We also reflect on the three lessons learned, namely: the active role of the care worker in promoting the engagement with the game, the competition between players during the games, and the overall acceptance of the games. Lastly, we report the analysis of the exercise-related metrics extracted from the wearable devices, which enabled the evaluation of in-game performance analysis.

The remaining of the paper is organised as follows. Section 2 describes the prior art in games for fall prevention. Section 3 details the design of the fall prevention solution. Section 4 describes the field trials conducted, and Sect. 5 reports the resulting main findings. Section 6 discusses this work and Sect. 7 highlights the main conclusions and opportunities for future work.

2   Related Work

Exercising through video games, or playing exergames, is a recent concept that combines the fun component of playing a video game and physical exercising [7,21]. It is generally acknowledged that exercise delivered through exergames is more acceptable by seniors than more clinical exercise strategies [7,17,18,21]. Exergames are promising for different rehabilitation purposes, including regaining functional ability [7,17], improving mobility [7,17,18], preventing cognitive decline [7], and promoting social inclusion [7,18]. However, there is a lack of validated solutions, specially regarding the adherence and engagement of seniors [7].

---

[1] Mini-games are small games that are contained inside a larger game plot.

Examples of exergames in the market include Dance Dance Revolution (DDR), Sony Playstation II Eye Toy, and Nintendo Wii Sports. These particular platforms have been tested with seniors in short term pilots, obtaining interesting results in terms of users' acceptance [7,15,22]. However, most of these solutions were originally designed for entertainment and recreation purposes and thus do not present a strong effectiveness [15,21] as is expected from fall prevention interventions. Moreover, overloaded interfaces, small fonts, game complexity, and lack of personalized goals can hinder these platforms from achieving consistent engagement when used by seniors [7,11,21].

There are some exergames in the market that were specifically designed for seniors. Examples include Corehab [8], Rehametrics [16], 3D Tutor [10], or SilverFit 3D [19]. These solutions target rehabilitation rather than fall prevention and were designed to be used by individuals at home or by healthcare providers at clinics. The only example we could find where seniors were expected to use the system in a senior care center was in PEPE [20], a robot developed to stimulate physical activity, with whom seniors play individually in front of the group.

Specifically designed to prevent falls of seniors we find two prototypes in the literature: FCC-Exergames [17] and Dance Don't Fall [18]. Both solutions were designed to be used by seniors at home. FCC-Exergames is an individual game and Dance Don't Fall enables two seniors to play together at home. Nevertheless, systematic reviews report a discrepancy between the number of available solutions that target exercising in groups compared to exercising alone [21]. With this context in mind we present a novel solution, the FallSensing games, designed to be used at senior care centres to reinforce group exercise practices for fall prevention and promote social interactions among seniors.

3 FallSensing Games

The FallSensing games include three mini-games to be played by two teams, with up to three players each, competing against each other, alternately. Players wear one wearable inertial sensor to track the movement execution. This sensor can be placed in the thigh, on the ankle, or on the top of the foot, depending on the game. Each game has its own rules and gameplay experience depending on the requested movement, which is based on a set of OEP [4] exercises. The movements to be executed are recurrently explained to promote their safe performance. Movement data is evaluated by the system to animate the avatar.

The OEP is a set of leg muscle strengthening and balance retraining exercises, that has shown to be effective in reducing by 35% the number of falls. Given this evidence for fall prevention, this programme was selected to be implemented as a set of mini-games. Strengthening exercises focus on major lower limb muscles. Balance retraining exercises focus on reinforcing body balance recovery using lower body exercises. The combination of OEP exercises into mini-games aimed to group exercises with the same sensor position on the body, to avoid sensor's re-position, and to combine exercises that reinforced the same group of muscles.

The game was designed around the Antarctic theme and the main actors are penguins. We chose to use penguins as avatars because they can be modelled to perform the required exercises, while keeping a fun factor for users. There are three mini-games inside the main screen. Each mini-game combines up to three physical exercises. In choosing which games to pair we minimized the changes in positioning the wearable (to sustain the gameplay), we balanced the relative effort of exercises, and considered the distance among the players and between the players and the display.

There are two types of users in the system: players and administrator. Players are seniors who wear the sensor on the limbs and perform exercises. The game administrator can also be a senior, but in most cases will be a care worker from the institution who works with the seniors. Game administrators start the system on a computer and select the players who will play for each team.

3.1 Requirements

Based on previous research on exergames for seniors and TV user interfaces for this audience [3,11,12] we identified the following game design requirements:

1. **The game administrator should be able to select players or enter new players that are not in the system,** to enable different people in the institution to play (and be individually monitored).
2. **The system should monitor the execution of movements continuously and reflect it in real-time through the avatars' animations.** Immersion in the game and identification with the characters depends on a clear alignment of the players' movements and the avatars' actions.
3. **Exercise instructions should be clear and easy to follow.** Players need to understand which movement to perform, when to do it, and how many times to repeat it, while being immersed in the game. In this regard, it should be noted that the speed of some exercises animations were reduced to better fit the playing rhythms of seniors.
4. **The user interface should be usable at a distance.** Seniors need to read the text in the interface comfortably on a distant TV, thus appropriate font-type and font-size need to be considered. Used graphics should also have appropriate dimensions and contrast to be understood at a distance.
5. **The visual feedback of the performance should be complemented with sounds.** Similar to the previous requirement, this one focuses on addressing common characteristics that arise with age, such as eyesight limitations and decreased cognitive processing speed. Auditory feedback can complement the game experience by helping players to notice changes in the game. Moreover, sounds and music increase the fun factor of the system.

3.2 Mini-Games

The following description explains the three mini-games, respectively, regarding the exercises to be performed, the position of the inertial sensor, and their respective goals (avatars vs player). It is worth noting that the penguins (i.e., avatars) are differentiated by the colour of their clothes and accessories: blue, green, or yellow. Sensors are also coloured in the same scheme.

Mini-game 1: This game includes Knee Bends and Sit-to-Stand exercises, monitored with a sensor on the thigh. Penguins start a walk on the snow, and when they encounter lakes, users need to bend their knees to enable the penguins to jump over the lake (Fig. 1). If the exercise is performed incorrectly or out of tempo, the penguin falls into the lake, and the player looses some time. After jumping the lakes, each penguin needs to pick up with their beaks 10 fishes from a pile. To catch the fishes each player must do the exercise Sit-to-Stand properly; otherwise the penguins will not be able to catch all the fishes on time. The objective is to perform all activities (jump all the lakes and pick all the fishes) in the shortest time possible.

Fig. 1. A: space required to perform exercise; B: instructions to help fixing the sensor; C: exercise instructions to follow; D: Mini-game 1; E: Mini-game 2; F: Mini-game 3.

Mini-game 2: This game includes Lateral Hip Abduction (Side Hip), Frontal Knee Extension (Front Knee) and Backwards Knee Flexion (Back Knee) with the sensor on the ankle. The penguins have a big lake to swim but before entering in the lake they have to warm up, lifting laterally their left and right paw five times. To do it, each player must do the right and left Lateral Hip Abduction exercise five times. If the exercise is well done the penguins conclude the warm up and enter the lake. To start the breaststroke swimming each player must do the Frontal Knee Extension exercise to enable the penguin to swim forward (Fig. 1). Arriving to the end of the lake, the penguin will return doing the backstroke swimming movement; each player must do the Backwards Knee exercise for this action. If seniors perform the movement steadily and slowly, as instructed, the penguin swims faster, while if they perform exercises too fast or incorrectly, the penguin will go slowly. We added this time-related feature in the game because OEP recommends strength exercises to be performed slowly, i.e. 3 seconds for the ascendant phase and 5 seconds for the descending phase. Using this strategy, each player needs to do 10 repetitions to swim each side of the lake, otherwise, players need to perform even more repetitions to travel the same distance. Still, the objective of the game is to travel all the lake in the shortest time possible.

Mini-game 3: This game includes Calf and Toe Raises with sensors on top of the foot. The penguins have a path to run on top of a snowball. They have to roll the ball forward until the first target, without loosing their balance (Fig. 1). The players must do the Calf Raises exercise correctly to enable the penguins to move forward with the ball, otherwise the penguins will lose their balance and run slowly. After reaching the first target, the penguins have to do the backward path rolling backwards until the finish line. The players need to do the Toe Raises exercise effectively to accomplish this action, otherwise, and once again, the penguins will lose their balance and run slowly to the finish line. Similarly to Mini-game 2, a mechanism to control exercise execution speed was employed for this mini-game aiming for the slow execution of each exercise repetition. At least 5 exercise repetitions are needed in order to run each side of the course. Once more, the objective is still to cross the finish line in the shortest time possible.

4   Methods

To explore how participants used the developed solution, we organized three different field trials. During trials, we used semi-structured interviews, observations, and/or the System Usability Scale (SUS) [2]. The participants were presented with the FallSensing Games, that were explained to them prior to the execution of the mini-games. It was also explained the main goal of the games was to retrain fall prevention strategies. The first trial was conducted during an afternoon in a day-care centre with 21 seniors (19 female). Participants played a single game during the time we spent there. After the game sessions, every participant answered the Portuguese of the SUS questionnaire, and additionally participated in a short interview to understand the perceptions of the gaming experience (e.g., encountered difficulties, expected outcomes, hedonistic and utilitarian value expectations) with questions regarding acceptance, difficulties, obstacles, outcomes, and feelings during the game. The average age of this group was 80.3 ± 8.05 years old.

The second trial was conducted in a day-care centre with 10 female seniors. The participants played 3 mini-games twice a week for 3 weeks (6 sessions). On

average, each session lasted half an hour. The average age of this group was
69.4 ± 11.15 years old. This group also attended gymnastics sessions in parallel
to the fall prevention games. Only observations notes were taken during this
trial.

The third trial was conducted in a nursing home with 6 female seniors. Participants engaged in 15 sessions, with an average duration of 20 min per session.
The tests were performed twice a week, during 7 weeks. The average age of
participants in this group was 83.5 ± 8.22 years old. This group also attended
gymnastics sessions in parallel to the fall prevention sessions.

In the third trial, we also monitored the quality of the performed exercises. In
particular, we compared the recognition of the exercises by the system with the
evaluation of an external observer. An exercise repetition was only considered
when the user started the desired movement, reached a minimum target joint
angle, and returned to the initial orientation. Tracking changes in the orientation of the moving limb was performed by using data from the wearable sensor
accelerometer and gyroscope (sampling frequency: 50 Hz) within a sensor-fusion
based second order complementary filter [5,14]. This enabled the characterization of the whole movement including the collected metrics such as: (i) number
of completed repetitions, (ii) maximum reached joint angle (range of motion),
and (iii) repetition cycle duration. The target joint angle was previously defined
according to the literature and with the help of a group of physiotherapists which
took into account the advanced age of this group [9].

5   Results

5.1   Overall Experience with the Platform

The participants considered the games easy to understand and to play, despite
their physical challenges. They indicated that the game interface clearly communicated the game objective, saying that "the games' screens always told them
what to do, so they could easily accomplish the games' objectives". Most participants considered the games fun and they appreciated the penguins avatars as
well. Placing the wearable devices on the body was considered difficult to be performed alone and the fact that sometimes the bracelet moved away from the right
place and interfered with the games bothered them. While the majority of participants found the mini-games appropriate for their age, some elderly participants
indicated that the game movements were too challenging (e.g., uncomfortable
body movements, too fast) which interfered with their performance. One of the
participants mentioned that he was not comfortable in getting up from the chair
as fast as required by the game being played as a race. The majority of participants was comfortable with the text fonts, but a small number of participants
said it was too small for them (Fig. 2).

Participants mentioned they would like to play the games again in the future,
because it enabled them to exercise, play together, and pass time. Most of the
participants referred they have a very inactive lifestyle and that solutions such
as the one developed will provide them with opportunities to perform exercise.

Fig. 2. Seniors during field trial sessions.

A participant mentioned that *"It is so we can pass the time, instead of just being here talking to each other. It is a way of being entertained, a way to pass the time."*. Participants often commented that the games could contribute to training their memory. One participant commented that *"What would make me play, first, because I have to concentrate in what I am doing, and it is good for my brain. And because I like to play games on the computer [FallSensing games]."*.

Participants considered the interaction to be modern and enjoyed to interact with a "computer". They felt that playing the game was a way to get further informed about the latest technological developments, and also a way to learn about how to use novel technologies such as computers.

The SUS questionnaires conducted with 21 persons also confirmed the high usability of the system. The SUS global score of 80.12 characterises a highly usable and acceptable system.

Table 1. Extracted biomechanical metrics of playing FallSensing mini-games (MG).

MG	Exercise	Nr. cycles	ROM (°)	Target ROM (°)	Cycle time (s)
MG 1	Knee Bends	3.08 ± 1.83	38.00 ± 12.27	15	2.04 ± 0.99
	Sit to Stand	4.14 ± 4.12	n.d	-	3.23 ± 0.98
MG 2	Side Hip	5.16 ± 0.44	39.85 ± 6.97	15	1.58 ± 0.76
	Knee Extension	23.52 ± 4.32	73.11 ± 12.77	30	1.40 ± 2.76
	Knee Flexion	20.52 ± 3.56	81.20 ± 13.31	30	1.32 ± 0.83
MG 3	Calf Raises	8.57 ± 1.50	24.12 ± 7.04	10	1.80 ± 2.17
	Toe Raises	7.08 ± 1.78	15.34 ± 7.10	10	1.63 ± 2.49

5.2 Movements Analysis

Besides providing an appropriate experience to seniors, the system was also able to accurately identify the performed movements (Table 1). All users could perceive and effectively execute the proper exercise movements to control the avatar in quite a satisfactory way, with the worst case being the execution of the 3 out of 10 correct Knee Bends during Mini-game 1. Moreover, this result may be related with the increased complexity of this exercise, because each player has to perform Knee Bends and coordinate their execution with the proximity to the lake; otherwise the penguin falls into the lake. If players fail to coordinate the timing, the repetition does not count and their avatar is slowed down. This mini-game feature was designed to instruct the user to perform the desired exercise and train the reaction time to a stimulus (i.e., approaching the lake).

As for the remaining mini-games, the number of detected repetitions was larger than the proposed values, as expected. The larger values are due to the designed game mechanism which penalizes the users who performed strength exercises performed too quickly. This mechanism was designed to simultaneously fulfil an OEP requirement and encourage users to perform the movements correctly and slowly without compromising the playful nature of the game. However, the mentioned mechanism did not work as effectively as expected, since in some cases, participants needed twice more repetitions than projected to finish the game. Moreover, this is corroborated by the fact that for practically all mini-games, the average cycle duration was almost always less than 2 seconds, instead of the expected 8 seconds reference value (3 and 5 seconds for ascending and descending movements phases, respectively). Executing more repetitions is not necessarily a problem, however it can lead to muscle fatigue and discourage seniors to play the game in the long term. Therefore, an alternative and more intuitive solution should be sought in order to fulfil this requirement.

Exercises' range of motion (ROM) was also evaluated using these mini-games being the obtained ROM results in agreement with proposed values for this age group, namely 45° for hip abduction, 70° for knee extension, 90° for knee flexion, 30° for plantar flexion, 20° for plantar dorsiflexion, and 40° for knee bending exercise [9]. Range of motion together with muscle strength can be an indicator of functional disability or an increased fall risk level on seniors. Thus, by targeting muscle weakness and movement ROM using this set of exergames, seniors can continuously improve their physical abilities and recover proper ROM.

5.3 Role of Care Workers During the Game

Our observations led us to conclude that external motivators such as care workers play a valuable role throughout the gaming process. Physiotherapists and social educators from the centre often provoked seniors to play the game and provided great incentive while seniors were playing. During the first session, seniors would be reluctant to try the system. Physiotherapists or social educators would start playing the game, with one or two people, and after a couple of minutes, almost everyone was standing around the game and looking forward to play it. Our initial expectation was that care workers would help in choosing players or register them in the system, but their role was much more prominent. They were initiating participation, stimulating team spirit, and motivating participants throughout the game to perform at their best.

5.4   Placement of Wearable Sensor

The placement of the wearable was problematic in some situations. Older women from Portugal frequently wear skirts and to position the sensor on the thigh they would have to raise the skirt in front of the group, or to go to a side room to place it. None of these options offers a great experience, and since participants might place the sensor quickly, data collection may be compromised as the sensors is not well attached to the body. Placing the sensor in the thigh was essential for monitoring the execution of certain exercises, but we are considering choosing an alternative exercise or placing the sensor in an alternative place. Making players feel uncomfortable with placing the wearable is not the experience we want the game to provide.

5.5   Competition Versus Collaboration

Despite our intention to promote collaboration within a team, we observed competitive behaviour of the seniors not only among, but also within the teams. We believe the reason behind the competitive behaviour was that mini-games had a linear progression from one side to the other, with players going in the same direction. This probably led seniors to conclude that they were on a race with each other, and thus engaged in competitive behaviour.

6   Discussion

This paper described a multi-player fall prevention game for seniors to use in senior care centres. The FallSensing games are one of few systems to: (i) focus on fall prevention, (ii) promote group exercises, and (iii) target senior care centres; and is the only one addressing the three characteristics simultaneously.

Using an exercising platform in senior care centres was very different from the home interaction context. For example, the role of the care worker was found to be determinant in the senior care centre, but such a role does not exist at home and studies do not talk about a supporting role when designing or evaluating systems for the home setting [17–19]. The issue with placing the sensors also seems to be characteristic of the senior care centre. The home has one or more intimate places (e.g., rooms), and the smaller distances between rooms would easily enable people to place sensors in their thighs away from guests. Moreover, the senior care centre is well suited for multiplayer games, while at home, seniors may live alone. The expectation that people would be alone at home probably influenced existing solutions to focus on individual playing settings [21].

Regarding the overall system acceptance and since the threshold previously defined in the literature for comparison of SUS global score is 80.3 [2], our system scored almost this threshold, which is a very positive outcome and reinforce the conclusion that the system is perceived as being easy-of-use and provides a global positive measure of system satisfaction.

Regarding the effect of interventions in terms of exercise monitoring, the majority of solutions in the literature used a variety of outcome measures and study designs, making it difficult to directly compare them with our solution [21]. Moreover, balance is clearly the main focus across the majority of the commercially available solutions, among a wide range of physical functions that could be simultaneous evaluated and targeted [21]. Our solution was designed not only to address balance retaining but also to promote mobility and muscular strength targeting more than one physical function simultaneously which constitutes the major advantage in respect to most commercially available exergames.

7   Conclusions and Future Work

This paper presented multi-player fall-prevention games for seniors, which are fun, easy-to-use, and well accepted among seniors in senior care centres. The role of the care worker was found to be preponderant during the game play, and competition revealed to be pervasive over collaboration. We believe fall-prevention games in senior care centres have potential to help preventing falls considering the usability and acceptance of the system during the trials.

Acknowledgements. We thank all participants that collaborated in the trials as well as the physiotherapists and care workers involved. We also acknowledge funding from FallSensing: Technological solution for fall risk screening and falls prevention (POCI-01-0247-FEDER-003464), co-funded by Portugal 2020, framed under the COMPETE 2020 (Operational Programme Competitiveness and Internationalization) and European Regional Development Fund (ERDF) from European Union (EU).

References

1. Ambrose, A.F., Paul, G., Hausdorff, J.M.: Risk factors for falls among older adults: a review of the literature. Maturitas **75**(1), 51–61 (2013)
2. Brooke, J.: SUS - a quick and dirty usability scale. In: Usability Evaluation in Industry. Taylor and Francis (1996)
3. Brox, E., Konstantinidis, S., Evertsen, G.: User-centered design of serious games for older adults following 3 years of experience with exergames for seniors: a study design. JMIR Serious Games **5**(1), 1–14 (2017)
4. Campbell, A.J., Robertson, M.C., Gardner, M.M., Norton, R.N., Tilyard, M.W., Buchner, D.M.: Randomised controlled trial of a general practice programme of home based exercise to prevent falls in elderly women. BMJ **315**(7115), 1065–1069 (1997)
5. Carneiro, S., et al.: Inertial sensors for assessment of joint angles. In: Proceedings of the 4th Workshop on ICTs for Improving Patients Rehabilitation Research Techniques, pp. 9–12 (2016)
6. Chaccour, K., Darazi, R., El Hassani, A.H., Andrès, E.: From fall detection to fall prevention: a generic classification of fall-related systems. IEEE Sensors J. **17**(3), 812–822 (2017)
7. Chao, Y.Y., Scherer, Y.K., Montgomery, C.A.: Effects of using Nintendo Wii™ exergames in older adults: a review of the literature. J. Aging Health **27**(3), 379–402 (2015)
8. Corerehab: Riablo (2017). http://eng.corehab.it/products/rehabilitation/

9. Jung, H., Yamasaki, M.: Association of lower extremity range of motion and muscle strength with physical performance of community-dwelling older women. J. Physiol. Anthropol. **35**(1), 30 (2016)

10. MediTouch: 3DTutor (2017). http://meditouch.co.il/products/3dtutor/

11. Nunes, F., Kerwin, M., Silva, P.A.: Design recommendations for TV user interfaces for older adults: findings from the eCAALYX project. In: Proceedings of ASSETS 2012, pp. 41–48 (2012)

12. Ogonowski, C., et al.: ICT-based fall prevention system for older adults: qualitative results from a long-term field study. ACM Trans. Comput.-Hum. Interact. **23**(5), 1–33 (2016)

13. World Health Organization: WHO global report on falls prevention in older age (2018)

14. Pereira, A., Guimarães, V., Sousa, I.: Joint angles tracking for rehabilitation at home using inertial sensors: a feasibility study. In: Proceedings of PervasiveHealth 2017, pp. 146–154 (2017)

15. Rand, D., Kizony, R., Weiss, P.T.L.: The Sony PlayStation II EyeToy: low-cost virtual reality for use in rehabilitation. J. Neurol. Phys. Therapy **32**(4), 155–163 (2008)

16. RehabMetrics: Physical and cognitive rehabilitation (2017). http://rehametrics.com/en/physical-and-cognitive-rehabilitation/

17. Santos, A., Guimarães, V., Matos, N., Cevada, J., Ferreira, C., Sousa, I.: Multisensor exercise-based interactive games for fall prevention and rehabilitation. In: Proceedings of PervasiveHealth 2015, pp. 65–71 (2015)

18. Silva, P.A., Nunes, F., Vasconcelos, A., Kerwin, M., Moutinho, R., Teixeira, P.: Using the smartphone accelerometer to monitor fall risk while playing a game: the design and usability evaluation of Dance! Don't Fall. In: Schmorrow, D.D., Fidopiastis, C.M. (eds.) AC 2013. LNCS (LNAI), vol. 8027, pp. 754–763. Springer, Heidelberg (2013). https://doi.org/10.1007/978-3-642-39454-6_81

19. SilverFit: SilverFit 3D (2018). http://silverfit.com/en/products/silverfit-3d-camera

20. Simão, H., Bernardino, A.: User centered design of an augmented reality gaming platform for active aging in elderly institutions. In: Proceedings of the 5th International Congress on Sport Sciences Research and Technology Support, pp. 151–162 (2017)

21. Skjæret, N., Nawaz, A., Morat, T., Schoene, D., Helbostad, J.L., Vereijken, B.: Exercise and rehabilitation delivered through exergames in older adults: an integrative review of technologies, safety and efficacy. Int. J. Med. Inf. **85**(1), 1–16 (2016)

22. Smith, S.T., Sherrington, C., Studenski, S., Schoene, D., Lord, S.R.: A novel dance dance revolution (DDR) system for in-home training of stepping ability: basic parameters of system use by older adults. Br. J. Sports Med. **45**(5), 441–445 (2011)

23. Wattanasoontorn, V., Boada, I., García, R., Sbert, M.: Serious games for health. Entertain. Comput. **4**(4), 231–247 (2013)

Comedy in the Ludonarrative
of Video Games

Oskari Kallio and Masood Masoodian[✉]

School of Arts, Design and Architecture, Aalto University, Helsinki, Finland
{oskari.kallio,masood.masoodian}@aalto.fi

Abstract. Although humor is a prevalent component of numerous video games, thus far it has not been recognized as an established genre of its own. Comedy—the deliberate act to harness and perform humor—represents one, but an important segment of the emotional range that video games should aspire to cover. The challenge, however, lies in attempting to analyse various elements contributing to comedy, particularly with the inclusion of interactively as a fundamental element of video games. In this paper, we propose using the concept of *ludonarrative* as the basis for analysing comedy in video games. We approach ludonarrative comedy through examples that illustrate trends which can be discerned from games that introduce humor through their *narrative* and *ludic* (gameplay-related) elements.

Keywords: Computer games · Video games · Comedy
Humor · Narrative · Ludonarrative · Ludology · Narratology

1 Introduction

Comedy is the performance of humor, which is why comedy cannot be analyzed without the understanding of what humor is. Hookam and Meany [1] define humor as the "ability to perceive or express the intentional or unintentional comic elements of life", and comedy as the "intentionally structured cultural product that employs particular forms and conventions to create the affect of amusement in an audience." Martin [2] describes humor as "a ubiquitous human activity that occurs in all types of social interaction. It infuses meaning to the meaningless and takes it away from matters that are perhaps too meaningful."

Although various humor theories [3] attempt to describe what is at the core of a humorous experience, there is no accepted unified theory of funny, nor a precise formula for humor creation—only intuition.

If comedy is rather difficult to define, it is even more so when the element of interactivity of video games[1] is made part of the equation. It is not surprising then that, while words "comedy" and "humor" are commonly used to describe specific genres of films and books, they are hardly ever used to describe video

---

[1] In this paper, we use "video games" and "computer games" interchangeably.

© IFIP International Federation for Information Processing 2018
Published by Springer Nature Switzerland AG 2018. All Rights Reserved
E. Clua et al. (Eds.): ICEC 2018, LNCS 11112, pp. 115–126, 2018.
https://doi.org/10.1007/978-3-319-99426-0_10

games. Furthermore, although "humor" is a prevalent element in many games, only a few of them seem to warrant the "comedy" label. However, the few comic games that do exist, are proof of the comedic capability that the medium holds. In many ways the medium of video games is perfect for comedy—with the means of play, games can actually involve their audience in the comedy-making. Hookam and Meany [1] note that for video games comedy to be recognized as a genre, there must first be a consensus on the elements that contribute to such comedy.

In this paper, we analyze video games comedy using the concept of *ludonarrative*. The term "ludonarrative", coined by game designer Hocking [4], comes from the Latin word *ludus*—roughly translating to "game"—and *narrative*—referring to a meaningful recount of connected events. In short, ludonarrative refers to the junction of gameplay and narrative elements in video games. Here, we define the qualities that make ludonarrative comedy distinct from comedy in other media, identify the challenges involved in its execution, and discuss three dimensions for the design of ludonarrative comedy in video games: their visual style, their sources of comedy, and the elements of conflict in them.

2   Ludonarrative Comedy

Major literature reviews of humor and comedy in video games are rather scarce. Dormannn and Biddle [5] provide the first of such reviews, focusing primarily on the gameplay elements. Dormann [6] extends this work, while still keeping the focus on humor in gameplay. The most comprehensive review of humor in video games to date, however, is that of Grönroos [7], which identifies the role of player input in comedic aspects of video games, and relates this to game characters, game worlds, and game mechanics, as means of offering *emergent* humor. She also reviews the role of *scripted* (i.e. narrative) humor in video games.

These reviews show that video games provide a fitting, but an under-utilized, medium for comedy. However, Grönroos [7] suggests that this apparent lack of humor in video games may in fact be a question of recognition, with interactive humor taking new unfamiliar forms: "games use humor in ways that are unfamiliar from other media, and often humor elicits amusement instead of laughter."

Ludonarratives provide many opportunities for comedy. Games are enthralling, player-influenced and effort-requiring rule-based systems with variable and quantifiable outcomes that, while have values assigned to them, also have negotiable consequences [8]. Frasca [9] emphasizes that the "player agency" is what distinguishes interactive narratives from traditional narratives: "Observers are passive, the player is active. If the player does not act, there will be no game, and therefore no session at all." He also stresses that "play" and the "narrative" are not one, but play can lead to the creation of a narrative.

Ludonarrative comedy also generates its own unique design problems. For instance, comic timing—the fundamental and unforgiving factor in any kind of comedy—can be easily impaired by the player.

Therefore, designers of comedy games need to have an insight about the strengths and weaknesses of this particular medium. In comparing the neglected video games comedy to the established horror video games genre, Quinn [10] argues that the barriers to successful video games comedy are not mechanical in nature. She also points out that horror and comedy share many of the same qualities: they aspire to take their audience by surprise; with both there is usually a set-up and a pay-off; and the design problems are similar (e.g. the efforts to keep the material fresh). Quinn suggests that only by considering comedy as a mechanical foundation for gameplay, as well as having a firm understanding of what drives humor, the potential of video games comedy can be realized.

However, most developers still seem to avoid designing their games primarily around humor, and often use it like a seasoning to add flavor to the end result, with little relevance to the overall design. Pratchett (quoted in [11]) stresses that this sort of approach does not lead to true comedy: "Good humor needs to be built in. It should be the chocolate chips in the gooey cookie of gaming, rather than chocolate sprinkles on top."

Full commitment to comedy is seen as a risk because bad comedy has no value. A funny joke is a source of joy, but a bad one can be downright detrimental. Bell, having studied responses to failed humor [12], proposes that the reason a bad joke makes the listeners angry is because it is often taken as an insult to the audience's sense of humor: "When a joke is actually funny, listeners don't mind the disruption because there is a payoff: humor. Without the humor, listeners may become annoyed at the lame crack."

Furthermore, it is also difficult for non-integral comedy to make it all the way to the final product, simply because of the way most games are developed. A substantial part of the game development process involves the trial-and-error based playtesting. Constant playtesting equals repetition, which is known to sour even the funniest of jokes. Humor is a transient delight. Repetition—when used correctly—is a comic enhancer, but without variation it can make the humor disappear. Root (quoted in [13]) highlights that "Surprise is one of the keys to comedy, and it's difficult to pull off in a game with repeat plays." Schafer [14] also emphasizes that game designers must be hypersensitive about repetition: "There is an old expression, don't put humor on the inner loop. Nothing is funny that many times in a row. OK, I just made that up but it's true. Characters need to change up what they say, not just to keep the humor fresh, but to make the character seem more real." Quinn [10] compares playtesting for comedic games to stand-up comedians who are constantly refining their material with fresh audiences: "Test early, test often and with new people." Therefore, the role of playtesting should not be about discarding comedy, but making it funnier.

Abbott [15] argues that comedy is "cerebral, technical, and deeply human", and notes that, of those three factors, comedic video games often stumble in the "deeply human" department. Abbot supports his claim with the gradual disappearance of comedic games towards the beginning of the new millennium, when video game visuals started transitioning from primitive to more photorealistic. He links this observation to the "uncanny valley" theorem, which maintains that the closer a human replica gets to a real human, the more unnatural it appears to the (human) observer: "The uncanny valley is nobody's friend, but it's an especially harsh environment for comedy." When games fail the comedic *Turing test*, it is likely that something about their humor is too foreign or unrecognizable to be considered funny. While the player can be used to fill the "deeply human" void in ludonarrative comedy, there are many fundamental, and largely unaddressed, problems in using the player as a component in a comic gameplay. At the very least, in such cases when players' efforts result in failure, they are more likely to end up being disappointed rather than amused. Failure can be turned into comedy, as long as the players themselves are not the laughing stock.

So one of the key questions in ludonarrative comedy is how to make players to commit to comedy. Totilo [16] calls attention to the dualistic role a player is designated in a video game. Players are not only members of the audience, but are also playing the part of the lead actor. When the objectives of a game are clear and the gameplay revolves around active verbs, players can be expected to play their part, but when the concept of "nuance" is introduced, requirements for the players' performance increase. "It's easy for a game designer to make someone feel like Bruce Willis or Sly Stallone by putting a virtual gun in their hand. But how do you go about making someone feel like Charlie Chaplin or Bernie Mac", Totilo contemplates [16].

3   Visuality of Ludonarrative Comedy

Humor has an aesthetic dimension that has long been recognized. Morreall [17] claims that aesthetic experience is the basis of all humor, while Gordon [18] describes humor as being "aesthetic to the extent that it arouses the viewers' imagination, provides them with insights about human existence, and provokes them to think more critically and creatively." Because video games are a visual medium, aesthetics have an important role in their delivery of humor. They can either be used to tell visual jokes, or prepare the audience for comedic experiences. Visual cues, such as the overall visual style, character design, and animations can condition the audience to get into a humorous mood.

For instance, *Katamari Damacy*[2], utilizes all of the above mentioned enhancers to produce a playable visual gag. The game uses its psychedelic aesthetics to highlight the eccentricity of its ludonarrative. A small glimpse of the visuals is enough to reveal that the game is not to be taken too seriously. The delightful animations and overly simple geometry of the in-game objects contribute to the carnivalistic style. A visual gag is something that cannot be translated to any other form, and Katamari Damacy is a prime example of that.

Video games also share many similarities with animated films, as with both, the directors are by and large responsible for the finished product. The fantastical canvas of games and cartoons makes it possible for the director to portray any imaginable idea. Tex Avery, a longtime animation director for Warner Bros.[3] in the early 20th century, had an enormous influence on animated comedy. He is responsible for both inventing and institutionalizing a great number of visual

---

[2] Namco (2004), Playstation 2.
[3] https://www.warnerbros.com.

gags, that have since become standard visual language in narrative animation. Eyes popping out of the characters' heads when shocked, their jaws dropping to the floor in astonishment, and gravity playing tricks on them, are all part of Avery's trademark comedy. Avery knew that the audience is aware of the fact that everything that happens on the screen has been manufactured, and used the fictitious mould of animation for yet more comedy. For instance, some of his cartoons used black rotoscoped human silhouettes on top of the actual animation, that were meant to trick the movie audience into believing that somebody had stood up in the theater to chat with the characters of his films. His other films featured a drawn fluttering hair on screen, as if it was stuck inside the projector. Eventually a character would notice the hair and pull it out. The visual humor of Avery comes from the realization that the animation directors are not bound by the laws of the nature, and have the freedom to do whatever they wish with the format. In a like manner there is still much to be extracted from the freedom that comes with the unique properties of video games.

The *Outcast*[4] video game features comparable comic antics. The game jests at deficiencies of the digital medium with a pretend blooper reel with simulated bugs and glitches. The reel shows reactions of the in-game cast as the game soundtrack is playing too loud during conversations, characters colliding into each other during cutscenes, and the AI malfunctioning in amusing ways.

Tex Avery's heir at Warner Bros., Chuck Jones, distanced himself from the anarchy of the Avery era and emphasized creative discipline in cartoons [19]. Since the possibilities with animations were boundless, Jones established clearly defined systems and rules for his animations [20]. He found humor in strict conditions and animation systems that benefited the internal consistency of the cartoons. Jones concentrated on the smallest possible gestures and expressions in order to invoke mirth. "If you can't tell what is happening by the way the character moves, you're not really animating," he is quoted saying [21]. For video games, Jones' structural approach is easier to adapt than the boundlessness of Avery's method, because games themselves are closed formal systems.

Super Mario Odyssey[5] provides a good example of animations that instantly tell the player what is happening. Mario is able to "capture" various enemies in order to control them. With each creature behaving and controlling in a comically distinct manner, the player gets instant feedback of their abilities. Much of what is humorous about the game is in the visual design, things appearing comical rather than being actual, and explicit visual gags.

In video games idle animations are also a popular means to communicate a character's personality and mood to the player. They usually happen when the player does not touch the controls of a game for a fixed amount of time. Idle animations in most cases are simple, such as the character glancing around the scenery or scratching its rear-end. They can, however, be used for simple visual gags, like in *Rayman 2: The Great Escape*[6], where the joint-less protagonist takes

---

[4] Infogrames (1999), Windows.
[5] Nintendo (2017), Nintendo Switch.
[6] Ubisoft (2000), Windows.

its blob of a torso and uses it to practice basketball dribbles. In other cases, idle animations have been used for character and world building purposes. One of the earliest examples is in *Leisure Suit Larry in the Land of the Lounge Lizards*[7]. The game begins on a nightly city street where Larry is waiting for the player interaction. Upon the player not touching the controls, a dog slowly walks into the scene, mistakes the stationary Larry for a lamppost, and urinates on him.

Comedy can also be generated purposefully through bad visual design. Terry Gilliam's animation transitions in *Monty Python's Flying Circus*[8] remain a good example of such deliberately shoddy visual style. Similarly, the animation series *South Park*[9] has became famous for having a clumsy approach to cut-out animation. Weinstock [22] argues that a big part of the initial success of South Park was due to "the tension established between its relatively sophisticated dialogue and involved narratives and its extremely limited animation." These show that, when cleverly executed, sub-par visuals can elevate the humor of a production.

Many low-budget games, having realized this, utilize intentionally bad animations and character designs to amuse the player. For instance, *Surgeon Simulator*[10] uses its coarse visual presentation to promote its funny gameplay premise, and to differentiate itself from the more serious simulator games. The game is set in an operation room, but the visual design underscores the farcicality of the player being the surgeon, rather than the vulgarity of the surgical procedure. Similarly, *Enviro-Bear 2000*[11] elevates the comicality of its premise with purposefully cheap-looking visuals, and clunky controls. The game is about a bear driving a stolen a car on a mission to absorb as much nutrients as it can before winter starts and its hibernation begins.

4   Sources of Ludonarrative Comedy

The choice of who conducts the comedy in a video game largely defines the type of its ludonarrative comedy. Salen and Zimmerman [23] divide video game narratives into two types, *embedded* and *emergent narratives*. Embedded narrative is all the information the game wants to transmit to the player, whereas emergent narrative arises from the player interacting with the rules and the mechanics of the game. The two narrative structures overlap and are not always easily distinguishable as two different narrative experiences. Players not only experience an interactive story crafted for them, but also create their own personal narratives by engaging with the gameplay. Game designers have direct control over embedded narratives, but only indirect control over emergent narratives. Designers of course set the parameters of the game worlds and the functioning gameplay systems, but can never predict the exact actions the player will take.

---

[7] Sierra On-Line (1987), MS-DOS.
[8] Monty Python's Flying Circus (1969–1973), BBC1 (1969–1973) and BBC2 (1974).
[9] South Park (1997), Comedy Central.
[10] Bossa Studios (2013), Windows.
[11] Captain Games (2009), Windows.

Cook [24] postulates that game designers approach video game comedy design in similarly distinct ways. The first approach, *humor-through-storytelling*, is a traditional one in which comedy is executed through conventional means of story-telling, including humorous writing, comic scenarios, and visual jokes. According to Cook, this style of comedy is emulated from other forms of entertainment, and therefore it is easily identifiable. The second approach, *humor-through-mechanics*, is unique to the interactive entertainment. This method involves the player as part of the "comedy-making" process by establishing gameplay mechanics or activities designed to cause comical conflicts (this will be discussed in the next section). Cook maintains that because gameplay mechanics are capable of generating nearly endless number of unique comedic situations, such emergent comedy can result in "evergreen humor." The two approaches emphasize different aspects of the comedic premise: humor-through-game-mechanics empowers the player as the comedian, whereas humor-through-storytelling exposes players to specific pre-defined humorous ideas. Although emergent comedy is unique to the interactive medium, the more finely-tuned comic plot-lines and concepts demand auteurism that only humor-through-storytelling can provide. To a large extent, comedy is the curation of ideas. It is about setting a framework and broadcasting a humorous point of view to the audience. However, when the responsibility to produce humor is placed on the player, comedy becomes coincidental instead of being methodical.

The third type of ludonarrative comedy, *unintentional comedy*, is one without a clear agency. This type of humor is found in the corruption of the game itself, in the form of bugs and glitches. They represent what Knox [25] regards as the essence in all humor, "playful chaos in a serious world." Glitches can be infuriating when they hinder or halt the player's progress, but their incongruousness can also cause unexpected mirth. Because unintentional comedy is a surprise to both the player and the game designer alike, it is one of the more clear examples of *incongruous humor* in video games. Incongruity theory [3] considers laughter as an effect that arises from the friction of two or more contrasting concepts. The bisociation, as Koestler [26] calls it, is a result of a shock effect that occurs when the two incompatible matrices conflict with the mind's expected and create a comic effect.

However, the incompetency of a game (or its designer) to perform tasks—malfunctioning physics engine or outlandishly twitching animations—can turn a serious game into an accidental comedy. Švelch [27] suggests that games that strive to represent real life but end up failing may become a subject of ridicule. Accidental comedy comes at the cost of taking the player away from the intended experience, which is why games seldom wish to be the subject of ironic laughter.

5   Conflicts in Ludonarrative Comedy

Vorhaus [28] asserts that comedy lives in the gap between the comic reality and the real reality. He contends that the gap, or a comic premise, as it is referred to, is a deliberately chosen point of view that is meant to reveal something humorous in a situation. Vorhaus outlines three recurring types of comical conflicts that lead to the comic premise. The first of the conflicts, the *inner conflict*, is about a character at war with itself. The second type of conflict is an interpersonal dispute between two or more characters, which Vorhaus calls the *local conflict*. The third type, the *global conflict*, is a conflict between a character and the world it is part of. The local and global conflicts can be identified in most comedic games. The inner conflict, being the most introspective of the three, is probably the rarest one to encounter.

5.1   Inner Conflict

Vorhaus [28] outlines that the *inner conflict* is about exploration of the character and its emotions, making it a rich source for comedy and drama alike. Because the inner conflict is about the character being at war with itself as opposed to something external, the surrounding world does not often understand its behavior. To an external observer the actions of the character may seem absurd, as the comedy stems from its unusual and seemingly trivial aspirations. This often translates into comedy with low stakes, in which characters care too much about seemingly insignificant matters.

Incorporating the inner conflict as part of gameplay can make the player an active part of the character's psychological struggle. Dille and Platten [29] posit that through gameplay, a video game can show proportionality to the players and provide them with metrics by which they can measure their progress. By focusing on aspects of gameplay that are usually taken for granted, a game can make the players care about its low stakes. If turning everyday objects and scenarios into play is, as Bogost [30] argues, an inarguable strength of the medium, mundane circumstances can make a game as interesting as anything.

Octodad: Dadliest Catch[12] exemplifies how contrasting the players' intent with their actual performance can reveal something about the inner conflict of the playable character. The central character of the game, Octodad, is an undercover dad in a regular human family doing his utmost to conceal his true identity, which is that he is in fact an octopus.

The browser-based game *QWOP*[13] also subverts player's expectations, but through the way movements function in the game. The player is in control of an Olympic sprinter, who needs to reach the finish line in record time. The game uses four keyboard buttons, Q, W, O, and P, to control the calves and thighs of the sprinter (not its direction). Running does not require the use of directional controls, as the only thing that matters is propulsion-creating muscular tension in the correct parts of the leg. This makes QWOP almost impossible to control.

5.2   Local Conflict

Vorhaus [28] describes the *local* (interpersonal) *conflict* as being a battle between two individuals. Usually one of the characters is comical, and another character

---

[12] Young Horses (2014), Windows.
[13] Bennett Foddy (2008), Browser game.

contrasts it by being the more serious of the two. The characters involved might compete for a shared desire, or simply cross paths and collide while pursuing their own separate goals.

Untitled Goose Game[14] finds comicality in the colliding interests of two characters. The player controls a wayward goose whose only goal is to torment an unsuspecting groundskeeper trying to do his job. The setup reinforces the stereotype that geese are inexplicably mean animals. The player is assigned to do mischievous tasks: steal the groundskeeper's keys, throw his rake in the lake, and steal food and other accessories to organize a picnic. Greyson [31] describes the game as being more about creating setups than causing straightforward mischief. The goose's animations are amusingly true to nature, for example it realistically huffs and spreads its wings as a sign of aggression when the groundskeeper gets too close to it.

The interpersonal conflict is well-suited for communal comedy, where two or more people are assigned roles with unambiguous objectives. Simply situating players in the same space creates a conflict between them. Such is the case with *Who's Your Daddy*[15], an asymmetrical multiplayer game about the stress of babysitting. One person plays a parent in a race against the clock to baby-proof a household, while the other player controls an infant in an attempt to drain their health to zero in any imaginable way. The goal of the father is to prevent the death of the suicidal baby by relocating hazardous objects out of the baby's reach, who in turn attempts to avoid the father's supervision, locking themselves inside heated ovens, swallowing batteries or shards of glass, and so on. The roughness of the visual presentation contributes to the funniness. The exaggerated character archetypes with silly-looking models and awkward animations—in addition to the ludicrousness of the unfolding catastrophe—make it clear that the game is not to be taken seriously. The game is hilarious because there is some truth in the setup. Vincent [32] describes the emotional core of the comedy: "Babysitting is a hard job because babies are irresponsible. They'll drink whatever's under the sink and stick forks in power outlets. It's not that they don't want to live, they just don't understand how life works."

5.3 Global Conflict

Global conflict refers to the dispute between characters and the world they inhabit. Vorhaus [28] divides the global conflict into two scenarios: (1) where a normal character is part of a comical world, and (2) where a comical character is situated in a normal world. As video game worlds are all more or less fictional, the latter scenario, where the world is normal, is rare to come across.

Katamari Damacy (See footnote 2) is a portrayal of an interactive absurdist world. The storyline concerns a celestial little prince reconstructing the cosmos after his father, the flamboyant King of All Cosmos, had accidentally destroyed it while playing tennis. The re-assembling of the stars and the planets happens

---

[14] House House (Tentative release date 2018), Platforms no yet specified.
[15] Evil Tortilla Games (2015), Windows.

as the player rolls around a spherical object, called Katamari, that sticks any colliding objects to its surface. The rebuilding starts from a miniature scale, where the player is able to attach only small items, such as coins and butterflies, to the Katamari. As they keep on rolling, the snowballing sphere allows increasingly larger objects, such as stadiums and islands, or even rainbows, to stick to Katamari's surface.

Frog Fractions[16] challenges game design conventions by making its gameplay sequences illogical. Frog Fractions presents itself as a simple edutainment browser game that wishes to educate the player about mathematical fractions. The player controls a frog on a lily pad trying to catch insects with its tongue. The score is displayed in fractions, but the lesson about them remains unclear. The nature of the game changes drastically as the player gains access to power-ups. Upon obtaining a dragon power-up with the ability to warp-drive, the player starts flying through outer space, landing on Mars—now colonized by bugs—and navigating its underwater caves while listening to a narration about the history of boxing. Frog Fractions is a collection of different gameplay styles. The style fluctuates from a space shoot 'em up, to a courtroom simulator, to a text adventure, to a rhythm action game. It is unabridged absurdity in video game format—a circus that subverts the audience's expectations to the most fundamental degree.

6   Discussion and Conclusions

The settings in video games contextualize and justify the players' actions in them. Video game worlds are hypernormalized realms, or as Huizinga [33] and later Salen and Zimmerman [23] define it, artificial spaces that suspend and replace the reality of the world and what is considered normal in it. Every video game wishes its audience to accept the implausibility that these worlds hold, hoping that the players would not question their artificial rules and boundaries. Video games aim to fascinate the players, because due to their freedom of movement, narrative details may hinge upon the players noticing them. Comedy can be regarded as a powerful way of captivating the players' attention, as it is an exceptionally charismatic way of conveying ludonarrative information to the players.

In order for ludonarrative comedy to work as intended, it requires to be highlighted. In this paper we have demonstrated, using examples of existing video games, various means of achieving this goal. These range from: (1) adopting a particular visual style, to (2) choosing a primary source of embedded, emergent, or even unintentional comedy, to (3) creating one or more types of inner, local, or global conflicts.

Further to these primary means of creating ludonarrative comedy, video games can also provide various humor enhancers, not only to captivate the players' curiosity, but also to prepare them for the full experience of humor [34]. Through these enhancers, game designers can highlight the comic premise of a game, and indirectly address the current state of affairs of the game world to

---

[16] Twinbeard Studios (2012), Browser game.

the player. Despite their importance, we have not included a discussion of these types of comic enhancers here, due to the space limitations of this paper.

In summary, ludonarrative comedy seems to offer a lot of potential, but its inclusion creates unique challenges for game designers. Some of the main issues to consider in designing ludonarrative comedy are: (a) narratives are less linear compared to cinema and literature, (b) the element of gameplay should not only be taken into account, but utilized as the basis for every comedic part, (c) the pace is not controlled by the story architects, but by the player, and (d) the role of the game designer is often to just nudge the players in the right direction.

References

1. Hookham, G., Meany, M.: The spectrum of states: comedy, humour and engagement in games. In: Proceedings of the 11th Australasian Conference on Interactive Entertainment, CRPIT, vol. 167, pp. 25–34. ACS, Sydney (2015). http://crpit.com/confpapers/CRPITV167Hookham.pdf
2. Martin, R.: The Psychology of Humor. Academic Press, Cambridge (2006)
3. Vandaele, J.: Humor mechanisms in film comedy: incongruity and superiority. Poet. Today **23**(2), 221–249 (2002). https://doi.org/10.1215/03335372-23-2-221
4. Hocking, C.: Ludonarrative dissonance in bioshock (2007). http://clicknothing.typepad.com/click_nothing/2007/10/ludonarrative-d.html. Accessed July 2018
5. Dormann, C., Biddle, R.: A review of humor for computer games: play, laugh and more. Simul. Gaming **40**(6), 802–824 (2009). https://doi.org/10.1177/1046878109341390
6. Dormann, C.: Fools, tricksters and jokers: categorization of humor in gameplay. In: Reidsma, D., Choi, I., Bargar, R. (eds.) INTETAIN 2014. LNICST, vol. 136, pp. 81–90. Springer, Cham (2014). https://doi.org/10.1007/978-3-319-08189-2_10
7. Grönroos, A.M.: Humour in video games: play, comedy, and mischief. Master's thesis, Aalto University (2013)
8. Juul, J.: The game, the player, the world: looking for a heart of gameness (2003). http://www.jesperjuul.net/text/gameplayerworld/. Accessed July 2018
9. Frasca, G.: Ludology meet narratology: similitude and differences between (video) games and narrative (1999). http://www.ludology.org/articles/ludology.htm. Accessed July 2018
10. Quinn, Z.: Comedy games: an underexplored genre (2015). http://www.gdcvault.com/play/1021867/Comedy-Games-An-Underexplored. Accessed July 2018
11. Mackey, B.: No laughing matter: making humor work in games (2009). http://www.gamasutra.com/view/feature/132586/no_laughing_matter_making_humor_.php. Accessed July 2018
12. Bell, N.D.: Responses to failed humor. J. Pragmat. **41**(9), 1825–1836 (2009). https://doi.org/10.1016/j.pragma.2008.10.010
13. Gonzalez, L.: A brief history of video game humor (2004). https://www.gamespot.com/articles/a-brief-history-of-video-game-humor/1100-6114407/. Accessed July 2018
14. Pratchett, R., Schafer, T., Teti, J., Vanaman, S.: Make 'em laugh: comedy in games (2010). http://www.gdcvault.com/play/1012287/Make-Em-Laugh-Comedy-in. Accessed July 2018
15. Abbott, M.: Knock em dead (2010). http://www.brainygamer.com/the_brainy_gamer/2010/07/comedy.html. Accessed July 2018

16. Totilo, S.: Joystuck: why aren't video games funny? (2004). http://www.slate.com/articles/technology/gaming/2004/11/joystuck.html. Accessed July 2018
17. Morreall, J.: Humor and aesthetic education. J. Aesthet. Educ. **15**(1), 55–70 (1981). http://www.jstor.org/stable/3332209
18. Gordon, M.: What makes humor aesthetic? Int. J. Humanit. Soc. Sci. **2**(1), 62–70 (2012). http://www.ijhssnet.com/journals/Vol2No1January2012/6.pdf
19. Furniss, M.: Chuck Jones: Conversations (Conversations with Comic Artists Series). University Press of Mississippi, Jackson (2005)
20. Barrett, R.: Chuck Jones' rules for writing road runner cartoons (2015). http://mentalfloss.com/article/62035/chuck-jones-rules-writing-road-runner-cartoons. Accessed July 2018
21. Zhou, T.: Chuck Jones' rules for writing road runner cartoons (2016). https://vimeo.com/133693532. Accessed July 2018
22. Weinstock, J.A.: Taking South Park Seriously. State University of New York Press, Albany (2008)
23. Salen, K., Zimmerman, E.: Rules of Play: Game Design Fundamentals. The MIT Press, Cambridge (2003)
24. Cook, D.: Opinion: a theory about humor in games (2012). http://www.gamasutra.com/view/news/39433/Opinion_A_Theory_About_Humor_In_Games.php. Accessed July 2018
25. Knox, I.: Towards a philosophy of humor. J. Philos. **48**(18), 541–548 (1951). http://www.jstor.org/stable/2020793
26. Koestler, A.: The Act of Creation. Hutchinson & co., London (1964)
27. Švelch, J.: Comedy of contingency: making physical humor in video game spaces. Int. J. Commun. **8** (2014). http://ijoc.org/index.php/ijoc/article/view/2687
28. Vorhaus, J.: The Comic Toolbox: How to be Funny Even If You're Not, 1st edn. Silman-James Press, Los Angeles (1994)
29. Dille, F., Platten, J.Z.: The ultimate guide to video game writing and design. Lone Eagle, Los Angeles (2007)
30. Bogost, I.: Video games are better without stories (2017). https://www.theatlantic.com/technology/archive/2017/04/video-games-stories/524148/. Accessed July 2018
31. Grayson, N.: The a**hole goose game is fun to play (2017). https://kotaku.com/the-asshole-goose-game-is-fun-to-play-1820622256. Accessed July 2018
32. Vincent, B.: Keep your infant son from death in 'who's your daddy' (2015). https://motherboard.vice.com/en_us/article/z43vew/keep-your-infant-son-from-death-in-whos-your-daddy. Accessed July 2018
33. Huizinga, J.: Homo ludens: A Study of the Play-Element in Culture. Beacon Press, Boston (1967)
34. Marszalek, A.: Humorous worlds: a cognitive stylistic approach to the creation of humour in comic narratives. Master's thesis, University of Glasgow (2012)

Physiological Affect and Performance in a Collaborative Serious Game Between Humans and an Autonomous Robot

Petar Jerčić[1]([⊠]) (ID), Johan Hagelbäck[2] (ID), and Craig Lindley[3] (ID)

[1] Blekinge Institute of Technology, 371 79 Karlskrona, Sweden
petar.jercic@bth.se
[2] Linnaeus University, 351 95 Växjö, Sweden
johan.hagelback@lnu.se
[3] CSIRO ICT Centre, Hobart, Australia
craig.lindley@csiro.au

Abstract. This paper sets out to examine how elicited physiological affect influences the performance of human participants collaborating with the robot partners on a shared serious game task; furthermore, to investigate physiological affect underlying such human-robot proximate collaboration. The participants collaboratively played a turn-taking version of a serious game Tower of Hanoi, where physiological affect was investigated in a valence-arousal space. The arousal was inferred from the galvanic skin response data, while the valence was inferred from the electrocardiography data. It was found that the robot collaborators elicited a higher physiological affect in regard to both arousal and valence, in contrast to their human collaborator counterparts. Furthermore, a comparable performance between all collaborators was found on the serious game task.

Keywords: Autonomous robots · Serious games · Collaborative play
Robot-assisted play · Emotions · Physiology · Affect

1 Introduction

An interest of Human-Robot Interaction (HRI) lies in the investigation of robots and their emotional abilities through an interaction with peers or colleagues [6]. Such *proximate interaction* includes factors (e.g., gaze, expressions, gestures, speed, distance) which are perceived to elicit affect in humans, and used to attribute emotional states to robots [11]. Robots have been found to be as engaging as humans [7]. Furthermore, engaging physical non-humanoid robot collaborators have been found to elicit emotional responses [11]. Evidence shows that emotions critically influence human decision-making and performance [20]. Humans use the mechanisms from Human-Human Interaction (HHI) to perceive robots as autonomous social agents [11]. These propositions motivate this investigation to take into consideration both HHI and HRI, in the investigation of the elicited physiological affect.

© IFIP International Federation for Information Processing 2018
Published by Springer Nature Switzerland AG 2018. All Rights Reserved
E. Clua et al. (Eds.): ICEC 2018, LNCS 11112, pp. 127–138, 2018.
https://doi.org/10.1007/978-3-319-99426-0_11

Various emotional models have been reported in the literature, while Russell [18] classified emotions through a combination of their independent components, arousal and valence. In his model, the level of excitement has been represented by arousal, while valence defined whether the current emotional state is positive or negative. Studies have found a strong correlation between *electrocardiography* (ECG) and physiological valence [24]. There have been multiple findings of a linear correlation between *galvanic skin response* (GSR) and physiological arousal [5]. Evidence suggests that people are sensitive to the *proximate interaction* factors of collaborating robots [13] (i.e., gestured motion and speed [9]), where they have been found to elicit emotions in their human partners [25]. Previous investigations employed gestured motion and speed of the collaborating robots, from a direct path at a fixed speed to a variable speed in gestured motions [25].

Many traditional games have been played in the physical world and require a tangible interaction, in contrast to a certain popularity of electronic games in the current research methods [23]. This study uses a traditional Tower of Hanoi (ToH) game which provides an easy measurement of performance through a sequential set of steps. Physical collaborators might support higher motivation and better performance in contrast to the traditional collaboration-based digital serious games [15], especially for the robot collaborators in serious games [14]. In contrast to the traditional collaboration-based digital serious games where one is playing together with a computer (a virtual entity), HRI-enhanced serious games present a physical entity eliciting diverse behaviors and stronger emotional responses in participants [14].

The purpose of this study is to investigate the decision performance of human participants, collaborating with robot partners in their proximate interaction on a shared serious game task. This paper attempts to investigate how a small subset of *proximate interaction* factors elicits physiological affect underlying such human-robot proximate collaboration, in an attempt to investigate how these influence performance on a serious game task. Moreover, it aims to understand the role of affect in decision–making performance by mapping the participants' physiological responses towards the collaborating robot. Following this goal, this paper sets out to investigate the effects of the elicited physiological affect on proximate interaction, in an attempt to inform the design of robot collaborators in serious games and to optimize the decision performance on collaborative tasks.

2   Hypothesis

Following up on given propositions, this study extends the previous research [11] to take into consideration the human collaborator condition, taking into account the elicited physiological affect in response to the human and robot collaborators. Therefore, the following hypothesis is presented:

Hypothesis 1: The collaborator condition (i.e., human, robot) will affect the performance on the game task (H1).

This study manipulated the collaborator conditions by varying the *proximate interaction* factors eliciting physiological arousal, through speed and gestured motions. Following on the previous findings [8] that the conditions of proxemic collaborators would influence elicited physiological arousal in participants and therefore performance on a game task, the following hypothesis is presented:

Hypothesis 2: Elicited physiological arousal will be affected by the collaborator condition (H2a), which in turn will affect the performance on the game task (H2b).

While physical collaborators have been found to elicit a higher motivation on a task, which is correlated with positive emotions [10], previous studies have not found a strong correlation between physiological valence and performance [8]. To expand on these findings, the following hypothesis is postulated:

Hypothesis 3: Elicited physiological valence will be affected by the collaborator condition (H3a), which in turn will have no significant effect on the performance on the game task (H3b).

3 Methodology

3.1 Participants

This study included 70 participants, 58 were males and 12 females. The age of participants ranged between 19 and 31, with a mean of (23.60 ± 2.34). Demographic data (i.e., familiarity with the ToH game task, board games in general, and solving mathematical problems) were collected and they were given a movie ticket as a reward for participating. Participants were students of Blekinge Institute of Technology. The Ethical Review Board in Lund (reference number 2012/737), Sweden, has approved all experiments conducted in this PsyIntEC ECHORD project (FP7-ICT-231143).

3.2 Experimental Setup

A crossover study with controlled experiments has been conducted in a laboratory setting. The lighting and temperature conditions were controlled in such a way that artificial fixture light was used throughout the experiment while the temperature was held constant at $23\,^{\circ}\mathrm{C} \pm 1\,^{\circ}\mathrm{C}$. The participants were seated in a chair with a fixed height and a predefined position. The height and position were constant during the experiment. The two experimenters were always present in the laboratory room to monitor the experiments, but they were completely hidden behind the screen.

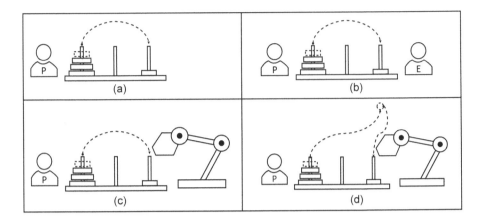

Fig. 1. Experiment conditions: (a) the *Solo* condition in which the participant is playing the game on his own; (b) playing with the *Human Collaborator* emulating the direct robot collaborator condition, with direct path at fixed speed; (c) the *Direct Robot Collaborator* condition, always moving in a similar fashion with a direct path at fixed speed; (d) *Non-Direct Robot Collaborator* condition which had one additional non-direct random point inserted in its path when performing the moves at varying speeds.

Study Stimuli. The ToH game (Fig. 2(d)) was used as the serious game for the study to investigate the elicited human physiological affect in collaborative HHI and HRI, and bring it in relation to the performance on a collaborative serious game task. Most of the participants were naive to the ToH serious game. The game was easy for the robot to handle since an optimal solution to the game exists, and it was a reasonable challenge for most of the participants. ToH was originally a single player game. In a collaborative gameplay, human-human or human-robot took turns to complete the game. The rules were explained in [17]. In short, the ToH is a mathematical game consisting of three rods and a number of disks of different sizes that can slide onto any rod. The goal of the game is to start from a given configuration of the disks on the leftmost peg and to arrive in a minimal number of moves at the same configuration on the rightmost peg [17]. In this study, the serious game started from a given configuration of the four disks, which was the same for all participants and referred to the beginning configuration in the game definition above. The individual trials consisted of moving any single disc to a next legal position, interchangeably between a participant and a collaborator until the final configuration of disks was reached on the opposite peg from the start. The participants always started first. At every move in the ToH game, the participants had an option to take a binary decision placing a disc on one of the two available legal pegs. This decision consisted of just one possible optimal step to move a disk towards the final configuration, and a non-optimal step which would be corrected by the collaborator, providing an immediate feedback on the outcome of a decision. The participants always had an option to take this optimal step as their next move, while it was mandatory for the collaborators. Therefore, only the participants had an option to take the non-optimal step to move a disk in any other legal position, which would not necessarily lead towards the final configuration.

The elicitation of physiological affect was achieved by the gestured motions and the speed of the collaborating robot. In particular, humans prefer that a robot moves at a speed slower than that of a walking human [9]. The gestured motions were composed from a direct path at fixed speed of 30 cm/s (30% of robot speed) between the two endpoints of a current disc movement, for the *Direct Robot Collaborator*, to a random path and speed between 5 cm/s up to 70 cm/s (5% to 70% of robot speed). A random path and speed were generated online for the *Non-Direct Robot Collaborator*. A non-direct path is generated using the two endpoints of a current disc movement in between which a random point in space above the disks was inserted, randomized on each game move robot arm makes, which totals in three virtual positions the robot arm has to follow while making its move. The robot was passing through all the specified positions before having arrived at a final disc movement position.

Main Manipulations. The main manipulations (see Fig. 1) were: (a) the *Solo* condition where no collaborators were present and in which a participant was playing the game on his own; (b) the *Human Collaborator* condition emulating the direct robot collaborator condition, with a direct path at fixed speed; (c) the *Direct Robot Collaborator* control condition, where the participants played together with the robot which was always moving in a similar fashion with a direct path at fixed speed; (d) the *Non-Direct Robot Collaborator* condition which had one additional non-direct random point inserted in its path moving at varying speeds. The experiment setup was identical between the trials and participants, where human participants played the turn-taking ToH game together with a robot or human collaborator, which allows for a pace participants feel most comfortable with. The goal of the game task was to move the disks from the starting to the final configuration. The collaborators were playing optimally on each move, following the algorithm. The experimenter has been trained to interact the same way with every participant according to a well–rehearsed procedure.

3.3   Experiment Procedure

The participants were allowed for six minutes of rest in total between the trials. As performed in the study from [8], the four conditions (*Solo, Human Collaborator, Direct Robot Collaborator* and *Non-Direct Robot Collaborator*) were presented to each participant. For each of the four conditions a participant repeated each condition three times one after the other (thus in all, a total of 12 ToH games were played per participant). Each experimental session took around 90 min to complete.

3.4   Data Collection

The physiological signals were acquired using Biosemi Active Two[1] physiological data acquisition system and its accompanying ActiView 9 software. ECG was measured at the chest using two 16-mm Ag/AgCl spot electrodes in a three-lead unipolar modified chest configuration: the two active electrodes were placed on the right collarbone and the lowest rib on the left side, and the ground electrode was placed on the left earlobe. GSR was measured using surface electrodes attached to the palmar surface of the middle phalanges from the middle finger and the index finger of the non-dominant hand (to reduce mechanical pressure susceptibility).

3.5   Data Reduction and Analysis

The data reduction was performed using Ledalab software for GSR [3]. Furthermore, Kubios software [21] and the HRV Toolkit[2] were used for ECG. This data were compared across the condition differences (*Solo, Human Collaborator, Direct Robot Collaborator* and *Non-Direct Robot Collaborator*) and the individual differences for the same trials (comparing the responses across individual moves for each condition).

In continuous stimulus settings, the most common measures of GSR are skin conductance level (SCL) and skin conductance response (SCR), where their changes are thought to reflect general changes in autonomic arousal [5]. The authors stated that the SCR signal is suitable for assessing the intensity of single (phasic) emotions, but changes in the overall (tonic) level are rather inert, thus valid for the trials longer than two minutes, such as the overall session in this experiment. Changes in arousal within periods shorter than two minutes are not likely indicated using the SCL. This problem is particularly limiting in trials shorter than two minutes. When the SCL temporal precision is insufficient, the rapidly reacting phasic changes (NS-SCR) seem to indicate a more promising focus: their number during a given time period is a prominent phasic-based indicator of arousal [4], such as a collaborator condition trial in this experiment.

Heart rate variability (HRV) is highly correlated with emotions [16]. Two measures of HRV are the standard deviation of normal-to-normal heartbeat intervals in the time domain (SDNN) and the ratio of low and high frequency powers (LF/HF) [1]. Wang and Huang [22] stated that SDNN and LF/HF were employed as two dimensions in the physiological valence/arousal model, where evidence revealed that SDNN was a good physiological indicator of valence [12]. The total variance of HRV increased with the length of analyzed recordings [19]. Thus, in practice, it was inappropriate to compare the SDNN measures obtained from the recordings of different durations. However, the duration of recordings used to determine the SDNN values (and similarly the other HRV measures) were standardized to a minimum of 5 min recordings for the short-term. Generally, the SDNN levels for the participants with positive affect were found to

---

[1] http://www.biosemi.com, accessed 05/05/2018 09:16.
[2] http://physionet.org/tutorials/hrv-toolkit, accessed 05/05/2018 11:36.

be higher than for negative one [12]. For even shorter recordings, main spectral components of the LF/HF ratio were distinguished in a spectrum calculated for the short-term recordings from 2 to 5 min [2].

4   Results

The participants reported previous experience with robotics on a seven-point Likert scale, where 1 meant "no experience" and 7 meant "familiar experience" ($\mu = 1.7$ $\sigma = 1.095$ $N = 70$). The differences between the participants were analyzed based on the reported values and the experienced outliers were identified. Six participants from the experienced outliers group were removed from the analysis to exclude the effects of participants' familiarity on the experience with the robot collaborators, which resulted in the 64 valid data samples. Moreover, 43 of 70 participants have not had any previous experience with the ToH.

4.1   Collaborator Conditions and Performance (H1)

There was no statistically significant difference in the total number of moves between the human and robot collaborator condition groups ($F(1,569) = 3.705$, $p > .05$), shown in Fig. 2(a), where a higher value reflects worse performance. However, a higher number of moves in the *Solo* condition in contrast to any of the collaborator conditions was expected since the participants were not expected to know the most optimal solution for the ToH game task. The difference was statistically significant between the groups ($F(3,751) = 20.807$, $p < .001$).

4.2   Physiological Arousal (H2)

The serious game used in this study was found to elicit the relative physiological arousal value (measured with SCL) of 765.209 muS ($\sigma = 835.545$ muS) where the overall arousal value was normalized against the baseline. Therefore, this result suggested that the serious game elicited a high physiological arousal overall. Furthermore, there was a statistically significant difference between the collaborator conditions ($F(3,744 = 58.881$, $p < .001$). A Tukey post-hoc test revealed that the physiological arousal indicator NS-SCR was statistically significantly higher for the *Non-Direct Robot Collaborator* (19.59 ± 8.05, $p = .03$) compared to the *Direct Robot Collaborator* (17.43 ± 6.76) condition. Both robot collaborator conditions were statistically significantly higher (18.51 ± 7.49, $p < .001$) than the *Solo* condition (11.62 ± 9.11) and the *Human Collaborator* condition (11.01 ± 6.08), as shown in Fig. 2(b). From these results the participants seemed to elicit a higher physiological arousal in the *Non-Direct Robot Collaborator* condition.

The worse performing participants reported higher arousal values after each round, as the Pearson product-moment correlation was run to determine the relationship between the participant's number of moves and their physiological arousal indicator NS-SCR. There was a strong, positive correlation between the

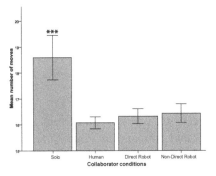

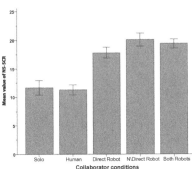

(a) Average number of moves per trial in the ToH serious game for each collaborator condition with 95% confidence interval. Stars (***) indicate a significant difference between the Solo condition in contrast to any of the collaborator conditions, at the p <.001 probability level.

(b) The average physiological arousal values measured by NS-SCR variable in the ToH serious game for each collaborator condition with 95% confidence interval. A significant difference ($p < .001$) is observable for both robot collaborators in comparison to the *Solo* and *Human Collaborator* conditions, where the physiological arousal indicator NS-SCR was statistically significantly higher ($p = .017$) for the *Non-Direct Robot Collaborator* compared to the *Direct Robot Collaborator* condition.

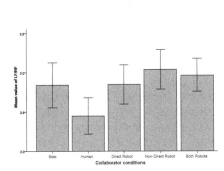

(c) The valence indicator LF/HF was statistically significantly higher ($p = .008$) for the *Non-Direct Robot Collaborator* compared to the *Human Collaborator* condition. While both robot collaborator conditions were statistically significantly higher ($p < .001$) than the *Solo* condition and the *Human Collaborator*, there was no statistically significant difference ($p > .05$) between the *Solo* and the *Direct Robot Collaborator* condition.

(d) Demonstration of the experimental setup where a human and the robot are collaborating on the ToH serious game, sharing the same physical space.

Fig. 2. Results and ToH serious game demonstration

number of moves per round and the physiological arousal indicator NS-SCR values, which was statistically significant ($r = .179$, $N = 739$, $p < .001$).

There was a significant interaction between the effects of the collaborator conditions and physiological arousal on the number of moves ($F(2,556) = 8.902$, $p < .001$). The simple main effects analysis showed that the collaborator conditions significantly affected the performance when physiological arousal was lower ($p < .001$), with better performance associated with both robot collaborators compared to the *Human Collaborator*. Between the robot collaborators, better performance was associated with the *Non-Direct Robot Collaborator*, after which comes the *Direct Robot Collaborator* one ($p < .001$).

4.3   Physiological Valence (H3)

The serious game task environment presented in this study was found to elicit the relative physiological valence score (measured with SDNN) of .624 s ($\sigma = 1.07$ s), where the overall physiological valence value was normalized against the baseline. Therefore, this result suggested that the serious game elicited a high (positive) physiological valence overall. Furthermore, there was a statistically significant difference between the collaborator conditions ($F(3,732) = 3.575$, $p = .014$). A Tukey post-hoc test revealed that the valence indicator LF/HF was statistically significantly higher for the *Non-Direct Robot Collaborator* (3.081 ± 1.869, $p = .008$) compared to the *Human Collaborator* (2.453 ± 1.724). Both robot collaborator conditions were statistically significantly higher (2.967 ± 1.841, $p = .007$) than the *Human Collaborator* condition (2.453 ± 1.724), as shown in Fig. 2(c). There were no statistically significant differences between the *Solo* and the *Direct Robot Collaborator* ($p > .05$), as shown in Fig. 2(c).

Overall in the experiment, the participants were found to perform the task equally well regardless of the physiological valence found, as no significant correlation was found between the valence indicator LF/HF and the number of moves ($p > .05$).

5   Discussion

Considering the H1, as the difference in the participants' performance was not statistically significant between any of the collaborator conditions, indicating that the collaboration with robot partners might be as effective as collaboration with human ones. It is possible that the participants may have been highly focused on the game task since the collaboration with a physical entity eliciting diverse behaviors and strong emotional responses might have promoted a higher focus on the task [10,14]. As the worst performance was found in the *Solo* condition, it is possible that the participants left to their own skills had more room for the non-optimal moves, since the help of the collaborators was not available.

The relevance of the previous claims is further supported through the H2a and the H2b, exploring the performance in regard to the elicited physiological arousal on the collaborative serious game task. The robot collaborators elicited a higher physiological arousal than the human ones, while the *Non-Direct Robot Collaborator* elicited a higher physiological arousal when compared to the *Human Collaborator*. The results indicate that people are sensitive to the robots' *proximate interaction* factors regarding physiological arousal in the context of collaborative serious games, supported by the previous investigations on *proximate interaction* factors in the context of HRI [9,13]. The results indicate that high physiological arousal is associated with worse performance in the context of collaborative serious games, supported by the previous investigations on the connection between arousal and performance on a task [10]. The authors state that the performance is positively correlated with physiological arousal up to the point when the level of arousal becomes too high and the performance decreases. Possibly there was a high physiological arousal elicited in this study, especially if we consider the "lower" physiological arousal group which was the only one that showed the statistically significant effect of collaborator conditions on the performance. The other "higher" physiological arousal group had no statistically significant effect on the performance. These findings indicate that serious games might elicit high physiological arousal which may have disrupting effects on the performance on the game task.

Regarding the H3a and the H3b, investigating on the performance in regard to the elicited physiological valence on a collaborative serious game task. The *Non-Direct Robot Collaborator* elicited higher (positive) physiological valence compared to the *Human Collaborator*, indicating as well that people are sensitive to robots' *proximate interaction* factors regarding physiological valence in the context of collaborative serious games. As the participants performed equally well regardless of the elicited physiological valence, this may suggest that physiological arousal has a more profound effect on the performance than physiological valence in the context of collaborative serious games, as supported by the previous studies exploring characteristics of robot behavior in HRI [9,13].

6   Conclusion

Overall, the collaborators in this study created a physiologically arousing, high (positive) physiologically valenced serious game environment. As a number of moves per trial in the serious game were consistent across all the collaborator conditions studied, these findings indicate that the participants' performance on the serious game task is comparable between the human and robot collaborator conditions. Regarding autonomous robots, this study found evidence of higher physiological affect elicited (arousal and valence) in contrast to their human collaborator counterparts, while still indicated a comparable performance on the game task between them. These findings motivate the introduction of autonomous robots as partners in the context of collaborative serious games, where the same performance benefits may be achieved as with using human ones. The *Non-Direct Robot Collaborator* condition elicited a higher physiological arousal and a (positive) valence, compared to the *Human Collaborator*. Moreover, it elicited a higher physiological arousal than the *Direct Robot Collaborator* condition, indicating that the careful design of *Direct Robot* partners can leverage different social cues to elicit target physiological arousal in the context of collaborative serious games. Furthermore, such context my witness a more positive valence elicited when using *Non-Direct Robot* partners instead of human ones. This study found evidence that the better performance was associated with the robot collaborators compared to the human ones, only for the "lower" physiological arousal group which was the only one showing the statistically significant effect of the collaborator conditions on the performance. The current study supports the notion that understanding physiological affect underlying such collaborative HRI from the human perspective, it would be possible to design more personalized serious games with intelligent robots which act together with human partners eliciting relevant physiological affect. This may contribute to improving the quality of HRI informing the design of such collaborative serious games. On the other hand, one has to be careful when designing serious games which elicit high physiological arousal, as such high levels of physiological arousal may be correlated with lower performance [10]. In contrast, physiological valence may not have such a significant effect.

Future studies should investigate the recognition of participants' emotions on–line using physiological measurements to adapt the robots' behavior in a closed-loop social interaction. Moreover, such future study should consider further physiological changes in participants by allowing for a non-optimal solution to the game, which would increase participants' autonomy and involve a more relaxed collaborator's behavior insisted of an optimal one. Furthermore, the *Human Collaborator* condition might have been too restrictive with emulating the direct robot collaborator condition. While this allowed for comparison between the collaborator conditions, it may miss the elements of HHI collaborative play. Future studies should allow for a more natural HHI collaborative interaction.

References

1. Acharya, U., Joseph, K., Kannathal, N.: Heart rate variability: a review. Med. Biol. Eng. Comput. **44**(12), 1031–1051 (2006)
2. Akselrod, S., Gordon, D., Ubel, F.: Power spectrum analysis of heart rate fluctuation: a quantitative probe of beat-to-beat cardiovascular control. Science **213**, 220–222 (1981)
3. Benedek, M., Kaernbach, C.: Decomposition of skin conductance data by means of nonnegative deconvolution. Psychophysiology **47**(4), 647–658 (2010). https://doi.org/10.1111/j.1469-8986.2009.00972.x
4. Boucsein, W.: Electrodermal Activity, 2nd edn. Springer, Boston (2012). https://doi.org/10.1007/978-1-4614-1126-0
5. Braithwaite, J., Watson, D.: A guide for analysing electrodermal activity (EDA) and skin conductance responses (SCRs) for psychological experiments. Psychophysiology **49**, 1017–1034 (2013)
6. Breazeal, C.: Designing Sociable Robots. The MIT Press, Cambridge (2002)

7. Burgoon, J., Bonito, J.: Interactivity in human-computer interaction: a study of credibility, understanding, and influence. Comput. Hum. Behav. **6**(16), 553–574 (2000)
8. Burgoon, J., Bonito, J.: Testing the interactivity principle: effects of mediation, propinquity, and verbal and nonverbal modalities in interpersonal interaction. J. Commun. **52**(3), 657–677 (2002)
9. Butler, J., Agah, A.: Psychological effects of behavior patterns of a mobile personal robot. Auton. Robot. **10**(2), 185–202 (2001)
10. Csikszentmihalyi, M., Bose, D.K.: Flow: The Psychology of Optimal Experience. Harper Perennial, London (1990)
11. Fiore, S.M., Wiltshire, T.J., Lobato, E.J.C., Jentsch, F.G., Huang, W.H., Axelrod, B.: Toward understanding social cues and signals in human-robot interaction: effects of robot gaze and proxemic behavior. Front. Psychol. **4**(NOV), 1–15 (2013). https://doi.org/10.3389/fpsyg.2013.00859
12. Geisler, F., Vennewald, N., Kubiak, T., Weber, H.: The impact of heart rate variability on subjective well-being is mediated by emotion regulation. Pers. Individ. Differ. **49**(7), 723–728 (2010)
13. Goodrich, M.A., Schultz, A.C.: Human-robot interaction: a survey. Found. Trends Hum.-Comput. Interact. **1**(3), 203–275 (2007). https://doi.org/10.1561/1100000005
14. Hocine, N., Gouaich, A.: Difficulty and scenario adaptation: an approach to customize therapeutic games. In: Serious Games for Healthcare: Applications and Implications, 1st edn, p. 30. IGI Global, Hershey (2013). https://doi.org/10.4018/978-1-4666-1903-6
15. Kiesler, S., Hinds, P.: Introduction to this special issue on human-robot interaction. Hum.-Comput. Interact. **19**(1), 1–8 (2004)
16. Lane, R., McRae, K., Reiman, E., Chen, K.: Neural correlates of heart rate variability during emotion. Neuroimage **44**(1), 213–222 (2009)
17. Lucas, E.: Récréations mathématiques. Gauthier-Villars, Paris (1893)
18. Russell, J.: A circumplex model of affect. J. Pers. Soc. Psychol. **39**(6), 1161–1178 (1980)
19. Saul, J., Albrecht, P.: Analysis of long term heart rate variability: methods, 1/f scaling and implications. In: Computers in Cardiology, 1988 edn, pp. 419–422. IEEE Computer Society press, Washington (1987)
20. Shiv, B., Loewenstein, G., Bechara, A., Damasio, H., Damasio, A.R.: Investment behavior and the negative side of emotion. Psychol. Sci. **16**(6), 435–9 (2005). https://doi.org/10.1111/j.0956-7976.2005.01553.x
21. Tarvainen, M.P., Niskanen, J.P., Lipponen, J.A., Ranta-Aho, P.O., Karjalainen, P.A.: Kubios HRV-heart rate variability analysis software. Comput. Methods programs Biomed. **113**(1), 210–20 (2014). https://doi.org/10.1016/j.cmpb.2013.07.024
22. Wang, H.M., Huang, S.C.: Musical rhythms affect heart rate variability. Adv. Electr. Eng. **2014**, 14 (2014)
23. Xin, M., Sharlin, E.: Playing games with robots-a method for evaluating human-robot interaction. In: Sarkar, N. (ed.) Human-Robot Interaction, September 2007, p. 522. INTECH Education and Publishing, Vienna (2007)
24. Xu, Y., Liu, G., Hao, M., Wen, W., Huang, X.: Analysis of affective ECG signals toward emotion recognition. J. Electron. (China) **27**(1), 8–14 (2010)
25. Zoghbi, S., Parker, C., Croft, E., der Loos, H.V.: Enhancing collaborative human-robot interaction through physiological-signal based communication. In: Proceedings of Workshop on Multimodal Human-Robot Interfaces at IEEE International Conference on Robotics and Automation (ICRA 2010). IEEE (2010)

Analysis of the Effect of Number of Players on the Excitement of the Game with Respect to Fairness

Sagguneswaraan Thavamuni[1(✉)], Hadzariah Ismail[1], and Hiroyuki Iida[2]

[1] Universiti Malaysia Sabah, Labuan International Campus, Labuan, Malaysia
bi14110317@student.ums.edu.my, had@ums.edu.my
[2] Japan Advanced Institute of Science and Technology, Nomi, Japan
iida@jaist.ac.jp

Abstract. Games can be played alone or with multiple people. We often assume that the game is more fun if played with someone, but we do not know much about how the number of players in a game affects the enjoyment of a fair game. From this research, we outlined that more players in a game increase the unpredictability of the game and its excitement overall. By applying the game refinement theory, we can see how the number of players can affect the excitement of a game. We also look at the pressure of a game on the players by utilizing the force-in-mind theory to further understand how games can motivate players without causing them too much stress.

Keywords: Fairness · Number of players · Pressure in games
Game refinement theory · Force-in-mind theory

1 Introduction

The act of playing games initially was something done during free time, to either have fun or relax after a busy day. However, as time went on, people started being more competitive over games. They started playing the game, practicing for long hours to hone their skills and master the game itself. Having more skills often meant that they will most certainly win the game. However, this would probably be not too interesting for viewers if these games are too one-sided. Ben-Naim et al. [5] have done a research to find the most competitive game. From their research, they found that a game with a higher upset probability is much more competitive game. In this research, they categorized the team into two sides, the team with a better performance record is considered the favourite, while the team with a worse performance is the underdog. The upset probability is the chances for the underdog team to win the game and hence, the closer the upset probability to 0.5, the more competitive the game is. Hence, games often introduce luck or chance elements to help balance the game [12].

E. Clua et al. (Eds.): ICEC 2018, LNCS 11112, pp. 139–151, 2018.
https://doi.org/10.1007/978-3-319-99426-0_12

By implementing luck and chance in a game design, this gives the underdogs a chance to win, and in turn makes it interesting for both the players and viewers, as the outcome of the game will be more uncertain. However, incorporating too much luck would make the game into a game-of-chance like children or gambling games [12]. A good balance between skill and luck in game design must be configured to make the game interesting, competitive and fun for everyone.

Games are further divided into two categories, single-player games or multiplayer games. As the name suggests, single player games usually consist of only one player while multiplayer games consist of two or more players. With the existence of the Internet, multiplayer games have become the norm of many online games as players from all over the world can connect and play with each other. Examples of popular online multiplayer games are Dota 2, Diablo III, Counter Strike, FIFA Online and StarCraft II. These online games can usually consist of a massive number of players, ranging from two up to the hundreds. More players in a game would suggest that an individual will interact with other players more frequent, where the interaction can be cooperation or a stand-off to achieve a goal. These increasing interactions help make the game more interesting to players. With these many players in a game, the main concern that comes to mind is the fairness of the game. How is the game balanced to ensure that each player has the same resources to work with in the game without having huge advantage over the others?

In this paper, we look at how the number of players can influence a game with respect to fairness. In Sect. 2, we briefly look into the game refinement theory and force-in-mind theory. Section 3 shows how games incorporate skill and chance to create a perceived fairness. Section 4 then outlines the effect of more players in a game on the excitement of the game. Section 5 shows how pressure in mind can be estimated. Concluding remarks are then made to summarize this paper.

2   Game Refinement Theory

Game Refinement Theory is a theory which was proposed by Iida et al. [9]. The Game Refinement Theory focuses on the sophistication and the uncertainty of the outcome of a game which in turn increases the attractiveness of a game. This theory is not used to calculate winning strategies but is used to see the quality of the game and the amount of entertainment it can provide. The game progress is twofold, where one is the game speed or scoring rate while the other is the game information progress. Game information progress presents the degree of certainty of the game's results in time or steps. If one knows the game information progress, for example after the game, the game progress $x(t)$ will be given as a linear function of time t with $0 \leq t \leq t_k$ and $0 \leq x(t) \leq x(t_k)$ as shown in Eq. (1).

$$x\left(t\right) = \frac{x(t_k)}{t_k}t \tag{1}$$

However, the game information progress given by Eq. (1) is usually unknown during the in-game period. Hence, the game information progress is reasonably assumed to be exponential. This is because the game outcome is uncertain until the very end of many games. Hence, a realistic model of game information progress is given by Eq. (2).

$$x(t) = x(t_k) \left(\frac{t}{t_k}\right)^n \tag{2}$$

Here, n stands for a constant parameter which is given based on the perspective of the observer. If one knows the outcome of the game, then we have $n = 1$, where $x(t)$ is a linear function of time t. Iida [8] conjectured that the parameter n has a possible correspondence with the expected feeling of the player in the game as tabulated in Table 1. The parameter $n = 2$ is ideal as it is the most exciting setting.

Table 1. Correspondence of n with expected feeling

n	Expected feeling
0	Boring
1	A little challenging
2	Exciting
3	Very challenging
4	Too high challenge

Equation (2) is then derived twice to obtain the acceleration of the game information. Solving at $t = t_k$, we obtain Eq. (3).

$$x''(t_k) = \frac{x(t_k)}{(t_k)^n} t^{n-2} \, n(n-1) \mid_{t=t_k} = \frac{x(t_k)}{(t_k)^2} n(n-1) \tag{3}$$

It is assumed in the current model that game information progress in any type of game is encoded and transported in our brains. We do not know yet about the physics of information in the brain, but it is likely that the acceleration of information progress is subject to the forces and laws of physics. Therefore, we expect that a larger value of $\frac{x(t_k)}{(t_k)^2}$, the more exciting the game becomes due to the uncertainty of the game outcome. Thus, we use its root square $\frac{\sqrt{x(t_k)}}{t_k}$, as a game refinement ($GR$) measure for other games under consideration. Table 2 shows some of the GR values for variants of boardgames and scoring sports games [13, 16]. We can see that the GR values lie between a zone value of 0.07 to 0.08.

According to Newton's second law of motion, the vector sum of force F is equal to the mass m multiplied by acceleration a of the object as described in Eq. (4).

$$F = ma \tag{4}$$

We can assume that the Newton's second law can be applied to find the Force-in-mind, F_n. Force-in-mind can be defined as the force of the information that

Table 2. GR value of various games

Game	$x(t_k)$	t_k	GR
Chess	35	80	0.074
Go	250	208	0.076
Basketball	36.38	82.01	0.073
Soccer	2.64	22	0.073
Badminton	46.34	79.34	0.086
Table Tennis	54.86	96.47	0.077

is moving in our minds. A higher F_n signifies that the information is more interesting and has a higher momentum in our minds. To calculate the F_n, we need to find the acceleration-in-mind as well as the mass-in-mind. As Eq. (3) is the second derivative of Eq. (1), the expression can be said to be the acceleration-in-mind. The expression can be further simplified as shown in Eq. (5).

$$a = (GR)^2 \; n(n-1) \tag{5}$$

GR value shows the balance between the skill and chance aspects of a game. As the variable n stands for the difficulty of the game, we can say that the $n(n-1)$ in Eq. (5) is the variable for game difficulty. Mass-in-mind can be defined as the inverse of branching factor in board-games. In score based games, the mass-in-mind can be defined as the total score of a game Σg over the score of a player g [10]. Hence, the force-in-mind can be expressed in Eq. (6)

$$F_n = \frac{\Sigma g}{g} \; (GR)^2 \; n(n-1) \tag{6}$$

3   Fairness and Excitement

Fairness can be defined as the act of being impartial by giving equal treatment to everyone without any bias or favouritism. In a game context, this can be translated into giving equal rules to all players without advantages for any side, ensuring an equal winning probability for each side. If each player has an equal probability of winning, we can assume that the game will always lead to a draw. Van den Herik et al. [17] defined that a game is fair if the outcome of the game is a draw and both sides of the players have roughly an equal probability of making a mistake which can cause them in the game. Iida [7] also conjectured that the outcome of a sophisticated game is always a draw if both players are of sufficiently strong level. This implies that the perfect play by both sides of the game will always lead the game to a draw. To make the outcome of the game more unpredictable, certain games nowadays do not maintain total fairness by incorporating elements of luck and chance.

Lennart Nacke [12] explained on the significance and importance of the balance of skill and chance in game design. A fair game usually operates on balance of skill or chance. Games that run mainly on chance are usually children games like scissors-paper-stone or gambling. Games with a focus on luck and chance help create fairness for people of various skill level, making it possible for lower skilled players to still be able to win. This will make the game very unpredictable as anyone can win the game, regardless of their skill level. Games that operate mainly on skill are more deterministic and players can master the game if they know the most effective strategies. Games like this allow veteran players to have an advantage over a newer player. This can get very one-sided as the result of the game can be easily predicted before the game even ends. Therefore, games now incorporate both skill and chance elements to their game design. The element of chance helps create unexpectedness into the game, making it more exciting and attractive to players and viewers.

Game refinement theory has been studied mainly based on the game outcome uncertainty [9]. However, it essentially concerns about game length with respect to justification of game outcome. If the length is too short, the game outcome would be not justified, i.e. unfair. If the length is too long, the outcome would be more than stable, i.e. boring or unexcited. Thus, justification of game outcome postulates the appropriate game length to maintain fairness and excitement. Therefore, the measure of game refinement for sophisticated games is ranged in a zone value like 0.07 to 0.08, which may correspond to the lower limit (engagement) and upper limit (fairness) respectively. A game which has a low GR value shows that it is more skill based, while those with a high GR show that it is more chance based [13]. The ideal game refinement zone is between 0.07 and 0.08 which can be seen by various popular boardgames and sports. Hence, we can say that a game is most interesting at a balance of skill and chance to make the game competitive and exciting at the same time.

4   Influence of the Number of Players

In this section, we study on how the number of players can affect the excitement of a game in team games and non-team games. The GR value as explained above is used to describe the properties of the game, whether it is more deterministic or stochastic.

4.1   The Parameter k

Figure 1 shows a curve of $y = GR^2x^2$ and two linear lines of formula $y = x$ and $y = \frac{x}{2}$ respectively for values of $x \geq 0$. There are two intersection points in this graph, which are the intersection of the curved line with the line $y = x$ and the curved line with the line $y = \frac{x}{2}$. The value of x and y from the graph can be assumed as the total score (Σg) and the winner's score (g) of a score based game respectively. Hence, the line $y = x$ and $y = \frac{x}{2}$ can also be expressed as $g = \Sigma g$ and $g = \frac{\Sigma g}{2}$ respectively.

The line $y = x$ shows that the total score of the game is equal to the winner's score. This signifies that the game is very one sided. For example, in a game

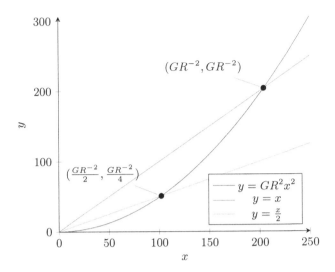

Fig. 1. Graph of $y = GR^2 x^2$

of soccer, if the score is 4:0, both the total score and the winner's score will be equals to four. The game may be too easy for the winning team.

The line $y = \frac{x}{2}$ shows that the winner's score is half of the total score. This signifies that the game is equally fair to both players. A similar example would be in a game of score with the score 2:2, where the total score is four while the winner/players' score is two. This shows that there is an equal distribution of score among the players.

If we draw a new straight line where $y = \frac{x}{3}$, this new line would signify that the players' score is one-third of the total score as $g = \frac{\Sigma g}{3}$.

Conjecture 1. The line $y = \frac{x}{k}$ is an even distribution of score for k number of players in an even and fair game scenario, where each player will have an equal win probability of $\frac{1}{k}$.

In Fig. 1 a curve $y = GR^2 x^2$ shows the progress of the game over time with respect to the score of the game. At the intersection of the curve with line $y = x$ at coordinates (GR^{-2}, GR^{-2}), the total score is equal to the winner's score, as was previously discussed above. The points on the curve after this point shows that the winner's score is higher than the total points. Hence, we can assume that the game ends at the intersection point of the curve and the line $y = x$ at point (GR^{-2}, GR^{-2}).

Figure 2 shows the curve of $y = GR^2 x^2$ with varying GR values from 0.06 to 0.09 and its intersections with the line $y = x$. As the GR increases, we can see that the intersection point of the curve and the line $y = x$ approaches the origin. A high GR value indicates that the game is more sophisticated and in turn, more exciting to the players and the observers. A higher GR value also indicates that the game has a more stochastic nature. A lower GR on the other

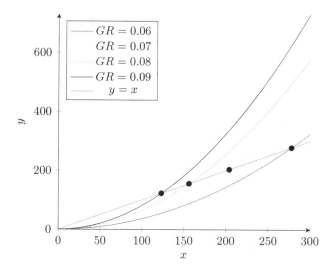

Fig. 2. Graph of $y = GR^2 x^2$ with varying GR values

hand shows that the game is more deterministic and requires more skills from the players.

Conjecture 2. The game is more exciting, sophisticated and stochastic in nature as the intersection points get closer to the origin. Conversely, if the points are further away, the game is much more deterministic and less sophisticated.

4.2   The Parameter k in Non-team Games

Figure 3 shows the same curve of $y = GR^2 x^2$ and five straight lines of line $y = \frac{x}{k}$ where k is equal to 2,3,4 and 10 respectively. The parameter k shows the number of players in the game. From the graph in Fig. 3, we can see that the intersection point between each of the straight line gets closer to the origin as the parameter k increases. It was conjectured previously in Conjecture 2 that as the intersection point approaches the origin, the game gets more stochastic and exciting to the players.

A previous research on the effect of number of players in an UNO game has been done by Ramadhan et al. [15]. UNO is a card game that can be played with multiple players for up to ten players, with the recommended number of players being four to six people. The finding from the research showed that the GR measure for the UNO game varied for different number of players. The GR measure increased as the number of players increased to four players, but showed continual decrease when the number of players gets more than four people. Hence, having four-players may be the optimum way to play UNO.

A research by Hainey et al. [6] showed that players who preferred multiplayer games over single player games were motivated by the amount of competition available in the game. Multiplayer games provide them with more competition,

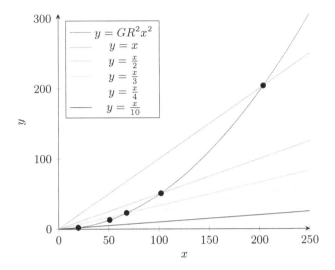

Fig. 3. Graph of $y = GR^2x^2$ with lines $y = \frac{x}{k}$

recognition, curiosity and cooperation which makes the game more interesting to the players.

Conjecture 3. The game gets more exciting and stochastic as the number of players increases in a game. Conversely, the game will be more deterministic if it has less players.

4.3   The Parameter k in Team Games

The parameter k is different for team-based or cooperative games. For example, in the previous example of UNO game, playing with four players would mean that the parameter $k = 4$ and the probability of each player to win under an equal fairness condition is $\frac{1}{k} = 0.25$.

In the case of a soccer game, there are two teams, where each team has 11 players. The total number of players in a soccer game is 22 people. However, the parameter $k \neq 22$ as each player does not have a win probability of $\frac{1}{22}$. Since there are two teams, the parameter k should be equal to 2, as each team has an equal probability to win of $\frac{1}{2}$. The players of each team have the same winning probability as their team, which is 0.5 under fair conditions.

Hence, the parameter k is not affected by the number of players in a team-based game but is only affected by the number of teams in the game.

5   Game Pressure on Players

In this section, we investigate how pressure in mind affects the excitement of a game and how it can be estimated.

5.1   Pressure

Pressure can be defined as force that is acted perpendicularly upon a surface area. Equation (7) shows the formula to calculate the pressure that is exerted on a surface. The unit for pressure is Newton per square meter (Nm^{-2}) or Pascal.

$$Pressure = \frac{Force}{Area} \tag{7}$$

Pressure is directly proportional to the amount of force applied and is inversely proportional to the surface area. Pressure acting upon a matter can change its properties or appearances. For example, if enough pressure is applied to gases, it can become a liquid. This can be seen in aerosol cans as the gas are compressed with high pressure to from liquid. Once it is sprayed and released to the atmosphere, the decrease in the pressure causes the liquid to revert back to gas.

Pressure is also known as stress. We often hear people complaining that their daily life is very stressful. This stress can come from various sources such as working long hours, heavy workload, being unhappy and much more. We do not know the physics in our brain, but we can say that our minds feel pressure from our daily activities.

5.2   Pressure in Games

Previously, we discussed that pressure existed in our minds, where we feel pressure from working on heavy workloads or working for long hours. Hence, playing a game should also exert pressure in our minds. Pressure in games can be said as the stress to earn score or win in a game. A difficult game might put more pressure on the players as it is significantly harder to earn points or score in those games. Conversely, an easier game would put less pressure on the players as scoring is much easier. The difficulty of the games can be seen in the parameter n of the force-in-mind formula shown in Eq. (6). Table 1 also shows the expected feelings of a player based on the parameter n. As the force-in-mind is directly proportional to the value of n, an increase in n would signify that more force will be applied by the game to our minds.

Abrantes et al. [3] showed the influence of the number of players on heart rate responses and physical demands in a small-sided soccer game. A small-sided soccer games are training drills used by coaches to ensure that their players are in top form. In their research, they analyzed the effects of the game type and number of players on the physical performances of each player. They found that the player's heart rate response and exertion of the players are much higher when it is a 3vs3 game compared to a 4vs4 game.

Owen et al. [14] explained that this is maybe due to the presence of less players made it so the players will have to move more with the ball and have a higher possession of the ball. They also pointed out that a high number of player in team will result in less technical actions performed by each player, but generally increases the technical actions performed in the whole game. The amount of technical actions performed by players can be assumed to be the player contribution to the game.

A player's contribution to the game can be generally evaluated as in Eq. (8).

$$Player\ Contribution = \frac{Team\ Score}{No.\ of\ Players} = \frac{g}{k_t} \tag{8}$$

Where k_t stands for the number of players in a team. Having more players in a game would signify that each player would contribute lesser to the team, and hence cause them to not feel much exertion.

Moreover, it is observed that heart beating rate usually increases when we are feeling excited, anxious or angry [1]. Previously, we conjectured that a higher number of players ensured that the game gets more exciting, but the number of players are not influenced in the case of a team game. Therefore, excitement might not be a major cause for the increase in heart rate [3]. The anxiety produced by the game may be the reason for the increase in heart rate. Anxiety is the feeling of fear, worry, or uneasiness that is a reaction from stress. Hence, we can assume that lesser players in a team game causes the stress on the players to increase as the 3v3 small-sided soccer game showed a higher heart rate. Referring to the pressure formula in Eq. (7), we can formulate a new model for calculating the pressure in our minds, assuming that k_t is the number of players in a team.

$$Pressure = \frac{F_n}{k_t} = \frac{\Sigma g\ (GR)^2\ n(n-1)}{g \cdot k_t} \tag{9}$$

Equation (9) suggests that pressure is directly proportional to the total score (Σg), game refinement value and parameter n but is inversely proportional to the player/team score (g) parameter k_t, which is the number of players in a team. When the player/team is losing, this would mean that more force and pressure is applied on the players. This would further explain why players feel frustrated when losing a game. Astor et al. [4] reported that a losing player's heartbeat rate drops when losing, suggesting that they felt negative emotions or frustration. Their findings also suggested that players experience a more intense emotion when losing than winning. These emotions may be caused by the pressure as explained above.

In the scenario of a non-team game like chess or shogi, the pressure is equivalent to the force-in-mind as $k_t = 1$. Games with high GR value are more sophisticated and exciting. This creates a pressure to the players to work harder to obtain the points or score in a game. However, an extremely high GR or n value may exert too much pressure to the player that may result in anxiety or choking. This can explain why players may feel frustration over an extremely high GR value.

Choking can be defined as performing poorly under pressure due to anxiety [11]. An intense amount of stress can also result in depression among players. An article [2] showed that there is an increasing numbers of athletes who are suffering from depression due to high stress due to the attention, expectations and money involved in the sports. Some of these athletes decided to quit the sports entirely to relieve themselves from the pressure while some even resulted into hurting themselves.

Low pressure in games would mean that there is not much force-in-mind or motivation for the players to score. Hence, it is better for the pressure to be a little bit higher to ensure a fun game experience. On the other hand, an extremely high pressure would cause frustration and anxiety among players, ruining their experience in the game. Therefore, the pressure of a game must be balanced and not be too high to ensure that the player will still have an enjoyable experience throughout the game.

6   Concluding Remarks

In this paper, we have looked at how the number of players can influence the enjoyment of the game. We conjectured that the games get more exciting and stochastic with more players. In a team game scenario however, the number of players do not affect the excitement of the game, but the excitement is only influence by the number of teams. We also applied the concept of pressure using the force obtained from the force-in-mind theory dividing the number of players in a team for a team based game. The pressure is directly proportional to the F_n, GR and the n values while inversely proportional to the number of players, k_t.

A high value of F_n, GR and n can cause the pressure to be high, causing negative effects on the player as it can cause them to perform poorly due to the stress induced from the game. Losing a game also creates negative emotions to the players resulting to frustration. This can cause the player to lose interest in the game itself and eventually quit. Hence, a good balance of game difficulty and force-in-mind must be discovered to ensure that the players will be continually motivated to continue playing the game.

In the model formulated to calculate pressure, we assumed that each player in a team will be exerted by an equal amount of pressure as they have the same contribution to the game. It should be noted that each player can have different levels of contribution to the game based on their roles in the game as well as their individual skill. In a game of soccer, players are generally divided into strikers, mid-fielders, defenders and goalkeepers. Each role will have different levels of contribution in a typical game of soccer. A striker will have a higher responsibility in scoring goals, while defenders and goalkeepers will have a higher responsibility in ensuring that the opponent does not score a goal. In a real game scenario, we cannot simply generalize that all players will have the same contribution to the game. Similarly, all players in a team may not always be of the same skill level. Higher skilled players will have a higher contribution to the game and hence have higher pressure exerted on them compared to the other players in the team. Hence, it is quite hard to generalize the pressure to be equivalent to the force divided by the number of players in the team.

More research has to be done on this domain to strengthen the model produced above for pressure. Future works will work on formulating a more accurate model for determining the pressure on players with varying roles and skill levels in a team, as well as look more deeply in to the interaction of the number of players, excitement and pressure of the game to determine the right balance of pressure to ensure that the game is balanced, fun and exciting to the players and viewers alike.

Acknowledgement. This work was carried out on a transfer scheme between Japan Advanced Institute of Science and Technology (JAIST) and Universiti Malaysia Sabah (UMS) Internship Program. This research is funded by a grant from the Japan Society for the Promotion of Science, within the framework of the Grant-in-Aid for Challenging Exploratory Research.

References

1. Heart rate and health. http://www.berkeleywellness.com/fitness/exercise/article/your-heart-beat-and-your-health
2. Pressure and the pro: why do so many of our top athletes suffer from, September 2011. https://www.independent.co.uk/life-style/health-and-families/health-news/pressure-and-the-pro-why-do-so-many-of-our-top-athletes-suffer-from-stress-424937.html
3. Abrantes, C.I., Nunes, M.I., MaÇãs, V.M., Leite, N.M., Sampaio, J.E.: Effects of the number of players and game type constraints on heart rate, rating of perceived exertion, and technical actions of small-sided soccer games. J. Strength Cond. Res. **26**(4), 976–981 (2012)
4. Astor, P.J., Adam, M.T., Jähnig, C., Seifert, S.: The joy of winning and the frustration of losing: a psychophysiological analysis of emotions in first-price sealed-bid auctions. J. Neurosci. Psychol. Econ. **6**(1), 14 (2013)
5. Ben-Naim, E., Vazquez, F., Redner, S.: What is the most competitive sport? arXiv preprint physics/0512143 (2005)
6. Hainey, T., Connolly, T., Stansfield, M., Boyle, E.: The differences in motivations of online game players and offline game players: a combined analysis of three studies at higher education level. Comput. Educ. **57**(4), 2197–2211 (2011)
7. Iida, H.: On games and fairness. In: The 12th Game Programming Workshop, pp. 9–11 (2007)
8. Iida, H.: Where is a line between work and play? Technical report 39(2018-GI-039), Information Processing Society of Japan, March 2018
9. Iida, H., Takeshita, N., Yoshimura, J.: A metric for entertainment of boardgames: its implication for evolution of chess variants. In: Nakatsu, R., Hoshino, J. (eds.) Entertainment Computing. ITIFIP, vol. 112, pp. 65–72. Springer, Boston (2003). https://doi.org/10.1007/978-0-387-35660-0_8
10. Kananat, S., Terrillon, J.C., Iida, H.: Possible interpretation of mass-in-mind: a case study using scrabble. In: eKNOW 2018: The Tenth International Conference on Information, Process, and Knowledge Management, pp. 26–31. IARIA (2018)
11. Masaki, H., Maruo, Y., Meyer, A., Hajcak, G.: Neural correlates of choking under pressure: athletes high in sports anxiety monitor errors more when performance is being evaluated. Dev. Neuropsychol. **42**(2), 104–112 (2017)
12. Nacke, L.: Chance and skill in game design, March 2015. http://www.acagamic.com/courses/infr1330-2014/chance-and-skill-in-game-design/

13. Nossal, N., Iida, H.: Game refinement theory and its application to score limit games. In: 2014 IEEE Games Media Entertainment (GEM), pp. 1–3. IEEE (2014)
14. Owen, A., Twist, C., Ford, P.: Small-sided games: the physiological and technical effect of altering pitch size and player numbers. Insight **7**(2), 50–53 (2004)
15. Ramadhan, A., Iida, H., Maulidevi, N.U.: Game refinement theory and multiplayer games: case study using UNO (2015)
16. Sutiono, A.P., Purwarianti, A., Iida, H.: A mathematical model of game refinement. In: Reidsma, D., Choi, I., Bargar, R. (eds.) INTETAIN 2014. LNICST, vol. 136, pp. 148–151. Springer, Cham (2014). https://doi.org/10.1007/978-3-319-08189-2_22
17. Van Den Herik, H.J., Uiterwijk, J.W., Van Rijswijck, J.: Games solved: now and in the future. Artif. Intell. **134**(1–2), 277–311 (2002)

The Influence of Digital Convergence/Divergence on Digital Media Business Models

Zvezdan Vukanovic$^{(\boxtimes)}$ (iD)

Abu Dhabi University, Abu Dhabi, UAE
zvezdan.vukanovic@adu.ac.ae

Abstract. The key objectives of this article is to analyze and discuss the influence of digital convergence/divergence on digital media business models. The identification of sustainable and hyper-competitive digital media business models is an urgent priority as continuing decline in audiences, collapse of traditional/old media organizations and the decrease of the economic and social influence of traditional media pose a major threat to media, democracy, ICT and telecommunications industry, with scholars agreeing that further erosion of media industry also have major implications for the advertising industry and a wide range of content producers. The successful digital media and ICT corporations will have to act more as corporate planners, as well as 'cloud', 'on-demand' and 'ubiquitous' content and distributor disaggregators, than traditional content and advertising providers.

In summary, the second decade of the 21st century digital media is apparently becoming increasingly interactive, mobile, immersive, and ubiquitous. Furthermore, the future of the media appears to be specifically oriented towards the establishment of, networked, 3D, on-demand, broadband and unicast as well as multimedia and hypermedia models of distribution, communication and content creation. Therefore, it is crucial that profitable digital media companies realize that media divergence can successfully perform as vendor lock-in a top-down corporate process and a bottom-up consumer-driven process. The digital business models influenced by digital convergence/divergence will focus on aggregate multi-platform distribution, complementarities, vendor lock-in, interoperable and networked media and ICT ecosystem, massive personalization/customization, user interface.

Keywords: Digital convergence digital media business models
Media market competition

1 Introduction - Contextual Background: The Need for the Application of Digital Media Business Models

One of the challenges of studying digital media business models in the age of media convergence is that the concept is so multifaceted and broad that it has multiple meanings. As a result, the academic and scholarly literature in this area is diverse and remains under-researched, under-explored and under-developed from both a theoretic

E. Clua et al. (Eds.): ICEC 2018, LNCS 11112, pp. 152–163, 2018.
https://doi.org/10.1007/978-3-319-99426-0_13

and an empirical perspective. This article reviews scholarly studies that identify the range of strategic options available for sustainable business models in digital media industry.

Identification of sustainable and hyper-competitive digital media business models is an urgent priority as continuing decline in audiences and collapse of traditional/old media organizations pose a major threat to media, democracy, ICT and telecommunications industry, with scholars agreeing that further erosion of media industry also have major implications for the advertising industry and a wide range of content producers.

Referred to in the industry as 'audience fragmentation' or 'disaggregation', this breakdown of large mass audiences of mass media is resulting in both advertising volume and rates falling within the dominant commercial media business model [1]. As Jenkins warns, 'monolithic blocks of eyeballs are gone' [2]. Notwithstanding, few media organizations have settled on a viable long-term strategy for making money in a sustainable fashion' [3]. As a result of this lack of foresight, media organizations – particularly news companies and departments – have not invested sufficiently in research and development to expand or update their product line over recent decades [3]. Importantly, many news media have invested less than 1 per cent of their operating budgets in R&D to develop new products and new business models. The cost of failing to recognize the potential and public demand for new forms of content and distribution methods has been that media organizations have not developed new products tailored to the Web 2.0 and Web 3.0 environment of social media and social networks or the changing media and ICT economy [4].

2 The Decrease of the Economic and Social Influence of Traditional Media

The lack of efficient development of new business models caused the decrease of the economic and social influence of traditional media (print, radio, TV, and printed books). Accordingly, eBooks (excluding educational publications) reached $8.2 billion in sales by 2017 and surpassed printed book sales, whose sales fall from $11.9 billion in 2012 to $7.9 billion in 2017. In addition, the number of e-books sold in the United States increased from 69 million in 2010 to 221 million in 2016. By contrast, the total weekday circulation of U.S. newspapers decreased during the last two decades for almost 50% (i.e. from 60 to 30 million).

3 Literature Review and Discussion on Recent Models of Convergence in Media Research

The concept of convergence is frequently used both in the academic field and within the media industry to denote the ongoing restructuring of media companies as well as to describe the latest developments in media forms, distribution, and consumption [5]. However, there is currently no generally accepted definition of the concept. Depending on the context, the meaning and connotations vary. It is generally accepted among media business scholars that convergence denotes the actual process toward a more efficient management of the media value chain. The use of the concept has therefore developed from being mainly connected with digitalization in media technology to also include elements of integration, combination, competition and divergence.

The digital media convergence is an ongoing and continuous process of media industry development based contrasted and complemented with the process of digital media divergence [5]. In the Table 1, the author provides the conceptual and applicative definitions of digital media convergence model.

Table 1. The conceptual and applicative definitions of digital media convergence model

Authors	Main digital media convergence model
Greenstein and Khanna [6, pp. 203–204]	Substitutes and complements
Jenkins [7]	Technological, economic, social or organic, cultural and global convergence
Lawson-Borders [8]	7 c: Communication, commitment, cooperation, compensation, culture, competition, and customer
Lee [9]	Data convergence Structural convergence Application convergence Industrial convergence
Dennis [10]	"Incremental awakening"—the 1980s, "early adoption"—early to mid-1990s, "uncritical acceptance"—late 1990s, and "presumptions of failure"—early 2000s
Huang, et al. [11]	- Content convergence, - Form convergence (or technological convergence) - Corporate convergence - Role (of producers and consumers) convergence
Meikle and Young [12]	Technological convergence Industrial convergence Social convergence Textual convergence

Jenkins [7] divides convergence into five areas, technological, economic, social or organic, cultural and global convergence. Technological convergence is the digitalization of all media content, economic convergence deals with the integration of the entertainment industry and the social or organic version of the process handles the consumers. According to Jenkins, cultural convergence is the explosion of new forms of creativity at the intersections of various media technologies, industries and consumers. Finally, global convergence is the cultural hybridity that results from the international circulation of media content. This definition is in line with the notion that convergence is an ongoing process, occurring at various intersections between media technologies, industries, content and audiences; it is not an end state [7]. The effects of the process of convergence are visible, measurable and possible to detect, while the actual process might not be [5].

Lawson-Borders [8] suggests another model of convergence, where the starting point is that convergence is a concept as well as a process. Lawson-Borders has identified seven observations. of convergence all beginning with the letter c: Communication, commitment, cooperation, compensation, culture, competition, and customer. These seven areas are partly overlapping and can serve as a guideline for best practices to expound on convergence both as a concept and a process Lawson-Borders [8]).

In addition, Lawson-Borders [8] believes that for convergence to succeed, media firms must:

(a) engage in high quality communication about what the organization is trying to accomplish;
(b) be committed to incorporating convergence into their organizational mission and philosophy;
(c) promote cooperation among everyone involved in the journalistic process "to share stories and ideas;"
(d) revise compensation plans to fairly compensate multimedia journalists for taking on the new roles and responsibilities required by convergence;
(e) facilitate the blending of different cultures in the newsroom (i.e., print, radio, television, and online) [13];
(f) develop strategies and alliances capable of allowing media firms to successfully compete in local markets and globally; and
(g) develop convergence strategies capable of serving evolving consumer needs in a dynamic and increasingly competitive/challenging marketplace (pp. 94–96).

Furthermore, Lee [9] describes four categories and eight levels of digital convergence:

1. Data convergence (Media convergence and Domain convergence)
2. Structural convergence (Architecture convergence and Infrastructure convergence)
3. Application convergence (Platform convergence and Device convergence)
4. Industrial convergence (Intra-industry convergence and Inter-industry convergence) [9]

Dennis [10, p. 7] identified four stages of communication industry convergence: "incremental awakening"—the 1980s, "early adoption"—early to mid-1990s, "uncritical acceptance"—late 1990s, and "presumptions of failure"—early 2000s.

Pavlik and McIntosh [14] state that there are four areas of implications due to convergence:

1. the content of communication,
2. the relationships between media organizations and their publics,
3. the structure of communication organizations and
4. how communication professionals do their work [14].

Greenstein and Khanna [6, pp. 203–204] define convergence in terms of substitutes and complements: "Two products converge in substitutes when users consider either product interchangeable with the other… . Two products converge in complements when the products work better together than separately or when they work better together now than they worked together formerly." Allison, DeSonne, Rutenbeck, and Yadon [15, p. 61] consider convergence as a "business trend where previously separate industries... are converging through megamergers, buyouts, partnerships and strategic alliances. [15] Allison, DeSonne, Rutenbeck, and Yadon [15]" Huang et al. [11] identify four categories of media convergence: content convergence, form convergence (or technological convergence), corporate convergence, and role (of producers and consumers) convergence.

Meikle and Young [12] observe that convergence can be understood in four dimensions:

- technological—the combination of computing, communications and content around networked digital media platforms;
- industrial—the engagement of established media institutions in the digital media space, and the rise of digitally-based companies such as Google, Apple, Microsoft and others as significant media content providers;
- social—the rise of social network media such as Facebook, Twitter and YouTube, and the growth of user-created content; and
- textual—the re-use and remixing of media into what has been termed a 'transmedia' model, where stories and media content (for example, sounds, images, written text) are dispersed across multiple media platforms.

Importantly, media convergence refers to an evolutionary process, not an endpoint. It is not simply a technological shift, but it alters relationship between existing technologies, industries, markets, genres, and audiences [2]. Furthermore, convergence alters the business operation of the digital media industry.

4 Driving Forces of Media Convergence

As the concept of media convergence appears to be multifaceted process there are apparently many driving forces behind convergence and the increased interest in the concept [16]. Most dominant driving forces include, but are not limited to:

(a) technological innovation, including the rise of the Internet and the digital revolution;
(b) the exponential growth of internet data, the computational power and the transfer of internet data
(c) deregulation/liberalization and globalization, including passage of the Telecommunications Act of 1996, formation of the European Union and the privatization of telecommunications and media around the world;
(d) changing consumer tastes and increased consumer affluence;
(e) technological standardization;
(f) the search for synergy (i.e., $1 + 1 = 3$);
(g) increasing global competition (which has resulted in high levels of merger and acquisition activity among media and telecommunication companies around the world); and
(h) repurposing of old media content for distribution via various forms of digital media [17].

5 Discussion: The Business and Technological Impact of Media Convergence/Divergence

In order to become flexible, adaptive, immediate and accessible digital media have to develop personalized, immersive, customized, innovative, engaging and user-friendly applications and, services that can be easily accessed as well as shared. Strategic shift of media business moves toward Internet of Smart Things, Web 3.0 and Web 4.0, cloud media, personalized, ubiquitous, software based, on-demand, wearable and database generated media and distributor of aggregated content (widgetization of media), flattening of distribution chain, content aggregators and multiplatform distribution. Content and multiplatform distribution aggregators are the winners in the digital future as the availability and the internet speed significantly reduces cost of media content as well as distribution.

Moreover, in the near future, contextual and behavioral micro targeting in advertising will be more prevalently supported by geospatial tagging, location-based marketing in which social interaction becomes a value. Digital media has to offer at the same time personal and, intimate as well as multifocalized experience firstly attempting to build a community, than a marketplace.

Accordingly, media consumption is not becoming exclusively about demand, but it is also becoming about choice that represents a prospective lock in and barrier entry into a digital media ecosystem. Miniaturization in media production and ubiquitous access will inherently favor usage of social media via mobile phones.

As a result of the digital media audience being more divergent due to the increase of media production and its content, the media market is increasingly fragmented and users' taste is more versatile than ever. Different services and applications on the social networks create their own terminal and multiplatform ecosystem that is becoming increasingly unreachable to consumers unless they pay for premium services/applications. What we are now seeing is the distribution platforms converging while the content diverges [18].

However, a positive side of digital convergence is that it leads to a democratization of content because of the development of web 2.0; where users generate and upload content for a public access [19]. On the other hand, media convergence represents a risk for content producers and distribution operators since most of digital media companies fear a fragmentation or erosion of their markets. Valerie Feldman in her monographic publication 'Leveraging Mobile Media: Cross Media Strategy and Innovation Policy for Mobile Media Communication' further substantiate the competitive and technological advantage of media divergence over media convergence by stating that:

"Multiple utilization of content in the divergent media is one possible leverage for media companies to raise revenue potentials from existing media content and establish multiple revenue streams. The precondition is the production of platform – neutral content that enables repurposing of content according to the syntax specifications of different distribution platforms. The profitability in the media divergent production and distribution is achieved as the content becomes disaggregated and re-bundled according to the characteristics of the medium" [20].

Thus, the development of multiple utilization of content decreases the technological and economic importance of media convergence. The proliferation of channels and the increasingly ubiquitous nature of computing and communications rather contributes to media divergence. Even on the device level, the plethora of specific devices does not suggest convergence, either, albeit digitization enforces technological convergence to some extent [21]. Yet, consumers' demand for context specificity as well as parallel media usage at the intersection of various media access modes, devices and contents rather suggest increase in media divergence [22].

Neverthless, Enlund and Lindskog [23] describe how the range of information from a consumer perspective has widened, as content now is available in many more media channels than before [23]. In this manner, interactivity and online media encourage divergence, but at the same time the technology behind the service and the production work flow, prior to distributing and broadcasting in the different channels, are converging [5].

Another important characteristic that further favourizes the media divergence over media convergence is the fact that in the digital media distribution channels and platforms the importance of intermediaries is largely minimized. However, one of the few media industry sectors that need media convergence in order to distribute efficiently its media content is IPTV – Internet Protocol Television. The reason for increasing interest in media convergence from IPTV industry viewpoint consists in the fact that IPTV channels are dominantly distributed to prospective subscribers via telecom multiplatforms. Despite its reliance on media convergence the industrial sector of IPTV has achieved limited commercial success as presently only 6% of the global TV viewers are pay IPTV subscribers. Moreover, the global future of IPTV market appears to be relatively uncertain as major international consulting and telecom agencies project that until 2018 the number of pay IPTV subscribers will increase approximately just 19 million per year. Moreover, with network providers pushing towards new digital payment models, and the idea of prioritizing consumer traffic related to online paying services, network neutrality seems to be an issue of the past, while the time of managed internet services has come [24]. This revenue business model trend will further diverge the audience market.

It is advisable to point out that media divergence is particularly profitable if the media company decides to use the 'cloud' vendor lock-in. The main competitive advantage of 'cloud' vendor lock-in is that it makes a customer dependent on a content producer/service/application or distribution channel/platform. This is explained that typical customers are unable to use another vendor without substantial switching costs or inconvenience. This is predominantly a case when there is a lack of compatibility or, interoperability between content producer/service/application and distribution channel/platform.

Although, both the old/traditional and digital media can reach small or large audiences, there are many fundamental differences in terms of the competitive advantage in distribution, production, technology, market targeting that favor digital media over old/traditional media. In the Tables 2 and 3 these marking differences are exposed in order to more effectively outline the major conceptual differences between digital and old media.

Table 2. The common denominators of major paradigmatic shifts in media business models before and after the digital convergence-divergence

Media business models before the digital convergence-divergence	Media business models after the convergence-divergence
Industrial media dominantly produced by large multinational corporations	Personal media primarily produced by internet users
Top-down content production	Bottom-up content production
Centralized framework for organization, production, and dissemination of media	Decentralized (network and on-demand) based media
One to many content distribution	Many to many content distribution
Linear, One-way media communication	Interactive and immersive media communication
Reaching the audience	Connecting the audience
Passive users - Users as Recipients	Active users - Users as participants
Static media	Mobile media
Economies of scale	Economies of scope (Long tail Economics)
One-sided platform distribution	More diversified multi-platform (hypermedia and multimedia) distribution, less hierarchical, and distinguished by multiple points of production and utility
Less available and accessible to the public, distribution costs and viewing is more expensive	Generally available and accessible to the public at little or no cost
The time lag between communications produced by industrial media can be long (days, weeks, or even months)	Capable of virtually instantaneous responses; only the participants determine any delay in response
Once created content, it cannot be altered (once a magazine article is printed and distributed changes cannot be made to that same article)	Easily altered content by almost instantaneously editing and writing comments
Less creative content creation	More creative content creation
Storage capacity for media content is relatively low	Storage capacity for media content is very high Acts as an online database
Low level of content categorization and sharing	High level of content categorization, annotation and sharing: Widgets, collaborative tagging, social classification, social indexing, and social tagging, folksonomy
Less peer-to-peer power Publisher-Centric	More peer-to-peer power User-Centric Model UGC – User generated content
Analogue	Digital media Digital convergence Mobile and wireless media Ambient media Augmented media Widget(ized) media Tagged media

Table 3. The common denominators of major paradigmatic shifts in media business models before and after the digital convergence-divergence

Two-dimensional media	3D media
Traditional market targeting (B2C and B2B marketing)	Better and more efficient market and consumer marketing (B2C and C2C) Nicheization Social network and online communities
Web 1.0 and Web 2.0	Web 3.0 (semantic web) and Web 4.0 (symbiotic web)
Value chain	Value network
Collaborative consumption	Collaborative creation
Producer	Producer
Broadcasting	Narrowcasting, microcasting and egocasting
Interactive media	Immersive media
Consumerism	Prosumerism
Top-down organizational structure	Bottom up organizational structure
Upstream supply chain (push marketing, low-cost producers)	Downstream supply chain (customization, targetization, high margins)
One to many distribution	Many to many distribution
Symmetric information flow	Asymmetric information flow
First build a marketplace, than a community	First build a community, than a marketplace.
Attention span is longer	Attention span is shorter
Owning the accessed content	Sharing the accessed content
Searching the data	Searching the metadata
Hardware based media	Software based (cloud) media
Demand is the king	Choice is the king
Industrial, Tangible Economy	Information, network, intangible, experience economy
Connect individual with the information/content/product	Share applications and experience among groups
Information based service	Conversation/Communication based service
Partial information access	24/7 information access
Place bounded media	Space bounded media
Individual/one screen media	Multi-screen media
Value is contained in transaction	Value is contained in relationship
Information based service	Conversation/Communication based service
Usage-based pricing	Access-based pricing

Table 4. Major Global ICT Corporations business models

Corporation	Business model
Apple	Consumer/Vendor Lock-in; On demand cloud applications; Closed/Proprietary Software, Product and Application Versioning; On demand cloud applications
Google	Complementarities, Open Proprietary Software, Product and Application Versioning; On demand cloud applications
Microsoft	Open and Closed/Proprietary Software, Product and Application Versioning; On demand cloud applications; Complementarities
Amazon	Open and Closed/Proprietary Software, Product and Application Versioning; Algorithmic Big Data Internet Intermediary
Facebook	On demand cloud applications; Algorithmic Big Data Internet Intermediary

6 The Future Research Perspectives, Outlooks and Implications

Importantly, the future application of business models in digital and ICT media will be focused on the following technologies: the Industrial Internet of Things - Industry 4.0 with its major five components: 1. Cyber-Physical Systems, 2. Internet of Things, 3. Smart Factory, 4. Internet of Services, 5. Smart Product, Internet of Services, autonomous vehicles, 3D printing, Smart Cloud, Quantum computing, nanotechnology, Big Data (Analytics), Smart Cloud, 5G, Cloud computing, edge and fog computing, artificial intelligence, collaborative robots (cobots), industrial robots, augmented reality, digital billboard advertising, USSD – Unstructured Supplementary Service Data, Predictive analytics, Quantum algorithm, Cognitive Computing, Quantum Computing, Cloud Computing, Biointerface & Gestural Interfaces, Quantifying Emotion, Geo targeting, Wearable technologies with biometric sensors, AI Art, Drone Journalism, Li-Fi, holography, smart grid, smart/intelligent city, Micro-electromechanical systems (MEMS).

7 Conclusion

The successful digital media and ICT corporations will have to act more as corporate planners, as well as 'cloud', 'on-demand' and 'ubiquitous' content and distributor disaggregators, than traditional content and advertising providers. Moreover, with all these changes, media will need to accommodate various consumer lifestyles. In an increasingly global and mobile digital media landscape, it is easier than ever to reach a large audience, but it is harder than ever to effectively connect with it. Therefore, old media traditional preoccupation was to reach the audience, however, in the age of digital media globalization, digital media companies have a twofold task to reach and connect the audience.

In summary, the second decade of the 21st century digital media is apparently becoming increasingly interactive, mobile, immersive, and ubiquitous. Furthermore, the future of the media appears to be specifically oriented towards the establishment of, networked, 3D, on-demand, broadband and unicast as well as multimedia and hypermedia models of distribution, communication and content creation. Therefore, it is crucial that profitable digital media companies realize that media divergence can successfully perform as vendor lock-in a top-down corporate process and a bottom-up consumer-driven process.

The digital business models influenced by digital convergence/divergence will focus on aggregate multi-platform distribution, complementarities, vendor lock-in, interoperabile and networked media and ICT ecosystem, massive personalization/customization, user interface.

References

1. Macnamara, J.: Remodelling media: the urgent search for new media business models. Med. Int. Aust. **137**, 20–35 (2010)
2. Jenkins, H.: Convergence Culture. Where Old and New Media Collide. MIT Press, Cambridge (2006)
3. Pavlik, J.: Media in the Digital Age. Columbia University Press, New York (2008)
4. Macnamara, J.: The 21st Century Media (R)evolution: Emergent Communication Practices. Peter Lang, New York (2010)
5. Appelgren, E.: Convergence and divergence in media: different perspectives. In: 8th ICCC International Conference on Electronic Publishing Brasilia - DF, Brazil, pp. 237–248, June 2004
6. Greenstein, S., Khanna, T.: What does industry convergence mean? In: Yoffie, D.B. (ed.) Competing in the Age of Digital Convergence, pp. 201–226. Harvard Business School Press, Boston (1997)
7. Jenkins, H.: Convergence? I Diverge. Technol. Rev. **104**(5), 93 (2001)
8. Lawson-Borders, G.: Integrating new media and old media: seven observations of convergence as a strategy for best practices in media organizations. Int. J. Med. Manag. (JMM) **5**(II), 91–99 (2003)
9. Lee, W.C.L.: Clash of the titans: impact of convergence and divergence on digital media. Unpublished doctoral thesis, Massachusetts Institute of Technology, June 2003
10. Dennis, E.E.: Prospects for a big idea—is there a future for convergence? Int. J. Med. Manag. **5**(1), 7–11 (2003)
11. Huang, E., Davison, K., Shreve, S., Davis, T., Bettendorf, E., Nair, A.: Facing the challenges of convergence: media professionals' concerns of working across media platforms. Convergence **12**(1), 83–98 (2006)
12. Meikle, G., Young, S.: Media Convergence. Palgrave, Basingstoke (2011)
13. Killebrew, K.C.: Culture, creativity and convergence: managing journalists in a changing information workplace. Int. J. Med. Manag. **5**, 39–46 (2003)
14. Pavlik, J.V., McIntosh, S.: Converging Media: An Introduction to Mass Communication. Pearson, London (2004)
15. Allison III, A.W., DeSonne, M.L., Rutenbeck, J., Yadon, R.E.: Tech Terms, 2nd edn. National Association of Broadcasters, Washington, DC (2002)
16. Wirth, M.: Issues in media convergence. In: Albarran, A.B., Chan-Olmsted, S., Wirth, M.O. (eds.) Handbook of Media Management and Economics, pp. 445–462. LEA Publishing, Mahvah (2006)

17. Wirth, M.O.: New media strategy: convergence-based driving forces & challenges. Paper presented at the Annual Convention of the Association for Education in Journalism and Mass Communication, Kansas City, KS, 31 July 2003
18. Lugmayr, A., Dal Zotto, C.: Media Convergence Handbook, vol. 2. Springer, Heidelberg (2016). https://doi.org/10.1007/978-3-642-54487-3
19. Diehl, S., Karmatin, M.: Media and Convergence Management. Springer, Berlin (2013). https://doi.org/10.1007/978-3-642-36163-0
20. Feldmann, V.: Leveraging Mobile Media: Cross-Media Strategy and Innovation Policy for Mobile Media Communication. Springer, Heidelberg (2006). https://doi.org/10.1007/b139034
21. Goldhammer, K.: On the myth of convergence. In: Groebel, J., Noam, E.M., Feldmann, V. (eds.) Mobile Media. Content and services for wireless communications. Lawrence Erlbaum Associates, Mahwah (2005)
22. Cole, J.: Multitasking bei der Internetnutzung. In: Zerdick, A., et al. (eds.) E-Merging Media. Kommunikation und Medienwirtschaft der Zukunft, pp. 82–83. Springer, Heidelberg (2004)
23. Enlund N., Lindskog T.: Nya redaktionella processer vid flerkanalspublicering. In: Hvitfelt, H., Nygren, G. (eds.) På väg mot medievärlden 2020. Studentlitteratur, Sweden (2000)
24. Lugmayr, A., Dal Zotto, C.: Media Convergence Handbook, vol. 1. Springer, Heidelberg (2016). https://doi.org/10.1007/978-3-642-54484-2

Sensor Ball Raffle – Gamification of Billboard Advertising: How to Engage the Audience?

Sari Järvinen[✉], Johannes Peltola, and Paul Kemppi

VTT Technical Research Centre of Finland Ltd.,
Kaitoväylä 1, 90570 Oulu, Finland
{sari.jarvinen, johannes.peltola, paul.kemppi}@vtt.fi

Abstract. In this paper, we present an interactive game for a large public display. Our focus was on experimenting new ways to enhance the effectiveness of a large, billboard size, display by adding a collaborative interaction mechanism for a user crowd. Working with a pop festival organizer, we developed a technology proof-of-concept of a multiplayer raffle game supporting crowd interaction with a large public display using an air-filled ball, equipped with an accelerometer and a barometer, as an interaction device. We experimented on its possibility to engage festival audience in live pilots in two occasions. Our observations showed that the audience enjoyed the raffle game and participated willingly. In addition, advertisers found the solution interesting.

Keywords: Interactive digital signage · Audience engagement
Interaction technologies

1 Introduction

In our daily lives, we are surrounded in public spaces with digital signage – small and large displays as well as huge billboards – with varying purposes. Public displays are being used e.g. for advertising, entertainment and infotainment, but it is not clear to what extent the public displays are able to deliver the intended message and if they have the expected impact or not. Interaction with the display and the presented content is often considered to improve the impact of the public displays.

In our work, the focus was on experimenting new ways to enhance the effectiveness of a large, billboard size, display by providing a collaborative interaction mechanism. In this case, the challenges were related to the development of an interaction mechanism for user crowds with low threshold for participation and to the design of a simple, but alluring, billboard application for a festival audience. Working with a pop festival organizer, we developed a technology proof-of-concept of a multiplayer raffle game supporting crowd interaction with a large public display and experimented on its possibility to engage festival audience during the intervals between different artist performances. The aim of our festival organizer partner was in this way to provide benefit for the advertisers improving the impact of the billboard advertisements. The interaction between the audience and the billboard display was implemented using a ball equipped with sensors monitoring the movement of the ball. In the next sections, we first discuss related work, and then describe our approach, the technology

E. Clua et al. (Eds.): ICEC 2018, LNCS 11112, pp. 164–174, 2018.
https://doi.org/10.1007/978-3-319-99426-0_14

components and details of the implementation. We present also the experiments done in real-world settings to evaluate the feasibility of the technology and design approaches, and finally our concluding remarks.

2 Related Work

Impact of digital signage has been studied extensively to evaluate the effect of the displays and the content presented. For example, Huang et al. [1] reported that in public spaces it is difficult to attract and hold the audience attention. People suffer from Display Blindness, when they expect display content to be uninteresting [2].

In the research community, interactivity is widely considered to enhance the impact of a public display and different interactive display solutions have been studied. Alt et al. [3] showed that with adoption of interactive content on public displays (1) the awareness of the content is increased, (2) the perception of public displays is more positive and (3) the information dissemination is improved. However, in order to have the desired impact the interaction method needs to be simple and clear to the user [4] and the application developers need to understand the user context related to public displays [5].

The focus in the research work is typically on medium sized displays (~ 55") and single person interaction. Common interaction technologies used include mobile devices, touch screens and gesture-based interfaces (e.g. Microsoft Kinect) [3].

Müller et al. [6] studied the user engagement in educational environment adopting interactive public displays with personal mobile devices. WallSHOP [7] demonstrated interactivity between multiple mobile devices and a public display. The purpose of the system was to combine the features of two device types to provide dynamic personalized content for advertisements. The user studies showed the feasibility of the solution, but also underlined challenges related to pairing of personal devices and the public display [8]. Different approaches (NFC, QR code, typing an URL, and connecting to a WiFi access point) to pair the personal device and the public display have been studied in [9]. Yamaguchi et al. [10] used a depth sensor installed at the public display and the mobile phone accelerometer to provide data for device pairing. After the device pairing, user could control the public display using his personal mobile device. In [11] mobile devices and a large display are used as an interaction medium between the audience and the orchestra. First commercial applications exist as well e.g. at movie theaters in Finland, before the movie, the audience can join a collaborative game on the screen using their mobile phones and the Leffapeli app. In average 5% of the audience joins in [12]. A comprehensive review on usage of mobile devices to interact with public displays is presented in [13].

In addition to explicit interaction with a public display, approaches to enable implicit interaction with digital content have been studied. For example, Tamaki and Hirakawa [14] present an approach to synchronize the content on a public display with the movement and height of the passerby. ReflectiveSigns has a scheduling system, which learns from audience behavior and adapts the display content accordingly [15].

3 Raffle Game for Festival Audience Engagement

Large public displays are used in pop festival context to live stream the artist performance, as with large audiences it is impossible for the entire audience to have a direct view on the artist. The artists perform for example for a period of 30–45 min and between the performances of different artists, there is an interval of 15–30 min. During this interval, the displays are used for advertising. Typically, advertisement content is displayed in predefined sequence and content is text, images, videos or animations.

The aim of our festival organizer partner was to provide benefit for the advertisers and have more interested clients for the display space during the intervals. As interactive digital displays have proven to have a stronger impact [3], we focused on interactive display solutions for user crowds. The requirements for the interaction method were following

- low threshold for participation, as we wanted to have as large as possible number of audience members interacting with the display
- ease of use, as the festival audience was unlikely to be interested in investing a lot of their festival time in learning an interaction method
- reliability, as the weather and lighting conditions could change drastically during the festival days or audience could behave unexpectedly.

Based on previous research, we evaluated usage of mobile phone based interaction methods and gesture interfaces. Even if in many occasions researchers have reached promising results related to usage of mobile devices as interaction interfaces with public displays, in our case we estimated that the number of audience members willing to install a specific application or use their phones in some other way to interact with the display would have been low. Previous research shows that the user willingness to interact with the display suffers if the process is time-consuming or complex [13].

Gesture-based interaction methods would be easier for the audience to start using. However, in a crowded situation such as audience gathered in front of a festival stage it would be difficult to implement a reliable gesture-based interaction solution. Most technology solutions for gesture-based interaction can operate with a maximum of 3–5 simultaneous users. In our case, the potential maximum number of simultaneous users was huge, thus the usage of a gesture-based interaction method would have limited the number of simultaneous users remarkably.

In the end, we selected an object on which we were able to attach a miniaturized sensor device to track the movement of the object. We considered the object-based interaction to be the best solution in our context.

The requirements already described for the interaction method were used again in the design process of the application. In addition, we wanted the application design to enable multi-brand advertising to add the number of possible clients for the festival organizer and minimize the possible hindering of the normal festival flow. Taking into consideration the nature of the event and the experience of the festival organizer, we estimated various possibilities including:

- controlling a cursor on the screen to complete a specific mission e.g. touching an virtual object visualized on the screen

– division of the audience into teams and a tennis-type of game between the teams
– tasks to throw the ball in specified ways e.g. height of 10 m.

Together with the festival organizer, we designed a simple application involving game features and a possible reward for the participation. The resulting application involves an air-filled ball equipped with a number of sensors, which when thrown keeps a raffle game wheel rolling on the screen. The advertised brands or products are presented on the rolling wheel. The raffle game is short, less than 30 s, and the festival presenter, who also invites the audience to play, initiates the game. The festival presenter throws the ball to the audience, which keeps the ball moving by throwing it from an audience member to another. The person holding the ball in the end of the game, when the raffle wheel stops and an audio signal is given, wins a prize.

4 Proof-of-Concept System Implementation

The system implementation (in Fig. 1) consists of four main components: sensors on the ball, large display with the raffle application, remote control software, and a centralized control application. The components operate on three different devices: sensor node attached to the ball, mobile phone for the remote control and a PC that hosts the raffle and control software and is directly connected to the public display.

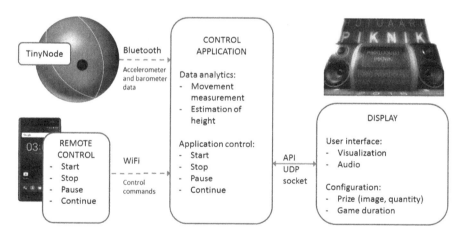

Fig. 1. System architecture

4.1 Sensor Ball

VTT Tiny Node sensor board [16] (in Fig. 2) is attached directly on the game ball. Tiny Node consists of integrated sensors including a 3D accelerometer, a barometer, a temperature sensor, and a humidity sensor. The Tiny Node communicates with other devices using a Bluetooth LE (BLE) data connection. The remote control application allows selecting a specific Tiny Node sensor and the control software opens a

Bluetooth connection for the selected Tiny Node. The communication in Bluetooth is initiated by activating the stream transmission of acceleration and barometer data from the sensor to the main control software for activity analytics.

Fig. 2. VTT Tiny Node: a battery operated sensor board.

4.2   Control Application

The control application maintains the state of the raffle system, passes messages between the components and performs the sensor data analytics for detecting if the game is played properly and the ball is moving. The festival presenter uses the mobile remote control to initiate the raffle game. During the raffle game, the sensor data from the sensor ball is analyzed by the control application to estimate the movement and height of the ball.

In addition, the pause and continuation of the game can be activated from the mobile remote control. This feature was implemented to overcome in live situation problems related to sensor data streaming and real-time analytics.

Measuring the Movement of the Ball. The sensor ball is equipped with a three-axis accelerometer and a barometer. The accelerometer data is used for measuring the magnitude of the movement of the sensor ball. The state of the ball motion is compared to the threshold and if the ball is not moving fast enough the game is put on hold.

For each received data block, a running sliding average of the accelerometer data is calculated. The average value is compared against a predefined threshold and if the movement does not exceed the threshold on a period of three seconds, the game is put on hold. Similarly, when the game is already on hold, the movement needs to continue similarly for three seconds, before the game initiates again and the raffle continues.

Estimating the Height of a Throw. The barometer sensor provides data for estimating the height of the throw. The height estimation is based on the barometric formula

$$h - h_0 = \frac{T_b}{L} \left(\frac{P_h}{P_b} \right)^{\frac{-LR}{g} - 1},$$

where h is the current altitude, h_0 is the reference altitude, T_b is the reference temperature, P_h is the current pressure, P_b is the reference pressure, L is the standard lapse rate (−0.0065 K/m), R is the universal gas constant (287 1/s2K), and g is the gravitational acceleration (9.80665 m/s2). The equation describes how the pressure (or density) of the air changes with altitude. The pressure drops approximately 11.3 Pa per meter in first 1000 m above the sea level. The reference temperature T_b was initialized manually to 15 °C and assumed to remain constant during the event. The reference pressure P_b is initialized and further updated every time when the detected still time exceeds a predefined threshold. The still time detection is based on the principle presented in [17]. The still time is incremented by the sample interval Δt on each time step, resetting to zero if the amplitude of the acceleration or the barometric pressure signal differs by more than a prescribed threshold from the average value of the signal since the current still time period began.

Together the acceleration and barometer data provide an automatic monitoring for the game so that the ball is constantly on a move and it reaches suitable height during the game. If someone tries to hold the ball and thus cheat the raffle, the game goes automatically on pause and the game continues only when the ball is back in the game.

4.3 Raffle Game

The game uses the X-Emitter Blender[1] game and particle engine for rendering the raffle unit. The game has a rolling wheel and the raffled prize is presented on the wheel in the end of the game. The rolling of the wheel is animated as well as shaking and lighting effects on the machine. The magnitude of shaking and the light effects is controlled by the movement activity of the ball sensor. The content of the advertisements on the wheel is managed on a configuration list. The list contains information about the game logic: how many prizes are available for each advertisement and what is the probability of each prize. In addition, the list contains technical information, such as texture of the logos and possible effects. The expected duration of the raffle is predefined, but the exact duration is random for each game so that participants cannot predict, when they should hold the ball in order to win the game.

4.4 Mobile Remote Control

The remote control software is implemented as an Android application and it consists of buttons to start, pause or continue the game and selecting the Tiny Node sensor when multiple game balls are in use. The mobile device needs to be connected to the same WiFi network than the computer hosting the control software. This eliminates the need of Internet connection and allows using a simple UDP socket for communicating the commands from the mobile device to the control application.

---

[1] www.blender.org.

5 Piloting at Music Festivals

To evaluate the feasibility of our approach from technical and design viewpoints we organized two live pilots in Oulu, Finland, together with our pop festival organizer partner. First, we piloted the solution during Rotuaari Piknik, which was an outdoor festival in downtown, Oulu, in July 2016 and second, in Pikkujoulu Piknik, which was a one-day festival organized in an indoor venue, in November 2016. Our main goal was to evaluate the technical functionality of the sensor ball as an interaction mechanism and audience response to this type of an interactive application.

Fig. 3. Rotuaari Piknik context: stage, screen and the ball (circled in the image)

5.1 Rotuaari Piknik – Outdoor Piloting

Rotuaari Piknik festival was organized on a square surrounded by buildings from three sides and by a stage from the fourth (Fig. 3). For each evening there were three artists performing each for approximately 45 min. Our pilot raffles were run for three evenings, when the overall festival operation permitted. Thus, we needed to be sure that the normal festival workflow (specially transferring music instruments for each artist) was not disturbed.

In our first festival pilot, the prizes in the raffle game were tickets to a music festival, movie tickets and gift vouchers for a hamburger restaurant. The range of the value of the prizes was from 10 to 150 euros. For each evening, there was one main prize and a number of smaller prizes. In this pilot, the ball used was a typical air-filled beach ball with a diameter of approximately 45 cm. We had multiple balls in use to keep the pace of raffle rounds fast in case it would take time to get the sensor ball back from the audience after the end of a raffle round.

We run the pilot raffle game multiple times each evening. Typically, 2–5 times before each performance resulting to 6–15 rounds each evening. The festival presenter encouraged the audience to participate informing about the prizes and giving instructions on how to play: 1. keep the ball moving, 2. hold on to it, when the raffle wheel stops and you hear an audio signal, 3. bring the ball to the presenter and retrieve your prize. The duration of the game was short: 20–30 s only to keep the interest of the audience high.

The evaluation of the technical functionality of the system and the audience reaction to the raffle game is based on our observations. We had two researchers observing the audience reactions and the game play for each raffle round.

Fig. 4. Audience engagement with the raffle game.

Our observations showed that after the first raffle round the audience understood the idea and participated eagerly (Fig. 4). Not all of the people were participating, but there was a large enough number of hands reaching for the ball to keep the game running. Some persons tried to hold on to the ball, but the system detected the misuse, the raffle wheel stopped and continued to roll only when the ball was moving again. The ball was moving well and the technical functionality of the system was in general acceptable. However, there were some problems with the signal transmission from the sensor ball to our receiver. We anticipated this, because, even if the range of the game was not too large for the BLE connection, the number of devices with radio interfaces in the area was high. Each evening there were more than 1500 persons in the area of a downtown square surrounded by buildings and most probably, all of them had a personal mobile device with them. Thus, we needed to use our remote controller, when the system did not receive the sensor data from the ball.

The companies present in the festival noted our interactive advertisement solution. During the first festival evening, two local businesses approached the festival organizer and wanted to be included in the raffle game. Therefore, for the second and third festival pilot evenings we reconfigured our system to support two new prizes: gift vouchers for two local restaurants with a value of 20–30 euros. For the festival presenter the game became a tool to gather the audience ready for the artist performing next.

5.2   Pikkujoulu Piknik – Indoor Piloting

The nature of the second festival was somehow different from the relaxed summer pop festival. Pikkujoulu Piknik was in practice a Christmas party with almost 5000 persons organized in a sport hall. The setup was similar: the audience in front of the stage and service points (bars, restaurants) surrounded the audience area (Fig. 5). The main difference compared to the summer festival was the absence of natural light – the evenings in July are bright in northern Finland. To overcome this challenge we used an air-filled ball with an integrated LED luminaire. The LED light ball was larger than the one used in first pilot, the diameter was more than 60 cm.

Fig. 5. Pikkujoulu Piknik context: stage, screen with the raffle game and the sensor ball

The presenter in Pikkujoulu Piknik was the same person as in the first pilot, thus the game was already familiar to the whole team and we repeated the same process as in the summer festival. The game configuration was similar to the summer pilot. The prizes included festival tickets, movie tickets and gift vouchers to multiple restaurants. All the advertisers included in the first pilot were willing to continue in the second pilot.

Two researchers observing the audience reactions and game play performed the evaluation. Our observations showed that the game was familiar also to a part of the audience after the summer pilot, which lowered even more the threshold to participate. The LED lights in the ball created a nice effect and there was no need to add environmental lighting for the ball to be visible. The audience participated actively to the game and there were even battles for the ball. We understood soon that the large size of the ball was a problem – multiple times more than one person was holding the ball, when the raffle stopped, and we had to improvise in selection of the winner. During this pilot, the radio interface between the ball and the raffle game application worked well. However, in one occasion, the audience ripped the sensor off the ball and the remote control was used to finish that specific raffle round in a controlled way. For the rest of the raffle rounds we changed the ball to a backup ball with a functioning sensor.

6   Lessons Learned

Our pilot observations showed that the sensor ball type of interaction method works well for a user crowd such as the pop festival audience. It requires minimal effort from the users and is easy to use. However, reliability of the communication interface between the sensor ball and the backend system is of utmost importance.

The game design was simple enough for the audience in this type of festival. The sensors worked well for controlling the movement of the ball and preventing the misplay of the game.

Piloting in real-world settings requires careful preparation for the unexpected, especially when the "show must go on" regardless of problems. Both the remote control and extra sensor balls were necessary and used during the pilots.

7   Conclusions and Future Work

We have presented an interactive digital signage application for a large billboard-sized screen aimed to engage the audience in a public event such as music festival. We have described our design and motivations behind our choices. We have given implementation details and demonstrated the feasibility of both the concept and the technical implementation. We have also reported our observations from multiple live pilot events, which proved that the audience enjoyed the game and advertisers found the game to be an interesting marketing channel.

For the future work, we will aim at organizing another pilot event to gather audience feedback with interviews. We will develop a solution to measure the effectiveness of the interactive digital signage application in communication of a marketing message to a crowd in a public event based on video analytics. We will also consider novel radio communication interfaces to improve the reliability of sensor data transmission between the ball and the control application.

Acknowledgements. This work was conducted in the context of "Innovative solutions for interactive environments - INSIST" project and was supported by Business Finland. We thank Pro Piknik Festivals for their contributions in design and piloting of the sensor ball raffle game. We also thank our colleagues for their invaluable help.

References

1. Huang, E.M., Koster, A., Borchers, J.: Overcoming assumptions and uncovering practices: when does the public really look at public displays? In: Indulska, J., Patterson, Donald J., Rodden, T., Ott, M. (eds.) Pervasive 2008. LNCS, vol. 5013, pp. 228–243. Springer, Heidelberg (2008). https://doi.org/10.1007/978-3-540-79576-6_14
2. Müller, J., et al.: Display blindness: the effect of expectations on attention towards digital signage. In: Tokuda, H., Beigl, M., Friday, A., Brush, A.J.B., Tobe, Y. (eds.) Pervasive 2009. LNCS, vol. 5538, pp. 1–8. Springer, Heidelberg (2009). https://doi.org/10.1007/978-3-642-01516-8_1

3. Alt, F., Schneegass, S., Girgis, M., Schmidt, A.: Cognitive effects of interactive public display applications. In: Proceedings of the 2nd ACM International Symposium on Pervasive Displays (PerDis 2013), pp. 13–18. ACM, New York (2013)
4. Brignull, H., Rogers, Y.: Enticing people to interact with large public displays in public spaces. In: Rauterberg, M., Menozzi, M., Wesson, J. (eds.) IOS Press (2003)
5. Finke, M., Tang, A., Leung, R., Blackstock, M.: Lessons learned: game design for large public displays. In: Proceedings of the 3rd International Conference on Digital Interactive Media in Entertainment and Arts (DIMEA 2008), pp. 26–33. ACM, New York (2008)
6. Müller, M., Otero, N., Alissandrakis, A., Milrad, M.: Increasing user engagement with distributed public displays through the awareness of peer interactions. In: Proceedings of the 4th International Symposium on Pervasive Displays (PerDis 2015), pp. 23–29. ACM, New York (2015)
7. Masuko, S., Muta, M., Shinzato, K., Mujibiya, A.: WallSHOP: multiuser interaction with public digital signage using mobile devices for personalized shopping. In: Proceedings of the 20th International Conference on Intelligent User Interfaces Companion (IUI Companion 2015), pp. 37–40. ACM, New York (2015)
8. Muta, M., Masuko, S., Shinzato, K., Mujibiya, A.: Interactive study of WallSHOP: multiuser connectivity between public digital advertising and private devices for personalized shopping. In: Proceedings of the 4th International Symposium on Pervasive Displays (PerDis 2015), pp. 187–193. ACM, New York (2015)
9. Vepsäläinen, J., et al.: Personal device as a controller for interactive surfaces: usability and utility of different connection methods. In: Proceedings of the 2015 International Conference on Interactive Tabletops & Surfaces (ITS 2015), pp. 201–204. ACM, New York (2015)
10. Yamaguchi, T., Fukushima, H., Tatsuzawa, S., Nonaka, M., Takashima, K., Kitamura, Y.: SWINGNAGE: gesture-based mobile interactions on distant public displays. In: Proceedings of the 2013 ACM international conference on Interactive tabletops and surfaces (ITS 2013), pp. 329–332. ACM, New York (2013)
11. Speicher, M., et al.: The audience in the role of the conductor: an interactive concert experience. In: Proceedings of the 5th ACM International Symposium on Pervasive Displays (PerDis 2016), pp. 235–236. ACM, New York (2016)
12. Leffapeli. http://www.finnkinob2b.fi/mediamyynti/leffapeli/. Accessed 02 July 2018
13. She, J., Crowcroft, J., Fu, H., Li, F.: Convergence of interactive displays with smart mobile devices for effective advertising: a survey. ACM Trans. Multimedia Comput. Commun. Appl. 10(2) 16 (2014). Article 17
14. Tamaki, N., Hirakawa, M.: Synchronizing digital signage content with the movement of passerby. In: Proceedings of the 8th International Symposium on Visual Information Communication and Interaction (VINCI 2015), pp. 150–151. ACM, New York (2015)
15. Müller, J., Exeler, J., Buzeck, M., Krüger, A.: ReflectiveSigns: digital signs that adapt to audience attention. In: Tokuda, H., Beigl, M., Friday, A., Brush, A.J.B., Tobe, Y. (eds.) Pervasive 2009. LNCS, vol. 5538, pp. 17–24. Springer, Heidelberg (2009). https://doi.org/10.1007/978-3-642-01516-8_3
16. VTT IoT Solutions (2015). http://www.vtt.fi/files/events/Teollinen_Internet_ja_Digitalisaatio_2015/TinyNode.pdf. Accessed 2 July 2018
17. Foxlin, E.: Pedestrian tracking with shoe-mounted inertial sensors. IEEE Comput. Graph. Appl. 25(6), 38–46 (2005)

Dance Dance Gradation: A Generation of Fine-Tuned Dance Charts

Yudai Tsujino[✉] and Ryosuke Yamanishi

Ritsumeikan University, Kusatsu, Japan
is0221rs@ed.ritsumei.ac.jp, ryama@fc.ritsumei.ac.jp

Abstract. This paper proposes a system to automatically generate dance charts with fine-tuned difficulty levels: Dance Dance Gradation (DDG). The system learns the relationships between difficult and easy charts based on the deep neural network using a dataset of dance charts with different difficulty levels as the training data. The difficulty chart automatically would be adapted to easier charts through the learned model. As mixing multiple difficulty levels for the training data, the generated charts should have each characteristic of difficulty level. The user can obtain the charts with intermediate difficulty level between two different levels. Through the objective evaluation and the discussions for the output results, it was suggested that the proposed system generated the charts with each characteristic of the difficulty level in the training dataset.

Keywords: Rhythm-based video games
Procedural content generation · Difficulty Adjustment

1 Introduction

There are so many genres of video games which are the popular entertainment in the world. Rhythm-based video games are one of the popular game genres. In most of the rhythm-based video games, players perform some actions corresponding to the displayed chart. Dance games, such as *Dance Dance Revolution*, are typical and popular rhythm-based video games all over the world. Playing dance games has attracted attention not only as a lot of entertainment but also fitness conditioning[1].

There are varied types of players, beginners to experts, for the rhythm-based video games. So, multiple charts for each difficulty level are prepared for the same song. The game creators manually compose these multiple charts in general. The difficulty level of the charts is discretely composed, thus there is sometimes too much distance between the difficulty levels. Some of the players, especially middle class players, are not enough satisfied with the charts because the charts

---

[1] https://www.engadget.com/2006/12/21/west-virginia-university-study-says-ddr-helps-fitness-attitude/ (Retrieved on Mar. 20, 2018.).

© IFIP International Federation for Information Processing 2018
Published by Springer Nature Switzerland AG 2018. All Rights Reserved
E. Clua et al. (Eds.): ICEC 2018, LNCS 11112, pp. 175–187, 2018.
https://doi.org/10.1007/978-3-319-99426-0_15

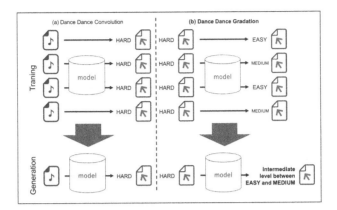

Fig. 1. The comparison of Dance Dance Convolution: the existing system (a) and Dance Dance Gradation: the proposed system (b). File icons with arrow show the charts with the corresponding difficulty level.

in the appropriate difficulty level for the player are not prepared. For example, if the easiest chart is too easy but the second-easiest chart is too difficult for a player, the player might require the intermediate difficulty level between those. In order to comply with such requests, the game creators have to compose an indefinitely large number of charts: that is impossible by the manual. We believe that automatic generation of fine-tuned charts has been demanded. *Dance Dance Convolution (DDC)* [2] is the system to compose dance charts automatically from audio tracks. In DDC, the big task of generating dance charts is divided into two subtasks; step-placement and step-selection tasks. DDC generates dance charts based on the relationships between acoustic features and the charts. The user can specify the difficulty level of the charts to be generated on five-level because the model in DDC has the one-hot vector for difficulty levels as the input. However, more detail tuning of difficulty levels cannot be supported in DDC. Moreover, it has been reported that the quality of the easier charts generated by DDC is not enough.

This paper proposes *Dance Dance Gradation (DDG)* that is a fine-tuning system for difficulty levels of dance charts. For the step-placement task, by blending the training dataset in different difficulty levels, DDG fine-tunes the difficulty levels of the generated charts. Figure 1 shows the concepts of DDC and DDG. Machine learning acquires the relation model between input and output in the training dataset. That is to say, the output of the learned model should have the averaged characteristics of the training dataset. As inputting multiple difficulty levels as the training dataset, the generated chart should be the averaged difficulty level based on the mixing ration of difficulty levels. Then, we propose the method to determine the threshold for onset detection considering the mixing ration.

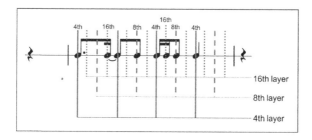

Fig. 2. The concept of the beat layer. The note should belong to the lowest layer. For example, the last note in this figure is assumed as the step in the 4th layer, though it also belongs to the 8th and 16th layers.

1.1 Definition

Some definitions key to this paper are as follows. A set of timing obtained by dividing a bar into n equal parts ($n \geqq 4$) is defined as "nth beat layer." Fig. 2 shows the idea of the beat layer and the corresponding musical score. Let the lowest layer in the layers which the timing where a given step exists belongs to be the lth layer, the step should belong to lth layer and defined as "lth step" or "the step in the lth layer"; here, "the lowest" means least n. This expression is defined as "beat layer" in this paper. The "4th" and "8th" above the notes in Fig. 2 shows the beat layer of each note. This expression does not strictly equal to a quarter note but is common in rhythm-based video games. This custom might arise from the note length not being taken into the consideration for playing the rhythm-based games.

If some steps belong to the higher layer, the sequence of steps should be more difficult and complex. Conversely, the sequence of steps belonging to the lower layer is easy to be sensed. Difficult charts have steps belong to the higher layer and easy charts consist of the steps belonging to lower layers.

In this paper, we used ITG dataset that is also used in the existing paper [2][2]. Table 1 shows statistics of the dataset. The multiple charts for different difficulty levels for a single audio track are contained in the dataset. Each chart is named as "Beginner (B)," "Easy (E)," "Medium (M)," "Hard (H)," and "Challenge (C)" in ascending order of difficulty.

1.2 Contribution

This paper offers the following contributions;

- We propose the system for constructing dataset with data which have different characteristics for supervised learning. Training with this dataset, the

---

[2] "In The Groove" http://stepmaniaonline.net/downloads/packs/In%20The%20Groove%201.zip and "In The Groove 2" http://stepmaniaonline.net/downloads/packs/In%20The%20Groove%202.zip (Retrieved on Nov. 28, 2017.).

Table 1. The statistics of the dataset (with reference to the existing paper by Donahue *et al.* [2]).

Dataset	ITG
Num authors	8
Num packs	2
Num songs	133
Num charts	652
Publishd year	2004–2005

learned model generates new data which reflects the strong point of each characteristic.

– We set the metric to evaluate how well-balanced output reflecting each characteristic. In this paper, we use this metric for determining the threshold to binarize the probability of step-placement.

2   Related Work

Procedural content generation (PCG) is a field of research for generating game contents automatically [7]. In PCG researches, the game is automatically generated depending on player's skill and behavior. Hastings *et al.* proposed *Galactic Arms Race* in which the weapon of the character is automatically evolved with player's behavior logs and preferences [3]. Pedersen *et al.* modeled the player's behaviors and proposed a method to generate suitable map for *Super Mario Bros.* [6]. This study can be categorized to one of those PCG researches with machine learning method.

Dynamic Difficulty Adjustment is a field of research for dynamically changing the difficulty levels of games based on the skills and actions of the players [4]. Andrade *et al.* resolve the problem of adjusting the actions of the computer-controlled opponent in the real-time games with reinforcement learning [1]. In this paper, we manually set the dataset for the training. If the training data would be set based on the players' skills, the difficulty levels can be dynamically and automatically adjusted. How to model the skills of the players and how to apply the model would be our future work for Dynamic Difficulty Adjustment in rhythm-based games.

This paper can be categorized not only the entertainment computing but also music information retrieval researches. In the field of music information retrieval, adjusting the difficulty levels for musical instruments has been a popular topic for a long time. For instance, Yazawa *et al.* proposed a method to generate guitar tablature adapting with player's level from the audio track [8] and Nakamura and Sagayama proposed a method to reduce piano score with merged-output hidden Markov model [5]. Though such reduction methods would be powerful for some particular instruments, different rules and features should be prepared for each instrument. On the other hand, a method based on machine learning with difficult and easy charts can be applied to other instruments if we collect huge corresponding easy and difficult charts. For actual musical instruments, it is a hard task to collect a lot of scores in different difficulty level for the same song. However, in the field of the rhythm-based games, that is the target of this paper, we can easily obtain the adequate amount of charts in different difficulty levels for the same song. The proposed system captures this specific characteristic of the rhythm-based games.

3   The Proposed System

This paper proposes *Dance Dance Gradation* (**DDG**). DDG is a system with training dataset in multiple difficulty levels to learn fine-tuned difficulty levels of dance charts for the step-placement task. Only charts with a unified difficulty level are used as the training data, the model should generate charts for that level. On the other hand, using the charts with multiple difficulty levels as the training data, the model should generate the charts moderately reflecting each characteristic of the difficulty level stored in the dataset. For example, if both Easy and Medium charts are used as the training data in 50% and 50%, the generated charts would be harder than Easy but easier than Medium. That is, DDG **gradationally** tunes the difficulty level of dance charts by arranging the training dataset.

Note, we use the same step-selection model as DDC with no modification, the chart is generated through step-placement and step-selection tasks, though. The details of step-selection model can be found in the existing paper [2].

3.1   Constructing Dataset for Training Characteristic of Each Difficulty Level

In dance games, the characteristic of charts is different depending on difficulty levels. Through the objective analysis for ITG dataset, we confirmed that the following score features related to the step-placement task are different depending on difficulty levels;

Feature 1: Frequency of steps. The more the number of steps the higher the difficulty level is; Beginner charts have approximately 0.6 steps per second on average while Challenge have approximately 4.9 steps per second.

Feature 2: Rhythm complexity. The rhythm in the easy chart is more likely to be more simple than the difficult chart; over 95% of steps in Beginner and Easy charts exist on 4th layer. 33% of steps in Challenge charts belong to 8th and 22% belong to 16th, where steps in easier charts hardly belong to.

Feature 3: Distribution in a bar. Steps in easier charts exist at some specified positions in a bar while steps in harder charts have a wide distribution; approximately 74% of steps in Beginner charts are placed at the beginning of a bar, where only 11% of steps in Challenge are placed.

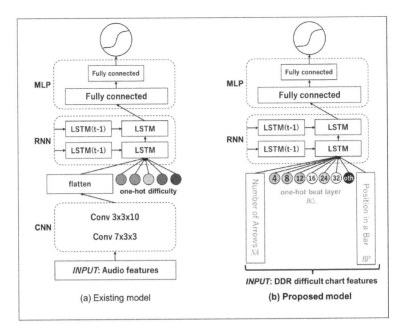

Fig. 3. Comparison of the existing model (a) and the proposed model (b).

DDG trains a model with different difficulty levels' charts. For indicating the usage rate of each difficulty level in the training dataset, we use 5-tuple vector: DR. Each element in DR shows the usage rate of charts for each difficulty level in the training dataset. For example, $DR = (1, 0.5, 0, 0, 0)$ with Challenge charts as input means that the model learns the relation of Challenge – Beginner with all tracks in the dataset and Challenge – Easy with the half of the tracks that are randomly selected from the dataset. Note, the model sometimes learns the relationships between the different output with the entirely same input.

3.2   Model

We use an LSTM model to adapt the difficulty level of charts while improving the model for step-placement in DDC [2]. Figure 3 shows the comparative image of the models for step-placement in DDC and this paper. In DDC, acoustic features obtained from the audio track with CNN and one-hot difficulty vector are used as the input for LSTM which estimates the probability that a step is placed in the chart. The proposed model uses the score features of the difficult chart at each time as the input instead of acoustic features and difficulty vector. The following three features are used as the score features based on the **features** mentioned in Sect. 3.1.

NA: **Number of arrows.** The number of arrows that are the required action for players at the time: non-negative integer in $[0, 1, 2, 3, 4]$. This feature is

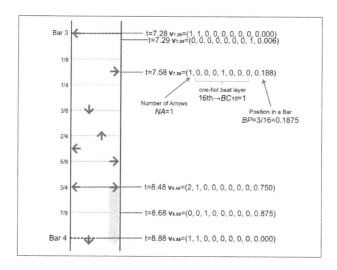

Fig. 4. Example of the score features. Score features can be expressed as 9-tuple vector for each time. The vector consists of features concerning the number of arrows, the beat layer and the position in a bar.

based on the idea that the probability of step would be low in the easy chart at the timing when the step does not exist in the difficult chart.

BC_L: **Beat layer.** The 7-tuple feature that is composed of the beat layer that the time belongs to (L: 4, 8, 12, 16, 24, 32, other). That is a one-hot vector in which the corresponding element would be 1. This feature is based on the **feature 2**.

BP: **Position in a bar.** The head and termination of the bar where a given time belongs to are each defined as 0 and 1, respectively. BP is the continuous value in $[0, 1)$. This feature is based on **feature 3**.

These features are connected as the input for the model. The input vector at time t: v_t is expressed as the following 9-tuple vector;

$$v_t = (NA, BC_4, BC_8, BC_{12}, BC_{16}, \\ BC_{24}, BC_{32}, BC_{other}, BP). \tag{1}$$

Figure 4 shows an example of the score features. We take $t = 7.58$ for a concrete example to explain the idea of the score features. There is only a right arrow at the time: $NA = 1$. To represent the time the note belongs to, the bar should be divided into 16 equal parts: $BC_{16} = 1$, thus the vector for beat layer should be $(0, 0, 0, 1, 0, 0, 0)$. The t exists at the position $\frac{3}{16} = 0.1875$ in the bar 3: $BP = 0.188$. The input vector at $t = 7.58$ would be $v_{7.58} = (1, 0, 0, 0, 1, 0, 0, 0, 0.188)$.

The output layer is the sigmoid function, and the output would be continuous value in the range $(0, 1)$. The target at each time is expressed in binary; a step exists at the time or not. The output value concern the probability that a step is placed at the time t: $SP(t)$. Estimating $SP(t)$ for all t in a given audio track, sequential data SP that is a sequence of step probabilities can be obtained.

3.3   Setting Threshold for Step-Placement: Especially for Blended Difficulty Level

The set of the timing for step-placement can be obtained from the series of the probability for steps SP detailed in Sect. 3.2. The number of steps dynamically influences the characteristics of charts as **Feature 1** in Sect. 3.1. Accordingly, the threshold for the step-placement should be appropriately determined.

   The proposed system learns multiple difficulty levels, thus it is expected that the output charts should have the characteristics of all of the learned difficulty levels. Then, the characteristics of each difficulty level should be reflected in the output chart depending on the usage rate of each difficulty level DR. For example, we expect that the output charts should have the characteristics of Beginner and Easy as fifty-fifty if $DR = (1, 1, 0, 0, 0)$, and the characteristics of the output charts should be mainly Beginner-like but a little bit a flavor of Medium if $DR = (1, 0, 0.2, 0, 0)$. Based on this idea, we evaluate;

Criteria 1. How much the output charts have the characteristics of each difficulty level used as the training data

Criteria 2. How much the balance of **Criteria 1** should be similar to DR.

   We use F-score as **Criteria 1** which can be calculated from the comparison between the ground truth and the output charts. As **Criteria 2**, we use the harmonic mean of F-score for each difficulty level that is weighted with DR. For all of the tracks in the validation data, the proposed system generates the charts while changing the threshold. And, the final threshold would be determined as the value that shows the best harmonic mean of F-score. The *threshold* is determined by the following procedures;

1. SPs for all of the tracks in the validation data are obtained.
2. All of the local maximum values are selected from SPs as the set of local maximum values.
3. The set of local maximum values is sorted in descending order of the value.
4. The threshold is determined by the stepwise approach as follows;
    for $n = 1$ to (size of the set of local maximum)
    (i). The nth local maximum is used as $threshold_n$, the local maximums over than $threshold_n$ are detected.
    (ii). Comparing the detected local maximums and the correct step-placement in each difficulty level, $\{F\}_n = \{F\text{-score}_B, F\text{-score}_E, F\text{-score}_M, F\text{-score}_H, F\text{-score}_C\}$ is calculated.
    (iii). Calculate the weighted harmonic mean of $\{F\}_n$ as HM. The weight is equal to DR.
5. The $threshold_n$ that shows the highest HM is determined as the *threshold*.

Table 2. List of the model name and DR. B, E, and M each mean Beginner, Easy, and Medium. The number following the initial shows the usage rate of the training data for each difficulty level. For example, M50 shows that 50% of Medium charts in the dataset is used as the training data.

Model name	Usage rate (%)		
	Beginner	Easy	Medium
B100	100	0	0
E100	0	100	0
M100	0	0	100
B100E100	100	100	0
B100M50	100	0	50
B100M100	100	0	100
B100E100M100	100	100	100
E100M100	0	100	100

For example, as learning a model for Beginner and Easy, let $\{F\}_a$ be as follows;

$$\{F\}_a = \{0.5, 0.4, NaN, NaN, NaN\},$$

here, if $DR = (1, 1, 0, 0, 0)$, the HM would be calculated as follows;

$$HM_{DR=(1,1,0,0,0)} = \frac{1+1}{\frac{1}{0.5} + \frac{1}{0.4}} \approx 0.44$$

if $DR = (1, 0.5, 0, 0, 0)$, the HM would be calculated as follows;

$$HM_{DR=(1,0.5,0,0,0)} = \frac{1+0.5}{\frac{1}{0.5} + \frac{0.5}{0.4}} \approx 0.46$$

Like the above examples, the HM is calculated according to DR.

4 Experiments

We trained the model with eight patterns of DR to verify the effectiveness of DDG. Table 2 shows the list of model name and DR used for the training. All model used Challenge charts as the input. None of the eight models used neither Hard nor Challenge charts as output; the 4th and 5th elements of DR are 0. In the ITG dataset, there are 120 tracks with five kinds of the chart and 13 tracks with four kinds of the chart. We randomly divided the tracks in the dataset as 80% (107 tracks) for the training data, 10% (13 tracks) for the validation data and 10% (13 tracks) for the test data.

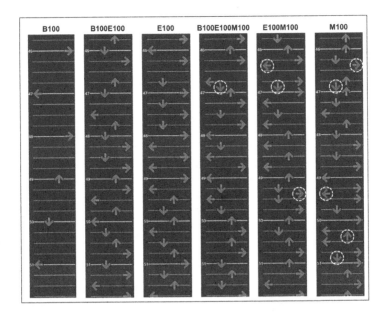

Fig. 5. Comparison of each model's prediction for the track *Queen of Light*

4.1 Training Methodology

The training methodology was same as Donahue *et al.* except for the termination condition. The target at each frame was the ground truth value. We calculated the updates using backpropagation through time with 100 steps of unrolling. The binary cross entropy is minimized by using stochastic gradient descent.

All models were trained with batches of size 256. We applied 50% dropout following each LSTM (only in the input to output but not temporal directions) and fully connected layer. All examples before the first step in the output chart or after the last step were excluded. The networks were trained for 100 epochs, but the learning was cut off if the loss function did not improve through 3 epochs in the validation data; all model finished learning within 69 epochs.

4.2 Results and Discussion

Figure 6 shows the charts for the track *Queen of Light* generated by six models. B100 model placed all steps at the beginning of the bar, and E100 model generated the sequence of 4th step. B100E100 model, which learned both Beginner and Easy charts, generated the sequence of 4th step with some quarter rests. It seemed that the chart generated by B100E100 was more difficult than the chart generated by B100 but easier than the one generated by E100. Three models using Medium generated the chart including some 8th steps (circled with dashed line). The frequency of 8th steps increased in order of B100E100M100, E100M100, and M100 model. It was suggested that the more Medium influenced the learning the harder the generated chart became.

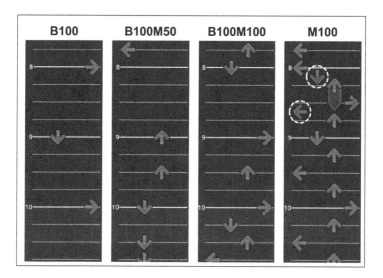

Fig. 6. Comparison of each model's prediction for the track *Lemmings on the Run*

Table 3. F-scores for each combination of model and answer difficulty level

	Beginner			Easy			Medium		
	F-score	Precision	Recall	F-score	Precision	Recall	F-score	Precision	Recall
B100	0.698	0.716	0.681	——	——	——	——	——	——
E100	——	——	——	0.699	0.546	0.971	——	——	——
M100	——	——	——	——	——	——	0.761	0.750	0.772
B100E100	0.408	0.270	**0.834**	0.648	0.552	0.786	——	——	——
B100M50	0.492	0.375	**0.716**	——	——	——	0.539	**0.833**	0.398
B100M100	0.436	0.300	**0.796**	——	——	——	0.649	**0.815**	0.540
B100E100M100	0.415	0.265	**0.956**	0.685	0.549	**0.912**	0.754	**0.795**	0.716
E100M100	——	——	——	0.436	0.300	**0.796**	0.649	**0.815**	0.540

Figure 6 shows the charts for the track *Lemmings on the Run* generated by B100, B100M50, B100M100, and M100 model. B100 model places all steps at the beginning of the bar as same as Fig. 5. The more the rate of Medium charts is increased the more the number of steps would be placed. B100M50 and B100M100 models did not place any 8th steps though M100 model placed several 8th steps. It was suggested that B100M50 and B100M100 models learned both characteristic of Beginner and Medium charts, and learn not to place 8th steps which were only seen in the Medium charts.

4.3   *F*-score

We calculated precision, recall, and F-score through all tracks in the test data to evaluate the effectiveness of each model. The charts for difficulty level used in the training were used as the ground truth for those metrics. For example, we calculated the metrics against Beginner and Easy charts for B100E100 model, which used charts of those level for the training.

It is expected the model which learned multiple difficulty levels generates the intermediate level charts. It means that the generated charts should cover all steps placed in easier ground truth and have extra steps. In other words, recall is more important than precision for easier ground truth. On the other hand, these charts do not have to cover all steps in harder ground truth but should not have extra steps. For harder ground truth, precision is more important than recall.

Table 3 shows the results of the proposed models. From the results, it was suggested that B100M50, B100M100, B100E100M100, and E100M100 models satisfied those requirements; it seemed that those models could tune difficulty level. From these results, we confirmed that DDG could generate the charts with a fine-tuned difficulty level. However, B100E100 model achieved high recall for both Beginner and Easy charts and low precision; it seemed that this model placed more steps than expected as the *threshold* for this model was set as too low.

5   Conclusion

In this paper, we present new task of fine-tuning difficulty level for rhythm-based video games. To tackle this task, we proposed a system that trains a model with multiple difficulty levels: *Dance Dance Gradation (DDG)*. For that system, we use the method to determine the threshold for nicely blending the characteristics of each learned difficulty level. Through the experiments, it was confirmed that DDG generated the appropriate charts of the averaged difficulty level reflecting on mixing ratio of learned difficulty levels.

Our future work is to use acoustic features as input combined with features of difficult charts. These features might help to generate more entertaining charts synchronized with the track.

Acknowledgement. This paper was supported in part by JSPS Grant-in-Aid for Young Scientists (B) #16K21482.

References

1. Andrade, G., Ramalho, G., Santana, H.S., Corruble, V.: Challenge-sensitive action selection: an application to game balancing. In: IEEE/WIC/ACM International Conference on Intelligent Agent Technology, pp. 194–200 (2005)
2. Donahue, C., Lipton, Z.C., McAuley, J.: Dance dance convolution. In: Proceedings of ICML 2017, pp. 1039–1048 (2017)
3. Hastings, E.J., Guha, R.K., Stanley, K.O.: Evolving content in the galactic arms race video game. In: Proceedings of CIG 2009, pp. 241–248 (2009)
4. Hunicke, R.: The case for dynamic difficulty adjustment in games. In: Advances in Computer Entertainment Technology, pp. 429–433 (2005)

5. Nakamura, E., Sagayama, S.: Automatic piano reduction from ensemble scores based on merged-output hidden markov model. In: Proceedings of ICMC 2015, pp. 298–305 (2015)
6. Pedersen, C., Togelius, J., Yannakakis, G.N.: Modeling player experience for content creation. IEEE Trans. Comput. Intell. AI Games $2(1)$, 54–67 (2010)
7. Shaker, N., Togelius, J., Nelson, M.J.: Procedural Content Generation in Games: A Textbook and an Overview of Current Research. Springer, Cham (2016). https://doi.org/10.1007/978-3-319-42716-4
8. Yazawa, K., Itoyama, K., Okuno, H.G.: Automatic transcription of guitar tablature from audio signals in accordance with player's proficiency. In: Proceedings of ICASSP 2014, pp. 3122–3126 (2014)

Short Papers

Playful Information Access Through Virtual Creatures

Kota Gushima[✉] and Tatsuo Nakajima

Department of Computer Science and Engineering,
Waseda University, Tokyo, Japan
{gushi,tatsuo}@dcl.cs.waseda.ac.jp

Abstract. This paper proposes Ambient Bot, an information notification system that presents practical everyday contents to people intimately and ambiently. Ambient Bot requires people to wear a head-mounted display (HMD). Users see a virtual creature in the real world via augmented reality technologies. The creature not only speaks but presents everyday information that people might be interested in only when they focus their attentions on the creature itself.

Keywords: Intimate notification · Eye contact · Playful interaction

1 Introduction

The recent progress of digital technologies dramatically increases one's cognitive overload. For example, a large amount of information is offered to citizens via public displays located on trains, stations and streets in our everyday commute in big urban cities. Modern social media try to steal our available attention with advanced computing technologies. To make everyday life more comfortable and peaceful, information should be more ambiently and playfully delivered to individuals only when the information is truly necessary.

This paper proposes a notification system named Ambient Bot that intimately and ambiently presents everyday information to people. It requires them to wear a head-mounted display (HMD) through which they see a virtual creature in the real world via augmented reality (AR) technologies. This creature speaks and presents everyday information of possible interest but only when they focus their attention on the creature itself.

2 A Basic Interaction in Ambient Bot

The goal of Ambient Bot is to offer an implicit light-weighted interaction method wherein it is easy to access necessary information, in the any places and situations of everyday life; for example, when a user is in a public space, such as a train station or when walking on the street. Ambient Bot adopts the his/her gaze as the basic input modality, while its visual text messages and spoken audio are the output modality. Interactions using eye contact cannot be used for accessing complex information, but

© IFIP International Federation for Information Processing 2018
Published by Springer Nature Switzerland AG 2018. All Rights Reserved
E. Clua et al. (Eds.): ICEC 2018, LNCS 11112, pp. 191–197, 2018.
https://doi.org/10.1007/978-3-319-99426-0_16

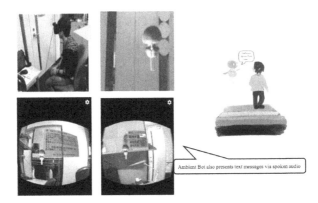

Fig. 1. An overview of Ambient Bot

these interactions can enable implicit natural interactions, bypassing explicit interactions like those related to the use of traditional controller devices.

Ambient Bot allows people to acquire information simply by using eye contact with a virtual creature that continually floats within their field of view when they really need information. The virtual creature not only speaks but also displays texts in a translucent window against an image of the real world. Figure 1 shows a user's perspective, i.e., what he/she sees via an HMD (Nexus 6 used as HMD and Microsoft HoloLens) when using Ambient Bot. When eye contact has not been made, the virtual creature automatically moves to a position that does not interfere with his/her view, ensuring that he/she is not strongly conscious of the creature's existence. To actualize interaction and for the creature to make an eye contact, it needs float around his/her field of vision as described above. The current design chose a jellyfish character as a floating virtual creature, as shown in Fig. 1 because it would be inappropriate to display humans, dogs or cats as floating creatures.

3   Accessing Multiple Information Sources in Ambient Bot

3.1   Pull-Based and Push-Based Interaction Methods

Two methods are investigated for people to access everyday information; the *pull-based* interaction method and the *push-based* interaction method. In the pull-based interaction method, people actively access information that they want to know. In the push-based interaction method, information is actively provided to people and they can passively access the information. The push-based interaction method includes not only notifications but also accidentally receiving information to make people mindless and frustrated. For example, people may acquire information about souvenirs via advertisements when they walk in a train station. Such interaction is classified as push-based interaction because they acquire the information passively from the outside world, and they may not expect to receive the information. We have developed two prototype implementations of Ambient Bot; one is based on the pull-based method and the push-based method is adopted by another.

3.2   Pull-Based Interaction in Ambient Bot

In the prototype based on the pull-based interaction method, since its user's objective is to access information intentionally, he/she needs to indicate to Ambient Bot what kinds of information he or she is currently seeking. In conventional information access services, people usually select a specific application on the desktop of a personal computer or a smartphone home screen, acquiring the information they want by clicking the target application's icon. For example, if a user wants to know the weather tomorrow, he/she usually picks up his/her smartphone, taps the weather forecast application icon, and thus, acquires the expected information. However, in the case of the basic Ambient Bot concept, user interaction instead entails making eye contact with a jellyfish. However, this eye-contact approach is likely insufficient for accessing complicated information because it is difficult to select the appropriate information with only eye contact.

Fig. 2. Accessing contents via multiple creatures

This basic interaction design as described in the previous section can be easily enhanced for accessing multiple information sources. A user can configure the types of contents to be accessed in advance, according to the time and situation. This design allows the user to acquire the desired information without hindering the implicit and natural interactions offered by the basic Ambient Bot interaction design. In the enhanced Ambient Bot, multiple virtual creatures appear around a user, with each virtual creature representing a different informational category. Figure 2 shows an overview of this interaction design. A user chooses a desired information category by selecting a virtual creature floating around him/her, and making eye contact with one of them. Showing multiple virtual creatures in the real world where a user is could lead to a cognitive overload, yet this load could also be reduced by carefully arranging the viewable positions of the creatures with respect to the time and specific situation.

3.3   Push-Based Interaction in Ambient Bot

In the prototype implementation based on the push-based interaction method, when Ambient Bot wants to provide information, a virtual creature appears in the real space, but the position is almost the edge of a user's view; thus, the creature's appearance does not consume his/her cognition too much.

When he/she makes eye contact with the creature, the creature provides information. In this prototype, the appearance of a virtual creature means that the creature wants to notify something to him/her. The creature moves out of his/her sight and disappears after providing the information or its user does not pay an attention to the creature for a certain time.

When a creature is appeared in his/her view, Ambient Bot shows a notification icon that indicates which content it wants to notify above the creature as shown in Fig. 3. For example, when a creature wants to notify a news message, the icon on the creature indicates that there is a news message for him/her. When he/she makes an eye contact on the creature, an appeared message window includes a news message.

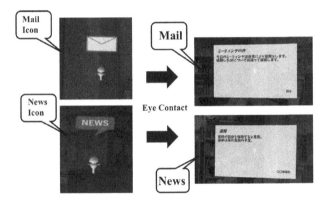

Fig. 3. A notification icon above a creature

4   User Studies

We conducted the first user study experiment to investigate the feasibility of the Ambient Bot's pull-based interaction design. We recruited ten participants, including eight males and two females, all of whom are university students between 21–24 years old who usually access information with their smartphones.

Participants freely used Ambient Bot at the beginning of the experiment. Then, they configured the system with the appropriate information, according to the current time and by matching the virtual creature with its corresponding content. Next, participants used Ambient Bot in the following three situations: working on daily tasks at a desk, sitting in a train, and walking outside.

Figure 4 shows results with respect to three situations based on their decisions regarding configurations that either displayed an article within an information window or read the article using a voice synthesizer. In the first situation, when working at the desk, nine out of ten participants displayed an information window, and whether or not they required that information to be voiced depended on the participants involved. Participants who rejected using the voice during work read only the critical part of the article, and then felt annoyed at listening to the entire article. On the other hand, a participant who wanted to listen to the article via voice said, "*I was less burdened when I used the voice assistance; rather than reading the whole article by myself, I could concentrate on my work*".

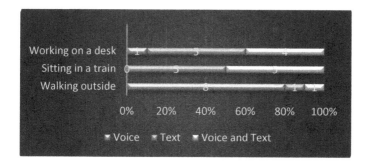

Fig. 4. Information delivery methods

In the second situation, when sitting in a train, all participants wanted to display an information window, yet their opinions about using the voice were divided. Participants who refused to use voice noted that, "*The voice conflicts with in-train broadcasting,*" while participants who wanted to use the voice noted that, "*The broadcast information on a train is not necessary for me to listen to.*" Unlike music, the reading of an article in a voice, seriously conflicts with in-train broadcasting. Using voice information in Ambient Bot may disturb those who normally use in-train broadcasting to provide their current location. On the other hand, for most of them, visual information on a train is unnecessary and displaying an information window did not disturb their activities on the train.

In the third situation, when walking outside, many participants refused to display an information window. To ensure people's safety while walking, they needed to carefully distinguish the necessary information from within their eye-sight. As a result, the presentation of a window to disturb their eye-sight, should be avoided.

The second user study to investigate the push-based interaction method was conducted using nine participants (8 males and 1 female, average age: 22.7). In this user study, participants chose their preferred display modes for three typical content types: newsflashes, e-mails and the user's schedule. For each type of content, the participants selected whether a notification icon is presented or not, and whether a message window is presented or not. The message window presents content, and the content may be read by the creature's voice.

In this user study, we interviewed the participants and asked them why they chose the configurations. Of course, some participants always turned the window on, but other participants changed the configuration to display the message window according to the content. The reason provided for turning the message window on was mostly because they may miss listening to content via voice only, and the reason for turning it off was because the content in the message window does not matter if participants missed listening or not. For e-mail content, all participants turned on the message window. From the interviews, they did not want to miss the email content. In addition, several participants said they do not need a function to read e-mails via a voice because e-mails are usually read by a user's eye, and not listened to by a voice.

The icon was turned on by most participants, except participant C. Several participants said, *"The icon was turned on in order that Ambient Bot informed what information would be presented."* Participant C selected to display the icon only when the message window was not displayed. He commented in the interview *"When the message window comes out, I can read the message quickly; thus, I can fully understand what content it is. In the case of only voice, the icon is displayed soon to see what content it is."* Hence, we understood through the interviews that all participants wanted to know at the beginning what type of content Ambient Bot wanted to present.

The results of the interviews suggested that the modality of information cues should be designed according to the existing services' modalities.

5 Related Work

Welbo [1] is an AR-based agent system similar to Ambient Bot, where a virtual agent appears in the real world, and the agent can talk to a user. However, in Welbo, a user needs to speak to the virtual agent for interacting with the agent. The approach is heavy weighted because speaking requires more human consciousness than eye contact that is adopted in Ambient Bot.

In past research, a concept named Pervasive Ambient Mirrors reflects people's current situations to influence their behavior [5]. In [4], slow technologies enable daily objects to ambiently represent some currently useful information for a user. Recently, push-based notifications on smartphones were studied [2] and an ambient notification method using an eyeglass device was reported [3].

6 Conclusion

Ambient Bot is a playful and ambient notification system that uses AR technologies to offer everyday information using casual interactions. This paper described some insights of Ambient Bot, that emerged from the two user studies.

References

1. Anabuki, M., Kakuta, H., Yamamoto, H., Tamura, H.: Welbo: an embodied conversational agent living in mixed reality space. In: Proceedings of the International Conference on Human Factors in Computing Systems, CHI 2000 Extended Abstracts (2000)
2. Costanza, E., Inverso, S.A., Pavlov, E., et al.: Eye-q: eyeglass peripheral display for subtle intimate notifications. In: Proceedings of the 8th Conference on Human-Computer Interaction with Mobile Devices and Services, pp. 211–218 (2006)
3. Elslander, J., Tanaka, K.: A notification-centric mobile interaction survey and framework. In: Jatowt, A., et al. (eds.) SocInfo 2013. LNCS, vol. 8238, pp. 443–456. Springer, Cham (2013). https://doi.org/10.1007/978-3-319-03260-3_38
4. Hallnäs, L., Redström, J.: Slow technology – designing for reflection. Pers. Ubiquit. Comput. 5(3), 201–212 (2001)
5. Nakajima, T., Lehdonvirta, V.: Designing motivation using persuasive ambient mirrors. Pers. Ubiquit. Comput. 17(1), 107–126 (2013)

Validating the Creature Believability Scale for Videogames

Nuno Barreto[✉], Rui Craveirinha, and Licinio Roque

CISUC, Department of Informatics Engineering,
University of Coimbra, 3004 516 Coimbra, Portugal
`nbarreto@dei.uc.pt`

Abstract. We present the validation of a scale to assess creature believability in videogames. We define Creatures as all zoomorphic entities not qualifying as fundamentally human-like, whether possessing or not anthropomorphic features. The scale, derived from a previous research, contains 26 items in 4 dimensions – Biological/Social Plausability, Relationship with the Environment, Adaptation, and Expression. The results of a Confirmatory Factor Analysis, using 19 subjects, originated a model with 4 factors, a CFI of 0.795, and RMSEA of 0.111. While not a good fit, it is very close to a mediocre fit, which is a potentially promising result. Further validation is needed with more subjects in the future.

Keywords: Believability scale · Creature design · Evaluation
Videogames

1 Introduction

Studies have shown believable actors are perceived to be more engaging than non-believable ones [4,11,21,24,25]. However, believability, as a construct, is still in its infancy [24]. Works by Loyall [15], Bates [4] and Mateas [17], transcribe their believability criteria from Disney's rules of thumb listed in "Illusion of Life: Disney Animation" [23], and are, in turn, used as basis for several agent architectures and algorithms (e.g. Warpefelt [25], Parenthöen et al. [18]). These criteria are used at face value, without any validation to assess how they measure believability, or if they do so at all.

Assessing believability has been discussed in Togelius et al. [24], arguing for subjective methods, such as self-reports used by Arrabales et al. [2]. This work adjusted a scale used to evaluate cognitive functions in avatars, and allowed assessing a form of believability. However, its range over other types of believability is reduced, since agents are judged as avatars for players, not simulated living beings.

This paper's contribution is the revision of the believability scale presented by Barreto, Craveirinha and Roque [3], providing a first attempt at validation through Confirmatory Factor Analysis.

© IFIP International Federation for Information Processing 2018
Published by Springer Nature Switzerland AG 2018. All Rights Reserved
E. Clua et al. (Eds.): ICEC 2018, LNCS 11112, pp. 198–204, 2018.
https://doi.org/10.1007/978-3-319-99426-0_17

We can foresee two applications for such a scale, at the moment: to aid the analysis and comparison of fauna, in game worlds, across presentation, autonomy and interactivity (even between different games), and as a set of heuristics to use during game development. This would allow game designers the means to evaluate how believable their creatures are, and consequently, the potential to improve their game's believability and engagement.

The paper's structure is as follows: Sect. 2 describes methodology. Section 3 presents Results and Scale Revision, where we perform a revision of the scale's underlying theoretical model within its Confirmatory Factor Analysis. Section 4 details conclusions.

2   Methodology

Aiming to provide an initial framework for the study of believability in creatures, a first believability scale was proposed in Barreto, Craveirinha and Roque [3]. After establishing a formal definition for creatures, an initial iteration was created with 46 statements. After a first round of Exploratory Factor Analysis, 26 statements achieved an acceptable loading value and thus made it into the existing model, grouped into 4 dimensions. Note however, there was no confirmation of the hypothesized model. As suggested in Spector [22], we now provide an additional validation and revision phase of the scale, through Confirmatory Factor Analysis.

As suggested in Togelius et al. [24], we designed an online self-report[1] where ten randomly sorted video clips (40 to 60 s long), from various videogame sources, were shown, each with at least one creature engaged in a specific activity. This duration allowed numerous, and time consuming (i.e. learning) creature activities to be demonstrated. After each clip, subjects answered a fail-safe question [13, 16], and scored each item in the scale.

We chose games that were recent, to reduce bias created by technological limitations, and that had creatures with extensive on-screen presence, to increase perceivable activity. The following creature/game pairs were selected: Radstags (Fallout 4 [6]), Wolves and Tigers (Life of Black Tiger [1]), Chop (Grand Theft Auto V [20]), D-Horse (Metal Gear Solid V: The Phantom Pain [14]), Aliens (No Man's Sky [10]), Sea Vulture (Risen [19]), Wolves (The Elder Scrolls V: Skyrim [5]), Deer (theHunter [8]), Trico (The Last Guardian [9]), Antilopes (The Witcher III: The Wild Hunt [7]).

Our survey was deployed online, with 19 users participating (12 Male and 7 Female). The sample is admittedly short, but we think that for the purpose of a first validation attempt, it can provide meaningful insight regarding the model. The average age was 31.5 ± 11.9. Distribution of level of education was: 11% with Highschool degree, 37% with Bachelor's degree, 47% with Master's degree, 5% with Doctorate degree. Academic background included Science, Technology, Engineering and Math (68%), Humanities (Literature, Social Sciences, etc.)

---

[1]   https://goo.gl/forms/VUbhu4lrvavk3W2X2.

(26%) and Arts (Illustration, Music, etc.) (5%). Average contact with media (videogames, movies, tv) per week was 20 h for 32% of users, 20 h to 40 h for 42%, 40 h to 60 h for 16%, and >60 h for 11%.

3   Results and Scale Revision

Each <subject, videogame> tuple was considered a separate answer, resulting in 190 entries (19 subjects × 10 clips), since each clip had its own context, creature(s) and activities. The data underwent a Confirmatory Factor Analysis (CFA) using a Maximum-Likelihood Path Analysis to test the scale's theoretical model's goodness-of-fit. Model data was compared using χ^2, $\frac{\chi^2}{df}$, CFI and RMSEA indexes.

A first structured equation model was considered (model 4F), transcribing the original scale [3]: its four dimensions were converted to latent variables, each with a covariance link to the remainder ones. These dimensions were also linked to their respective items, measured variables. The indexes obtained are listed in Table 1.

Observing the values, we first conclude the null model, as expected, provides a bad fit. Specifically, $\frac{\chi^2}{df}$ is above 5 (9.768), CFI is below 0.8 (0.000) and RMSEA is above 0.1 (0.215); all values lie within a bad fit on their respective ranges. Similarly, the original model (4F), also seems a bad fit. While its $\frac{\chi^2}{df}$ value was 4.594 (below 5 yet above 2), the others, CFI (0.630) and RMSEA (0.138) were above 0.6 and 0.1 respectively, suggesting a bad fit.

Table 1. Goodness-of-fit indexes for alternative models for the scale. (n = 190)

	Step	$\chi^2(df)$	$\frac{\chi^2}{df}$	CFI	RMSEA
	Null model	3174.497 (325)	9.768	0.000	0.215
1F	1 Common-Factor	1082.293 (291)	3.719	0.722	0.120
4F	4 Factors (w/o adj.)	1345.917 (293)	4.594	0.630	0.138
4FW	4 Factors (w/ adj.)	852.059 (264)	3.125	0.795	0.111

Since the original model seemed a bad fit for the data, we devised alternatives. One alternative involved a model (1F) which, unlike the previous, hypothesizes only 1-Common Factor, or dimension (Believability), to explain variances. Surprisingly, results are slightly better than 4F. Although $\frac{\chi^2}{df}$ (3.719) is also below 5 but above 2, its CFI (0.722), while still below, is closer to 0.8, the threshold for a mediocre fit (according to Hooper, Coughlan and Mullen [12]). Its RMSEA (0.120), while near 0.1, is still above it and a bad fit.

We also used hints from the estimates' modification indexes, formulating model 4FW as follows:

- We added covariances between residuals.
- Item 25 ("The creatures learn through imitation") was changed to reflect Adaption.
- While several items had a loading value inferior to 0.4, the conventional cut threshold, we opted to remove only item 16 ("The creatures' same-stimuli reactions change over time"), because of the item's sentence confusing wording.
- Data outliers were removed according to their Mahalanobis Distance p1 and p2 values (when both equaled zero).
- Removed the covariances between the latent variable pairs < "Relation with the Environment","Adaptation" > and < "Adaptation","Biological/Social Plausibility" > as their estimated value was nearly zero.

Comparing fit indexes with the alternative models, it is clear 4FW yields better results. Its $\frac{\chi^2}{df}$ is the highest at 3.2, within the mediocre fit range. The CFI (0.795) is close to 0.8 and it can be argued this borderlines a mediocre fit. The RMSEA (0.111) is around 0.1. However, while this model fares better than previous ones, all of them are bad fits or borderline mediocre fits. Therefore, additional experiments need to be conducted to expand these result; with this in mind, we propose model 4FW for a revision proposal, as it had the best results. The original model (4F) and the one we considered (4FW) are illustrated in Fig. 1, and Table 2 lists the revised scale.

Table 2. The revised believability scale obtained after the CFA.

Factor	Item	Factor	Item
Relationship with the Environment	1. The creatures interact with the environment	Adaptation	17. The creatures learn from past events
	2. The creatures control their body		18. The creatures are able to apply old behaviors to new, similar, situations
	3. The creatures direct their behaviors towards targets		19. The creatures change the way they look with age
	4. The creatures locate objects in the environment		20. The creatures change the way they sound with age
	5. The creatures expel material		21. The creatures change the way they behave with age
	6. The creatures' actions are appropriate to their context		25. The creatures learn through imitation
Biological/Social Plausibility	7. The creatures move by themselves		22. The creatures' expressions anticipate their actions
	8. The creatures' motions reflect their weight/size	Expression	23. The creatures show positive (or negative) emotions towards objects, or events
	9. The creatures make several simultaneous motions		24. The creatures show expressions to known stimuli
	10. The creatures react to stimuli		26. The creatures' body are adapted to their habitat
	11. The creatures focus on stimuli		
	12. The creatures coordinate with other creatures		
	13. The creatures communicate with other, same-species, creatures		
	14. The creatures engage in reproductive acts		
	15. There are signs of previous reproductive acts, such as eggs, cubs, pregnancy, etc.		

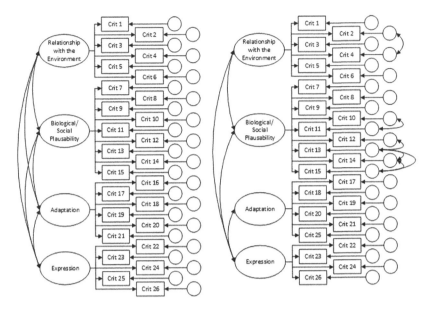

Fig. 1. Structured equation models of model 4F (left) and model 4FW (right). Ovals are the scale's construct's dimensions, rectangles are items and circles are residuals; single-headed arrows explain variance while the remaining show covariances.

4   Conclusion

We attempted to validate a Creature Believability Scale. After modeling the scale as a Structural Equation, we performed a Confirmatory Factor Analysis, leading to adjustments using three different approaches. From those, we chose one with an improved fit, taking into account the scale's future utility. With the selected approach, we revised the scale. After revision, 1 item was removed from the original 26-item scale, while one other switched dimensions.

The items' statements could also be revised by interviewing several subjects and assessing if they former are similarly interpreted across the latter. Revising the test setup altogether is also an option; for instance, using actual gameplay in lieu of video clips. Backtracking towards the scale's initial steps would allow reanalyzing the scale through an Exploratory Factor Analysis, though using a different, and larger, sample.

This research tries to provide a complementary insight into creature design. The existing literature on believability is either focused on humans or narratives, either centering on behaviors or expressions. This Creature Believability Scale provides a tool to assess believability of non-humanoid creatures, but also unifies several perspectives on how to convey believability.

The results show the scale, in its current form, needs further research. The model was deemed a borderline mediocre fit, so additional studies need to be conducted to understand why it is so. In the future, we will conduct a new

Confirmatory Factor Analysis phase with additional subjects (est. 300 to 500 required), to provide further validation.

We believe the revised scale is a step towards guidelines that improve design practices, allowing designers to evaluate their work's believability. While not ideal, we believe it is promising, and a first step towards the goal set for the research.

Acknowledgements. This work was supported by the FCT Ph.D. Grant SFRH/BD/ 100080/2014.

References

1. 1Games: Life of black tiger (2017)
2. Arrabales, R., Ledezma, A., Sanchis, A.: ConsScale FPS: cognitive integration for improved believability in computer Game Bots. In: Hingston, P. (ed.) Believable Bots: Can Computers Play Like People?, pp. 193–214. Springer, Heidelberg (2011). https://doi.org/10.1007/978-3-642-32323-2_8
3. Barreto, N., Craveirinha, R., Roque, L.: Designing a creature believability scale for videogames. In: Munekata, N., Kunita, I., Hoshino, J. (eds.) ICEC 2017. LNCS, vol. 10507, pp. 257–269. Springer, Cham (2017). https://doi.org/10.1007/978-3-319-66715-7_28
4. Bates, J.: The role of emotion in believable agents. Commun. ACM **37**, 122–125 (1994)
5. Bethesda Game Studios: The Elder Scrolls V: Skyrim. [DVD-ROM] (2011)
6. Bethesda Game Studios: Fallout 4. [DVD-ROM] (2015)
7. CD Projekt RED: The Witcher 3: Wild Hunt. [DVD-ROM] (2015)
8. Games, E.: theHunter (2005)
9. genDESIGN and SIE Japan Studio: The Last Guardian. [Blu-Ray] (2016)
10. Hello Games: No man's sky. [Blu-Ray] (2016)
11. Hingston, P.: Believable Bots: Can Computers Play Like People?. Springer, Heidelberg (2011). https://doi.org/10.1007/978-3-642-32323-2
12. Hooper, D., Coughlan, J., Mullen, M.R.: Structural equation modeling: guidelines for determining model fit. Electron. J. Bus. Res. Methods **6**(1), 53–60 (2007)
13. Kittur, A., Chi, E.H., Suh, B.: Crowdsourcing user studies with mechanical turk. In: Proceedings of the SIGCHI Conference on Human Factors in Computing Systems, CHI 2008, pp. 453–456. ACM, New York (2008)
14. Kojima Productions: Metal Gear Solid V: The Phantom Pain. [Blu-Ray] (2015)
15. Loyall, A.B.: Believable agents: building interactive personalities. Ph.D. thesis, Carnegie Mellon University Pittsburgh (1997)
16. Mason, W., Suri, S.: Conducting behavioral research on Amazon's Mechanical Turk. Behav. Res. Methods **44**(1), 1–23 (2012)
17. Mateas, M.: An oz-centric review of interactive drama and believable agents. Technical report, School of Computer Science Carnegie Mellon University, July 1997
18. Parenthöen, M., Tisseau, J., Morineau, T.: Believable decision for virtual actors. In: 2002 IEEE International Conference on Systems, Man and Cybernetics (2002)
19. Piranha Bytes: Risen. [DVD-ROM] (2009)
20. Rockstar North: Grand Theft Auto V. [Blu-Ray] (2013)

21. Rosenkind, M., Winstanley, G., Blake, A.: Adapting bottom-up, emergent behaviour for character-based AI in games. In: Bramer, M., Petridis, M. (eds.) Research and Development in Intelligent Systems XXIX, pp. 333–346. Springer, Heidelberg (2012). https://doi.org/10.1007/978-1-4471-4739-8_26

22. Spector, P.E.: Summated Rating Scale Construction: An Introduction. Sage, Thousand Oaks (1992)

23. Thomas, F., Johnston, O.: The Illusion of Life: Disney Animation. Hyperion, Santa Clara (1997)

24. Togelius, J., Yannakakis, G.N., Karakovskiy, S., Shaker, N.: Assessing believability. In: Hingston, P. (ed.) Believable Bots: Can Computers Play Like People?, pp. 215–230. Springer, Heidelberg (2011). https://doi.org/10.1007/978-3-642-32323-2_9

25. Warpefelt, H.: The non-player character - exploring the believability of NPC presentation and behavior. Ph.D. thesis, Stockholm University, Faculty of Social Sciences, Department of Computer and Systems Sciences, Stockholm, Sweden (2016)

The Programmable Drone for STEM Education

Patrik Voštinár[✉], Dana Horváthová, and Nika Klimová

Matej Bel University, Tajovského 40, 974 01 Banská Bystrica, Slovakia
patrik.vostinar@umb.sk

Abstract. Technologies in the current world are constantly changing. These changes are also reflected in teaching process. Computer Science subject uses mostly programming language Scratch in Slovak schools. We wanted to try out a new tool for pupils as a way for programming and STEM education – modular and programmable drone Airblock. In this contribution we wanted to present this drone which we think is suitable for teaching programming. Drones are very popular among people and that was the reason why we think drones can be used as a motivational tool in order to teach programming at schools. This was done by the extracurricular activity at the Matej Bel University and the pupils were from lower secondary schools in Banská Bystrica, Slovakia. The pupils developed many buttons with different behaviours. The Airblock drone could fly without pre-programmed buttons. The subject matter of this article is a presentation of robotic toy – programming of the flying drone Airblock suitable for teaching programming.

Keywords: Programming · Drone · Airblock · STEM education

1 Tangible Technological Devices

Nowadays technological devices are very popular. They are devices which provide interactivity, response and communication [1]. This includes programmable tools as well as programmable drones.

Technological devices should be included into early experiences because everyday technologies are controllable; engaging in control activities obliges pupils to deal with and to construct simple programs; control technology activities may help them to develop more general abilities to think and learn [2].

Programmable toys appeared to be a good choice because they are tangible technological devices and pupils can directly manipulate with them; they can stimulate problem-solving in real conditions of pupils' environment [3].

There are 3 ways of receiving information [4]: visual – sights, diagrams, symbols, pictures; auditory – words, sounds; kinaesthetic – touch.

We wanted to use these modalities into our learning process. It was important to include all of them and make our lessons tangible. Because of this, programmable drone Airblock meets our requirements.

It is generally known how much important a motivation is – especially internal motivation. While outside motivation can be added to the education process by the

© IFIP International Federation for Information Processing 2018
Published by Springer Nature Switzerland AG 2018. All Rights Reserved
E. Clua et al. (Eds.): ICEC 2018, LNCS 11112, pp. 205–210, 2018.
https://doi.org/10.1007/978-3-319-99426-0_18

teachers and family, the internal motivation needs to be awakened for the pupils regardless of the possible reward [5].

In Slovak schools Computer Science subject uses mostly programming language Scratch. This programming becomes more self-evident. Because of this reason we should be looking for a new motivation for teaching programming. New motivation could be Airblock: the modular and programmable drone.

2 Micro-project: Computer Science Extracurricular Activity

Micro-project: Computer Science extracurricular activity was realized with support of the Comenius Institute and the Department of Computer Science of the Faculty of Natural Sciences at the Matej Bel University in Banská Bystrica. There have been involved around 75% of future Computer Science teachers of all grades from our faculty. Our students had the opportunity to work actively with elementary and secondary children from the beginning of their bachelor study at the Department of Computer Science. Indicators of the progress of the participating students were reflection, self-reflection and assessment of individual pedagogical competences through assessment scales.

The Comenius Institute offers to Slovak teachers (including future teachers) one-year costless practice course with many workshops. There are chosen yearly only 20 participants. Nika Klimová (one of the authors) was chosen as the only future teacher of these 20 participants (the rest of them were teachers or principals). She received money to develop her micro-project – something special that could be used in the teaching process. She decided to buy a learning tool – drone Airblock: the modular and programmable drone. We supposed using this drone could increase interest of teaching programming. Because of our experimental lessons took place for the first year, we did not come to a more formal form of study on the curve of learning, efficiency and motivation, and therefore we cannot analyse our results with other teaching processes.

2.1 Airblock: The Modular and Programmable Drone

Airblock is the modular and programmable drone. It can be turned into a flying drone, hovercraft, water hovercraft, spider etc. It is made from engineering foam (it is indoor-friendly) and includes 1 main module (CPU) and 6 dynamic magnetic hexagons that can be assembled or disassembled without the need of tools (see Fig. 1). Drone can be programmed by "drag-and-drop" programming. Airblock was the winner of Reddot Award: Product Design 2017, Good Design Award 2017, K-Design Grand Prize 2017 and Idea Finalist 2017.

It is based on STEM education joining science, technology, engineering, and mathematics together.

Hovercraft mode allows Airblock to do a number of stunts, and by selecting two propellers from either side, it can generate specific movements. For instance, the two propellers located on the back of the hovercraft drive the hovercraft forward. The two propellers located in the front drive the hovercraft backward. Getting two propellers to push against each other enables the hovercraft to go left or right.

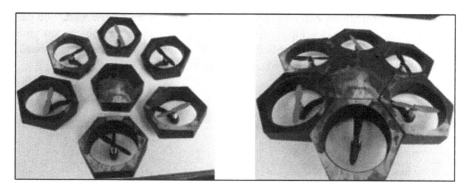

Fig. 1. Flying drone

For the programming drone we need a mobile device such as tablet or mobile phone (smartphone). We can download a mobile application Makeblock which could be downloaded for the operating system Android (free app at Google Play) and iOS (free app at App Store).

2.2 Programming Airblock

Programming in this environment is comparable to programming in Scratch. Simply drag-and-drop different blocks of commands – like forward, pause, turn, etc. and connect them together to create a seamless action.

In the application Makeblock it is possible to design your own environment of the controller. Into environment application can be added joystick control or predefined buttons for flying drone into circle, triangle, etc. Predefined buttons can be modified. It is possible to create your own buttons with different behaviours (see Fig. 2).

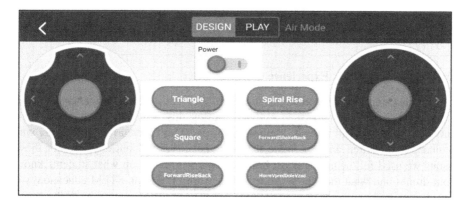

Fig. 2. Makeblock application – code environment.

The application allows two modes – design and play. In the *design mode* you can add some components or develop some behaviour. In the *play mode* you can test your application. Behaviour can be modified after some buttons if *design mode* is pressed.

Drag-and-drop blocks are divided into following categories (see Fig. 3):

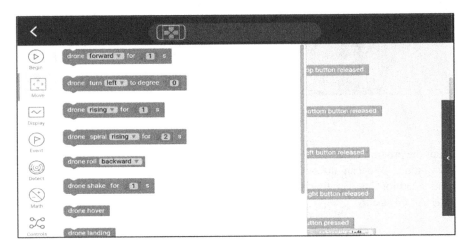

Fig. 3. App Makeblock – example of "drag-and-drop" blocks.

- **Begin** – what happens when button is pressed/released, power on/off.
- **Move** – motion of the drone – move, turn, rising, roll, shake, hover and landing drone.
- **Display** – offer possibility to set LED on the drone.
- **Event** – shake tablet, switch on/off tablet, tilt tablet.
- **Detect** – slider value, read gyro value, temperature, battery level
- **Math** – mathematics operation (addition, subtraction, Boolean value, change item, round, random integer, etc.)
- **Controls** – if condition, wait, repeat, break the loop, etc.

2.3   Drone Airblock – Experience

We were teaching lower secondary school children *Program your drone!* 5 lessons at Computer Science Extracurricular Activity. During this activity there were children from 8–12 years old, but it wasn't limited by the age. Our Extracurricular Activity was voluntary for children and for future teachers and it was without any fee. For these lessons we used following methods: brainstorming – to come up what students know about drones and what they think drones can perform. Based on STEM education, we were discussing how the drone can fly and students were trying out to build the drone into many flyable shapes. Then we were developing programs through [6]:

- algorithm and data structure planning,
- coding,

- testing,
- error detection,
- correction,
- efficiency control, quality control,
- documentation.

Brainstorming turned out that all of pupils know what a drone is and could describe drones e.g. can fly or move some lightweight objects.

We taught pupils in a group and algorithm planning was made similarly as brainstorming with having a task of what the drone should perform, e.g. a triangle in the air. Students came up how to program it. After that they coded it together with the support of the group (through discussion). Testing showed if the program is correct. In the case of performing triangle it was wrong, so we were finding an error which occurred in angles. We tested it again. Then we were discussing if the program can be more efficient. Finally, we documented it through a print screen. This method was used for all tasks.

Feedback showed that programming of the Airblock drone was very exciting for the pupils (see Fig. 4). They said they created a lot of different environments and programmed many drone behaviours. They also had "much fun" and the best part of the lesson was testing.

Fig. 4. Students were developing app for the drone. (Color figure online)

For example, they created buttons with following behaviour:

- **drawing 2D geometrical shapes** such as triangle, square, rectangle, circle, etc.,
- some of the students were able to develop **3D geometrical shapes such as** cube and rectangular prism,
- **traffic light:** drone turn on, shows the red colour for 1 s, wait for 1 s, change colour to orange for 1 s, wait for 1 s, change colour to green for 1 s and hover until 1 m, do spiral, land,
- **action** – repeat 10 times: rising for 1 s, wait for 1 s, set all LED colours to red, downward for 1 s.

3   Conclusion

In this article we described educational tool Airblock: the modular and programmable drone. This drone could be used for increasing motivation of pupils for teaching programming. Pupils can programme behaviour of the drone in blocked programming language similar to Scratch. They created many drone control environments with their own buttons. They "had much fun" and the best part of the lesson was testing.

We want to improve the teaching of drone at Computer Science Extracurricular Activity by improving pedagogical backgrounds and monitoring related research in the future.

Acknowledgements. This contribution has been processed as part of the grant project *Implementation of Blended Learning into Preparation of Future Mathematics Teachers*, project no. 003UMB-4/2017th and project *Interactive Applications for Teaching Mathematics at Primary Schools*, project no. 003TTU-4/2018.

This contribution has been supported also by the Comenius Institute and its donors:

References

1. Learning and Teaching Scotland: Early Learning, Forward Thinking. Learning and Teaching Scotland, Dundee (2003)
2. Siraj-Blatchford, J., Whitebread, D.: Supporting Information and Communications Technology in the Early Years, 4th edn. McGraw-Hill Education, London (2003)
3. Pekarova, J.: Using a programmable toy at preschool age: why and how. In: Proceedings of SIMPAR-2008, Simpar, Venice, pp. 112–121 (2008)
4. Felder, R.M., et al.: Learning and teaching styles in engineering education. Eng. Educ. **78**(7), 674–681 (1988)
5. Picka, K., Pešková, K.: Perception of digital games as educational media by lower secondary school pupils. J. Technol. Inf. Educ. **10**(1), 17–33 (2018)
6. Szlávi, P., Zsakó, L.: Methods of teaching programming. Teach. Math. Comput. Sci. **2**(7), 247–257 (2003)

A Taxonomy of Synchronous Communication Modalities in Online Games

Quentin Gyger[(⊠)] and Nicolas Szilas[(⊠)]

TECFA-FPSE, University of Geneva, 1211 Genève 4, Switzerland
Quentin.Gyger@etu.unige.ch, Nicolas.Szilas@unige.ch

Abstract. This paper discusses the benefits, limits and specificities of communication modalities in online video games and proposes a corresponding taxonomy. This taxonomy could serve as a guideline for game designers who want to integrate communication into the game mechanics.

Keywords: Synchronous communication · Taxonomy · Online video game
Game design · Communication modalities · Chat · Voice over internet protocol
Emote · Predefined message · Indicative signal

1 Synchronous Communication: Different Modalities

Online games have a social component by definition and since any social act requires communication, it's essential to understand how communication is addressed in online video games. This communication has different topics [1], dispatched to various modalities [2] that have their own benefits and limitations. Communication naturally occurs when it comes to achieve the game's goals, however, there is a greater amount of socioemotional discussion [1]. Victory and defeat being inherent to game's components, knowing how to communicate with different modalities in cooperative and competitive team games is essential. Even though the trend for online games is *Voice over Internet Protocol* (VoIP), there is still massive written communication in chat [3, 4] because of its own benefits such as persistence or the ability to easily follow who said what in a conversation [5]. Based on the analysis of most popular games [6] and additional independent games, we found that the communication modalities mainly present in online games consists of either a written chat, a VoIP (integrated or not in the game), emotes (messages often accompanied by an animation, performed via a command), or *predefined message* (PM) for basic exchanges (i.e. *say hi, good game, have fun*). In several games there are also *indicative signals* (IS), which are alerts (in the form of different signals) used to provide to the other players some pieces of information. Two common IS are pings which are "a combination of animation and sound indicating a point of interest" [7] and freely drawing line in a gamespace such as annotations in Dota 2 [7]. Pings could be more elaborate than just a general indication,

E. Clua et al. (Eds.): ICEC 2018, LNCS 11112, pp. 211–216, 2018.
https://doi.org/10.1007/978-3-319-99426-0_19

such as the *Smart ping*[1] in League of legends [8] which allows to make specific announcements. In addition, some of these modalities can be mixed, but they generally just coexist in games, according to the kind of game, the players' needs and the evolution of the games. Indeed, they can greatly influence the ability of players to communicate, to spend good time in games and reach their goal in an optimal way. Therefore, these modalities are important in game design.

2   Communication at Different Levels

In online games, the conversation may be *diegetic* or *extradiegetic*, depending on whether its elements transgress or not the fiction [9] established in the game. Diegetic conversations, also called *in character* (IC) or *in role-play* (IRP) conversations, place the players in their character's role. Extradiegetic conversations, also called *out of character* (OOC) conversations place the players as themselves playing a game. A modality of communication like in-game chat or VoIP (inbuild or independent) can be used as much for diegetic or extradiegetic discussions [10]. However, depending on the context of the game and the place given to the role-play, some modalities can take the player out of the game [5]. For example, if a young woman plays the role of an old wizard, voice communication can disrupt the other players' immersion. But the same modality embedded in the gameplay can be very immersive too, for example in DayZ (a 3D survival FPS game), the voice comes directly from the character and the player can speak for his or her character. Integrating communication as an element of game design in itself can allow the player to stay in the flow [11], but an extradiegetic discussion does not necessarily leave the player out of the flow. Indeed, in competitive games, players often communicate as players controlling a character and don't argue in role-play, but their discussions remain at the same diegetic level and a role-play communication could appear discordant. Therefore, the communication must be thought of in such a way that players can remain at the desired diegetic level or can travel to the different levels at the same time.

A distinction is necessary at this level: such a correspondence regarding the diegetic level does not mean that one should not make use of metalepsis, which introduces extradiegetic into a diegetic narration [12]. Indeed, the use of mastered metalepsis has interesting virtues, including in serious games [13]. The assumption here is that back and forth switches between different diegetic levels must be followed by the different players to maintain a consistent communication and keep them immersed in the game. Moreover, role-players frequently navigate back and forth between their IC and OOC status, and sometimes they even do meta-gaming (introduce OOC knowledge in their role-play).

---

[1] "Smart Ping is a radial menu that includes four alerts [(*danger, on my way, assist me, enemy missing*)]. These can be used to communicate with your team faster than taking the time to type and [break the] flow of gameplay" [8]. These alerts are displayed with sound and their own visual effect and are visible to teammates on the terrain and the minimap.

3 Benefits and Limits of Communication Modalities

All communication modalities have inherent advantages and limitations. The benefits and limits of the different communication modalities discussed in this section are intrinsic or technical characteristics and do not constitute an exhaustive list, but they highlight important particularities that are used in game design to reinforce specific aspects of a game.

A chat is a common feature in online games, it allows players to freely converse and this modality of conversation is easy to follow, because the messages remain displayed in sequence along with the utterer's name. In some games, conversations can also be displayed on top of the characters to add role-play immersion. The VoIP feature is very widespread, because it allows players to express themselves instantly without writing on a keyboard, which can provide an effective communication (without interrupting the gameplay). The predefined message mostly have a socioemotional role, but can also be task-oriented. They allow to exchange basic messages, essentially courtesy, without the need to moderate the words of the players. They are usually limited in number but quick to use like in Hearthstone[2] [14]. They can also be displayed in a radial menu such as *Communication wheel* in Overwatch [15] which offers eights communication's options and also allow to communicate on specific goals of the game (i.e. *say group up, need healing*). The emote feature consists of pre-recorded sentences (written in or spoken by the character) accessible to other players around the player character in the game (i.e. John thanks you for your help, John is pointing at you). This allows role-play players to take action on their characters. Some emotes have not only a written or spoken component, but also a visual animation (i.e. laughing, dancing, drinking) performed by the character. They are usually enabled by clicking on shortcuts or typing keywords in chat (i.e. dancing). Among IS, the ping feature has mainly a strategic communication function: it allows to quickly communicate information about some game's specific objectives. The information they give can be contextual if the player pings a specific object (i.e. tower, opponent or ally players) [7]. The drawing feature can also have the same purpose without the contextual part [7] and allow to give information about a direction or movement, they can also be used for socioemotional communication (i.e. *drawing a smiley or congratulations words*).

The benefits and limitations of these modalities will be assessed across five dimensions (see Fig. 1). The first dimension is called *gameplay coexistence* and represent the players' ability to communicate without interrupting their actions in the game. *Multicommunication* describes the possibility given to the player to follow multiple conversations through the same modality at the same time (without overload of the channel). *Persistence* represents the time interval during which the message will remain visible before disappearing. *Expressive power* represents the varieout restriction. *Multilingual* is the possibility to communicate with people who speak another

---

[2] "Short quotes that heroes can [utter]during a game. Each emote comes as a sound bite, and in a written form, displayed in a speech bubble next to the character's portrait." [13]. They're accessible by right-clicking on the portrait.

language without personal knowledge of this language (online games can be played in different countries). Figure 1 displays the characteristics of modalities according to these five dimensions.

Characteristics of modalities

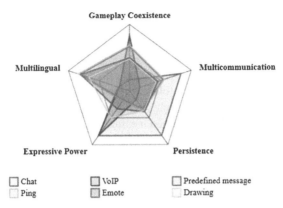

Fig. 1. Communication modalities' characteristics. This graphic has been made in relation to the intrinsic and technical properties of the different modalities and could be different depending on the context or the modalities' design.

4 Modalities of Communication: Towards a Taxonomy

The purpose of this section is not to define an exhaustive list of the modes of communication present in every kind of online games, but to give a current overview of communication in online video games [6] to inspire the game designers. Table 1 below is a proposal for classifying these different modalities using their characteristics (see Fig. 1) and characteristics of communication useful to cooperate, have fun or achieve goal in game. For this reason, we introduce in the taxonomy the diegetic aspect described in the Sect. 2 and the socioemotional and task-oriented function.

Socioemotional messages can be positive or negative and include message that show solidarities, tension relief, agreement, disagreement, tension or antagonisms. Task-oriented communication are asking for or giving an opinion, suggestion or task orientation [1]. Theses function are essentials for the communication of online games and can be reached with different modalities.

In online games such as Massively Multiplayer Online Games (MMORPG), Multiplayer Online Battle Arena (MOBA) and First-Person Shooters (FPS), to name a few, synchronous communication can be *written* in a chat or *vocal* when it occurs in inbuilt or independent VoIP (i.e. Discord, Ventrilo, Teamspeak). These competitive games may also contain IS (more or less elaborate) that could be *visual* and/or *audio* indications to communicate game's *tasks* through HUD (head-up display) alerts. Recent successful FPS like Fornite Battle Royal seems to prioritize vocal and PM through a radial menu, but a chat could also fulfill a valid communication function, as the modality and its restrictions would be the same for all players [16]. Other games without teamplay like Collectible Card Game (CCG), racing or fighting video games could prefer written PM to fulfill a basic socioemotional or task-oriented communication function. Games with Role-Playing (RPG) components could have emotes to give an immersive dimension and encourage players to have *diegetic* conversations. As we have seen above, the modalities have some *intrinsic characteristics*. Indeed, their *persistence* could be low as in VoIP and IS or high as in chat. *Multicommunication* could be described as the possibility for many people to communicate without saturating the discussion channel (i.e. many people can chat at the same time, while few can talk (VoIP) at the same time because channel's overload). The *gameplay coexistence* is an important component based on the ability of players to communicate without interrupting their action in the game. Especially in fast games, efficiency could be crucial in which case it's important that communication coexists with the gameplay. There are also some modalities' *technical characteristics* like the *Expressive power*, denoting the player's ability to communicate freely. It should be noted that a limited communication is not necessarily bad, because it could provide great moderation and the possibility to easily translate messages, which allows the game to be easily *multilingual*.

Table 1 doesn't constitute an absolute taxonomy of synchronous communication in online games, because some characterizations could be changed depending on the context or integration of the modality. Instead, Table 1 illustrates the common use of the communication modalities in online games.

Table 1. Taxonomy of synchronous communication in online video games. Modalities characteristics are classified by levels (L = low, M = medium, H = high).

	Synchronous communication in online games												
	Communication Characteristics								Modalities Characteristics				
	Sign-system					Function	Diegetic level			Intrinsic			Technical	
	Verbal		Non-verbal											
	Written	Vocal	Visual Static	Visual gestures	Audio	Task-oriented	Socioemotional	Diegetic	Extradiegetic	Gameplay Coexistence	Multicommunication	Persistence	Expressive Power	Multilingual
Chat	x					x	x	x	x	L	H	H	H	L
VoIP		x				x	x	x	x	H	L	L	H	L
PM	x					x	x		x	H	M	L	L	H
Emote	x	x		x			x	x		M	M	L	M	H
Ping			x		x	x			x	H	M	L	L	H
Drawing				x		x	x		x	M	M	L	M	H

5 Conclusion

Communication is an important component of game design, as it may reinforce game's qualities such as immersion, coordination, efficiency or sociability of players. In this article, after having identified 6 main synchronous communication modalities, we proposed a taxonomy of such modalities according to a series of dimensions and the communication's characteristics. This taxonomy could serve as a guideline for game designers who want to optimally integrate communication into the gameplay. In addition, the taxonomy proposes a design space in which some regions are unexplored in current online games, which may suggest new communication techniques to be invented in the future.

References

1. Peña, J., Hancock, J.T.: An analysis of socioemotional and task communication in online multiplayer video games. Commun. Res. **33**, 92–109 (2006)
2. Jensen, C., Farnham, S.D., Drucker, S.M., Kollock, P.: The effect of communication modality on cooperation in online environments. In: Proceedings of the SIGCHI Conference on Human Factors in Computing Systems, pp. 470–477 (2000)
3. Suznjevic, M., Dobrijevic, O., Matijasevic, M.: Hack, slash, and chat: a study of players' behavior and communication in MMORPGs. In: 2009 8th Annual Workshop on Network and Systems Support for Games (NetGames), pp. 1–6. IEEE (2009)
4. Chen, M.G.: Communication, coordination, and camaraderie in World of Warcraft. Games Cult. **4**, 47–73 (2009)
5. Smith, D.C.: Voice-to-text chat conversion for remote video game play (2010)
6. Most Popular Core PC Games | Global. https://newzoo.com/insights/rankings/top-20-core-pc-games/. Accessed 29 June 2018
7. Wuertz, J., Bateman, S., Tang, A.: Why players use pings and annotations in Dota 2. In: Proceedings of the 2017 CHI Conference on Human Factors in Computing Systems, pp. 1978–2018. ACM (2017)
8. Chipteck, Smart Ping. https://support.riotgames.com/hc/en-us/articles/201752974-Smart-Ping. Accessed 20 May 2018
9. Bordwell, D.: Narration in the Fiction Film. Routledge, Abingdon (2013)
10. Nevelsteen, K.J.L.: A Survey of Characteristic Engine Features for Technology-Sustained Pervasive Games. Springer, Berlin (2015). https://doi.org/10.1007/978-3-319-17632-1
11. Csikszentmihalyi, M.: Flow: The Psychology of Optimal Experience. HarperPerennial, New York (1990)
12. Genette, G.: Figures III, 286 p. Éd. Le Seuil, Paris (1972)
13. Allain, S., Szilas, N.: Exploration de la métalepse dans les" serious games" narratifs. Rev. des Sci. Tech. l'information la Commun. pour l'éducation la Form. **19** (2012)
14. Emote. https://hearthstone.gamepedia.com/Emote. Accessed 20 May 2018
15. Communication Wheel. http://overwatch.wikia.com/wiki/Communication_Wheel. Accessed 29 June 2018
16. Herring, S.C., Kutz, D.O., Paolillo, J.C., Zelenkauskaite, A.: Fast talking, fast shooting: text chat in an online first-person game. In: Proceedings of the 42nd Annual Hawaii International Conference on System Sciences, HICSS (2009)

Realtime Musical Composition System for Automatic Driving Vehicles

Yoichi Nagashima[(⊠)] [iD]

Shizuoka University of Art and Culture,
2-1-1 Chuo, Hamamatsu, Shizuoka, Japan
nagasm@suac.ac.jp

Abstract. Automatic driving vehicles (ADV) are drawing attention all over the world. ADV contains many realtime sensors. In the future, people (including the driver) will enjoy BGM without attention to ambient conditions, however, it will be much better than the BGM corresponding to the surrounding situation in real time - rather than being properly chosen from existing music. The author proposes an approach of a "realtime musical composition system for automatic driving vehicles" which generates music in real time without using existing music, so we are free from the copyright issue. The realtime composition system can arrange/modify its generating musical factors/elements with realtime parameters such as sensor information in real time, so it is the best solution for "music in ADV". This paper reports on the first prototype of realtime composition system for ADV - as collaborative research (2015–2017) with Toyota Central R&D Labs.

Keywords: Realtime composition · Automatic driving vehicle
Copyright free

1 Introduction

Automatic driving vehicles (ADV) are drawing attention all over the world. ADV contains many realtime sensors: (1) radar sensors and distance sensors for preventing collision, (2) video cameras for "drive recorders" and "monitoring blind spots", (3) GPS receiver, and (4) CAN (Controller Area Network) system with driving data - steering, brake, accelerator, speed, etc.

In the future, passengers in the car will enjoy BGM (BackGround Music) without attention to ambient conditions, however, it will be much better than the BGM corresponding to the surrounding situation in real time. For example, if we are in a car driving through a tunnel and the GPS knows that we will exit the tunnel and come out onto the coast, "BGM making us feel the beach" will be fantastic.

Here, we face a traditional problem, copyright matters. The author proposes an approach of using "realtime musical composition system for automatic driving vehicles" which generates music in real time. This is the same idea of "algorithmic musical composition" in the computer music field and it has a long history [1]. The realtime composition (algorithmic composition) system generates music in real time without using existing music, so we are free from copyright concerns. Also, the realtime

E. Clua et al. (Eds.): ICEC 2018, LNCS 11112, pp. 217–222, 2018.
https://doi.org/10.1007/978-3-319-99426-0_20

composition system can arrange/modify its generating musical factors/elements with realtime parameters such as sensor information in real time, so it seems to be the best solution for "music in ADV".

This paper reports the first prototype of realtime composition system for ADV in collaboration (2015–2017) with Toyota Central R&D Labs (TytLabs) [2]. Researchers of TytLabs contacted the author one day because they discovered a research report by the author (2005–2006) titled "FMC^3 (Free Music Clip for Creative Common)". This was a copyright-free music clip generation system for content creators (only in Japanese) [3].

At that time (2003–2004), "Flash movies" were explosively prevalent all over the world - satire, gags, art, etc. However the music part of these flash movies was "existing music" without copyright management, so they eventually disappeared from the internet. As a longtime composer and researcher in computer music the author worked on projects of "realtime composition" system for web content creators aimed without copyright invalidity. The basic policy of the system is the "importance of heuristics in music", so the output music has "4 measure loop music" with traditional/theoretical chord sequences and realtime musical transposition without "intro" nor "ending". The 55 types of chord sequence patterns are randomly selected, 3 types of music styles (8beat, 16beat, shuffle) [3]. This project with TytLabs inherited and expanded on these FMC^3's ideas.

2 Pre-test and Discussion

Before contacting the author, researchers of TytLabs had conducted experiments by themselves. For example, the output data of laser doppler sensors were assigned to musical sounds, then a piano melody was generated like a chime phrase. For example, the information from a video camera was converted to volume, so the sound expressed the brightness or complexity of the outdoors. However, they thought that was not music, but only sound realtime generated corresponding to the outside world. Then, they contacted the author, entered into a contract with the author's university and TytLabs and the collaborative research project began.

In the first year, one of young researcher's of TytLabs came to the author's lab once/twice per month and studied musical theory and cutting-edge computer music aesthetics/technology/theory, and we had some discussions about this challenging field. However, in the second year, the young researcher who studied music was suddenly transferred to another department, so TytLabs leader requested the author to develop a prototype of realtime composition system that substantially shifted from collaborative research to contract research.

We had a deep discussion about why the past experimental prototypes of TytLabs did not succeed. There was no musical construction - metrical structure, rhythm/beat and tonal structure. Although it had a scale corresponding to the output information from the sensor, it was a list of sounds, not a melody. As requested to develop new prototype, the author took a similar approach to FMC^3 that aimed at expanding musical heuristics. Finally we succeeded in design the rough system block diagram of realtime composition for BGM for automatic driving vehicles (Fig. 1).

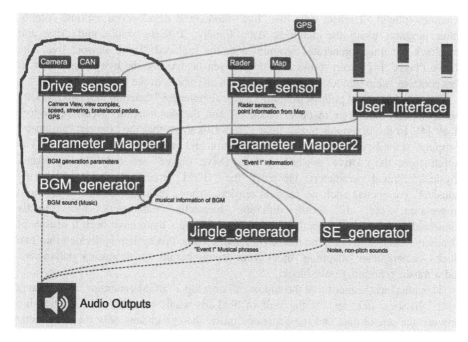

Fig. 1. System block diagram of the experimental prototype system (Color figure online)

3 System Description

The system of Fig. 1 has roughly two blocks. We call the left block "BGM block" and the right block "momentary event block". The latter is like TytLabs's prototype using doppler radar sensor and Map+GPS, which generates "momentary" sounds - musical (tonal) elements (Jingle generator) and noisy elements (SE generator). The former is an FMC[3]-like automatic composer using musical theory, know-how and heuristics with live camera and CAN data (driving, speed, etc.), and this block (red circled area) is reported on in this paper.

The important point is the connection from "BGM generator" to "Jingle Generator". This connection is the key of the total musical structure - metrical structure, rhythm/beat and tonal structure (chord, scale, tension). If the "Jingle Generator" works without this connection, the BGM and Jingle (small phrases) will collide and the music will be destroyed. The "BGM generator" sends the available chord/scale (information of tonality), so the total music is harmonized.

To develop and test collaboratively, the "BGM generator" was divided into three blocks, because the lab of the author (development) and TytLabs (testing) were distant from each other. The final prototype system will be mounted into a Toyota test car, but in the development process, the author could not get any "live" sensor data. So, the block "Drive sensor" was changed to a "Drive recorder" and a "Drive Player". At first, TytLabs staff drove the test car and recorded all sensor data into a movie file and a text data file using a "Drive recorder". Next, the author used a "Drive Player" which generates (plays) all sensor data like "live" mode, and developed a realtime composition program using the playback data. Finally, TytLabs staff could drive and test/check the music generator program with the replaced "Drive sensor" live. The "Drive Player" [4] screen shows considerable sensor data and the live camera view. It also contains "skip" buttons to jump to frames anywhere in the drive.

The next important point is dividing "musical generator" function into two blocks. - the upstream "Parameter mapper" block [5] and the downstream "BGM generator" block [4]. In the computer music field it is well-known that the concept "parameter mapping" is the key point in realtime composition and interactive performance [1]. The output from the "Drive sensor" or the "Drive player" are only driving-related physical/technical parameters. However, the "BGM generator" works with many "musical" parameters such as, musical tension, groove feeling, expectation of chord progression, etc. If these different hierarchy parameters are directly connected/transferred, the result will be a fatal failure - there have been a history of successive failures in compute music (in Japan). Thus, this system is divided into two blocks - a parameter "mapping" block from driving parameters to musical parameters, and a music generating only block.

This idea has the merit that the author can develop a "BGM generator" as separated from TytLabs's field test. If the staff of TytLabs wants to change the relationship between the sensor data and the generated music, he can change only the "Parameter mapper" block. Because the "BGM generator" is developed with pure musical theory/heuristics, to arrange/modify/change from the field request will perform badly in the project. Whole system was constructed on "Max7" [6] environment. The detail of the whole system (subpatches) are shown on the web [7].

4   Explanation of Musical Structure

This is the outline the musical structure of the realtime composition algorithm. There are four musical styles - called "8beat", "16beat", "ballad" and "shuffle" - these loop music styles are comfortable for all people. The tempo of BGM is fixed for each musical style, and never changes the while driving. The amateur will consider that if the car speeds up, the BGM will speed up (if the car slows down, the BGM will slow down), but this is very unnatural. The Volkswagen UK presented "Play the Road" system in 2013 [8], this system (not for ADV, but for the driver) also adopted the "constant tempo" concept, as the musical designer of "Play the Road" knew music well.

The BGM does not have an "intro" nor "ending", as the realtime composition works eternally. However, if the car stops at a traffic light the BGM volume decreases (diminuendo) and if the car starts again the BGM volume increases (crescendo) and sometimes the timbre of melody changes, or the musical style changes. The BGM is constructed as 4 measures loop music with a four chord sequence. From the deep musical consideration (space does not permit description here) [9], the 4-chord sequence is defined by 152 types (Fig. 2). For example, the chord sequence #63: [Bb7 - Eb7 - Dm7 - G7] (in the Key: C major) is constructed upon this theoretical reason: [Bb7 - Eb7] is "secondary dominant" sequence, [Eb7 - Dm7] is "sub(contrary) 5th" sequence, [Dm7 - G7] is "two-five" sequence, final [G7] (dominant 7th) wants to go to the tonal center root [C] ("dominant motion", all 4th chord of 152 types are G7 or Db7). 152 chord sequences have musical reasons backed by theory.

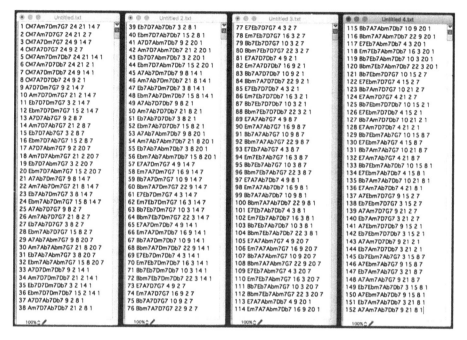

Fig. 2. 152 types of chord sequence in the prototype system

The BGM is constructed by "chord", "bass", "drums" and "melody" parts. In all loops, when the next chord sequence number is selected randomly at the final moment of the previous measure, all musical elements in the next four chords are combined by small-depth randomness (ad lib). For example, the "drums" part is generated corresponding to the musical style, and added with small variations randomly. The "bass" part is generated corresponding to the musical style and chord of each measure (1–4) using root/5th/7th notes of the chord with small variations of the bass phrases. The "chord" part is generated correspondingly to the musical style and chord of each measure, not played at once but played sequentially like "arpeggio" to prevent the sound from overlapping/distorting at the first moment. The "melody" (named for this project only, not a proper melody) part is generated corresponding to the musical style and chord of each measure, like an improvisational "ad lib" phrase with small variations of rhythm randomly. The available notes are - chord notes, available tension notes in JAZZ musical theory. The appearance probability of tension notes is changed randomly with the musical parameter "musical tension" from the "Parameter mapping" block.

5 Conclusions

After the development and test-run, we had a concluding discussion. The first objective, "musical level of the BGM" was successful, however, "music that makes us feel the surrounding situation" was not satisfactorily created yet. The reported prototype system only generated the BGM-part, so we could not combine the system with "Jingle Generator" and "SE Generator" which generates "momentary" sounds, this is one reason of the dissatisfaction. This means the "program music" in traditional classic music, and is opposite to loop music that we can listen to comfortably. The classical "program music" has exaggerated intros and endings, and the tempo changes by the way. Music is eternal and we faced the essence of music.

The musical know-how gained in this project is effectively utilized in the place of music education for designers. And, the author will demonstrate the system at short paper presentation session in ICEC2018. This first project has finished, and we hope to contribute to the fantastic future of ADV music.

Acknowledgments. The author would like to express his appreciation to Nobushige Fujieda, Yoshiyuki Akai and Hisanori Uda (Toyota Central R&D Labs. Human Science Research Area, Expand-Senses Program).

References

1. Roads, C.: The Computer Music Tutorial. MIT Press, Cambridge (1996)
2. Toyota Central R&D Labs. https://www.tytlabs.com/
3. Nagashima, Y.: FMC^3. http://nagasm.org/FMC3/
4. http://nagasm.org/ASL/Max7_5/fig4/003.jpg
5. http://nagasm.org/ASL/Max7_5/fig4/004.jpg
6. Max. https://cycling74.com/products/max
7. http://nagasm.org/ASL/Max7_5/fig4/005.jpg – http://nagasm.org/ASL/Max7_5/fig4/026.jpg
8. Play the Road. http://www.youtube.com/watch?v=3flwZ8OpXBY
9. Nagashima, Y.: Towards a "realtime musical composing" system for autonomous vehicle. http://nagasm.org/ASL/paper/SIGMUS201802.pdf. (in Japanese)

Circus Noel: A Case Study into Interaction and Interface Design for Cinematic VR

Mirjam Vosmeer[(✉)] and Alyea Sandovar[(✉)]

Play and Civic Media, Amsterdam University of Applied Sciences,
Amsterdam, Netherlands
m.s.vosmeer@hva.nl, alyea@tinthue.com

Abstract. In this paper, we present the case study *Circus Noel*, a VR tight rope walking act with which the use of movement in cinematic VR was explored. We use the notion of spatial presence as discussed by Ryan, and its potential to induce an 'illusion of non-mediation'. Seven users were interviewed about their experience. The results of this case study provide insight into the way a user's body. may be represented in cinematic VR by two moving feet, without disrupting the sense of presence.

1 Introduction

Cinematic VR – referring to VR that is recorded with a 360° camera as opposed to VR that is generated with software - provides the user with a new way to experience interactive entertainment in a cinematic setting. Users may experience a previously unknown feeling of being surrounded by the movie that they are watching. At times, users may even be able to interact with the setting and the characters of the storyline that they are involved in. However, to enable these interactions, producers are still exploring the possibilities of interface and interaction design for cinematic VR. A key concept that is influenced by the quality of these designs is *spatial presence* (Schubert et al. 2001). While the notion of presence has been discussed extensively long before cinematic VR was developed; the kind of presence that this particular medium offers seems to differ from presence experienced in other media (such as movies, books or video games). The sensation of being surrounded by a movie induces a sense of presence that is more physical than emotional. Ryan (2015) has identified this distinction as a 'technology-induced experience of being surrounded by data' on one hand and a 'narrative experience of being imaginatively captivated by a story world' on the other. However, the physical aspect and the possibility of gazing 360 degrees creates the expectation in users that they should be able to see their own body, use their hands to touch objects or even walk around in the VR environment.

This paper presents a VR project, *Circus Noel* (2017) in which the possibility of movement in cinematic VR was explored. We will discuss the results of a small explorative study. Through the study, we have aimed to collect some further insights into the ways that walking can be integrated in the interface design of a cinematic VR experience.

E. Clua et al. (Eds.): ICEC 2018, LNCS 11112, pp. 223–227, 2018.
https://doi.org/10.1007/978-3-319-99426-0_21

2 Presence, Movement and Interface Design

The term presence is usually defined as the 'sense of being there' (Ryan 2015). It is differentiated from immersion by defining immersion as an objective criterion that refers to the medium itself, in this case a VR movie, while presence is a characteristic of the user experience (Roth 2016). Lombard and Ditton (1997) have described presence as a 'perceptual illusion of non-mediation', indicating that in an ideal experience of presence, the user is no longer aware that there is technology involved. In a recent research study, it was also asserted that the two main dimensions of immersion are technical and narrative (Elmezeny et al. 2018), confirming the previously cited descriptions by Ryan (2015). The authors propose that the first category may be influenced by body centered interaction (Slater et al. 1994), while the second is more connected to narrative transportation (Phillips and McQuarrie 2010). The current study is concerned with this technical aspect of immersion, and how body centered interaction may influence the sense of presence, ultimately leading to situation in which the context of technology is indeed temporarily forgotten.

In order to not disrupt the immersive experience that VR offers and thus optimize the 'illusion of non-mediation', interface design for VR should be as non-intrusive as possible (Pakkanen et al. 2017). In his paper Gillies (2014) poses this question: *What is Movement Interaction in Virtual Reality for*? He proposes Slater's (2009) theory of Place Illusion, in which Slater states that the immersive quality of VR depends on the ability of the interactive design to reproduce the same sensorimotor contingencies as the real world. A number of examples exist that show that movement interaction appears to increase the sense of presence in VR (Steinicke et al. 2013). In a study conducted in Usoh et al. 1999 found that walking in a digital environment created a stronger sense of presence than using a joystick. Of course, due to limitations of 1999 technology, the visual aspects of virtual simulations have since improved dramatically. Norman (2010) has stated that in the case of walking in VR, the limitation may be the direction of movement. For instance, the user is only able to walk within the scope of the computers overview.

A recent study by Born and Masuch (2018) closely relates to our current study. Their goal was to understand whether virtual representation (having a body or hands in virtual reality) could increase the experience of presence. Their VR experience requires the user to walk a plank between two islands and conclude that spatial presence was significantly higher for users with full body representation. The authors recommend that in a further study to use a tracking technology that allows a rendering with the same refresh rate as the head movement device. Thus, the body movement would be just as smooth as the hand and head movements. In their analysis of VR interaction paradigms, Pakkanen et al. (2017) had their participants compare three ways of interacting within a 360° video including: hand gesturing, head orientation pointing and remote-control use. It was found that the use of hand gestures was significantly more problematic than the other two types of interaction. This result possibly reflects that hand gestures which are 'new' to the users, are therefore more difficult to learn and to remember than the use of a remote control or head pointing.

It is the point of our study to explore how smooth movement in cinematic VR can be embedded in the interface and interaction design for this particular medium and thus increase spatial presence, ultimately leading to an 'illusion of non-mediation' (Lombard and Ditton 1997).

3 Case Study: *Circus Noel*

Circus Noel was as a collaborative project between three students, an academic researcher, and two industry partners; a television broadcasting company (AVRO-TROS 2018) and a VR production company (WeMakeVR 2018). It is presented as a virtual tightrope walking act and was developed as a 'VR companion piece' to a Dutch national television series for children in December 2017. Although the installation was built with a children's audience in mind, the VR experience was also successfully presented to adult audiences at Dutch festivals and at demo sessions. The goal of the project was to create a cinematic VR experience that allowed the user to physically walk through a VR scene. The installation differs from previous studies, in that our goal was to develop a smooth walking simulation with filmed footage. The experience is somewhat similar to certain computer-generated VR experiences, such as *The Walk* by Sony (2016) or *Richies's Plank Experience,* by Toast (2016). The *Circus Noel* VR experience was filmed in an real-life circus with the 360° camera sliding high through the air along a rope. In the VR experience, users can imagine themselves as a tightrope walker who is performing a circus act while fellow circus performers watch and cheer as the mission is accomplished. Producing a VR walking experience filmed with a 360° camera, however, was a technical and conceptual challenge not often undertaken. While it falls beyond the scope of this paper to go into the technical details that made smooth movement in cinematic VR possible, it can be stated that the developers succeeded in creating the right viewing position of the moving user on the rope within 360-degree filmed footage. This includes the right position, to the correct time, and the circus performance in 'sync' with the current position of the user on the rope. To give the user a realistic sense of movement a physical installation was build that features a thin bar on the floor, between two platforms. Users wear a HTC Vive headset and HTC Vive trackers that are attached to both ankles.

In the introduction scene, a circus assistant hands the user a pair of shoes, after which the viewer is transported onto a platform high in the circus tent. Looking down, the user can see the circus ring, in which other circus performers are present, and a rope that stretches towards the other side of the tent. The two shoes that were handed over before are seen below, and as the movements of her feet are monitored by the trackers, she can now imagine herself walking high in the air on the rope; while in reality she is walking on a thin bar, just a few centimeters above the ground. The circus setting within the VR experience mimics a real-life experience, but the tightrope as it is shown beneath the user, the two platforms that she walks between and her 'own' feet are 3D rendered. To accomplish the blending of the two realities, the filmed material was projected within a sphere using Unity, after which the rope, platform and shoes were added.

4   Study Design and Methodology

A total of 7 adults between the ages of 20 and 39 were interviewed about their experience in this exploratory study. We opted for an open-ended qualitative reflexive approach in which the goal was to understand how to improve the immersive experience of 'walking in VR' with filmed footage. Our aim was to gather information on whether the user experience had felt real, how walking in VR felt to the user, and whether the visualization of just two feet was enough to create an immersive experience for users. We wished to understand whether having the two feet (with no body), felt to users like the entire body was involved in the movement.

5   Results and Discussion

To start from the perspective of entertainment, walking in cinematic VR appears to offer an enjoyable and exciting interactive entertainment experience. When users were asked to describe their experience with Circus Noel, their responses mostly seem to reflect Ryan's (2015) concept of 'technology-induced experience being surrounded by data'. For example, comments reflect the embodied experience: "I really felt like I was up there." Another comment described the feelings the experience induced: "I thought it was scary and exciting. When I was walking the bar, I felt like I would fall down because it seemed really high." In many cases, from the phrases that the users used to describe their rope-walking adventure, it can be deduced that they indeed experienced an 'illusion of non-mediation'. For instance, if someone is referring to 'my feet', or is expressing a fear of falling, or is indeed feeling difficulty to keep their balance, this indicates that they are no longer quite aware of the medium itself. When users were asked about their point of view and level of identification with their 'avatar feet', they responded that indeed the movement of their feet in the VR experience and their real feet did correspond one to one: "I felt that I really was walking."

As Born and Masuch (2018) also assert, the interface design that consists of creating movement by moving your feet – which can be seen as 'natural feet gestures' - instead of for instance having to use a controller or learn hand movements (Pakkanen et al. 2017); can help to optimize an immersive entertainment experience. In this particular situation, Norman's (2010) comments on the fact that walking in VR is limited by the scope of the computers overview is overruled – because of the realistic sense of height that the tightrope walking act provides, users hardly ever wish to step off of the rope. In Circus Noel, users do not seem to miss the representation of their whole body. This is an important result to cinematic VR. Though the industry is growing, it will remain challenging for some time to include a satisfactory image of a user's own body (primarily as a user's body cannot be filmed beforehand). The introductory scene in which the circus assistant hands over two shoes, that in the next scene symbolize the users own feet, may indeed have helped to create this illusion.

There were several limitations to this study, the most important being the limited number of participants and the rather non-systematic set-up of our investigations. However, we consider this first study an exploratory project, that will lead to a larger research study. We will systematically explore *spatial presence* and the ways it can be influenced by physical movement. Our next steps are to gather insights from a group of VR experts through a focus group format, in order to discuss theoretic notions of this specific experiment. Subsequently, we will explore the use of questionnaires such as the IPQ (igroup presence questionnaire) to eventually set up a larger experiment and further investigate isolated elements from this experience. Our goal is to eventually determine which elements influence the sense of presence and their role in the creation of an optimal 'illusion of non-mediation' within cinematic VR.

References

AVROTROS (2018). https://www.avrotros.nl

Born, F., Masuch, M.: Increasing presence in a mixed reality application by integrating a real time tracked full body representation. In: Cheok, A.D., Inami, M., Romão, T. (eds.) ACE 2017. LNCS, vol. 10714, pp. 46–60. Springer, Cham (2018). https://doi.org/10.1007/978-3-319-76270-8_4

Circus Noel: Amsterdam University of Applied Sciences (2017). https://www.youtube.com/watch?reload=9&v=DijFgtmfAho&feature=youtu.be

Elmezeny, A., Edenhofer, N., Wimmer, J.: Immersive storytelling in 360-degree videos: an analysis of interplay between narrative and technical immersion. J. Virtual Worlds Res. **11**(1) (2018)

Lombard, M., Ditton, T.: At the heart of it all: the concept of presence. J. Comput.-Med. Commun. (1997)

Norman, D.A.: Natural user interfaces are not natural. Interactions **17**(3), 6–10 (2010)

Pakkanen, T., et al.: Interaction with WebVR 360° video player: comparing three interaction paradigms. In: 2017 IEEE Virtual Reality (VR), 18 March 2017, pp. 279–280. IEEE (2017)

Phillips, B.J., McQuarrie, E.F.: Narrative and persuasion in fashion advertising. J. Consum. Res. **37**(3), 368–392 (2010)

Roth, C.: Experiencing interactive storytelling. Ph.D. thesis (2016). http://dare.ubvu.vu.nl/handle/1871/53840. Accessed June 2017

Ryan, M.-L.: Narrative as Virtual Reality 2: Revisiting Immersion and Interactivity in Literature and Electronic Media. JHU Press, Baltimore (2015)

Schubert, T., Friedmann, F., Regenbrecht, H.: The experience of presence: factor analytic insights. Presence Teleoperators Virtual Environ. **10**(3), 266–281 (2001)

Slater, M., Usoh, M., Steed, A.: Depth of presence in virtual environments. Presence: Teleoperators Virtual Environ. **3**(2), 130–144 (1994)

Slater, M.: Place illusion and plausibility can lead to realistic behaviour in immersive virtual environments. Philos. Trans. R. Soc. B: Biol. Sci. **364**(1535), 3549–3557 (2009)

Sony: The Walk (2016). http://www.sonypictures.com/movies/thewalk/vr/

Steinicke, F., Visell, Y., Campos, J., Lécuyer, A.: Human walking in virtual environments, pp. 199–219. Springer, New York (2013). https://doi.org/10.1007/978-1-4419-8432-6

Toast (2016). https://toast.gg/plank/

Usoh, M., et al.: Walking > walking-in-place > flying, in virtual environments. In: Proceedings of the 26th Annual Conference on Computer Graphics and Interactive Techniques, pp. 359–364. ACM Press/Addison-Wesley Publishing Co (1999)

WeMakeVR (2018). http://wemakevr.com/

Reorientation Method to Suppress Simulator Sickness in Home VR Contents Using HMD

Yuki Ueda[1(✉)], Kazuma Nagata[1(✉)], Soh Masuko[2], and Junichi Hoshino[1]

[1] Graduate School of Systems and Information Engineering, University of Tsukuba, 1-1-1, Tennodai, Tsukuba-shi, Ibaraki, Japan
{ueda,nagata}@entcomp.esys.tsukuba.ac.jp,
jhoshino@esys.tsukuba.ac.jp
[2] Rakuten, Inc., Rakuten Institute of Technology, Rakuten Crimson House, 1-14-1, Tamagawa, Setagaya-ku, Tokyo, Japan
so.masuko@rakuten.com

Abstract. While home-use HMD including Oculus Rift has been widely spread in the market today, simulator sickness mainly caused by difference between visual information and body sensation has taken up as a problem. Even though it has been proved that simulator sickness is reduced by reflecting actual physical movement to a VR space, many of approaches ever proposed had various restrictions and mechanisms easy to cause simulator sickness. In the current study, such an approach for moving within a VR space is proposed for home-use HMD that is less likely to cause simulator sickness.

Keywords: Virtual reality · Walking · Redirection · Simulator sickness

1 Introduction

With the spread of the home-use HMD today, various VR contents will be experienced at home. The applications of VR games, which gives high sense of immersion, to the open world games are expected. The latter enjoys growing popularity as the user can freely explore within a big stage. Also, if VR is utilized in online shopping, it would be possible to create the experiences that give the user the feeling of actually being in a shopping mall while at home, enjoying shopping within the VR showroom in which various information such as the user's preferences and the purchasing purpose, as well as the best-selling items and limited-time sales are reflected.

However, the foregoing experiences may cause the VR sickness accompanied by the symptoms such as fatigue, headache, eye strain, dizziness and nausea, because the user are made to be wandering about within the VR space for a long time. The discomfort with the VR sickness that makes long-hour VR experience painful for the user has also become an unavoidable obstacle for the developers delivering the content. While the cause of the VR sickness is still under discussion, one of the current leading theory is that it is mainly caused by the gap in somatic sensation between the real world and the VR space [1]. Although a lot of methods with which the user can move within the VR space by actually moving his body have been proposed so far aiming to

© IFIP International Federation for Information Processing 2018
Published by Springer Nature Switzerland AG 2018. All Rights Reserved
E. Clua et al. (Eds.): ICEC 2018, LNCS 11112, pp. 228–234, 2018.
https://doi.org/10.1007/978-3-319-99426-0_22

enhance the immersive sensation or suppress the aforementioned gap in the somatic sensation, many of them have not been suitable for the VR experience at home as they require a big space and large-scale equipment. When moving within VR space using the position estimation technology with the help of a redirection method such as Redirected Walking [2] and Reorientation Technique [3], you can actually travel within the VR space by walking without being required to prepare a big experience space and large-scale equipment. However, the mechanism of correcting the direction when arriving at the end of the walkable area might cause the gap in somatic sensation and induce the VR sickness.

Therefore, in this study, we are proposing the redirection method that may be used in VR experiences at home, which enables the correction of direction without causing the gap in somatic sensation to realize the traveling method within the VR space which suppresses the VR sickness.

2   Related Work

The studies on the trend and countermeasures for the VR sickness that occurs when using the military simulator have been conducted based on the data obtained from many subjects. Kennedy et al. has developed the Simulator Sickness Questionnaire (SSQ) that is a subjective evaluation method using questionnaires [4]. The SSQ is designed to make the subjects evaluate themselves for the items about 16 body abnormalities using four grades, which enables measurement of VR sickness level with 4 types of indices; SSQ-TS (Total Score), SSQ-N (Nausea), SSQ-O (Oculomotor) and SSQ-D (Disorientation). The SSQ is still used in many studies as an effective indicator to measure the level of VR sickness with various symptoms.

LaVopla Jr. examined the mechanism causing VR sickness from a medical point of view and discussed three hypotheses [1]. Among them, the sensory conflict theory that is a hypothesis that the VR sickness is caused by the difference in somatic sensation is said to be the most widely accepted hypothesis.

Prothero et al. demonstrated the fact that It is possible to alleviate the VR sickness by making the user perceive as if the foreground environment is moving around him rather than he is traveling within the VR space by placing the Independent Visual Background [5] that can be glanced over from him, within the VR space when he is viewing an immersive image in a static state.

Llorach et al. compared the level of VR sickness with SSQ, between the cases where a game controller is used and where the user is traveling within VR space by actually walking with HMD leveraging a location estimation technology. The result showed that the sickness was alleviated when the user was actually walking leveraging a location estimation technology. However, the real-world situations in which this method could be used were limited because as big space as the one to be used within the VR space must be prepared [6].

Razzaque et al. proposed Redirected Walking (RDW) that is a traveling method within VR space, which dan deliver the user the sense of keep walking by going back and forth within the limited experience space [2]. With RDW, the user must pass through the checkpoints set within the VR space while walking. This technique enables the user to move within a bigger VR space than the experience space by making a gap in the rotation angle between the VR space and the real world when the user is correcting the direction at checkpoints. However, the user cannot travel freely because it requires settings of checkpoints within the VR space, thus the walking path is limited by it. Also, in comparison to the traveling method using a controller, the same lever of VR sickness had been observed with this technique in the SSC score. This may be due to the gap in the rotation angle generated when correcting the direction.

3   System Overview

In this study, we have defined the following four requirements for the traveling method that suppresses the VR sickness caused by home-use VR contents and considered the basic methods to be used.

1. Traveling within the VR space is enabled by actually walking.
2. The big experience space is not required.
3. The traveling path is not limited.
4. The gap in somatic sensation is not created.

To meet the foregoing requirements, we decided to take the approach that gives the user the sense of continuously walking within a big VR space by walking back and forth within the small walkable area. In the traditional studies on such as Redirected Walking [2] and Reorientation Technique [3], the traveling path is limited and the rotation angle that is different from the actual angle is visually delivered not to make the user perceive they are correcting the direction. On the other hand, in this study we have tried to alleviate the VR sickness by intentionally make the user recognize he is correcting the direction and let him perceive the proper rotation angle.

For this purpose, first we decided to rotate the foreground, a view seen from the user within the VR space when he is correcting the direction, in line with the rotation by the user so that he can keep traveling after correcting the direction. However, only rotating the foreground in line with the user's rotation will end up making the user see the static scenery despite the fact that he is rotating in the real world. Thus, in this study, based on our insight to the independent visual landscape [5], we have positioned the visual background fixed to the world coordinate system within the VR space to be seen by the user as shown in Fig. 1. With this, the sensation as if the foreground is rotating in line with the user's body is generated when he is correcting the direction, and the redirection method that does not cause the gap in somatic sensation due to the rotation angle may be realized. Based on this idea, we have implemented a system.

The system is consisted of a PC to draw VR environment, HTC vive; a home-use HMD that has a position estimation function, a base station for HTC vive and a flat floor. The user is freely transitioning between the following two phases by manipulating the controller for HTC vive.

(1) **Traveling phase.** In the traveling phase, the user can freely walk within the walkable area. While the user is walking, the position and orientation of the HMD is tracked, and directly reflected in his view within the VR space. When the user

arrives at the edge of the walkable area, the grid indicating the walkable area is shown on the HMD, indicating it is impossible to go further ahead. To go further ahead within the VR space, the user must transition to the rotation phase by manipulating the controller to correct the direction.

(2) **Rotation phase.** The user corrects the direction under the state where the foreground and the user's position are fixed. This has been enabled by rotating the foreground around the HMD position coordinate at the center, by the range of the rotation around the yaw axis of the HMD. The visual background fixed to the world coordinate system is shown to the user to provide the visual information without any gap in rotation angle. This delivers the sensation to the user as if the foreground is rotating with his body when correcting the direction. This time, as in Fig. 2, the visual background was made to be always seen from the user during the rotation phase by rendering the Sphere positioned to cover the whole foreground like a wire frame. The Sphere was fixed to the world coordinate system independent of the user's movement and rotation. During the rotation phase, an arrow that indicates the user's rotation direction is shown on the controller. On completion of the direction correction, the user is transitioned to the traveling phase after being notified as in Fig. 3.

visual background fixed to the world coordinate system

Fig. 2. Visual background from user's view

rotating the foreground synchronized with user's rotation

Fig. 1. Fixed visual background

Fig. 3. Completion of the direction correction

4 Experiments

This time, in place of the rotation phase for the proposed system, we have prepared a model created based on the conventional method, which involves the redirection method that enables correction of direction by creating a gap in the rotation angle to compare the proposed method and the conventional redirection method.

For the evaluation experiment, we have used the PC built-in with NVIDIA GeForce GTX 970 4 GB as CPU to generate the VR space. As shown in Fig. 4, while experiencing the system, the subject was holding the controller to transition between the phases with his right hand and walking within the flat area of 3.0 m × 1.5 m. The subject was accompanied by an assistant to watch the cable not to be entangled with his body during the experiment.

We had 10 male subjects in their 20's participated in the experiment. They are divided into two groups of 5 people. Both groups experienced the proposed system and the conventional method model alternately with 30 min break in between, so that everyone is experimented with both redirection methods. For this experiment, the scene mimicking the VR showroom as shown in Fig. 5 below had been prepared. These subjects were given the task to walk through the path that had been explained beforehand to reach the goal point. The arrows to indicate the direction to walk toward were shown on the floors and shelves in the scene. The pathway walked through by the subjects is shown in Fig. 6. The total walking distance is about 50 m. The two redirection methods were compared in terms of the time to reach the goal, the time to correct the direction and the number of direction corrections, the SSQ [4] evaluation value right after the experiment and the contents of the hearing from the subjects.

The time to finish the task, the time to correct directions, the average number of direction corrections and the standard deviations for the subjects are shown in Table 1. With this experiment, it has been found that for the proposed system, the time to correct directions is 34% shorter and the time to complete the task is 21% shorter than the conventional method model. It is obvious that the difference of the time required to complete the task between two methods corresponds to the difference of the time taken to correct directions. As a result of the t-test that supports each element, significant differences have been shown for all of the time to complete ($t(9) = 2.716$, $p < .05$), the time to correct directions ($t(9) = 3.647$, $p < .01$) as well as the number of direction corrections ($t(9) = 2.358$, $p < .05$).

Also, the evaluation values on SSQ-TS (Total Score), SSQ-N (Nausea), SSQ-O (Oculomotor) and SSQ-D (Disorientation) are shown in Table 2 below. Furthermore, as a result of the non-parametric Wilcoxon signed-rank test for each evaluation value, the proposed system has shown a significantly low value on SSQ-D ($T = 1$, $p < .05$)

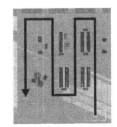

Fig. 4. Scene of experiments

Fig. 5. VR showroom setup

Fig. 6. Pathway walked through by the subjects

compared to the conventional method model. Although significant differences were not shown on other scores, there was a dominant trend for the better on the subjects participated in this experiment.

Table 1. Comparison of times

	Conventional method		Proposed method	
	Average	SD	Average	SD
Time to finish tasks*	298 s	58 s	236 s	37 s
Time to correct directions**	131 s	37 s	87 s	17 s
Average number of corrections*	31 times	4.1 times	27 times	3.5 times

(*...$p < .05$, **...$p < .01$)

Table 2. Comparison of SSQ score

	Conventional method		Proposed method	
	Average	SD	Average	SD
SSQ-TS	48.25	47.35	23.19	19.78
SSQ-N	33.39	40.31	14.31	14.93
SSQ-O	35.63	34.08	20.47	16.97
SSQ-D*	65.42	59.07	27.84	31.74

(*...$p < .05$)

The time to correct directions is shorter for the proposed system compared to the conventional method model. This is because while the conventional method model recommends the rotation direction with bigger rotation angle to minimize the gap in somatic sensation upon correction of direction, the proposed system recommends the direction that can complete correction of direction within the minimum time. The shorter time to correct directions helps suppressing sickness from the rotation. It also helps suppressing VR sickness due to the shortened total experience time.

The reason why a significant difference was shown in the number of direction corrections would be because the user lost sight of the planned path before the direction change and unable to systematically select the path as seen in the many opinions, which says, "turning around within the VR space made me forget which way I wanted to go after correcting the direction."

From the result of SSQ, it has been turned out that the proposed system had a significantly better result compared to the conventional method model as for the disorientation after the experience (indicated by SSQ-D). Based on this result as well as the fact found through the hearing that the majority of them had perceived the difference in rotation angle with the conventional method model and most of them had felt uncomfortable, we think that the proposed system could suppress the VR sickness from disorientation better than the traditional method. Also, the shorter time to correct directions in the proposed system compared to the conventional method may have been contributed to suppress the VR sickness. However, if the rotation direction with narrow rotation angle is recommended to shorten the time to correct directions in the conventional method model, the gap in somatic sensation would become very big, leading to the bigger difference in the disorientation score. Also, for other scores, while no significant differences were shown from the test, the proposed system showed lower scores for each SSQ index compared to the conventional method model. Thus, we think that the level of VR sickness was suppressed with the proposed system. Although there seems to be some differences in the average SSQ scores between these systems at a glance, no significant difference has been shown on the scores except for SSQ-D. This result may be caused by the short experience time and the light task, which ended up with light level of sickness for both methods. For this reason, we think significant difference may be observed between both systems in other evaluation values as well by imposing heavier task.

5   Conclusion

In this study, the redirection method that make the users perceive the correct rotation angle by showing them a static background upon change of direction had been proposed and its effectiveness has been revealed with the experiment. With this experiment, it is shown that the traveling method that can suppress VR sickness is enabled within the experience space prepared at home. However, the user must stop the main VR experience every time when changing the direction for both methods. Therefore, in terms of timeliness, these methods may be inferior to other traveling method. As such, these methods would be preferable to be used in the games with less action element, or for the shopping experiences in the VR showroom dealing with the items that is not for sale or limited.

References

1. LaViola Jr., J.: A discussion of cybersickness in virtual environments. ACM SIGCHI Bull. **32** (1), 47–56 (2000)
2. Razzaque, S., Kohn, Z., Whitton, M.: Redirected walking. In: EuroGraphics 2001 (2001)
3. Peck, T., Whitton, M., Fuchs, H.: Evaluation of reorientation techniques for walking in large virtual environments. In: 2008 Virtual Reality Conference, VR 2008. IEEE (2008)
4. Kennedy, R.S., Lane, N.E., Lilienthal, M.G.: Simulator sickness questionnaire: an enhanced method for quantifying simulator sickness. Int. J. Aviat. Psychol. **3**(3), 203–220 (1993)
5. Prothero, J.D., Draper, M.H., Furness, T.A., Parker, D.E., Wells, M.J.: The use of an independent visual background to reduce simulator side-effects. Aviat. Space Environ. Med. **70**(3), 135–187 (1999)
6. Llorach, G., Evans, A., Blat, J.: Simulator sickness and presence using HMDs: comparing use of a game controller and a position estimation system. In: Proceedings of the 20th ACM Symposium on Virtual Reality Software and Technology, VRST 2014, pp. 137–140 (2014)

A.R.M. - Augmented Reality Muscularity

Dirk J. J. Sweere, Martin P. Hughes, Martijn G. van Laar,
and Lisa E. Rombout[✉]

Tilburg University, Warandelaan 2, 5037 AB Tilburg, Netherlands
l.e.rombout@uvt.nl

Abstract. The theory of embodied cognition states that cognition is influenced by the body we inhabit. Research on embodiment illusions has confirmed that our perceived body affects our behavior and disposition. Virtual and augmented reality applications make the experience of ownership over a different body more accessible, but these virtual bodies are seldom fully utilized. Instead, the focus often lies on the scenario or the virtual surroundings. As an initial exploration of the effectiveness of embodiment illusions within the domain of exergaming, we embodied participants with a virtual muscular arm. Results show that weight perception is not directly affected by this manipulation. However, we theorize that body alterations like this might affect players' motivation.

Keywords: Augmented reality · Virtual body · Embodiment
Experience design · Exergaming · Serious gaming · Embodied cognition

1 Introduction

The field of embodied cognition encompasses several theories on how cognitive processes are rooted in the body [1]. Generally, it states that our mental constructs and task performance are influenced by the body we inhabit. Experience design in serious games is not commonly focused on the virtual body and its properties. Embodiment through virtual or augmented reality (VAR) might provide an additional psychological mechanism in creating effective gaming solutions.

1.1 Experience Design in Exergaming

Within serious games in general and exergaming in particular, the experience design often focuses on the narrative, the virtual surroundings, and the objects presented in the game. If a virtual body is present, it is often designed to either fit the task or to be a generic stand-in for the player. Merely the presence of a virtual body can already affect the player, for instance by reducing body-image anxiety [2], increasing the intention to engage in exergaming in the future [3], and heightening enjoyment of the game [4]. More enjoyable exergames can lead to longer periods of interaction, leading to positive health benefits [4].

E. Clua et al. (Eds.): ICEC 2018, LNCS 11112, pp. 235–240, 2018.
https://doi.org/10.1007/978-3-319-99426-0_23

However, altering the virtual body in specific ways could potentially lead to enhanced effectiveness of the experience. For example, differences in an avatars' body size affects motivation and physical activity [5,6]. Game performance can be improved by designing a body that is strongly associated with excellence on the task in the game [7,8]. Within exergames, one area strongly associated with stereotypical body-types is weight-lifting. Weight perception has been shown to be at least partly a top-down process [9]. For example, a dumbbell that has a bright color overlay induces less fatigue than a dark color [10]. Therefore, embodying a muscular virtual body could potentially also affect weight perception.

1.2 Embodiment Illusions

Embodiment can be defined as 'the ensemble of sensations that arise in conjunction with being inside of, having, and controlling a body' [11]. The rubber hand illusion [12] shows that our sensation of embodiment is flexible and that we can feel embodied in artificial body parts, even if their location is slightly off. The illusion can be similarly evoked using VAR techniques [13], and show that multi-sensory input can override explicit knowledge of the body-image [14–16].

VAR technologies hold enormous potential in the domain of serious games, because of the tendency users have of treating the VAR environment as real, described as 'presence'. Presence correlates positively with task performance in virtual environments [17]. Induced embodiment is related to presence and can be an important contributor to the effectiveness of VAR experiences [18,19].

However, the effects of embodiment illusions go further than that. Several studies show that behavioral tendencies—both in-game [7] and afterwards [20]—can be altered by placing the user in a certain type of body, making use of implicit associations the user has with that body-type. Similarly, these illusions can affect implicit biases [21] and attitudes [22]. Embodiment illusions thus allow us to alter a VAR experience in several meaningful ways.

The current study was designed to take a first look at the effects of an embodiment illusion with a muscular virtual arm through augmented reality. An AR application, rather than a VR one, has the potential to only change the elements of interest, and could safely be used in a gym during a real exercise [23]. We hypothesized that embodiment with a muscular arm would affect participants' weight perception in such a way that objects seem to weight less.

2 Pilot Study

A small scale pilot study was conducted to test the setup and the virtual arm. 10 participants (7 female, 3 male) were randomly divided in a control group ($n = 5$) and an experimental group ($n = 5$). The participants' right arm was blocked from direct view. The control group saw their real arm on a screen, whereas the experimental group saw an overlay of a virtual arm. This 3D poly-model was created with the program MakeHuman and Blender 3D modeling software. It was attached to a marker using the Vuforia plug-in for Unity. Participants were instructed to close their eyes before a 150 g apple was placed in the palm of their hand. For the experimental group, the virtual overlay changed to include a virtual apple. Both groups then looked at the screen and estimated the apples' weight. The experimental group lastly answered 3 embodiment questions, one on perceived strength, and one on naturalness, on a 7-point Likert scale [17].

The mean estimated weight of the apple was 200 g (SD = 61.24) in the control group, and 129 g (SD = 83.40) in the experimental group. Based on the questionnaire, the embodiment (M = 3.6, SD = 1.67) and naturalness (M = 3.8, SD = 1.1) seem to be comparable with the literature, but there was a lower score on perceived strength (M = 2.2, SD = .84). This might indicate that any effects are likely to be subconscious. The participants generally found it difficult to estimate the weight of the apple, reporting that they mainly used their knowledge of the weight of apples to make their guess. We concluded therefore that, although the virtual arm was sufficient to induce embodiment, the object to be weighted needed to be unknown to the participants.

3 Methods Main Study

Fig. 1. The AR condition

30 undergraduate students (17 female, 13 male), recruited at Tilburg University, were randomly divided in a control group (n = 15) and an experimental group (n = 15).

Participants were seated in front of the full screen application running on a computer screen, with their right arm on the other side of a barrier. For the experimental group, the marker was attached to their lower arm using a stretch band. No changes were made to the model of the virtual arm. The camera was positioned just above the right shoulder (see Fig. 1).

Participants made a few movements with their arm (side-to-side and up and down), and were then asked to close their eyes. A glass paperweight (309 g) was placed in the participant's hand. A second video camera filmed their arm from the side to measure the arm drop, as a measurement of unconscious weight estimation. With their eyes still closed, participants were asked to estimate the weight of the object and for how long they believed they could hold it (added as a potentially more intuitive weight estimation). Afterwards the circumference of their arm was measured directly below the elbow, to control for how much the virtual arm diverged from their real arm. Lastly, the participants in the experimental group were asked to complete an extended embodiment questionnaire (8 items, 7 point Likert scale) [12].

4 Results

A Shapiro-Wilk test showed that for both conditions the estimated holding time did not follow a normal distribution (Control: M = 8.87, SD = 8.06, Virtual Arm:

M = 10.93, SD = 15.62). Therefore the non-parametric Mann-Whitney test for independent samples was used, showing no significant difference between conditions (p = .85).

The arm drop was measured from video by two independent observers. 2 participants were excluded due to their hand touching the desk during the drop. Both arm drop (C: M = 2.95, SD = .88, VA: M = 2.68, SD = 1.09) and weight estimation (C: M = 873.33, SD = 686.83, VA: M = 530.00, SD = 301.66) had a normal distribution. An independent samples t-test showed no significant differences of weight estimation (p = .09) and arm drop (p > .1) between conditions.

An ANOVA for estimated holding time with condition and gender as between-subjects factors when controlling for arm circumference showed no significant main effects for both condition and gender. However, a significant disordinal interaction effect between condition and gender on estimated holding time was found (F(1, 25) = 7.52, p = .01, η^2 = .23). Analysis of variance showed no significant effect of condition and gender on both weight estimation and arm drop when controlling for arm circumference.

There was a significant correlation between arm drop and holding time (r(28) = .44, p = .02). The three weight estimation measurements and the embodiment questionnaire score (M = 38.33, SD = 4.67) were not correlated.

5   Discussion

There were no significant differences between the two conditions for any of the weight perception measurements, and for the augmented condition none of the weight perception measurements were correlated with the embodiment questionnaire scores. Embodiment with a muscular virtual arm does not seem to influence participants' perceived or actual ability to hold and lift objects, and does therefore probably not influence weight estimation.

The interaction effect of condition and gender on estimated holding time could suggest that the virtual muscular arm was experienced as more compatible with male body-types, resulting in higher embodiment for men. However, a direct comparison of mean embodiment scores showed no significant difference. Alternatively, the extremely muscular arm could have induced stereotype threat. This type of priming can cause gender conforming behavior [24,25].

Since the arm drop is a physical reaction, unaffected by verbal cognition and knowledge about objects, its correlation with reported maximum holding time might indicate that an indirect estimation of weight is a more accurate measure for weight perception than a direct estimate.

A few limitations of this study have to be considered. Handedness of the participants was not recorded. All experiments were done using the right arm, so the sense of embodiment of left-handed participants may have been impacted. Additionally, measurements of the biceps might have been more informative than lower-arm circumference, since that muscle is used for lifting the forearm.

Although this study did not find a difference in weight perception using a virtual muscular arm, similar embodiment illusions might have different effects.

VAR exercising applications have been shown to mainly affect enjoyment, motivation, and attitude [26, 27], while psychological advantages are also enhanced by exercising in VR [28]. Exergaming is rated as more enjoyable and effective if the game focuses on entertainment [29]. Therefore, it is possible that the main effects of embodiment are also more attitude-based. Future studies could therefore focus more on the effects of embodiment illusions on motivation and enjoyment.

Embodiment illusions provide other interesting possibilities within exergames. For example, the virtual body could be used as a more intuitive feedback provider, where the body changes shape if the user engages with the experience. Feedback positively influences adherence to exercise [26], but is usually provided abstractly in the virtual environment instead of on the virtual body. Furthermore, the virtual body could be personalized in such a way that it provides the individual user with the benefits they need most. Entertainment technologies such as virtual and augmented reality hold the potential for the creation of personalized experiences, and the virtual body is an integral part of that.

References

1. Wilson, M.: Six views of embodied cognition. Psychon. Bull. Rev. **9**(4), 625–636 (2002)
2. Song, H., Kim, J., Lee, K.M.: Virtual vs. real body in exergames: reducing social physique anxiety in exercise experiences. Comput. Hum. Behav. **36**, 282–285 (2014)
3. Kim, S.Y.S., Prestopnik, N., Biocca, F.A.: Body in the interactive game: how interface embodiment affects physical activity and health behavior change. Comput. Hum. Behav. **36**, 376–384 (2014)
4. Mellecker, R., Lyons, E.J., Baranowski, T.: Disentangling fun and enjoyment in exergames using an expanded design, play, experience framework: a narrative review. Games Health: Res. Dev. Clin. Appl. **2**(3), 142–149 (2013)
5. Peña, J., Khan, S., Alexopoulos, C.: I am what I see: how avatar and opponent agent body size affects physical activity among men playing exergames. J. Comput.-Med. Commun. **21**(3), 195–209 (2016)
6. Li, B.J., Lwin, M.O., Jung, Y.: Wii, myself, and size: the influence of proteus effect and stereotype threat on overweight children's exercise motivation and behavior in exergames. Games Health: Res. Dev. Clin. Appl. **3**(1), 40–48 (2014)
7. Kilteni, K., Bergstrom, I., Slater, M.: Drumming in immersive virtual reality: the body shapes the way we play. IEEE Trans. Vis. Comput. Graph. **19**(4), 597–605 (2013)
8. Osimo, S.A., Pizarro, R., Spanlang, B., Slater, M.: Conversations between self and self as Sigmund Freud a virtual body ownership paradigm for self counselling. Sci. Rep. **5**, 13899 (2015)
9. Ellis, R.R., Lederman, S.J.: The golf-ball illusion: evidence for top-down processing in weight perception. Perception **27**(2), 193–201 (1998). PMID: 9709451
10. Ban, Y., et al.: Augmented endurance: controlling fatigue while handling objects by affecting weight perception using augmented reality. In: Proceedings of the SIGCHI Conference on Human Factors in Computing Systems, CHI 2013, pp. 69–78. ACM, New York (2013)

11. Kilteni, K., Groten, R., Slater, M.: The sense of embodiment in virtual reality. Presence: Teleoperators Virtual Environ. **21**(4), 373–387 (2012)

12. Botvinick, M., Cohen, J.: Rubber hands feeltouch that eyes see. Nature **391**(6669), 756 (1998)

13. IJsselsteijn, W.A., de Kort, Y.A.W., Haans, A.: Is this my hand I see before me? The rubber hand illusion in reality, virtual reality, and mixed reality. Presence: Teleoperators Virtual Environ. **15**(4), 455–464 (2006)

14. Blanke, O., Metzinger, T.: Full-body illusions and minimal phenomenal selfhood. Trends Cogn. Sci. **13**(1), 7–13 (2009)

15. Slater, M., Spanlang, B., Sanchez-Vives, M.V., Blanke, O.: First person experience of body transfer in virtual reality. PLoS One **5**(5), e10564 (2010)

16. Lenggenhager, B., Tadi, T., Metzinger, T., Blanke, O.: Video ergo sum: manipulating bodily self-consciousness. Science **317**(5841), 1096–1099 (2007)

17. Schuemie, M.J., Van Der Straaten, P., Krijn, M., Van Der Mast, C.A.: Research on presence in virtual reality: a survey. CyberPsychology Behav. **4**(2), 183–201 (2001)

18. Biocca, F.: The Cyborg's dilemma: progressive embodiment in virtual environments. J. Comput.-med. Commun. **3**(2), JCMC324 (1997)

19. Tamborini, R., Skalski, P.: The role of presence in the experience of electronic games. In: Playing Video Games: Motives, Responses, and Consequences, pp. 225–240 (2006)

20. Rosenberg, R.S., Baughman, S.L., Bailenson, J.N.: Virtual superheroes: using superpowers in virtual reality to encourage prosocial behavior. PLoS One **8**(1), e55003 (2013)

21. Peck, T.C., Seinfeld, S., Aglioti, S.M., Slater, M.: Putting yourself in the skin of a black avatar reduces implicit racial bias. Conscious. Cogn. **22**(3), 779–787 (2013)

22. Banakou, D., Groten, R., Slater, M.: Illusory ownership of a virtual child body causes overestimation of object sizes and implicit attitude changes. Proc. Natl. Acad. Sci. **110**(31), 12846–12851 (2013)

23. Riva, G., Baños, R.M., Botella, C., Mantovani, F., Gaggioli, A.: Transforming experience: the potential of augmented reality and virtual reality for enhancing personal and clinical change. Front. Psychiatry **7**, 164 (2016)

24. Spencer, S.J., Steele, C.M., Quinn, D.M.: Stereotype threat and women's math performance. J. Exp. Soc. Psychol. **35**(1), 4–28 (1999)

25. Nguyen, H.H.D., Ryan, A.M.: Does stereotype threat affect test performance of minorities and women? A meta-analysis of experimental evidence. J. Appl. Psychol. **93**(6), 1314 (2008)

26. Annesi, J.J.: Effects of computer feedback on adherence to exercise. Percept. Mot. Skills **87**(2), 723–730 (1998). PMID: 9842630

27. Daniel, R., Ewald, M., Maiano, C.: Virtual reality and exercise: behavioral and psychological effects of visual feedback. Annu. Rev. Cybertherapy Telemed. **2011**, 99 (2011)

28. Plante, T.G., Aldridge, A., Su, D., Bogdan, R., Belo, M., Kahn, K.: Does virtual reality enhance the management of stress when paired with exercise? An exploratory study. Int. J. Stress Manag. **10**(3), 203 (2003)

29. Lyons, E.J., Tate, D.F., Komoski, S.E., Carr, P.M., Ward, D.S.: Novel approaches to obesity prevention: effects of game enjoyment and game type on energy expenditure in active video games. J. Diabetes Sci. Technol. **6**(4), 839–848 (2012). PMID: 22920810

Virtual Reality as e-Mental Health to Support Starting with Mindfulness-Based Cognitive Therapy

Koen H. B. Damen and Erik D. van der Spek[✉]

Department of Industrial Design, Eindhoven University of Technology,
Eindhoven, The Netherlands
k.h.b.damen@student.tue.nl, e.d.vanderspek@tue.nl

Abstract. Mindfulness-based cognitive therapy (MBCT) is used in mental health therapy but requires effort by the patient. This paper describes a preliminary design exploration of Open-MindEd, a Virtual Reality (VR) application specifically designed to support starting with MBCT. In collaboration with a mental health institute, two prospective users from the target group gave longitudinal input for the design, leading to the formulation of aspects how a VR application could serve as a tool to support people starting with mindfulness. Subsequently, a single-blind experiment (N = 30) was performed to evaluate whether Open-MindEd could stimulate starting with MBCT. No significant positive effects were found. Despite several limitations, this paper shows some potential design considerations of VR as e-mental health to support MBCT.

Keywords: Virtual Reality · e-Mental health
Mindfulness-based cognitive therapy · Transtheoretical Model

1 Introduction

According to the World Health Organization, around 20% of adolescents in the world suffer from mental health disorders [18] with the most up to date inventory showing similar numbers for the Netherlands [7], where this study was performed. To combat rising costs, mental health organizations such as the GGZ (Dutch Association of Mental Health and Addiction Care), are exploring the possibilities of using e-mental health [6] for cognitive behavior therapy

Many e-mental health applications are based on cognitive behavior therapy [17]. A relatively novel form of cognitive behavior therapy is mindfulness-based cognitive therapy based on the work of Segal, Williams and Teasdale published in 2002 [16]. Mindfulness is *"the awareness that emerges through paying attention on purpose, in the present moment, and nonjudgmentally to the unfolding of experience moment by moment"* [9]. There are two types of mindfulness programs: mindfulness-based stress reduction (MBSR) [10] and mindfulness-based cognitive therapy (MBCT) [16]. At the GGZ, MBSR is an eight-week group program that uses mindfulness meditation to reduce suffering associated with (chronic) physical psychosomatic and psychiatric

E. Clua et al. (Eds.): ICEC 2018, LNCS 11112, pp. 241–247, 2018.
https://doi.org/10.1007/978-3-319-99426-0_24

disorders [4]. MBCT is a manualized intervention based on the MBSR program. It incorporates elements of cognitive therapy that focus on detaching or decentering the view of one's thoughts. It is designed to prevent recidivating depression [1].

In practice, e-mental health for mindfulness is currently limited to online instructions for relaxation exercises and explanation of homework assignments [17]. However, homework assignments require effort by the patient, for cognitive therapy arguably even more so than stress reduction exercises, and failure by the patient to initiate this effort can thus harm the efficacy of the therapy. Therefore, new low-cost technologies are sought that can stimulate both starting with and sticking to therapy from home [17]. After a discussion with the GGZ, it was decided that Virtual Reality (VR) could be a possible avenue here, as it is relatively novel and can be used for persuasion [3].

1.1   VR as a Tool to Stimulate Uptake of Mindfulness Based Cognitive Therapy

VR could be useful to stimulate self-management of MBCT from an ecological as well as a content perspective. First, it is hypothesized that people will be more compliant to start doing VR homework than currently due to the novelty effect of VR. While this would not lead to lasting change, for the setup of getting current patients to begin mindfulness training, we contend it is a viable effect. Subsequently, wearing a VR headset, the patient is unable to look away and so cannot get distracted by other stimuli.

Furthermore, a VR exercise system could increase intrinsic motivation for executing mindfulness exercises by (1) enabling users to "unlock" new exercises (stimulating competence [5]), and (2) providing the possibility to choose how long, how often and when to execute exercises, and which exercises to execute (stimulating autonomy [5]).

As we are primarily interested in improving the uptake of self-managed MBCT, the Transtheoretical Model (TTM) can be used to describe the moment that is most relevant for an intervention. The TTM lists stages of change to integrate processes and principles of various behavior change theories [14]. It consists of six stages of change: precontemplation, contemplation, preparation, action, maintenance, and termination. The steps between precontemplation and action best describe starting with a therapy.

Prochaska and Diclemente [13] found that the sample item "*I tell myself I am able to quit smoking if I want to*" is the best representor of self-liberation (making a firm commitment to change). Translating this to our research, "*I tell myself I am able to start with mindfulness if I want to*" best describes a commitment to behavior change. Therefore, the questionnaires used in the studies will stay close to this template.

1.2   Related Work

A number of works have already examined VR for mindfulness, showing positive restorative results. VR mindfulness stress reduction exercises can reduce perceived pain for chronic patients [8], elicit deeper relaxation [11], reduce state anxiety in children [15], reduce urges of self-harm [12], and reduce the amount of complicated grief in grieving patients [2]. While evidence for the potential merit of VR stress reduction exercises for clinical settings is therefore rising, to the best of our knowledge the potential of VR to improve the uptake of mindfulness-based cognitive training, as well as its potential for self-management in home settings, has so far not been scrutinized.

2   Open-MindEd

In order to explore the design space and whether MBCT uptake for home users could be stimulated by VR in the context of therapy, *Open-MindEd* was developed. It consists of three different mindfulness attention exercises, co-designed with two participants currently undergoing MBCT and based on expert meetings with a therapist. In the co-design sessions, the participants among others said that they appreciated a feeling of safety in the environment while performing mindfulness exercises, and that VR could help with visualizing objects and environments. The exercises can be seen in Fig. 1. One is a passive animation (no user interaction), where the patient had to focus on a sprout blooming into a flower. Users can set the time for the flower to bloom and thereby train shorter or longer-term attention. Another exercise is set in a forest and allows you to move in the direction that you are looking to (minimal interaction). It was designed to connect to the mindfulness experience of 'remembering to be', or being present in the environment. Lastly, a physics-based puzzle of placing an assortment of stones in the correct order on top of each other was developed (interaction with game mechanics); as this is a task that takes some effort to get right, it signified dealing with obstacles.

Fig. 1. Three exercises: a walk through a forest (minimal interaction), placing stones on top of each other (interactive with game mechanics), watching a flower grow (passive).

3   Case Study on the Design and Perceived Value

With the help of a mindfulness trainer, a group of eight who just started with an eight-week MBCT-training (i.e. who were in the preparation stage of the TTM) were approached for a longitudinal case study. After being given the informed consent form a week in advance, two people volunteered; P1: F, 37, with persistent burn-out and anxiety feelings; P2: M, 24, mild social phobia. They were given a Galaxy S6 or S8 with *Open-MindEd* pre-installed, one Samsung Gear VR and a manual. Exercises were handed out in week 2 (nature walk), week 3 (stone stacking) and week 4 (focus on flower), with a subsequent semi-structured interview the week after each exercise. The interviews were audio recorded, transcribed and thematically analyzed according to the method of Zürn et al. [19]. The interviews gave some useful insights into the design. However, since only two persons participated they should be treated as anecdotal and in lieu of space constraints, we will only highlight some of the insights. A more detailed analysis is available upon request to the authors.

Exercise 1: The Virtual Forest
P1: *"Because of that combination of the three sounds [wind, chirping birds, and water], you really think like: 'I am in the forest'."* P2 said: *"Immersion, the fact that you are really submerged into [the environment], also with your thoughts, that works really well."* An advantage of this exercise is that *"this makes it [mindfulness] quite tangible in my opinion"* (P2). P1 said that *"thanks to those goggles you are much more occupied with: 'What is happening now? What is happening at this moment?' It is almost literally that you are wearing blinkers."*

Exercise 2: Stacking Stones
P1 found the touchpad controls frustrating, but regarded this as a good mindfulness exercise, as *"you are quite focused on the here-and-now, because you are purely focusing on those stones"*. P2 really liked this exercise but he found it too easy as he was done quickly. That is why he suggested *"when you have finished [stacking] it, that you immediately offer a new one."*

Exercise 3: The Virtual Flower
The exercise was not really clear to P1. She thought that *"it took quite long before something happened"*. However, when the leaves appeared on the stem *"you suddenly get intrigued like: 'How is it going to look like?'"* Therefore, P1 felt rewarded for waiting: *"You are indeed rewarded for waiting for so long"*. P2 conversely found it difficult to focus: *"my thoughts wandered off quite a lot"*. However, he managed to return his thoughts, *"especially near the end when there was something to see"*. P1 believed that for *"people who have real problems with executing breathing exercises, this might be a real good one"*. This exercise might also be very appropriate for people who have a lot of (ruminating) thoughts going on, according to P1. A disadvantage of this exercise would be that *"it might be a visual meditation, but there might be not enough happening"* (P2).

General Remarks
P1 liked that there were different exercises as it allows the user to try them all out and one can decide for him/herself what works best. Also, P1 liked *"that you have something that you can grab and that centralizes you for a moment"*. However, she does *"not know if I would immediately use VR goggles, because it also shuts you off quite drastically"*. According to P2, the reason *"why this works really well with mindfulness, in my opinion, is because you can go to another environment in no-time. That is why [you can] leave your thoughts behind for an instance and return to them later."*

Both participants mentioned they would have liked to continue using the VR application for the training and, with some usability improvements, after as well.

4 Experiment on the Persuasive Potential of VR Mindfulness

A small-scale experiment was performed to evaluate if *Open-MindEd* makes starting with executing mindfulness exercises more appealing for people without experience with mindfulness. As not enough people with similar mental health issues could be found for sufficient power, we chose to measure the effect on a general student population.

Participants

The participants were students from Eindhoven University of Technology (TU/e) with little to no experience with respect to mindfulness. N = 30 Participants were randomized evenly in an experiment group (10 female, mean age 21.3, SD 1.8), and a control group (7 female, mean age 21.1, SD 1.5). Familiarity with mindfulness and VR were not significantly different between the groups [resp. $F(1,28) < 1$ and $F(1,28) = 2.63, p = .12$].

Procedure

Students were incentivized by having a chance of winning 3x10 euros. After obtaining informed consent, participants were asked to rate the pre-intervention statements. Then the control group would execute a regular breathing exercise for ten minutes. The experiment group would execute the passive virtual flower exercise of *Open-MindEd* (see Sect. 2) for ten minutes using a Samsung Gear VR with a Samsung Galaxy S6. This exercise was chosen because it did not introduce interactivity as an additional variable, therefore only comparing the VR modality of the exercise to that of a control group.

Measurements

Participants were asked to rate eight statements pre-intervention and twelve statements post-intervention about their ability and desire to start with mindfulness. Post-intervention, we also queried their opinion on the use of VR for mindfulness exercises. All statements were 7-point Likert scale items, with 1 being "strongly disagree", 4 being "neutral" and 7 being "strongly agree".

4.1 Results

Table 1 shows the pre- and post-intervention statement scores. ANCOVAs with the pre-intervention scores as covariates show no significant effect of the condition on post-intervention scores [I would like to start with mindfulness: $F(1, 27) < 1$; I am open to execute mindfulness exercises: $F(1, 27) < 1$; I am able to start with mindfulness: $F(1, 27) = 1.22, p = .28$].

There was also no effect of the condition on how difficult the students found it to keep their thoughts focused $F(1, 28) = 3.45, p = .07$, or how boring they found the exercises $F(1, 28) = 1.76, p = .20$. We also measured subjective stress levels. All stress levels dropped but here too an ANCOVA with prior stress as covariate showed no significant effect of condition on post intervention stress levels $F(1, 27) < 1$.

Table 1. Pre- and post-intervention statement scores.

Statement	Control group (M, SD)		VR group (M, SD)	
	Pre	Post	Pre	Post
I would like to start with mindfulness	4.50 (1.38)	4.65 (1.44)	4.93 (0.94)	5.10 (1.04)
I am open to execute mindfulness meditation exercises	5.63 (0.97)	5.73 (.80)	5.73 (0.86)	5.47 (.92)
I am able to start with mindfulness if I want to	5.25 (1.56)	5.83 (1.08)	5.10 (1.24)	5.47 (.72)

5 Conclusion

From the experiment, no proof was found that the VR exercises persuaded participants to go from the precontemplation to the contemplation phase of MBCT exercises. Therefore, any novelty effect from the VR modality to motivate picking up mindfulness exercises should be considered negligible. If VR would make focusing thoughts easier and less boring, we also could not find evidence for that in our 10-min experience. At the same time, it should be noted that the Flower focusing exercise used in the experiment was a passive VR experience, did not have competence enhancing game elements, nor did the experiment provide autonomy to choose exercises.

The case study with people that were already in the preparation phase conversely did show some interesting insights on how VR could be used to improve MBCT exercises for the target group. People could be supported to start with Mindfulness training by:

1. Shutting off users from their direct environment with the VR goggles, allowing them to focus on the here-and-now more easily;
2. Making mindfulness more tangible by providing clear assignments and visual representations;
3. Making it possible to go "somewhere else" in an instant and focus on something completely different, enabling users to break (negative) thought cycles;
4. Introducing exercises one at a time, while teasing users that more are coming soon;
5. Incorporating multiple exercises, without forcing users to execute an exercise more than once, so that users are able to pick the exercises that they like doing and work for them;

Due to the case study only having two participants, these points should however be considered anecdotal for now, and still require future testing.

References

1. Baer, R.A.: Mindfulness training as a clinical intervention: a conceptual and empirical review. Clin. Psychol. Sci. Pract. **10**(2), 125–143 (2003)
2. Botella, C., Osma, J., Palacios, A.G., Guillen, V., Banos, R.: Treatment of complicated grief using virtual reality: a case report. Death Stud. **32**(7), 674–692 (2008)
3. Chittaro, L., Zangrando, N.: The persuasive power of virtual reality: effects of simulated human distress on attitudes towards fire safety. In: Ploug, T., Hasle, P., Oinas-Kukkonen, H. (eds.) PERSUASIVE 2010. LNCS, vol. 6137, pp. 58–69. Springer, Heidelberg (2010). https://doi.org/10.1007/978-3-642-13226-1_8
4. Fjorback, L.O., Arendt, M., Ørnbøl, E., Fink, P., Walach, H.: Mindfulness-based stress reduction and mindfulness-based cognitive therapy – a systematic review of randomized controlled trials. Acta Psychiatr. Scand. **124**(2), 102–119 (2011)
5. Gagné, M., Deci, E.L.: Self-determination theory and work motivation. J. Organ. Behav. **26**(4), 331–362 (2005)
6. GGZ Nederland website: e-mental health in the Netherlands. http://www.ggznederland.nl/uploads/assets/20130514%20Factsheet%20eHealth.pdf. Accessed 17 March 2017
7. De Graaf, R., Ten Have, M., Van Gool, C., Van Dorsselaer, S.: Prevalentie van psychische aandoeningen en trends van 1996 tot 2009; resultaten van NEMESIS-2. Tijdschrift voor Psychiatr. **54**(1), 27 (2012)
8. Gromala, D., Tong, X., Choo, A., Karamnejad, M., Shaw, C.D.: The virtual meditative walk: virtual reality therapy for chronic pain management. In: Proceedings of the 33rd Annual ACM Conference on Human Factors in Computing Systems, pp. 521–524. ACM (2015)
9. Kabat-Zinn, J.: Mindfulness-based interventions in context: past, present, and future. Clin. Psychol. Sci. Pract. **10**(2), 144–156 (2003)
10. Kabat-Zinn, J.: Full Catastrophe Living: Using the Wisdom of the Body and the Mind to Face Stress, Pain and Illness. Dell, New York (1990)
11. Kosunen, I., Salminen, M., Järvelä, S., Ruonala, A., Ravaja, N., Jacucci, G.: RelaWorld: neuroadaptive and immersive virtual reality meditation system. In: Proceedings of the 21st International Conference on Intelligent User Interfaces, pp. 208–217. ACM (2016)
12. Nararro-Haro, M.V., et al.: The use of virtual reality to facilitate mindfulness skills training in dialectical behavioral therapy for borderline personality disorder: a case study. Front. Psychol. **7**, 1573 (2016)
13. Prochaska, J.O., DiClemente, C.C.: Toward a comprehensive model of change. In: Miller, W.R., Heather, N. (eds.) Treating Addictive Behaviors, pp. 3–27. Springer, Boston (1986). https://doi.org/10.1007/978-1-4613-2191-0_1
14. Prochaska, J.O., Redding, C.A., Evers, K.E.: The transtheoretical model and stages of change. In: Health Behavior and Health Education: Theory, Research, and Practice. 4th edn, pp. 97–122. Wiley, San Francisco (2008)
15. Van Rooij, M., Lobel, A., Harris, O., Smit, N., Granic, I.: DEEP: a biofeedback virtual reality game for children at-risk for anxiety. In: Proceedings of the 2016 CHI Conference Extended Abstracts on Human Factors in Computing Systems, pp. 1989–1997. ACM (2016)
16. Segal, Z.V., Williams, J.M., Teasdale, J.D.: Mindfulness-Based Cognitive Therapy for Depression: A New Approach to Preventing Relapse. Guilford Press, New York (2002)
17. Smeets, O.: E-mental health. Bijblijven **32**(5), 359–363 (2016)
18. World Health Organization. http://www.who.int/features/factfiles/mental_health/mental_health_facts/en/. Accessed 20 May 2018
19. Zürn, X., Damen, K., van Leiden, F., Broekhuijsen, M., Markopoulos, P.: Photo curation practices on smartphones. In: Cheok, A.D., Inami, M., Romão, T. (eds.) ACE 2017. LNCS, vol. 10714, pp. 406–414. Springer, Cham (2018). https://doi.org/10.1007/978-3-319-76270-8_28

Engagement in Interactive Digital Storytelling: Sampling Without Spoiling

Sergio Estupiñán[✉], Kasper Ingdahl Andkjaer, and Nicolas Szilas

TECFA-FPSE, University of Geneva,
Bd. du Pont-d'Arve 40, 1205 Geneva, Switzerland
{sergio.estupinan,kasper.andkjaer,
nicolas.szilas}@unige.ch

Abstract. Interactive Digital Storytelling (IDS) enables users to influence the unfolding of a story at the plot level using Artificial Intelligence techniques for generating and balancing narrative paths on the fly. Despite their promise, most IDS systems are still unable to consistently deliver engaging user experiences. To further understand the characteristics of this new media, particularly user engagement, we apply the concept of Continuation Desire to an existing Interactive Narrative to dynamically sample engagement during a play session. We use a comparative study to assess the effects of interrupting users during gameplay. This study found no evidence that, if done properly, interrupting the experience spoils it. We find no significant impact on the desire to play again as a result of introducing interruptions either.

Keywords: Interactive Digital Storytelling · Evaluation · Engagement
Continuation Desire · Disruptiveness · Replayability · User research

1 Introduction

Interactive Digital Storytelling (IDS) is a relatively new media whose rationale is to empower users to influence the course of narrative events of a computer-based system [7, 8]. The unfolding narrative is dynamically generated using Artificial Intelligence (AI) for narrative generation and balancing. In IDS, users would 'feel' the unfolding story as being their own, since it is the outcome of their own actions that drives it.

The high degree of freedom, increasing complexity, and range of possible narratives, makes it difficult to keep the structure of the narrative engaging and meaningful. Such variability is also problematic from an evaluation perspective. The focus of evaluation must be on the Interactive Narrative Experience (INE), not the final product.

Current evaluation of IDS systems has mainly focused on the global appreciation of the INE inquiring users about their experience after a play session using surveys and standardized questionnaires. There is, however, a lack of research in the IDS community into the factors that determine, during run time, if and why an IDS system is perceived as meaningful and engaging by the users at a given time.

In game studies, one such concept is engagement [11], which has been used to explain the user involvement with the system, albeit not specifically with a narrative focus. Engagement theories have previously been used to measure games as processes,

© IFIP International Federation for Information Processing 2018
Published by Springer Nature Switzerland AG 2018. All Rights Reserved
E. Clua et al. (Eds.): ICEC 2018, LNCS 11112, pp. 248–253, 2018.
https://doi.org/10.1007/978-3-319-99426-0_25

and given their narrative focus, they could fit well with IDS. This article introduces a method inspired by engagement research and performs a comparative study to measure the impact of such a method on users.

2 Related Work

Early research on the evaluation of IDS has provided basic results beyond the mere display of output examples [3] and the evaluation of the product. Ad-hoc question-naires have been used in an attempt to evaluate the general qualities of systems (e.g. eval. B in [1]). Another line of research used objective metrics to measure the user experience (e.g. aggregating interaction logs). Qualitative studies have also been conducted based on interviews and content analyses [12]. In the video games domain, related research has focused on the evaluation of in-game metrics as well as fine-tuning parameters within games [13]. Log analyses [5] and interrupting questionnaires have also been used, although not necessarily in relation to the narrative dimension. It is only with the IRIS project [6] that a IDS-specific evaluation framework was proposed, focusing on the general assessment of users' Interactive Narrative Experience after using an IDS system [9].

   While all of the above self-report approaches are *a posteriori*, there are other methodologies which have proceeded differently. To tackle the problem of measuring engagement in a condensed way, Continuation Desire (CD) attempts to perform sampling during an experience: users are interrupted and asked to quantify to which extent they want to continue the experience, what they want to do next and why they want to continue [10, 11]. This approach produces a continuous CD curve and accounts of the narrative, making it possible to trace the evolution of CD as the Interactive Narrative unfolds.

   The multiple facets associated with the term engagement, including flow, immersion, and enjoyment, share this common trait: the willingness to continue taking part in the activity, which is what Continuation Desire measures. It has therefore been argued that CD acts as an indicator of engagement [11], although the relation is one-way.

   This answer to the problem of *a posteriori* approaches does not come without problems however: Injecting questionnaires into an experience could disrupt and bias the experience, which should be avoided [10]. This study addresses this problem.

3 Engagement in Interactive Digital Storytelling

Given the unsuitability of relying only in non-disruptive or psychophysiological measures for engagement research, the challenge becomes to minimize the disturbance of more intrusive methods so as not to bias the results. The scope of this article is limited to designing and implementing an in-game Continuation Desire evaluation approach and to measure the disruption caused. We believe that such a method should meet these requirements: (1) Gather fine-grained data during the interaction with an IDS system, and (2) The measuring instrument should not bias the results.

4   Experiment Design

To test the hypothesis that introducing interruptions during the experience will not have a significant negative impact on the experience, we implemented a CD questionnaire into the IDS system "Nothing For Dinner"[1] and set up a comparative study using self-reporting metrics disruptiveness and replayability desire. Two independent groups were recruited using a scientific crowdsourcing platform[2]: Interruption group (N = 35), and Control group (N = 42). There were 36 males and 41 females, 18–40 years old (M = 27.3 y/o, SD = 5.95 y/o), speaking English as a first language. There was no recruitment requirement for computer proficiency or gaming profile. Compensation was 1.50 £ for around 23 min, the study was taken online on their own computers.

4.1   Metrics

The content of the interruption questionnaire is not evaluated in this article, it is mentioned as a proposal for a way to measure user appreciation of the INE. The relevant metrics for this experiment are: (1) *Disruptiveness*; how much users felt the interruptions were in the way of the experience (measured in the Interruption group), and (2) *Replayability desire*; how willing the user was to try the experience again (sampled in both groups).

4.2   Interruption Design

Triggering. The moment of interruption must be chosen to avoid generating user discomfort (e.g. while the user is reading or selecting an action) and also since actions may occur in parallel in the system (e.g. agents may decide to interact with each other or with the player). We implemented the following interruption triggering algorithm:

```
1) Play session starts
2) Wait 'x' seconds
3) Wait until all User-Initiated Actions (UIA) are completed
4) Watch for new UIA
5) Wait until UIA is completed
6) Wait for system dialogs to end
7) Wait 'y' seconds
8) Is there any active UIA?
YES) Go to 6
9) Trigger interruption, pausing the system
11) Has the interruption appeared 'z' times? NO) Go to 2
12) Wait for 't' seconds
13) End
```

In step 5, the algorithm waits for all User-Initiated Actions (UIA) to finish so the user can see the outcome of their actions prior to each interruption.

---

[1] http://nothingfordinner.org/.

[2] https://prolific.ac/.

User Interface. We consider that the UI design should meet the following characteristics: (1) Users can observe the state of their session while the questions are asked, so they feel they are in the system (non-masking interface), and (2) The elements giving questions, as well as users' means of answering, should mimic the existing system to ensure continuity between system and sampling.

4.3 Questionnaire Contents

Continuation Desire. The Engagement Sampling Questionnaire (ESQ) [11] was presented in each interruption: (1) "Do you want to continue the experience?" (Likert scale), (2) "What makes you want/not want to continue the experience?", and (3) "What do you want to do next in the game?". The last question is relevant from a narrative perspective since it assesses the audience's anticipatory behavior, a core property of narratives [4].

Affective State. Users reported their affective state during each interruption using the Self-Assessment Manikin (SAM) [2], a validated cross-cultural affective assessment tool in three dimensions (Valence, Arousal, Dominance). Chosen for its fast learning curve and rapid reporting, users were shown SAM in the preliminary phase of the study. The affective results are not in the scope of this article.

4.4 Procedure

Upon being informed about the financial compensation and accepting the research consent, participants started the experiment by being redirected from the scientific crowdsourcing website to the study website. The procedure was:

1. Training questions (Interruption group): SAM is introduced and explained.
2. Anticipation: (1) "I want to begin playing" (Likert scale). (2) "What makes you want or not want to begin playing?" (freeform text).
3. The experience is presented in full. When the interruption procedure has run its course or time is reached for the Control group, the post-questionnaire is presented.
4. Post-game question.: "I want to try the game again" (Likert scale).
5. Regarding the interruptions (Interruption group): "The in-game interruptions spoiled my gaming experience" (Likert scale), "Overall, filling out the interruption questions was:" (Very difficult - Very easy, Single Ease Question).

We used seven-point Likert scales since they provide a good balance between degrees of freedom and ease of use. Participants received the compensation at the end.

5   Results

Interruption Distribution: From the start of the experience to *Interruption 1*, two clusters were found: C1, size = 20, 5.63 min elapsed in average (SD = 51.32 s), results interval [222, 400] s, and C2 2, size = 15, 8.50 min elapsed in average (SD = 63.9 s), results interval [426, 650] s (Fig. 1).

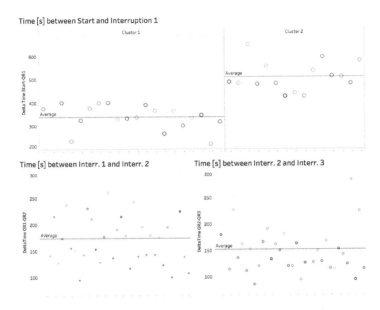

Fig. 1. Elapsed time between question rounds in seconds.

Next, 97% of *Interruption 2* triggered around 2.90 min in average (SD = 55.52 s) interruptions being evenly distributed around 94 and 261 s after the first interruption. Finally, 94% of *Interruption 3* triggered around in average 2.54 min after *Interruption 2* (SD = 51.73 s), uniformly spaced around 85 and 227 s.

Disruptiveness: Participants in the Interruption group had a neutral opinion of interruptions having spoiled their experience, with an average of 4.11 (SD = 1.61), 95% Confidence Interval ranging from 3.57 to 4.63 (4 = Neutral, 5 = Agree a little).

Difficulty: The perceived difficulty filling out the interruption questionnaire was calculated using the Single Ease Question, scoring 5.79 (Moderately easy) in average (SD = 1.12). The calculated 95% Confidence Interval ranged from 5.42 to 6.16, where 4 corresponds to Neutral, and 7 to Very easy.

Replayability Desire: The Control group scored 3.07 whereas the Interruption group 2.82 (Disagree a little) in average. An independent two-tailed t-test was performed, finding no significant difference (p = 0.536). The calculated Cohen's d is 0.1362, so the effect size is very small.

6 Discussion and Conclusion

The main objective of this article is to assess the disruptiveness of the proposed approach for measuring Continuation Desire (an indicator of the presence of engagement) within the Interactive Digital Storytelling domain. A comparative experiment was made using the IDS system "Nothing For Dinner" with an Interruption group (N = 35) and a Control group (N = 42), each session lasted around 23 min.

The obtained results indicate that the interruption triggering system performed consistently, spreading the interruptions evenly over the entire session. More importantly, it was found no major perception of disruptiveness when using the proposed approach for the sampling of Continuation Desire. In terms of replayability, we found no statistically significant effect when introducing the interruptions. The content of the interruption questionnaire was not analyzed in this article, it remains the basis for future work assessing its usefulness compared to existing evaluation approaches. These findings support the notion that in-experience sampling could be performed without creating major impact on users. It remains our long-term goal to advance the evaluation of IDS, for which we consider this study a first successful step.

References

1. Barber, H., Kudenko, D.: Generation of adaptive dilemma-based interactive narratives. IEEE Trans. Comput. Intell. AI Games **1**(4), 309–326 (2009)
2. Bradley, M., Lang, P.J.: Measuring emotion: the self-assessment manikin and the semantic differential. J. Behav. Ther. Exp. Psychiatry **25**(I), 49–59 (1994)
3. Cavazza, M., Charles, F., Mead, S.J.: Characters in search of an author: AI-based virtual storytelling. In: Balet, O., Subsol, G., Torguet, P. (eds.) ICVS 2001. LNCS, vol. 2197, pp. 145–154. Springer, Heidelberg (2001). https://doi.org/10.1007/3-540-45420-9_16
4. Eco, U.: Lector in fabula: Le rôle du lecteur ou la Coopération interprétative dans les textes narratifs. Grasset, Paris (1985)
5. Kim, J.H., Gunn, D.V., Schuh, E., Phillips, B.C., Pagulayan, R.J., Wixon, D.: Tracking real-time user experience (TRUE): a comprehensive instrumentation solution for complex systems. In: CHI 2008 Proceedings of the SIGCHI Conference on Human Factors in Computing Systems, pp. 443–451 (2008)
6. Klimmt, C., Roth, C., Vermeulen, I.: The UX-tool: measurement device and documentation for empirical assessment of the UX in IS, January 2012
7. Molnar, A., Kostkova, P.: Interactive Digital Narrative. Routledge, London (2015)
8. Murray, J.H.: Hamlet on the Holodeck: The Future of Narrative in Cyberspace. MIT Press, Cambridge (1997)
9. Roth, C.: Experiencing interactive storytelling. Ph.D. thesis, VU University Amsterdam (2015)
10. Schoenau-Fog, H., Birke, A., Reng, L.: Evaluation of continuation desire as an iterative game development method. In: Proceeding of the 16th International Academic MindTrek Conference, pp. 241–243. ACM, New York (2012)
11. Schoenau-Fog, H.: Hooked! – evaluating engagement as continuation desire in interactive narratives. In: Si, M., Thue, D., André, E., Lester, J.C., Tanenbaum, J., Zammitto, V. (eds.) ICIDS 2011. LNCS, vol. 7069, pp. 219–230. Springer, Heidelberg (2011). https://doi.org/10.1007/978-3-642-25289-1_24
12. Seif El-Nasr, M., Milam, D., Maygoli, T.: Experiencing interactive narrative: a qualitative analysis of Facade. Entertain. Comput. **4**(1), 39–52 (2013)
13. Sundstedt, V., Bernhard, M., Stavrakis, E., Reinhard, E., Wimmer, M.: Game Analytics (2013)

Playing with Empathy Through a Collaborative Storytelling Game

Sindre B. Skaraas, Javier Gomez, and Letizia Jaccheri[✉]

Department of Computer Science, NTNU, Trondheim, Norway
sibsen@live.com, {javier.escribano,letizia.jaccheri}@ntnu.no

Abstract. This project aims to provide increased understanding about how t o positively affect empathy by storytelling experience. This experience consists of a group of people that collaborate on telling a story by using a serious educational game. This study reports about the early evaluation of a serious educational game about empathy. By having players collaborate on telling a story, the game aims to exercise their empathic abilities. This study shows the exploratory phase aimed at proving the game concept and identifying points to be further developed. The game was evaluated in a workshop trial with 12 participants. This evaluation showed enough potential to warrant development into a more focused version that facilitates empathic responses.

Keywords: Serious games · Affective learning
Empathy · Collaborative storytelling

1 Introduction

One of the most common qualifiers to measure how we deal with the world is empathy. As children will grow up, their opinions and perspectives will be formed largely based on their ability to understand other people's motives, emotions and views. Storytelling is a natural and reoccurring way for humans to develop empathy [18]. In fact, novels are one of the main forms of communication cultures have had to share different perspectives and to build empathy in their population. Despite this, the role of empathy in video games is a topic that has often received more negative attention than positive [1,10]. This project aims to provide an activity that will positively affect empathy by emulating a storytelling and story creation experience. This activity will consist of a group of people that will collaborate on telling a story. By making each player understand and add to the story, they are forced to put themselves into the story and to have an empathic response to the character [15]. This is done in a way of collaborative learning, which is found to be more interesting to the players and to promote critical thinking [9]. The development is directed by certain guidelines for educational games, as presented by Annetta [2], to make sure the users can achieve heightened engagement and affective learning.

© IFIP International Federation for Information Processing 2018
Published by Springer Nature Switzerland AG 2018. All Rights Reserved
E. Clua et al. (Eds.): ICEC 2018, LNCS 11112, pp. 254–259, 2018.
https://doi.org/10.1007/978-3-319-99426-0_26

The game is presented in [17]. The research question is whether such a relation exists between the game experience and the players' empathy. The game uses storytelling as a way to exercise the ability to form an empathic understanding to an imagined situation. The players then show that they can interpret the story, build on it, and explain it to the group. In this stage, the study takes an informal approach. The aim is to explore the possibilities of the game with a real audience and to gather feedback to take the concept further. So because of that preliminary form, the game study exists mainly as a proof-of-concept. It is a combination of a digital system and a real-world activity of oral storytelling. The digital aspect is simply a conduit that provides communication tools and a structure to the play. The "game" in its true sense is determined when the players interact with each other and decide how they will develop the story. Because of this reliance on the group dynamic, there is an element of uncertainty to the game design. This is why the study also takes an exploratory approach, seeking the aid of the players to further develop the prototype.

The study reported in this paper is part of a larger ecosystem of projects. This ecosystem is formed under the novel of "The Little Doormaid: Tappetina" [12]. This novel also lends its name to the game in this study. Starting as a way to interpret the story of the novel into a digital game, this project has since evolved into a collaborative storytelling platform. The ecosystem is an initiative to encourage nuanced views of people. It is formed under to combat the stigma that surrounds women entering male-associated fields such as technology.

The structure of this paper is as follows: Sect. 2 will look at a collection of works that serves as background for this research project. Section 3 outlines the evaluation process and discussion of its results. And Sect. 4 then talks about how the game will be developed for improvement and more focused research.

2   State of the Art

There has been a fair amount of studies that set out to prove the effectiveness of game-based learning. Smiley [19] suggests how the research field is now beyond simply asking if game-based learning can be effective. The author shows how several application areas exist where instructional games are proven to be more effective than ordinary instruction, something echoed by a more recent literature overview by Susi et al. [3]. So instead, Van Eck [19] argues studies should look more at why they are effective, and how – which is to say, "when, with whom, and under what conditions". This is where the core motivation for this research proposal lies – to further explore how the to-be developed game can drive learning. Key to the research is uncovering the landscape of ideas that seems promising and that are grounded in theory. Regarding the educational content games may have, there is again the literature overview by Connoly et al. [8]. Here, they analyze different (positive) impacts of games, which include different learning outcomes such as: affective learning, knowledge acquisition, perceptual/cognitive skills and behavior change.

Since a narrative is central to the game development of this project, it would be useful to find how stories are related to games in general. The basis for that discussion is found in an article by Jenkins [13] that clears up the question of what the role between games and narrative really is. The work connects games and movies in that game narratives are not linear nor essential thing in games as it is in cinema. It's also showed here how the game designers are not storytellers, but "narrative architects". This is because their real role is creating game spaces that facilitate narrative experiences, or spatial stories. Four approaches to such environmental storytelling is suggested: (1) making spaces that evoke narratives the player is already familiar with, (2) enacting the narrative at certain spots of the game, (3) revealing the plot by embedding bits of info in the environment, and (4) letting narratives emerge spontaneously within the game. This fourth approach is what lead to coming up with the concept of the game activity in this study.

In [1], Anderson et al. describes how much research has been dedicated to make a link between violent video games and decreased pro-social behavior. Recently, more research has been going in the opposite direction, to investigate the positive effect of games on empathy. So-called pro-social games are shown by Greitemeyer et al. in [10] to increase empathy along with a reduction in being pleased at someone else's misfortune, or *schadenfreude*. Greitemeyer et al. then shows support for the positive aspects of the General Learning Model (GLM) of Buckley et al. [5]. The GLM is an generalized version of the General Aggression Model (GAM), which was solely used to just look at the negative effects of violent games. With the GLM, games are portrayed as a media that when exposed to, one's mental state can be affected, leading to possible reactions in behavior. In [4], Belman et al. makes an overview of different efforts to promote empathy in social sciences, and recommends how to extend these studies to creating "games for good" that try to promote certain ethical values. Of note, two dimensions are identified in these studies. Firstly, Dispositional vs Induced Empathy, where studies may look behavior affected by empathy vs how empathy can itself be changed. The second dimension is Low- vs High-Involvement. In a game, this would determine how much the player is immersed in terms of time, engagement and building relationships in a player community.

As for popular entertainment games, there exists those that use different forms of storytelling and empathy in their mechanics: An older game genre that features collaborative storytelling is tabletop role-playing games, such as Dungeons and Dragons [11]. In this game, the story is created by a central narrator as each players take on a character and role dice to determine results. Other games will have all players contribute equally to creating the story, such as Once Upon a Time [14] by Atlas Games, which combines fairy tales and more traditional, competitive card playing. These games and others serve as inspiration to design the digital game and associated activity. Empathy games, on the other hand, take several forms: Some may deal with exploring one's identity (Who Am I? Race Awareness Game [16]) or to simulate social interaction (Hall of Heroes [6] - helps teens adapt to middle school). Games that combine storytelling and empathy do so often by teaching problem-solving (Four Little Corners - An interactive storybook app about friendship [7]), but may be too inflated to be properly studied in terms of the exact relationship to empathy. This space is where this game wishes to fill. By simplifying the story structure, it may give the players the reins to exercise their empathic abilities.

3   Evaluation

Since the study at this stage was determined to not require a formal experiment, the methodology was loose and not very controlled. So, instead of formal data collection, it was deemed that having a researcher heavily involved in and observing the activity would grant the most insight. This way the feasibility can be evaluated by interacting with participants. This gives rise to investigating feedback and examining what points need improvement. The main form of getting feedback was observation and note-taking. The researcher played the game together with the participants. This means that while taking part in the story building, he could talk to the players and get an insight into how well they engage with the game. Since the researcher participated in the game, it was not a blind trial. The participants were to be informed of the goals of the game and given some guidance on how to play, when needed. Data collection methods included recording audio of the activity, a short questionnaire, plus the game data: the complete constructed story and their individual solutions. The data results allowed one to look back on the trial and effectively reconstruct the interaction and story building process.

The evaluation was held during the workshop "Games, culture and science for boys and girls". This event took place at the Gunnerus Library (Trondheim, Norway). It was conducted by NTNU researchers and aimed at teenagers. The objective of the workshop was to introduce teenagers to research and the current games developed at the University. Having this workshop as the context of the evaluation made it less of a typically controlled research environment. Instead, everyone was open to comment, share their experience, and play however they liked. "Tappetina's Empathy" was among several games to be presented here. Around 30 people in total were present to play the games. Teenagers were also brought in to help organize the activities as well as participate themselves. This lead to a relaxed and jovial atmosphere, which was further contributed to by encouraging the participants to pick the games they wanted to try out. Before the activities, each game project got to present their goal and agenda, informing everyone about what the game would be like. The first batch of players would be pre-determined, followed by a period of walking around to the games that each found interesting. In addition to the game trials, there were art installations and brief history lessons, as this was a hosted in an old library.

Because of the number of workshops and time constraints, only 12 players played the game activity in groups of 4 people. Most of them were teens of age 13 or older, some joined by their parents. Their point of initiative was mixed between being lead to the game by the organizers and electing to play this game over others after hearing the presentation. Similarly to the other games, "Tappetina's Empathy" received its own isolated room for the players to sit in a circle. Here, the players could speak and focus without distractions.

Among the data points observed is engagement. That is, how much fun the experience was for the players. Looking at the questionnaire data, there were varying amounts of engagement: When asked how much they enjoyed playing the game, most players answered 4 out of 5 stars. Going by the observations and the audio recording, players displayed different emotional reactions and level of focus. A couple of younger kids were naturally more boisterous with friends or siblings present, showing great willingness to build onto the story with numerous details. Others were reserved and silent, but could eventually offer a constructive story addition.

Players had also different ways of interacting with the story and the game tools. The most timid could at times do nothing but repeat the cue they selected. The majority of participants showed an innate ability to use their fantasy to build onto the story. Some would even put elements of their own life into the character and story, displaying a desire to form real-world, empathetic connections to the fiction. Players showed differences in their comprehension of the game structure. This can be interpreted through time spent selecting and how they expressed that the choices were difficult. There did seem to be a hint of relation between this comprehension and the player's age and self-rated empathy. When it comes to the correlation to empathy, some hints were gathered about a possible relationship here. In the question form, the players were asked to rate their empathy ability. Looking at all the answers for this, and comparing them to their respective answers for enjoyment, we see a 0.73 average distance. While this is hardly enough for a proof in its own terms, it does grant an indication that further research can look at. To be adapted, the game's design would need to focus even more on requiring the player to form an emotional understanding to succeed and have fun. As it is, there is not enough agency in the player's hands to properly shape the story. This may be because of a overly simplistic structure, or that the Story Tag events themselves are too descriptive.

4   Taking the Game Further

The trial was considered enough of a success that the game is to be further developed. The overall response from the players was positive, who were intrigued by the concept. A couple players even showed a desire to download the game and play it with their friends. The main goal was however to determine if it could be used to make a stronger connection to empathy. This was also determined to be fulfilled enough to warrant a more focused approach. Finally, some improvements and changes would be in order to better influence or be influenced by empathic abilities.

Acknowledgment. This work has been partially supported by NTNU ARTEC and by the ERCIM fellowship program. The authors would like to thank Alexandra Angele-taki for organizing the international experiment workshop at the Gunnerus library of NTNU. The project has been recommended by the Data Protection Official for Research, Norwegian Social Science Data Services (NSD). For the development of the game, the Unity Engine and editor was utilized, as developed by Unity Technologies.

References

1. Anderson, C.A., et al.: Violent video game effects on aggression, empathy, and prosocial behavior in eastern and western countries: a meta-analytic review. Psychol. Bull. **136**(2), 151 (2010)
2. Annetta, L.A.: The "I's" have it: a framework for serious educational game design. Rev. Gen. Psychol. **14**(2), 105 (2010)
3. Backlund, P., Hendrix, M.: Educational games-are they worth the effort? A literature survey of the effectiveness of serious games. In: 2013 5th International Conference on Games and Virtual Worlds for Serious Applications (VS-GAMES), pp. 1–8. IEEE (2013)
4. Belman, J., Flanagan, M.: Designing games to foster empathy. Int. J. Cogn. Technol. **15**(1), 11 (2010)
5. Buckley, K.E., Anderson, C.A.: A theoretical model of the effects and consequences of playing video games. In: Playing Video Games: Motives, Responses, and Consequences, pp. 363–378 (2006)
6. Centervention: Hall of Heroes game (2016)
7. DADA Company: Four little corners - an interactive storybook app about friendship (2013)
8. Connolly, T.M., Boyle, E.A., MacArthur, E., Hainey, T., Boyle, J.M.: A systematic literature review of empirical evidence on computer games and serious games. Comput. Educ. **59**(2), 661–686 (2012)
9. Gokhale, A.A.: Collaborative learning enhances critical thinking. J. Technol. Educ. **7**(1) (1995)
10. Greitemeyer, T., Osswald, S., Brauer, M.: Playing prosocial video games increases empathy and decreases schadenfreude. Emotion **10**(6), 796 (2010)
11. Gygax, G., Arneson, D.: Dungeons and Dragons, vol. 19. Tactical Studies Rules, Lake Geneva (1974)
12. Jaccheri, L.: The Little Doormaid: Tappetina. CreateSpace Independent Publishing Platform (2016)
13. Jenkins, H.: Game design as narrative. Computer **44**, 53 (2004)
14. Lamber, R., Rilstone, A., Wallis, J.: Once upon a time: the storytelling card game (2003)
15. Manney, P.J.: Empathy in the time of technology: how storytelling is the key to empathy. J. Evol. Technol. **19**(1), 51–61 (2008)
16. Playtime Interactive: Who Am I? Race Awareness Game (2010)
17. Skaraas, S.B., Gomez, J., Jaccheri, L.: Tappetina's empathy game: a playground of storytelling and emotional understanding. In: Proceedings of the 17th ACM Conference on Interaction Design and Children, IDC 2018, pp. 509–512 (2018)
18. Smiley, J.: Thirteen Ways of Looking at the Novel. Alfred A. Knopf Incorporated, New York (2005)
19. Van Eck, R.: Digital game-based learning: it's not just the digital natives who are restless. EDUCAUSE Rev. **41**(2), 16 (2006)

Construction of Mixed Reality Story Environment Based on Real Space Shape

Kazuma Nagata[1(✉)], Soh Masuko[2], and Junichi Hoshino[1]

[1] University of Tsukuba, 1-1-1 Tennodai Tsukuba Ibaraki,
Tsukuba 305-8573, Japan
{nagata.kazuma, jhoshino}@entcomp.esys.tsukuba.ac.jp
[2] Rakuten, Inc, Rakuten Institute of Technology, Rakuten Crimson House,
1-14-1, Tamagawa, Setagaya-ku, Tokyo, Japan
so.masuko@rakuten.com

Abstract. We propose a system to construct Mixed Reality (MR) environments based on actual environments. Our goal is to develop MR content in which users and characters can coexist in an actual room and experience a story. This study represents a preliminary step in the development of such an MR experience. We proposed a method to construct an MR environment that uses three-dimensional information acquired from the actual environment based on rules. We extract valid plane information from three-dimensional information and use it. Virtual objects used for MR content can be placed in real space automatically. Rules are created by specifying the area and height of the plane of the real space. In this study, we placed seven types of objects in two types of rooms and confirmed that it is possible to construct an environment using a transmission-type head mount-ed display. However, under the current system, users cannot experience a story.

Keywords: Mixed Reality · 3D recognition · Dynamic construction

1 Introduction

Storytelling content allows users to experience various stories through a character's active behaviors [1–3]. By matching a real space, the user can feel as if the character is in the same world. If the user can experience an Mixed Reality (MR) story of their room as a character world setting, this may increase the reality of the experience. It is thought that interaction, such as being able to change to the story through room remodeling, is possible. For example, when routes to obtain items differ depending on the shape of the room or the furniture arrangement, it is possible to use furniture to place a bridge (Fig. 1). Everything in the room can be used as a tool to experience the content. This study proposes a method to build an MR environment tailored to the room in preparation for developing a system that can realize an experience in which the user senses that they are living in the same room as the character.

E. Clua et al. (Eds.): ICEC 2018, LNCS 11112, pp. 260–265, 2018.
https://doi.org/10.1007/978-3-319-99426-0_27

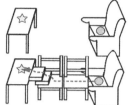

Fig. 1. (left, right) Image that makes room a character world stage. (center) Creating a road using furniture.

2   Related Work

One study into the story experience is Steven's AR Façade [4], which explored communicating with characters and experiencing a story in real space using a transparent HMD based on Facade [3]. Façade is the story content in the house where the character lives. The AR Façade reproduces the same placement in real space. Nakevska used the CAVE environment and projected images onto the walls of a room in order to perform the story experience of Alice in Wonderland [5]. In a room, the user can experience a story by acting on objects in the room or projected images; however, such methods cannot be incorporated into a user's own room because such a real environment is special.

Another method sets a virtual object that matches a real environment measured using a depth camera to create a character world tailored to an arbitrary room. Misha's Oasis [6] detects a walkable region from three-dimensional information of walls and floors to build a VR space adapted to that region. That is not story content. The proposed method also measures a real environment.

With the proposed method, we aim to create MR story experiences in arbitrary environments by setting virtual objects according to measured information.

3   Construction of Mixed Reality Space

3.1   Overview

We construct an MR space that matches the shape of the three-dimensional data of a real space acquired by scanning. We define the floor, tables, etc. as a "horizontal plane," walls, shelves, etc. as a "vertical plane," and inclined planes as a "slope." We define this classification as a "region." We place a CG object on the surface classified into each region based on the rule. A CG object placed in a certain region is defined as a "stage." In this procedure, three-dimensional data of the physical space are classified into each region, and the stage is arranged in a region according to the rule.

3.2   Obtaining Surface Meshes

Note that the mesh shape of the obtained three-dimensional data is incomplete, and there are extra meshes and holes caused by the ceiling and measurement error. Data resampling is performed because it is difficult to judge the appropriate region. Note that subsequent processes can be simplified by acquiring data as a single plane mesh. We performed data resampling so that we could handle only the confirmed surface from the top of the room model (Fig. 2). First, we sufficiently cover the room model and prepare a fine rectangular mesh relative to the room model mesh. Move from the top of the room model to the bottom and fix each vertex at the point where it hits the mesh of the room model. Thus, it is possible to acquire a mesh of the surface.

Fig. 2.   Retrieving the surface mesh by resampling.

3.3   Region Classification

To classify the re-sampled three-dimensional data into each region, clustering is performed based on the inner product of the normal vectors of the mesh vertices. The inner product of the normal vectors of adjacent vertices is taken to find the angle between the normal vectors. Clustering performs vertices with angles less than a threshold as the same region. To make vertices classified in each cluster a mesh, a Delaunay triangulation is created from the group of vertices. Thus, it is possible to divide the three-dimensional data of the real space into planes. The plane is estimated using the RANSAC algorithm on the divided planes, and the inclination of the plane is obtained from the estimated plane equations. Each region is classified using the inclination and area of the plane (Table 1). For visibility, we change the color according to the region (Fig. 3).

3.4   Stage Placement

We place stages based on the rules in each region, and a stage is placed in a region or between regions. Note that placement is performed based on different rules.

Rules for placing stages in regions. Region: Region type. (e.g. FLOOR, HPLANE, VPLANE...), Area: Sort by Region area. (e.g. 1, 2, 3..., unspecified), Height: Sort by Region height. (e.g. 1, 2, 3..., unspecified), Number of Regions: Number of regions to place the stage. (e.g. 1, 2, 3..., unspecified), Number of Stages: Number of Stages placed in the Region. (e.g. 1, 2, 3..., unspecified).

Table 1. Region classification.

Region	Plane type	Condition	Color
FLOOR	Horizontal	Maximum area	
HPLANE	Horizontal	-	
VPLANE	Vertical	-	
LSLOPE	Slope	Low inclination	
HSLOPE	Slope	High inclination	

Fig. 3. Region classification

Rules for placing a stage between regions. Target Stages: Stages where areas are placed. (e.g. Tent-Lab), Number of placement: Number of stages to be connected from one stage. (e.g. 1, 2, 3..., unspecified).

The placement rule is determined by combining these. When multiple stages satisfy the condition, they are placed in the same region. In addition, the placement position is determined randomly within a range not outside a region but also not in contact with another mesh; however, in the case of a very narrow area, it does not depend on it.

3.5   Result of Placement

Stages (Fig. 4) were placed in two real environments (room1 and room2) according to the rules (Tables 2 and 3). The scan data are shown in Fig. 5, and the placement results are shown in Fig. 6. Note that they were also confirmed using Microsoft HoloLens (Fig. 7).

Tent   Lab   Rocket   Windmill   Mushroom   Grass   Bridge

Fig. 4. Stage models.

Table 2. Placement rule of the stage on the region.

Stage	Region	Area	Height	Number of regions	Number of stages
Tent	HPLANE	1	0	1	1
Lab	HPLANE	2	0	1	1
Rocket	HPLANE	3	0	1	1
Windmill	HPLANE	4	0	1	1
Mushroom	HPLANE	0	1	5	1
Grass	FLOOR	0	0	1	100

Table 3. Placement rule of the stage between regions.

Stage	Target stages	Number of placement
Bridge	Tent – Lab	1
Bridge	Tent – Rocket	1

Fig. 5. Scanned data. (left: room1, right: room2)

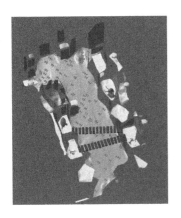
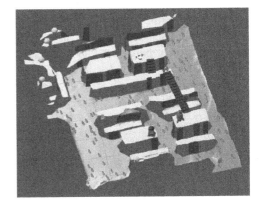

Fig. 6. Result of stage placement. (left: room1, right: room2)

Fig. 7. Confirmation by Microsoft HoloLens (left: room1, center and right: room2)

4 Discussion and Future Work

The purpose of this study was to experience MR in an arbitrary environment by scanning a real space. Note that we did not achieve completely automatic placement; however, we were able to place objects according to the environment. Note that not all components of this system work automatically. For example, parameters must be changed according to the given environment. Therefore, it is necessary to acquire an appropriate threshold and automatically change the shape and size of the model at the time of placement according to the given environment. In addition, this work represents an incomplete implementation of an environment construction system; thus, this work does not represent a method that can provide a true story experience. Therefore, it is necessary to implement a story system that changes with user interactions and the environment. We think that it is possible to experience an MR story as if the character actually lives with the user by enhancing the completeness of the system.

References

1. Cavazza, M., Charles, F., Mead, S.J.: Character-based interactive storytelling. IEEE Intell. Syst. **17**, 17–24 (2002)
2. Nakano, A., Koumura, J., Miura, E., Hoshino, J.: Spilant world: interactive emergent story game using episode tree. J. Soc. Art Sci. **6**(3), 145–153 (2007)
3. Mateas, M., Stern, A.: Façade: an experiment in building a fully-realized interactive drama. In: Game Developer's Conference: Game Design Track (2003)
4. Dow, S., Mehta, M., Lausier, A., MacIntyre, B., Mateas, M.: Initial lessons from AR Façade, an interactive augmented reality drama. In: ACM SIGCHI International Conference on Advances in Computer Entertainment Technology (2006)
5. Nakevska, M., van der Sanden, A., Funk, M., Hu, J., Rauterberg, M.: Interactive storytelling in a mixed reality environment: the effects of interactivity on user experiences. In: Pisan, Y., Sgouros, N.M., Marsh, T. (eds.) ICEC 2014. LNCS, vol. 8770, pp. 52–59. Springer, Heidelberg (2014). https://doi.org/10.1007/978-3-662-45212-7_7
6. Sra, M., Garrido-Jurado, S., Schmandt, C., Maes, P.: Procedurally generated virtual reality from 3D reconstructed physical space. In: Proceedings of the 22nd ACM Conference on Virtual Reality Software and Technology, pp. 191–200. ACM (2016)

Digital Therapies

Robert J. Wierzbicki[✉]

University of Applied Sciences Mittweida, Mittweida, Germany
robert@wierzbicki.org

Abstract. Today, digital transformation and virtualization processes profoundly affect societies; not only in terms of socio-economic disruption, but also in terms of rising mental health problems. This paper focuses on the design aspects and the use of "nurture games" as a social utility of preventive measures (that is referred to in this paper as "*Digital Therapies*"), in the realm of nurturing and public school education, supporting therapeutic benefit and well-being. The Cognitive Behavioral Therapy (CBT), employed for treating a large number of mental problems, is considered here as a fundamental psychotherapeutic approach, which needs to underpin the design of games aiming to improve mental health and support the prevention of challenging behaviors in youth.

Keywords: Digital therapy · Cognitive behavioral therapy · Mental health
Behavior · Game design · Nurture games · Game-like settings
Blended nurture · Therapeutic benefit · Well-being · Digital transformation
Society

1 Behavior in Humans

Human behavior is the result of different factors, including, amongst others, the organism's genetic composition and the interaction between heredity and environment [1]. The nature/nurture debate is still ongoing [2, 3], even if some geneticists might have declared it to be over [4].

Today, not only children and adolescents reveal emotional and behavioral problems [5]. Stress in the modern world can substantially bias the development of cognitive control processes in adults as well. This may not only increase the overall vulnerability to depression, anger and anxiety disorders, but also decrease one's ability to cope with unexpected stressful and tragic life events [6]. Dysfunctional patterns may help to cope with these situations but in the long term, they may cause severe or irreversible mental problems and result in abnormal behaviors as well as socialization styles and finally leading finally to mental self-destruction.

2 Mental Health in the Internet Age

Human mental health condition and behavior are caused by a combination of genetic, biological, environmental, psychological, and, last but not least, technological factors. Internet, the greatest invention of the past few decades, has definitely made some

© IFIP International Federation for Information Processing 2018
Published by Springer Nature Switzerland AG 2018. All Rights Reserved
E. Clua et al. (Eds.): ICEC 2018, LNCS 11112, pp. 266–273, 2018.
https://doi.org/10.1007/978-3-319-99426-0_28

negative impact on society. Moreover, relationship between internet technology and the individual has become increasingly problematic [3, 7]. As the virtualization of human life and the convergence of life and technology continue, more and more problems arise, depriving many of us of positive human qualities. Even good people may turn bad online [8]. Ever-changing subcultures and the behavioral transformation societies undergo is dramatically more accelerated and more psychologically formative than any previous technological transformation [9] Mental health problems in young people seem to have increased considerably over the past 20 years. They are predominantly rooted in social change, including disruption of family structure, growing youth unemployment as well as increasing educational and vocational pressures [10]. The identification of mental health problems and disorders is complicated. Even the ones concerned may not be aware of a mental balance distortion already present. The list of mental health problems is long. It includes, among others, social anxiety, panic, depression, substance abuse, separation anxiety disorder, attention-deficit/hyperactivity disorder (ADHS), oppositional defiant disorder, pervasive developmental disorders (PDD) and post-traumatic stress disorder (PTSD) [11–13]. Many negative effects in mental health are caused or reinforced by the internet, tech usage and media consumption. Actions that children observe through the media become examples to follow [14]. Bringing up children in the internet age has become a great challenge. Letting children use tech products from an early age disturbs their overall development and distorts their perception of reality [15]. Tech ban, on the contrary, may result in problems integrating juveniles into digital society later in life. The long academic debate on the impact of violent games on behavior is finally over. It has been proven that violent video games are a causal risk factor for increased aggressive thoughts and behavior, decreased empathy, and decreased prosocial behavior in youths [16].

Internet-based problems like virtual violence and cyberbullying impact not only mental health but also the safety of teens and may result in their social isolation and sometimes even in suicide [17]. The prevalence of childhood psychiatric disorders appears to have been underestimated for a long time [18]. It seems more than obvious that preventive actions need to be taken.

3   Psychotherapy

Psychotherapy focuses on the significance or the relevance of our early childhood in our thinking and behavioral patterns [19]. Modern psychotherapy has been proven very useful for people who are struggling with longstanding difficulties. Especially psychoanalysis [20] and psychodynamics [21] have been accepted as useful in handling complex personality and behavior problems, even if modern psychology might find the therapy techniques not very effective in particular cases and the scientific evidence in support of the therapies may sometimes appear to be ambiguous [22].

Psychoanalysis emerged as a method of making the unconscious conscious, restoring the unity of the mind and its capacity for self-regulation [23]. The goals of psychodynamic therapy are a client's self-awareness and understanding of the influence of the past on present behavior [24].

Psychodynamic therapy, as opposed to psychoanalysis, does not need to include all analytic techniques (interpretation, transference analysis, technical neutrality and countertransference analysis [25]), and does not necessarily need to be conducted by psychoanalytically trained analysts.

4   Cognitive Behavioral Therapy

Cognitive Behavioral Therapy (CBT) is considered a holistic combination of both psychotherapy and behavioral therapy, the latter emphasizing on the close equation between our psychological problems, behavior patterns and thoughts [26]. CBT is a technique used to teach individuals to change their unwanted behaviors. A key cognitive concept in CBT is "guided discovery" [27] – a therapeutic stance which involves trying to understand the patients' view of things and help them expand their thinking, so that they become aware of their underlying assumptions, and discover alternative perspectives and solutions for themselves [28] (Fig. 1).

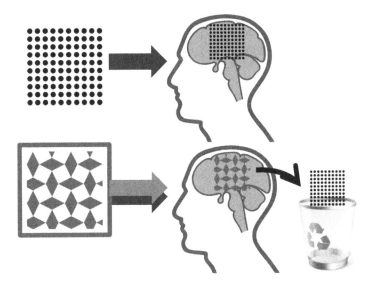

Fig. 1. The principle of changing behavioral patterns in a cognitive behavioral therapy.

CBT is a collaborative approach. The therapist and client are regarded as equal members of a team, and the client takes substantial ownership over the direction of the course of treatment [29]. Different distressing feelings in humans relate to the neurotransmitter activity in the brain [30], attributed to physical sensations, and physiological and emotional input. Cognitive behavioral treatments can alter our perception of unpleasant sensations by altering sensory processing in the cortex [31]. Cognitive interventions, among others, may include exercises in perspective taking [32], distraction techniques [33], methods of relaxation (e.g. guided imagery [34], enhancing both physical and mental performance), rational problem solving [35], and the use of adaptive self-statements [36].

Many studies have assessed the efficacy of CBT interventions [37]. Originally developed for the treatment of depression, cognitive therapy has been applied successfully to a number of psychiatric conditions, including anxiety and mood disorders among children and youth [38]. The concept behind CBT refers to the so-called "cognitive restructuring" [39, 40] and is based upon an identification of factors affecting the individual's difficulties.

Powerful cognitive behavioral treatments with children and adolescents include stories, metaphors and analogies [41, 42]. Metaphors in CBT help understand complex reasoning behind conscious and subconscious decisions and help to cognitively restructure distorted schemas [43].

5   Game as a Communication Channel

Today, teaching in schools relies on different standard communication channels such as printed texts, workbooks, paper-and-pencil exercises or chalkboard demonstrations.

In addition, there are mobile technologies, e-mails, messenger services, forums, and social networking, which are the most prominent from the digital area.

The choice of communication channels depends essentially on the instruction strategy, curriculum to be taught, type of blended learning arrangement, goals to be achieved and the media available.

Game as a communication channel is one of the latest technology-based additions to learning aids and tools, capable of enhancing the learning process in many areas. Serious games in education may serve as effective learning tools that engage and motivate learners [44]. It is, however, important to differentiate between a game *sensu stricto* and a "game-like" interactive setting. The first requires players to engage in an artificial conflict, defined by rules, that results in a quantifiable outcome [45]. An effective digital nurturing interactive setting may require a different perception of a "game", in which, for example, no quantifiable outcome needs to be generated. The focus may simply be put on playfully acquiring sensory impressions, emotive experiences, discovery and generating deep reflective thoughts – all aspects of cognitive behavioral therapy. The perception of such an environment as a game, no matter if single or collaborative, is still present because the action therein is rooted in game mechanics.

In one of my previous papers, I discussed an approach I call "Blended Nurture" [14], a concept that aims at changing social or personal behavior through participation in "nurture games" combined with a moderated live part settings which contain both the virtual and the real components (Fig. 2).

A coach (therapist) must ensure that experiences are correctly classified and that

BLENDED NURTURE ARRANGEMENT

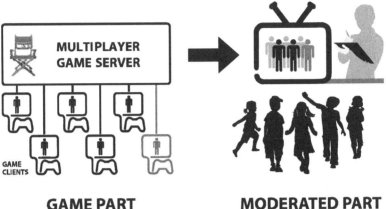

GAME PART   **MODERATED PART**

Fig. 2. "Blended Nurture" arrangement [14].

correct behavioral patterns become embedded in the cognitive structures of the brain. A setting like this reflects the classical cognitive behavioral therapy model and is thus predestined as school-based prevention and intervention measures aimed at strengthening socialization, personality development, and mental health in young people. This requires, however, collaboration between schools and psychologists, which not always can be achieved.

Nurture game concepts often rely on common sense rather than on in-depth psychological knowledge and CBT-expertise. This is the reason, why games like these do not always fulfil the promise of boosting efficacy in education, especially at tackling mental health problems. Sometimes wrong assumptions are made. Always complying to the standard definition of a game formulated by Salen and Zimmerman [45] is in my option a mistake. Relying on "get started" reports utilizing this definition (e.g. [46]) tempt game designers to think in terms of competitive settings, rules, scores, winning and losing, rewards and measurable outcomes, which is not the best starting point for the development of games in question. Another thing is that sometimes simple interactions and decision making, accentuated with appropriate (from the CBT point of view) storytelling contexts and metaphors, allow to achieve more than what a sophisticated multiplayer game may offer.

6 Conclusion

In this paper, I have discussed some basic aspects underlying creation and utilizing of "nurture games" as school-based prevention and intervention measures, aimed at strengthening socialization, personality development, and mental health in young people; "nurture" being understood as upbringing processes, promoting the development of children and adolescents on the way to adulthood.

Cognitive Behavioral Therapy (CBT) has been recognized in this paper as a fundament for the creation of games, which tackle psychological problems within a preventive context. Digital therapies, the CBT-based approaches in a digital domain, can help to cope with different social problems, sensitize to ethical questions, promote "correct" behavior as well as social and moral values. They can also help to reduce stress, relieve symptoms of depression and boost feelings of joy and well-being.

I claim that the standard definition of a game by Salen and Zimmerman [45] needs some refinement. It might be reasonable to recognize *collecting experiences through interaction* as a core aspect of a "game" rather, than gaining scores and achieving a quantifiable outcome. The modified perception of a game could perhaps provide a more consistent and unified view on what a game actually is, and would also allow to avoid debating on terminology and differentiation between "games", "serious games", "game-like environments" etc.

References

1. DiLalla, L.F., Gottesman, I.I. (eds.): Behavior Genetics Principles. Perspectives in Development, Personality, and Psychopathology, Decade of behavior, 1st edn. American Psychological Association, Washington, DC (2004)
2. Robinson, G.E.: Beyond nature and nurture. Science (2004). https://doi.org/10.1126/science.1095766
3. Wierzbicki, R.J.: The convergence of life and technology from the nurturing perspective. Int. J. Adv. Smart Convergence **3**(1), 7–10 (2014)
4. Horgan, J.H.: Eugenics revisited. Sci. Am. **268**(6), 122–131 (1993)
5. Gullotta, T.P., Plant, R.W., Evans, M.A. (eds.): Handbook of Adolescent Behavioral Problems. Evidence-Based Approaches to Prevention and Treatment, 2nd edn. Springer, Boston (2015). https://doi.org/10.1007/978-1-4899-7497-6
6. Zarb, J.M.: Developmental Cognitive Behavioral Therapy with Adults. Routledge, New York (2007)
7. Gackenbach, J. (ed.): Psychology and the Internet. Intrapersonal, Interpersonal, and Transpersonal Implications, 2nd edn. Elsevier, Amsterdam (2007)
8. Vince, G.: Why good people turn bad online: Experts reveal how the internet boosts the 'personal rewards of expressing outrage' (2018). http://www.dailymail.co.uk/sciencetech/article-5578675/Why-good-people-turn-bad-online-Experts-say-internet-amplifies-rewards-expressing-outrage.html
9. Birkerts, S.: Changing the Subject. Art and Attention in the Internet Age. Graywolf Press, Minneapolis (2015)
10. Michaud, P.-A., Fombonne, E.: Common mental health problems. BMJ (Clin. Res. Ed.) (2005). https://doi.org/10.1136/bmj.330.7495.835
11. Costello, E.J., Mustillo, S., Erkanli, A., Keeler, G., Angold, A.: Prevalence and development of psychiatric disorders in childhood and adolescence. Arch. Gen. Psychiatry (2003). https://doi.org/10.1001/archpsyc.60.8.837
12. Ford, T., Goodman, R., Meltzer, H.: The British child and adolescent mental health survey 1999: the prevalence of DSM-IV disorders. J. Am. Acad. Child Adolescent Psychiatry (2003). https://doi.org/10.1097/00004583-200310000-00011
13. Fombonne, E.: Epidemiological surveys of autism and other pervasive developmental disorders: an update. J. Autism Dev. Disorders **33**(4), 365–382 (2003)

14. Wierzbicki, R.J.: Blended nurture. In: Kim, T., et al. (eds.) ASEA 2011. CCIS, vol. 257, pp. 643–649. Springer, Heidelberg (2011). https://doi.org/10.1007/978-3-642-27207-3_70
15. Spitzer, M.: Digitale Demenz. Wie wir uns und unsere Kinder um den Verstand bringen. Droemer, München (2014)
16. Anderson, C.A., et al.: Violent video game effects on aggression, empathy, and prosocial behavior in Eastern and Western countries: a meta-analytic review. Psychol. Bull. (2010). https://doi.org/10.1037/a0018251
17. Kowalski, R.M., Limber, S., Agatston, P.W.: Cyberbullying. Bullying in the Digital Age, 2nd edn. Wiley-Blackwell, Malden (2012)
18. Ramchandani, P.: Prevalence of childhood psychiatric disorders may be underestimated. Evid.-Based Mental Health **7**(2), 59 (2004)
19. Bor, R., Palmer, S. (eds.): A Beginner's Guide to Training in Counselling & Psychotherapy. SAGE Publications, Thousand Oaks (2002)
20. Freud, S.: General introduction to psychoanalysis. Createspace Independent. [Place of publication not identified] (2012)
21. Ahles, S.R.: Our Inner World. A Guide to Psychodynamics & Psychotherapy. Johns Hopkins University Press, Baltimore (2004)
22. Fonagy, P.: The effectiveness of psychodynamic psychotherapies: an update. World Psychiatry: Official J. World Psychiatric Assoc. (WPA) (2015). https://doi.org/10.1002/wps.20235
23. Diamond, M.J., Christian, C.: The Second Century of Psychoanalysis. Evolving Perspectives on Therapeutic Action. CIPS Series on the Boundaries of Psychoanalysis. Karnac, London (2011)
24. Haggerty, J.: Psychodynamic Therapy. Psych Central (2018). https://psychcentral.com/lib/psychodynamic-therapy/
25. Kernberg, O.F.: The four basic components of psychoanalytic technique and derived psychoanalytic psychotherapies. World Psychiatry: Official J. World Psychiatric Assoc. (WPA) (2016). https://doi.org/10.1002/wps.20368
26. Muntau, G.: Cognitive Behavioral Therapy: Master Your Brain, Depression and Anxiety. CreateSpace Independent Publishing Platform (2017)
27. Padesky, C.A.: Schema change processes in cognitive therapy. Clin. Psychol. Psychother. (1994). https://doi.org/10.1002/cpp.5640010502
28. Fenn, K., Byrne, M.: The key principles of cognitive behavioural therapy. InnovAiT (2013). https://doi.org/10.1177/1755738012471029
29. Wenzel, A., Kleiman, K.R.: Cognitive Behavioral Therapy for Perinatal Distress. Routledge/Taylor & Francis Group, Routledge/New York (2015)
30. Panksepp, J.: Affective Neuroscience. The Foundations of Human and Animal Emotions. Series in Affective Science. Oxford University Press, Oxford (2005)
31. Chisholm-Burns, M., Schwinghammer, T., Wells, B.G., Wells, B., Malone, P., Dipiro, J. (eds.): Pharmacotherapy Principles and Practice, 3rd edn. McGraw-Hill Publishing, New York (2013)
32. Harwood, M.D., Farrar, M.J.: Conflicting emotions: the connection between affective perspective taking and theory of mind. Br. J. Dev. Psychol. **24**(2), 401–418 (2006)
33. Briers, S.: Brilliant Cognitive Behavioural Therapy. How to Use CBT to Improve Your Mind and Your Life, 2nd edn. Pearson, Harlow (2012)
34. Ackerman, C.J., Turkoski, B.: Using guided imagery to reduce pain and anxiety. Home Healthcare Nurse **18**(8), 524–530 (2000)
35. Nezu, A.M., Nezu, C.M., D'Zurilla, T.: Problem-Solving Therapy. A Treatment Manual. Springer, New York (2012)

36. Cristea, I., Szentagotai-Tatar, A., Lucacel, R.: Differential effects of self-statements following a self-esteem threatening situation. J. Evid.-Based Psychotherapies **14**, 39–52 (2014)
37. Herbert, J.D., Forman, E.M. (eds.): Acceptance and Mindfulness in Cognitive Behavior Therapy. Understanding and Applying the New Therapies. Wiley, Hoboken (2011)
38. Reinecke, M.A., Dattilio, F.M., Freeman, A. (eds.): Cognitive Therapy with Children and Adolescents. A Casebook for Clinical Practice, 2nd edn. Guilford Press, New York (2003)
39. Ellis, A.: Reason and Emotion in Psychotherapy. Lyle Stuart, Oxford (1962)
40. Beck, A.T.: Cognitive Therapy and the Emotional Disorders. International Universities Press, New York (1976)
41. Blenkiron, P.: Stories and analogies in cognitive behaviour therapy: a clinical review. Behav. Cogn. Psychother. (1999). https://doi.org/10.1017/s1352465804001766
42. Wierzbicki, R.J., Bohnke, P.: Exploiting convergence of life with technology to tackle real-life problems by means of computer games. Int. J. Adv. Smart Convergence (2013). https://doi.org/10.7236/ijasc2013.2.2.1
43. Spiegler, M.D., Guevremont, D.C. (eds.): Contemporary Behavior Therapy, 5th edn. Wadsworth, Cengage Learning, Belmont (2010)
44. Li, J.: Video games in classrooms: an interview with Zack Gilbert. Horizon (2016). https://doi.org/10.1108/oth-03-2016-0009
45. Salen, K., Zimmerman, E.: Rules of Play. Game Design Fundamentals. The MIT Press, Cambridge (2010)
46. Baranowski, T., Buday, R., Thompson, D., Lyons, E.J., Lu, A.S., Baranowski, J.: Developing games for health behavior change: getting started. Games Health J. (2013). https://doi.org/10.1089/g4h.2013.0048

Posters

Data Reduction of Indoor Point Clouds

Stephan Feichter and Helmut Hlavacs[(⊠)]

Entertainment Computing Research Group, University of Vienna, Vienna, Austria
helmut.hlavacs@univie.ac.at

Abstract. The reconstruction and visualization of three-dimensional point-cloud models, obtained by terrestrial laser scanners, is interesting to many research areas. This paper presents an algorithm to decimate redundant information in real-world indoor point-cloud scenes. The key idea is to recognize planar segments from the point-cloud and to decimate their inlier points by the triangulation of the boundary, describing the shape. To achieve this RANSAC, normal vector filtering, statistical clustering, alpha shape boundary recognition and the constrained Delaunay triangulation are used. The algorithm is tested on various large dense point-clouds and is capable of reduction rates from approximately 75–95%.

Keywords: Point-cloud · Decimation · Plane detection · Triangulation

1 Introduction

The use of digital three-dimensional models of real-world environments has become popular in a variety of fields, including environment-based game design, serious gaming, robot navigation, professional civil engineering, architecture, documentation of historical structures or interior design. Terrestrial laser scanners (TLS) measure distances by laser with very high precision. For indoor environments TLS can efficiently produce complete high quality 360° scans, using and combining only a few scan positions [10,11]. The output of a TLS, is a dense point-cloud (x, y, z) spanning large areas or entire floors, that exceed millions of points. Due to the sheer amount of data, these large datasets lead to difficulties in processing, visualization and real-time use [2,7]. In indoor scenes the majority of redundant information is captured in planar surfaces like walls, floors or ceilings. These surfaces end up being over-represented by thousands of points, when they could be represented more efficiently by a primitive shape, with only a few parameters [7,8]. This paper explores a way to reduce point-cloud data size by plane segmentation, normal vector based filtering, statistical clustering, alpha shape boundary recognition and constrained Delaunay triangulation. The proposed approach is evaluated on six different real-world 3D scans of indoor environments.

2 Related Work

Data segmentation is defined as the grouping of elements into regions with similar properties. There are three main segmentation approaches for point-clouds:

E. Clua et al. (Eds.): ICEC 2018, LNCS 11112, pp. 277–283, 2018.
https://doi.org/10.1007/978-3-319-99426-0_29

region growing, clustering of features and model fitting. The region growing method is achieved by identifying a seed element and growing it within some specific patterns in the data [1]. The clustering of features method identifies patterns in the data, based on their attributes and combines them into clusters. The model fitting method is driven by estimating a mathematical model to fit the data. Such models can be geometric primitive shapes like planes, spheres or cylinders [1]. Two widely used model fitting algorithms are Random Sample and Consensus (RANSAC) and hough-transform. For the accurate representation of indoor environments in games or virtual reality, the following works have been found: In the paper of Shui et al. [11], the point-cloud first is coarse segmented by a gaussian map region growing algorithm. Then it is fine segmented using RANSAC, followed by a boundary generation. At the end a semantic graph structure for the segments is created. This is then imported into Unity3D and manually enhanced with textures. Ma et al. in [6] describe a hybrid reconstruction solution. Planar surfaces are segmented by a flatness based region growing method, then the planar surfaces and all residual objects are reconstructed differently. The objects are reconstructed by the Greedy Projection Triangulation. The planes are reconstructed with a Quad-Three-Based algorithm. At the end, object meshes and plane meshes are combined to achieve the full reconstruction of the point-cloud.

3   System Overview

The first step of the proposed pipeline is to detect and remove sparse outliers with an algorithm from Rusu et al. [5]. The second step in the pipeline is the segmentation process. Man-made structures are dominated by planar surfaces. To detect these, the concept of RANdom SAmple Consensus (RANSAC) [3], is used [12]. To define a plane, three points are needed. RANSAC selects these three points randomly and generates a plane model. Then, the algorithm detects all points belonging to the plane model within a given threshold, also known as the plane thickness. This gets repeated until the best-fit plane in the 3D point-cloud is found. This is where the highest number of inlier points fit the candidate plane model. Due to the plane thickness, the obtained point-cloud segment may contain points, belonging to other objects or planes. These points generally are found at the borders of the planes and have a different normal vector direction than the plane model. We first estimate the normal vector of each point in the point-cloud by an algorithm proposed by Hoppe et al. [4]. Then we calculate the angle between each point normal vector and the plane model normal vector. The angle is then used to filter each point by a defined threshold. The next step in the pipeline is a clustering. The filtered plane segments of the point-cloud may contain different disconnected surfaces. To further process these areas separately, a statistical clustering technique is applied. As every extracted segment has a diverse topology, an algorithm that works with no a priori knowledge of the number of clusters is necessary. The algorithm used is the k-means clustering, which separates the data points into k different clusters. With help of the elbow method and the gap statistics, the used cluster algorithm can choose the optimal number of clusters automatically [5,9]. To decimate the inlier points of each planar cluster, the boundary points of each cluster, containing all necessary information of its shape, are calculated. To achieve this, an alpha-shape-based boundary algorithm is used [6]. The algorithm repeats to assign a polygon around the points, using a set of circles. With this method, cavities of the shape, can be captured. The edge points are then connected with straight edges and are considered as the boundary [8]. The obtained boundary points get then triangulated to form a connected mesh. This is achieved by using the ordered boundary vertices as a constraint for the constrained Delaunay triangulation. At this point the proposed algorithm has processed one plane segment, found by the RANSAC algorithm, into one or more meshes. The algorithm repeats this procedure on the residual point-cloud, as long as the next found RANSAC segment contains a minimum number of point-cloud points. When the segmentation process ends, an output file (.ply) is generated, containing the generated meshes and the points of the residual point-cloud.

4 Results

The sample set to evaluate the proposed system, contains six different dense point-clouds of TLS scanned indoor environments (Fig. 1). All experiments were performed on an Intel Core i5 laptop with 3.1 GHz and 16 GB RAM. The pipeline was implemented in MATLAB R2017b, due to its ease of use and its cross platform compatibility. Each sample was fed into the pipeline with predefined parameters. The algorithm achieves acceptable results for every sample, resulting in reduction ratios from 73.15% to 96.50%. Table 1 gives a quantitative overview of the plane segments found by RANSAC, the total point count of the original TLS scan, the number of the residual point-cloud points and triangulated faces, the processing time and the point reduction rate for each sample. The visual results for each sample are depicted in Fig. 2. To achieve a full reconstruction, the residual point-cloud points have to be triangulated with for example, the greedy projection triangulation.

Table 1. Point-cloud reduction results

Nr.	Name	#Planes	#Total pts.	#Residual pts.	Faces	Duration[h]	Reduction
1	Ballroom	11	25,793,831	5,189,432	33,360	20:03	79.88%
2	Bedroom	11	20,133,594	2,834,338	13,036	6:53	85.92%
3	Loft	7	13,500,000	2,973,802	7,358	5:46	77.97%
4	Boardroom	8	13,476,844	3,618,515	12,654	5:14	73.15%
5	Construction	10	11,686,367	1,161,448	7,284	4:11	90.06%
6	Officeroom	9	8,550,825	299,445	9,593	5:45	96.50%

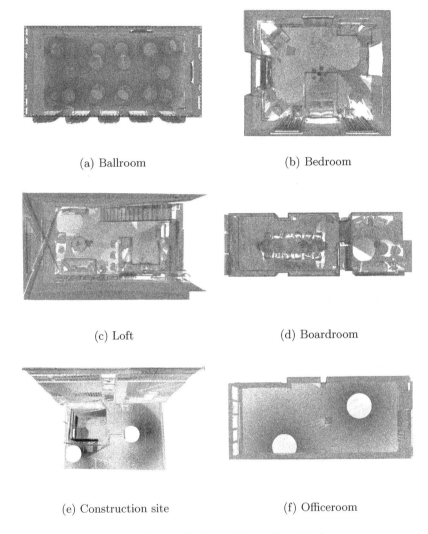

(a) Ballroom

(b) Bedroom

(c) Loft

(d) Boardroom

(e) Construction site

(f) Officeroom

Fig. 1. Point-cloud sample set (top view).

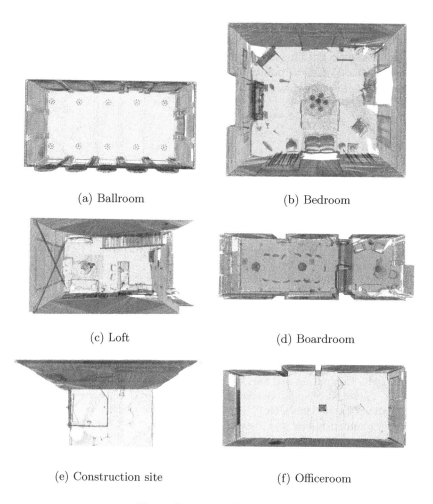

(a) Ballroom

(b) Bedroom

(c) Loft

(d) Boardroom

(e) Construction site

(f) Officeroom

Fig. 2. Result set (top view).

5   Conclusion

In this paper, we have developed an automatic system for 3D point-cloud processing, which is capable to reduce the number of points of real-world indoor environments produced by terrestrial laser scanner. After denoising, planar segments of the point-cloud are extracted. By normal vector filtering and clustering of the segments, a number of planar clusters can be obtained. The boundary points, which describe the shape of the planar clusters, are then triangulated. This reduces the number of interior points and simplifies the output mesh, but preserves its geometry. The experiments on six different TLS scanned indoor scenes with 8 to 25 million points and varying characteristics are quantitative and visible acceptable. We were able to reduce the total point count by approximately 75–95%.

References

1. Awwad, T.M., Zhu, Q., Du, Z., Zhang, Y.: An improved segmentation approach for planar surfaces from unstructured 3D point clouds. Photogramm. Rec. **25**(129), 5–23 (2010)
2. Deschaud, J.E., Goulette, F.: A fast and accurate plane detection algorithm for large noisy point clouds using filtered normals and voxel growing. In: Proceedings of the 5th International Symposium on 3D Data Processing, Visualization and Transmission (3DPVT 2010) (2010)
3. Fischler, M.A., Bolles, R.C.: Random sample consensus: a paradigm for model fitting with applications to image analysis and automated cartography. Commun. ACM **24**, 381–395 (1981)
4. Hoppe, H., DeRose, T., Duchamp, T., McDonald, J., Stuetzle, W.: Surface reconstruction from unorganized points, vol. 26. ACM (1992)
5. Liu, X., Zhang, X., Cheng, S., Nguyen, T.B.: A novel algorithm for planar extracting of 3D point clouds. In: Proceedings of the International Conference on Internet Multimedia Computing and Service, pp. 142–145. ACM (2016)
6. Ma, L., Favier, R., Do, L., Bondarev, E., de With, P.H.: Plane segmentation and decimation of point clouds for 3D environment reconstruction. In: 2013 IEEE Consumer Communications and Networking Conference (CCNC), pp. 43–49. IEEE (2013)
7. Ma, L., Whelan, T., Bondarev, E., de With, P.H., McDonald, J.: Planar simplification and texturing of dense point cloud maps. In: 2013 European Conference on Mobile Robots (ECMR), pp. 164–171. IEEE (2013)
8. Michailidis, G.T., Pajarola, R.: Bayesian graph-cut optimization for wall surfaces reconstruction in indoor environments. Vis. Comput. **33**(10), 1347–1355 (2017)
9. Nguyen, A., Le, B.: 3D point cloud segmentation: a survey. In: 2013 6th IEEE Conference on Robotics, Automation and Mechatronics (RAM), pp. 225–230. IEEE (2013)
10. Sahin, C.: Planar segmentation of indoor terrestrial laser scanning point clouds via distance function from a point to a plane. Opt. Lasers Eng. **64**, 23–31 (2015). https://doi.org/10.1016/j.optlaseng.2014.07.007. http://www.sciencedirect.com/science/article/pii/S0143816614001791

11. Shui, W., Liu, J., Ren, P., Maddock, S., Zhou, M.: Automatic planar shape segmentation from indoor point clouds. In: Proceedings of the 15th ACM SIGGRAPH Conference on Virtual-Reality Continuum and Its Applications in Industry, vol. 1, pp. 363–372. ACM (2016)
12. Yang, M.Y., Förstner, W.: Plane detection in point cloud data. In: Proceedings of the 2nd International Conference on Machine Control Guidance, Bonn, vol. 1, pp. 95–104 (2010)

Designing 'Wall Mounted Level' – A Cooperative Mixed-Reality Game About Reconciliation

Kyoung Swearingen[(⊠)] and Scott Swearingen[(⊠)]

Department of Design, The Ohio State University, Columbus, OH 43210, USA
{swearingen.75,swearingen.16}@osu.edu

Abstract. 'Wall Mounted Level' is a cooperative mixed-reality game that leverages multimodal interactions to support its narrative of 'reconciliation'. In it, players control their digitally projected characters and navigate them across a hand-drawn physical sculpture as they collaborate towards a shared goal: finding one another. The digital and physical characteristics of the game are further reflected in the ways in which players interact with the software and one another through 'touch'. This paper discusses the design choices we made in creating the varying modes of player collaboration through both digital and physical engagement.

Keywords: Game design · Art · Mixed-reality

1 Introduction

The game begins with a cut scene of the two player-characters having an argument with one another. Shortly after, it resolves to the 'Next Day' where the players take control of the characters and seek to reunite them under the guidance of supporting audio and visual cues. The fractured landscape doubles as a metaphor for the characters' internal struggle as they navigate a fragmented space filled with obstacles of memories past and other puzzles as they strive to reach one another. The space is composed of interiors and exteriors that reveal and conceal not only the characters, but also obstacles that are meant to be avoided. These obstacles are the remains of the argument that took place 'the day before', and need to be navigated around as they patrol the environment. More so, they also reveal in some cases the path that players must take, and should be considered carefully as they make progress. Additionally, lights will turn on as you enter buildings to help guide you, as well as the NPCs which are scattered throughout the environment. In 'Wall Mounted Level', knowing the position of the other player (your goal) is just as important as knowing where your own character is. Thus we decided to connect the characters visually with a digital string that also turns red when either one of them touches an obstacle. This visual language parallels the collaboration between the players themselves who are also connected to one another physically.

E. Clua et al. (Eds.): ICEC 2018, LNCS 11112, pp. 284–288, 2018.
https://doi.org/10.1007/978-3-319-99426-0_30

2   The Environment

The game environment is a hand drawn cityscape that was laser-cut and assembled into a paper relief sculpture. Serving as a metaphor of the characters' internal struggles, we decided to further fragment the sculpture and create a deeper relief out of it. Other materials that we considered for the construction of 'Wall Mounted Level' included cardboard, chipboard, wood, and acrylic plexiglass, but ultimately, we favored the inherent quality of paper as a tangible, vulnerable, interactive medium. These qualities also resonated with the characters' fragile relationship while inspiring interaction between the players.

The flatness of the paper, however, too closely resembled the 2D screenspace of monitors and flat screens. Wanting to leverage the physical quality of the material, we were compelled to abstract the level into 3D space which resulted in the creation of a relief sculpture. Using a laser cutter, we separated the level into six distinct chunks that we cut and reassembled into a wooden frame to be hung on a wall (Fig. 1).

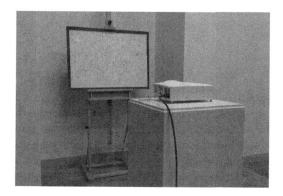

Fig. 1. 'Wall Mounted Level' (24" × 36", laser-cut illustration board and paper). Sitting on an easel in front of projector. Testing dimensions and footprint of entire setup. November, 2017.

3   Mechanics

All of the digital elements are projected onto 'Wall Mounted Level' using projection mapping and other compositing techniques. As characters move through interior spaces, we mask them by projecting black pixels onto a sorting layer in front of them. At the same time, windows and doors light up in a sorting layer behind them to indicate which building they are currently located in. This helps the players keep track of their own location as they move throughout the level. Roaming NPC's and enemy AI (the remnants of the argument that took place 'the day before') also help to describe the overall flow of the level.

As enemy AI patrol the level and attempt to thwart player progress, 'good memories' (the blue orbs) are scattered throughout the level which can be picked up, listened to, and used to revive the characters' health. Tethering characters to one another also reinforces our narrative of connectedness while prompting deeper cooperation and collaboration between the players themselves (Fig. 2).

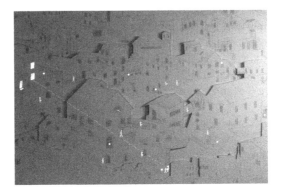

Fig. 2. 'Wall Mounted Level'. Players in pursuit of one another while being trailed by enemy AI. Lit interiors help to guide them. Note the blue tether that connects the characters to one another. November, 2017. (Color figure online)

4 Technology

Because the level was no longer flat after abstracting it into 3D space, single-exposure projection was not a suitable option given the range of depths. Using the software Isadora [1] allowed us to project multiple exposures at the same time and corner-pin them independently. This provided us the flexibility to further fragment the level while yielding greater agility in designing it.

Unity 3D handles our player collision, game logic and scripting in addition to managing and compositing all visible elements including the characters, their tether, enemy AI, NPC's, pick-ups, lighting, and black pixels used for masking. Employing two handheld controllers and a Makey Makey [2] for player input, Unity sends its live feed through a Syphon client to Isadora for handling projection mapping.

5 Modes of Engagement

The modes of player interaction parallel the sculpture itself in terms of digital and physical engagement. Digital interactions account for lateral movement as each player steers their own character through the environment using an analog stick. Moving up and down ladders and transitioning between floors requires players to touch one another and complete a 'Makey Makey' circuit that they are connected to, which in turn sends the appropriate input message to the software that is listening for it. However, this input message is shared between both players and will affect them equally if they are in valid positions (e.g. at the top of a ladder, or at the base of a stairwell) when the message is sent. Employing both digital and physical interactions in this manner also provides opportunities for symmetrical and asymmetrical collaboration. As a collaborative effort, lateral movement is an asynchronous interaction whereas vertical movement is a synchronous one that affects both players equally and at the same time. As a result, player collaboration intensifies in tandem with this multimodal experience. Similar to the physical quality of the sculpture, the verbal communication and physical coordination that takes place between the players is especially important to us in terms of human-facing interactions as it extrends the narrative of 'reconciliation' (Fig. 3).

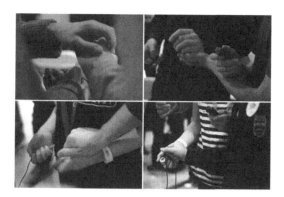

Fig. 3. Close-up of player interactions. November, 2017.

6 Motivation

Our motivation for creating 'Wall Mounted Level' was to embrace tangible surfaces as mediums for digital games to exist in, and for the interactions between players to occur in person. Utilizing real, physical surfaces for our environment helps to secure the sense of presence between the players, thereby increasing opportunities for empathy to exist between them. Furthermore, we increase the value of these human-facing inter-actions by promoting 'meaningful choice' through a game that involves some risk and other shared experiences. Throughout its development, 'reconciliation' served as the underlying narrative and concept that drove aesthetic choices, gameplay, and the interface not only between the players and the game, but between the players them-selves. It was important to us that the game required the physical presence of the players to embolden the collaboration between them. This aided in establishing a deeper connection between the players and the game world itself which is a tangible, physical object. In conclusion, 'Wall Mounted Level' is a cooperative multiplayer game that uses mixed-reality to support its narrative, interactions, game-play and aesthetic elements to promote multimodal collaboration between its players.

References

1. Isadora. https://en.wikipedia.org/wiki/Isadora_(software)
2. Makey Makey. https://en.wikipedia.org/wiki/Makey_Makey

3. Link, S., Barkschat, B., Zimmerer, C.: An intelligent multimodal mixed reality real-time strategy game. In: Virtual Reality (VR). IEEE (2016)
4. Seif El-Nasr, M., et al.: Understanding and evaluating cooperative games. In: CHI 2010 Proceedings of the SIGCHI Conference on Human Factors in Computing Systems, pp. 252–262 (2010)

Automatic Generation of the Periodic Hair Motion of 3D Characters for Anime Production

Kenji Furukawa$^{(\boxtimes)}$ and Susumu Nakata

Ritsumeikan University, Kusatsu, Shiga, Japan
is0279fe@ed.ritsumei.ac.jp

Abstract. Many Japanese animation products benefit from the techniques of computer graphics. In the animation process, three-dimensional (3D) characters are often rendered so that the characters move according to a Japanese traditional animation style called limited animation or anime. The hair of the characters is modeled as a set of bunches and the motion of each bunch should also be defined in the manner of limited animation, which is different from its physically correct motion. We present a method to produce a hair motion for 3D characters that is appropriate for limited animation under the assumptions that the hair motion is periodic and other objects, including the camera, remain stationary. We present a mathematical formulation of this hair motion based on a typical technique used in traditional hand-drawn anime and apply the motion to each bunch of hair of an example 3D character.

Keywords: Hair motion · Animation · Computer graphics

1 Introduction

Most Japanese animations are created following to the traditional hand-drawn style called "limited animation," which is a set of techniques for expressing motion using a small number of images [1]. Such products are often called "anime," and, in this style, the depicted motions of characters and objects are different from the motions predicted by real physics. The motions of characters and objects are depicted in a way specific to limited animation and, as a result, the motions are determined differently from typical computer graphics (CG) motions. A typical example of such an expression is hair motion. The hair of a character is often depicted as a set of bunches, each of which moves according to the style of limited animation.

The purpose of this study is to develop a method that determines the hair motion of CG characters in the style of limited animation. We assume that hair motion is periodic and we formulate the periodic motion of each bunch of hair as a function by observing hand-drawn animes. In addition, we provide a technique to discretize the periodic motion over time so that it is suitable for limited animation.

There are related studies that have tried to reproduce the shape and motion of hair. Sakai et al. [2] reproduced the shape of hair as a three-dimensional (3D) surface model. Yeh et al. [3] developed a method to generate the motion of illustrated hair based on

E. Clua et al. (Eds.): ICEC 2018, LNCS 11112, pp. 289–292, 2018.
https://doi.org/10.1007/978-3-319-99426-0_31

fluid simulation. Our method is suitable for the creation of CG-based animation in which the motion is defined according to style of the limited animation.

2 Proposed Method

The first step is to identify the approach needed to depict hair motion as a set of still pictures used in traditional limited animation. In this study, we assume that the hair motion is periodic and, for simplicity, we assume neither the character nor the camera moves. In the late 1940s, a guideline for depicting periodic hair motion for anime production was presented by Masaoka Kenzo, a creator in the early days of Japanese anime production. Our investigation, conducted using discussion with professional animators and some animation textbooks, shows that most current animes inherit this traditional approach, which mainly consists of two techniques: a hair line is drawn as if a mass of air moves under that line (Fig. 1, left) and periodic motion is depicted by repeatedly applying a few still pictures. The number of pictures is typically between three and eight per cycle.

The second step is to formulate the hair motion. We assume a given 3D hair model that consists of a set of bunches. Moreover, a skeleton without branches is assigned to each bunch (Fig. 1, right). Our approach is to define the shape of a horizontal hair line as a function of time and position, discretize it in time and space, retrieve rotation angles, and then apply them to the nodes of the 3D skeleton. We define the shape of a horizontal hair line as follows:

$$f(x, t) = -\frac{a}{s}\left(\frac{x}{\pi}\right)^p \left(\cos\left(\frac{x}{k} - \frac{2\pi}{T}t\right) + \frac{1}{s}\right) \quad (0 \leq x \leq \pi), \tag{1}$$

where x is the relative distance from the root of the hair line, t is time, and T is the period of hair motion. Parameters a, k, and s respectively determine the amplitude and spatial period of waving hair and the strength of gravity. The remaining parameter p determines the proportions of the wave amplitudes at the root and tip.

The third step is to determine the discretization of (1) in time. We assume that the frame rate of the produced movie is N_{FPS}, which is typically 24 frames per second. In limited animation, the number of pictures is lower than N_{FPS}. Hence, one still picture is used for two or three consecutive frames, even if the characters are in motion. Let N_{Dup} be the standard number of frames over which a single still picture is duplicated. Note that the number of duplicate frames is typically two or three and changes depending on the scene. In this step, we determine the t at which still pictures are required for the given constants T, N_{FPS}, and N_{Dup}.

The given frame rate leads to the fact that $N_{Frame} = [N_{FPS}T]$ frames are used for one cycle of the periodic hair motion, where the $[\cdot]$ operator denotes rounding to the nearest integer. Such rounding is a requirement for depicting periodic motion by repeatedly using still pictures and, as a result, the period of a produced movie N_{Frame}/N_{FPS} is slightly different from the given period T. In other words, this difference is a requirement of the style of limited animation.

We define the number of still pictures in a cycle as $N_{Pict} = \lceil N_{Frame}/N_{Dup} \rceil$, where the $\lceil \cdot \rceil$ operation denotes rounding up. This number is determined so that the number of frames to which a still picture is assigned does not exceed the value of standard duplication N_{Dup}. As a result, a still image is assigned to N_{Dup} or $N_{Dup} - 1$ frames. Consequently, we define the interval for the time discretization as $\Delta t = T/N_{Pict}$. Finally, we duplicate the former $N_{Pict} - K$ pictures N_{Dup} times and we duplicate the remaining pictures $N_{Dup} - 1$ times, where $K = N_{Dup}N_{Pict} - N_{Frame}$. As a result, all the pictures are assigned to N_{Frame} frames to depict one cycle of hair motion.

We spatially discretize the shape of hair defined in (1) at each discrete time point, obtain the rotation angles at all the discrete positions, and apply the angles to the nodes of the skeleton to determine the pose corresponding to each still picture. The final movie is given by repeating N_{Frame} frames using the N_{Pict} pictures rendered according to the above process.

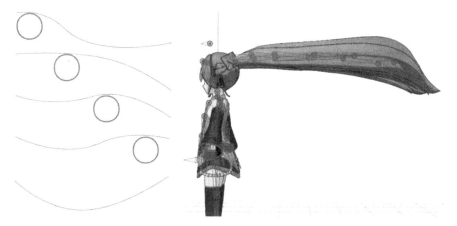

Fig. 1. Left: example of hair motion in Japanese anime style created by professional animator Shotaro Imai. Right: example of a skeleton model of "Hatsune Miku," a character created by Crypton Future Media, Inc. (http://www.piapro.net).

3 Experiment

Figure 2 shows a set of still images produced using our method with $N_{FPS} = 24$, $N_{Dup} = 2$, and $T = 0.45$. In this example, we use the model called "Tune-chan," provided by G-Tune, which has 14 hair bunches. As a result, six pictures are generated to depict a cycle and are assigned to 11 frames. For the error analysis, we defined a skeleton corresponding to a bunch of hair in each scene of some hand-drawn anime products, applied our method to the skeleton, and measured the angular errors and node displacements. Table 1 shows the angular errors and the relative node displacements. In addition, we measured the error between one of the hand-drawn animes and the skeleton obtained using the physics engine provided in MikuMikuDance, a software tool for 3D character animation, to compare the accuracy of our method with that of a physics engine. The average angular error of our method is 11.4° while that of the physics engine is 27.1°. These results indicate that our method provides hair motion that is similar to that of hand-drawn animation and, as far as the above case is concerned, the motion is more accurate than that given by a physics engine in animation software.

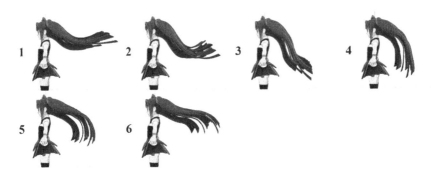

Fig. 2. Example of one cycle of hair motion with $s = 1.2$, $k = 1.0$, $a = 0.8$, and $T = 0.45$. The model "Tune-chan" was provided by G-Tune (http://www.g-tune.jp/campaign/10th/mmd/).

Table 1. Error of generated hair motion

Studio	Title	Angular error	Position error
Sunrise	My-HiME (2004) Ep. 26, 12:47	18.1°	13.8%
Diomedea	KanColle: The Movie (2016) 53:27	10.9°	7.0%
Diomedea	KanColle: The Movie (2016) 58:09	7.4°	4.7%
Satelight	Symphogear AXZ (2017) Ep.1, 7:26	10.6°	5.7%
Satelight	Symphogear AXZ (2017) Ep.2, 8:54	9.8°	7.5%

4   Conclusion

We developed a method to produce the anime-like hair motion of a 3D character model with a skeleton when both the character and camera are stationary. We define the motion of a horizontal line as a function of position and time, discretize the motion in time according to the style of limited animation, and apply the node angles to the 3D skeleton to obtain the hair motion of the character.

References

1. Lamarre, T.: The Anime Machine: A Media Theory of Animation. University of Minnesota Press, Minnesota (2009)
2. Sakai, T., Savchenko, V.: Skeleton-based cartoon hair modeling using blobby model. In: SIGGRAPH Asia 2013, Article No. 17. ACM (2013)
3. Yeh, C., Jayaraman, P.K., Liu, X., Fu, C., Lee, T.: 2.5D cartoon hair modeling and manipulation. IEEE Trans. Vis. Comput. Graph. **21**, 304–314 (2015)

An iTV Prototype for Content Unification

Jorge Abreu[(⊠)] ⓘ, Pedro Almeida ⓘ, Ana Velhinho ⓘ,
Sílvia Fernandes ⓘ, and Rafael Guedes ⓘ

University of Aveiro, DigiMedia, Aveiro, Portugal
{jfa,almeida,ana.velhinho,silvia.fernandes,
rafaelguedes}@ua.pt

Abstract. This paper addresses an iTV prototype able to offer contents from different sources over a unique and common user interface. The prototype was developed under the UltraTV project, formed by a consortium that gathers the industry and the academy to develop a new digital entertainment approach to the iTV ecosystem. The high-fidelity prototype runs on an Android set-top box and combines TV programs with Over-the-top (OTT) videos (from YouTube, Facebook Videos, and Netflix). The system focuses on unification, recommendation and profiling features, able to accommodate the demands of younger viewers. Adopting a User-Centered Design methodology, the development of the prototype benefited from continuous feedback obtained on different validation phases, namely a review by experts, laboratory tests, and a field trial.

Keywords: Unification · Interactive TV · Personalization · UX
Usability

1 Research Problem and Motivational Factors

The goal of the team was to build a Set-top box (STB) based application that allowed for the unification of TV content, aiming to enhance the entertainment experience offered to different consumer profiles, including younger generations – on the one hand by providing content beyond the traditional broadcast channels to the classic TV consumers (promoting the diversification of their choices), and on the other by aiming to regain the attention in TV content and improve the quality of OTT content viewing on the large TV screen for those who are used to watch videos on their computer and mobile devices. Targeting a different approach to content 'surfing', the prototype aims to foster the discovery of content from different players and sources.

2 iTV Content Unification Demo

2.1 UCD Prototype Development

By following an approach that included identifying the users' needs and specifying the context of use by means of characterization surveys, the development followed an iterative and continuous process. This approach allowed for the incorporation of the

E. Clua et al. (Eds.): ICEC 2018, LNCS 11112, pp. 293–296, 2018.
https://doi.org/10.1007/978-3-319-99426-0_32

users' suggestions and opinions. This way, the UltraTV project followed a User-Centered Design methodology and took into consideration a participatory Design approach.

This process occurred across several months in which the development went through different design stages: hand drawn and digital sketches, low fidelity prototypes, mid-fidelity and high-fidelity STB deployments. Throughout these stages, assessments of the UI design, usability and overall User Experience were made. Following the internal validations of first sketches and low fidelity mock-ups, the research team adopted an evaluation methodology that included a review by experts [1, 4], a UX lab testing phase [2] and a month-long field trial with end-users [5]. The assessment was made using several UX evaluation methods and metrics and interviews. Following laboratorial testing and continuing an iterative product design development, a functional STB-based prototype was built, supported by the user experience responses to the previous mid-fidelity prototype [3]. Usability and control issues were solved based on observation and the analysis of previous results.

2.2 Functional Requirements and User Interface

The Luna™ framework[1], an application engine optimized for the development of context-oriented television interfaces, was chosen as the implementation platform due to its performance, graphic raw speed and time to product implementation. Luna includes a graphic engine and an API targeted to the development of TV user interfaces. Considered as a 'TV Browser', Luna allows to maximize GPU (Graphics Processing Unit) performance when compared to other HTML5 browsers. In graphical terms, it presents as main features text rendering, a set of built-in effects, 'frame-accurate' animations; resolutions up to 4 K; and the support for 'video texture'.

Within an IPTV (Internet Protocol for Television) framework supported by the operator's channel offer, the high-fidelity version of the prototype incorporates the backend with a Web API that feeds the application with the operator's live content and video on demand, and access to the OTT sources YouTube, Facebook Videos, and Netflix. These features, when presented on a profile based TV user interface, are the starting point to create a dynamic delivery of contents, based on the user profile and consumption behaviors.

The UltraTV main screen unifies the content on a single UI (Fig. 1). This allows the user to, in a grid based navigation, have access to a diversified bundle of content with a reduced number of interactions. Content is displayed on thumbnails and cards, showing up to 140 different previews of shows, movies, and videos with no visual differentiation of the content sources. The home screen is structured into columns of content that are placed either according to genre/type of content, source or live TV. The center column displays a list of live TV channels, arranged in a traditional numbered sequence to attend to the operator's policies, while two "Suggestions" columns (TV and Web) display content based on the user's profile and viewing history.

---

[1] Craftwork Homepage, https://www.craftwork.dk/products/luna/index.html, last accessed 2018/06/01.

Fig. 1. Home screen interface

A unified search engine, with predictive keyboard, retrieves results from Catch-up TV and OTT sources sorted in rows, presenting labeled card-based thumbnails of the content for quick scan and access (Fig. 2).

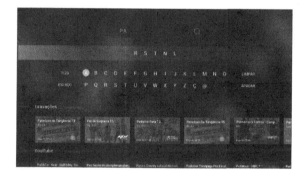

Fig. 2. Unified search interface

Additional content from different sources is suggested by several means. In full screen, the user has access to a side menu with cross reference recommendations (e.g. a YouTube video related to the TV show that's being watched) or an item page that offers similar content for the available on-demand, DVR or online sources. As shown in Fig. 3, in the home screen the user has access to another level of content by selecting a "see more" card, that takes him to a grid of the same category (e.g. the "see more Shows" section will offer every TV show available on catch-up TV and VoD, organized in different genres, according to the relevant suggestions for the active profile). Both these options create the chance for the user to explore beyond the traditional IPTV operator offer and discover new content from alternative content sources.

Furthermore, to provide a unique user experience for each profile, the suggestions are made by taking into consideration the users' choices and viewing habits. By assigning favorites or blocking content that they do not want to watch (Fig. 4), the users enhance the recommender system by directly curating their preferences. More than liking or disliking the content, the user is making the choice to save it on a favorites list (displayed in a "My Content" section), or to ask the platform to ignore it on its grid.

Fig. 3. "See more" card on the home screen (left), second level grid for "See more shows" (right)

Fig. 4. Full screen menu with "Favorite" (left) and "I don't want to see this" (right) options

Acknowledgments. This paper is a result of the UltraTV - UltraHD TV Application Ecosystem project (grant agreement no. 17738), funded by COMPETE 2020, Portugal 2020 and the European Union through the European Regional Development Fund (FEDER).

References

1. Abreu, J., Almeida, P., Silva, T., Velhinho, A., Fernandes, S.: Using experts review to validate an iTV UI for the unification of contents. In: Proceedings of the 12th International Multi-Conference on Society, Cybernetics and Informatics (IMSCI 2018). Springer (2018)
2. Almeida, P., et al.: Iterative user experience evaluation of a user interface for the unification of TV contents. In: Abásolo, M.J., Abreu, J., Almeida, P., Silva, T. (eds.) jAUTI 2017. CCIS, vol. 813, pp. 44–57. Springer, Cham (2018). https://doi.org/10.1007/978-3-319-90170-1_4
3. Almeida, P., Abreu, J., Silva, T., et al.: UltraTV: an iTV content unification prototype. In: Proceedings of the ACM International Conference on Interactive Experiences for TV and Online Video - TVX 2018. ACM (2018)
4. Almeida, P., de Abreu, J.F., Oliveira, E., Velhinho, A.: Expert evaluation of a user interface for the unification of TV contents. In: Proceedings of the 6th Iberoamerican Conference on Applications and Usability of Interactive TV - jAUTI 2017, pp. 59–70. Universidade de Aveiro (2017)
5. Almeida, P., Jorge, A., Fernandes, S., Oliveira, E.: Content unification in iTV to enhance user experience: the UltraTV project. In: Proceedings of the ACM International Conference on Interactive Experiences for TV and Online Video - TVX 2018. ACM (2018)

Content Unification: A Trend Reshaping the iTV Ecosystem

Jorge Abreu$^{(\boxtimes)}$ ⓘ, Pedro Almeida ⓘ, Sílvia Fernandes ⓘ,
Ana Velhinho ⓘ, and Ana Rodrigues ⓘ

DigiMedia, University of Aveiro, Aveiro, Portugal
{jfa, almeida, silvia.fernandes, ana.velhinho,
ana.rodrigues}@ua.pt

Abstract. Changes in the viewer's habits, such as getting linear and nonlinear content, anytime and anywhere, are reshaping the behaviors of watching TV. In this context, many commercial stakeholders, of both Managed Operated Networks (MON) and Over-the-Top solutions (OTT), have been offering new content unification features supported by innovative user interfaces, including natural language interaction, to turn the TV viewing experience more pleasurable and engaging. Beyond the providers' commercial interests of preserving their walled gardens, the need for retention of customers is pushing channels, operators and OTT players to match each other's offers. Solutions are multiplying on leading services towards a personalized experience that aggregates several sources of content in the same interface, enriched with emergent interaction models such as voice control. Such industry trends, paired with empirical academic research, support the development of new unification-based UI solutions, that promise to have a central role in the future of the TV.

Keywords: iTV industry · Unification · User interface · OTT
Voice interaction

1 Introduction

Over the last decade, we have been witnessing a revolution in the Interactive Television (iTV) domain, with the emergence of new content delivery technologies and the increasing penetration of Over-the-Top (OTT) content. The result is the blurring of boundaries, between linear and non-linear content, the improvement of the features, and a considerable impact on the viewer's behaviors [1–3]. While providing flexibility regarding content access and consumption, new technologies have diversified interaction models and User Interfaces (UI). To map the current iTV domain, two surveys conducted under the scope of R&D projects developed in partnership with an IPTV industry player, gathered data about interaction models [4], and UI design trends [5]. This paper increments the referred studies with recent releases. After this introduction, the next section presents the state of the art of the unification trend with a focus on the iTV UIs. The third section introduces an empirically validated iTV prototype for the unification of content, developed under an R&D consortium. Finally, the main contributions of this study are drafted in the conclusion section.

© IFIP International Federation for Information Processing 2018
Published by Springer Nature Switzerland AG 2018. All Rights Reserved
E. Clua et al. (Eds.): ICEC 2018, LNCS 11112, pp. 297–300, 2018.
https://doi.org/10.1007/978-3-319-99426-0_33

2 Current Unification Trends in iTV Industry

Recently, online players have developed niche business models relying on OTT streaming technology. To face these OTT newcomers, cable Pay-TV subscriptions have started to offer additional On-Demand services. Despite the fast growth of such players, limitations on getting traditional TV channels and live content [6] kept them from taking over the TV market. Those restrictions prevent a seamless UX, perpetuating a behavior of using multiple apps displaying different settings and UIs. The lack of integrated search and cross-source recommendations is also a limitation that leads to users having a scattered audiovisual consumption across devices. The interdependent dynamics between channels and Pay-TV operators and OTT providers is bringing both sides closer together in favor of more balanced solutions regarding a personalized and content-first viewing experience. With the aim to address the most recent unification trend in the iTV domain (2017–2018 releases), this document highlights prominent operator-based versus OTT-based solutions that offer cutting-edge approaches to unification.

2.1 Sky Q

A pioneer unification partnership between UK cable company Sky and Netflix could be the beginning of a paradigmatic change. In March 2018, Sky announced that the complete Netflix catalog would be made available to their Sky Q customers in a single, unified user interface[1], allowing the user to switch between live and Netflix content seamlessly (see Fig. 1). This is a significant example of how the iTV domain is becoming more and more intertwined with an inescapable unification of sources, with both cable and OTT providers coming to terms with the benefits of a cross-content approach.

2.2 Hulu

Hulu has also rebranded its VOD platform to include a new set of live content and channels alongside their original content[2]. Hulu Live supports a "Lineup" area that presents personalized content from their on-demand and live content to each profile (see Fig. 1). Although it offers on-demand, what truly differentiates Hulu is the integration of live channels in a distinctive graphical interface. A traditional grid is replaced by lists, with contemporary gradients act as filters, setting Hulu apart from other platforms.

2.3 YouTube TV

Offering a device-independent proposal, YouTube launched the YouTube TV app in 2017[3]. While the app started out as a mobile solution to the new ways of watching TV

---

[1] Sky Group, http://bit.ly/2LcigCg, last accessed 2018/06/01.

[2] Hulu Homepage, https://www.hulu.com/live-tv, last accessed 2018/06/01.

[3] YouTube TV Homepage, http://www.tv.youtube.com, last accessed 2018/06/01.

or online audiovisual content, by combining live channels to its ever-growing catalog of user-generated content, YouTube TV has become a stand-alone product in its commercial offer of online and live content (see Fig. 1). As a streaming platform, the YouTube TV is becoming a key app for other devices, as it is now available for mobile, browser, or as an app for smart TVs. Highly flexible but limited to the USA, it is an ambitious product that will continue to grow.

Fig. 1. Sky Q (left), Hulu (center), YouTube TV app for Roku devices (right)

3   An Operator-Based Prototype for Content Unification

The product of the synergy between industry and academy, the UltraTV prototype targets the new TV generation focused on the unification and personalization [7, 8]. The prototype (Fig. 2) combines on the same UI and UX, TV content and OTT content (YouTube, Facebook videos, Netflix). With a MON-based framework supported by the operator's offer, it provides a unified access to a diversified bundle of content sorted by genres and sources. Content is displayed on a card-based grid with axis navigation and a fluid blob menu redirecting to the system's main features: "My Content" area (favorites and keep watching), filtering, profiles, unified search, and settings. Cross-content recommendations are also offered to foster the discovery of content.

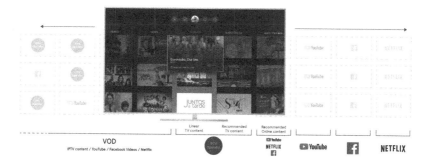

Fig. 2. UltraTV home screen interface architecture

4   Conclusion

Recent releases in the iTV industry confirm growing expectations towards personalization and unification features, favoring the aggregation of sources, merging linear with non-linear videos. The single UI horizontal unification shows a different path from existing solutions that provide content in proprietary apps. While operator-based solutions strive to accommodate in their offers streaming services (e.g. Sky Q), OTT players steadily conquer the TV market by adding live broadcast confined by restrictions (e.g. Hulu, YouTube TV). Without a fully integrated solution available on the market, research projects are developing solutions that envision enhanced viewing experiences boosted by profile-based recommendations and content discovery on a single UI. Supported by feedback of end-users and recognizing industry trends, these contributions may provide valuable user and content-centered insights agnostic to players' interests to push the next generation of television, including advanced interaction by natural language (as the project CHIC – Cooperative Holistic view on Internet and Content).

Acknowledgments. This paper is a result of the CHIC – Cooperative Holistic for Internet and Content (grant agreement number 24498), funded by COMPETE 2020 and Portugal 2020 through the European Regional Development Fund (FEDER).

References

1. Abreu, J., Nogueira, J., Becker, V., Cardoso, B.: Survey of Catch-up TV and other time-shift services: a comprehensive analysis and taxonomy of linear and nonlinear television. Telecommun. Syst. **64**, 57–74 (2017)
2. Nielsen-Company: Screen wars: The battle for eye space in a TV-everywhere world, New York (2015)
3. Ericsson-Consumerlab: TV and Media 2017: A consumer-driven future of media, Stockholm (2017)
4. Silva, T., Almeida, P., Jorge, A., Oliveira, E.: Interaction paradigms on iTV: a survey towards the future of television. In: The 9th International Multi-conference on Complexity, Informatics and Cybernetics. IMCIC, Orlando (2018)
5. Abreu, J., Almeida, P., Varsori, E., Fernandes, S.: Interactive television UI : industry trends and disruptive design approaches. In: Proceedings of 6th Iberoamerican Conference on Applications and Usability for Interactive TV, pp. 213–224. UA Editora, Aveiro (2017)
6. Waterman, D., Sherman, R., Wook Ji, S.: The economics of online television: industry development, aggregation, and "TV Everywhere". Telecomm. Policy **37**, 725–736 (2013)
7. Almeida, P., Jorge, A., Fernandes, S., Oliveira, E.: Content unification in iTV to enhance user experience: the UltraTV project. In: Proceedings of the ACM International Conference on Interactive Experiences for TV and Online Video - TVX 2018. ACM, Seoul (2018)
8. Almeida, P., et al.: UltraTV: an iTV content unification prototype. In: Proceedings of the ACM International Conference on Interactive Experiences for TV and Online Video - TVX 2018. ACM, Seoul (2018)

Creating Art Installation in Virtual Reality. The Stilleben Project

Jan K. Argasiński[✉]

Department of Games Technology and UBU Lab,
Jagiellonian University, Krakow, Poland
jan.argasinski@uj.edu.pl

Abstract. The purpose of this paper is to present piece of interactive, Virtual Reality art that was created in UBU Lab at Jagiellonian University in Krakow, Poland. The work is presented in the context of transmedial design. The main challenge and motivation was to create immersive and affective/aesthetically intensive work with engagement of only simple, minimal resources. "The Stilleben" project was based on real-life artworks (graphics, installations, albums) by the artist Jakub Woynarowski and is example of exploratory design created in interdisciplinary, cultural computing laboratory just established at the Jagiellonian University.

Keywords: Virtual reality · Interactive art · Transmedial narrative

1 Motivation

In late 2015 with the support of Polish Ministry of Science and Higher Education there was established the laboratory for creative computing at the Jagiellonian University in Krakow. The idea was to gather group of the interdisciplinary scholars and creators to engage in activities from the borderline of exploratory programming and electronic art.

In his 2016 book [1] Nick Montfort from MIT distinguished the terms "exploration" and "exploitation" in programming. The first style of coding "is not supposed to provide the single solution or 'one true way' to approach computing (. . .) it's meant, instead, (. . .) to bring the abilities of the computer to address one's important questions, artistic, cultural, or otherwise".

Among other projects carried out in the lab, such as various literary text generators or demoscene productions, there is one piece dedicated to new paradigm in interactive, transmedial storytelling [2] which is Virtual Reality. The project name is "the Stilleben" and it is being designed by an artist Jakub Woynarowski and developed by computer scientist Jan K. Argasiński.

"The Stilleben" is part of *Creative Computing. The laboratory* K/PMI/000260, National Programme for the Development of Humanities grant funded by the Polish Ministry of Science and Higher Education.

E. Clua et al. (Eds.): ICEC 2018, LNCS 11112, pp. 301–304, 2018.
https://doi.org/10.1007/978-3-319-99426-0_34

2   The Stilleben

The idea behind "the Stilleben" is to transform existing, minimalist, graphic art and installation into similar VR experience.

The guiding principle of Woynarowski's art is always an abstraction in it's board sense. His projects focus on fragile balance between objects being perceived as everyday, ordinary things and their contextual symbolic meaning. His well known work *Hikikomori* (2007) is specific kind graphic novel/album that creates sort of visual alphabet of common objects that are taken out of everyday meaning by alien intervention of an unidentified, organic substance that breaks into the space of an isolated apartment (see Fig. 1).

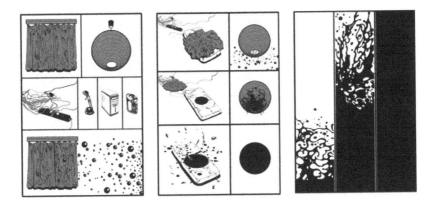

Fig. 1. J. Woynarowski, *Hikikomori*, excerpts

Hikikomori is Japanese term for "internal confinement" or "isolated entity". This word is used to describe behaviour that consists of withdrawal from public space, social life, seeking isolation. In the album and later in the art installation (2012, see Fig. 2) Woynarowski explores state of self-confinement disrupted by presence of oranic, animated substance which interferes in the hermit's space and seizes it.

"The Stilleben" is continuation and development (in a slightly different direction) of the ideas contained in *Hikikomori*. This time it referes to the concepts inspired by 17th century still life paintings (ger. *Stilleben*) and their depiction of inanimate matter in the state of half-death, being kind of *silent life*. Still life paintings and their three-dimensional equivalents - cabinets of curiosities, with their allegorical valence and somewhat disturbing conotations are interesting parallels of modern databases or even computers (17th century cabinets were able to perform various tasks, they even contained simple games).

Fig. 2. J. Woynarowski, *Hikikomori*, art installation in the Museum of Contemporary Art in Krakow (MOCAK), 2012

3   Designing "the Stilleben"

As it was said before, Woynarowski - the designer of "the Stilleben" is interested in objects elevated to the level of abstract symbols. In dialtectics of what is outside and what is inside. Synthetic self-confinement versus organic intrusiveness. In "the Stilleben" user finds himself in simple, sterile white cube that later in time becomes luxuriant garden (see Fig. 3). The evolution of "the Stilleben's" single room interior refers to tradition of visual "hexamerons", depicting the stages of Genesis process. The presented story is universal tale of the passage of energy and impermanence of forms, which disintegrate and keep reviving in new shapes.

One of the most important project challenges was to create adequate user experience in Virtual Reality [3,4]. The planned effect was to simulate a sense of *Unheimlich* (German word for uncanniness, weirdness). Un-heimlich relates to German *Heim* - a house; it can be interpreted as *un-settle*, to *not feel like home*. Wanted effect was achieved thanks to minimalistic graphic design of the installation and, partially, thanks to the creation of a special space in UBU lab (see next paragraph).

4   The Implementation

The Stilleben was implemented by Jan K. Argasiński. The application was created in Unity game engine [6] and VR hardware used was HTC Vive connected to state of the art PC computer. "The Stilleben" was scripted in C# programming language. VRTK - *Virtual Reality Toolkit* libraries were used to support the basic SteamVR platform.

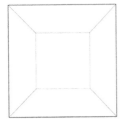  

Fig. 3. J. Woynarowski, *Stilleben*, storyboards for VR application (stages: 1st, 10th and 27th of total 30)

As integral part of the installation dedicated room was built inside UBU lab at the Jagiellonian University in Krakow. The room has exact same dimensions as the VR installation resulting in real confinement of the user. When "spectator" is immersed in VR wearing the headset - he still can move around real space and feel real, non movable objects around him. It allows for deeper influence of the virtual narrative [5]. The key effects occur when the boundary between what is virtual and what is real is broken by the interference of the organic substance. The substance is intangible, untouchable, permeates objects, floats in the air like dust, flows down the walls. Its presence, however is perceived by the user as real. A fully virtual object appears only in the final sequence when the substance explodes with vegetation eventually leading to a complete darkening of the vision.

5   Conclusion

The advanced working prototype of "the Stilleben" can be experienced in the UBU Lab at the Faculty of Management and Social Communication of the Jagiellonian University in Krakow, Poland. We believe our work to be interesting piece of art and an informative undertaking in the field of exploratory design. In investigating the boundaries of new medium.

References

1. Montfort, N.: Exploratory Programming for Arts and Humanities. MIT Press, Cambridge (2016)
2. Bolter, J.D.: Writing Space: Computers, Hypertext and the Remediation of Print, 2nd edn. Routledge, Mahwah (2001)
3. Grau, O.: Virtual Art. From Illusion to Immersion. MIT Press, Cambridge (2003)
4. Kac, E. (ed.): Signs of Life. Bio Art and Beyond. MIT Press, Cambridge (2007)
5. Kwon, M.: One Place After Another. Site-Specific Art and Locational Identity. MIT Press, Cambridge (2002)
6. Linowes, J.: Unity Virtual Reality Projects. Pactk Publishing, Birmingham (2015)

Design of a Mixed-Reality Serious Game to Tackle a Public Health Problem

Tiago França Melo Lima[1,2]([⊠]) (iD), João Paulo Ferreira Beltrame[1],
Carlos Ramos Niquini[1], Breno Gonçalves Barbosa[1],
and Clodoveu Augusto Davis Jr.[2] (iD)

[1] Federal University of Ouro Preto (UFOP), João Monlevade, MG, Brazil
tiagolima@decsi.ufop.br
[2] Computer Science Department, Federal University of Minas Gerais,
Belo Horizonte, MG, Brazil
clodoveu@dcc.ufmg.br

Abstract. Despite the emergence of several game-based initiatives in health, aiming to train students and professionals and to support patients rehabilitation, some public health problems remains neglected. Mosquito-borne diseases are a global public health concern. Education and awareness of population are an important intervention strategy and should be part of public health policies, given that individuals behavior may affect the transmission dynamics of diseases. For instance, improper storage of water can become a breeding site for the *Aedes aegypti* mosquito, the vector of dengue, zika, chikungunya and urban yellow fever viruses. Most of *Aedes* foci are in or near people's homes and the control of mosquitoes population is essential to prevent these diseases. We believe that games are a powerful tool and can be used to support awareness and behavioral changes regarding public health issues. This paper presents the current development stage of a serious game designed to support actions based on education and engagement of population aimed at vector surveillance and control. A mix of a 2D game with augmented and virtual reality modules and the real world itself will provide the proper environment to offer fun with the purpose of helping to deal with this complex problem. The development is based on agile principles, with short cycles involving activities of conception, design, construction and evaluation. Some partial results are game design, prototypes and demos. Future work includes designing and conducting an experimental study to evaluate effectiveness and efficiency regarding knowledge acquiring and behavioral changes.

Keywords: Serious games · Dengue · *Aedes aegypti* · Awareness
Education · Public health · Gamification

The authors acknowledge the support from CNPq, FAPEMIG, IFIP Digital Equity Committee and UFOP.

E. Clua et al. (Eds.): ICEC 2018, LNCS 11112, pp. 305–309, 2018.
https://doi.org/10.1007/978-3-319-99426-0_35

1   Introduction

Powerful tools to face some real-world problems, approaches based on games have been applied in different areas and contexts for varied purposes. An example is gamification – the use of game design elements in a non-game context [3] to achieve motivation and engagement [4]. Another example are serious games – those in which the primary purpose is other than offering fun and entertainment [9]. For instance, they can be designed to promote learning and behavioral changes [2,5,9]. Education and health are popular subjects for serious games. However, more specific but also important themes such as public health and mosquito-borne diseases remain neglected.

Dengue is a mosquito-borne viral disease and a global public health concern. Its primary vector is the *Aedes aegypti* mosquito, which also transmits chikungunya, yellow fever and zika viruses. Human behavior can contribute to the growth of vector population [10], and consequently, to the spread of diseases. For instance, improper stocks of water and inappropriate disposal of solid waste can become vector breeding sites. Thereby, citizens have an important role and must be included in public health policies to prevent and control dengue [8,11].

Population awareness is generally based on traditional media advertisement and educational campaigns (e.g. classes, talks, theater) in schools and public places [1,7]. Game-based approaches are powerful tools to support education, awareness, engagement and behavior changes [2,5,12]. In this context, serious games and gamification could also be used to enhance the outcomes of education-based policies for public health. In this project, we propose a serious game to support education and awareness about dengue, which can be used as an alternative strategy to assist vector surveillance and control.

2   Development and Results

Research and game development activities were performed. A survey and analysis of serious games aimed at the areas of public health, vector-borne diseases, and more specifically, related to dengue was conducted. However, few examples of games were found. The game development process is based on agile principles, with short cycles (biweekly) involving conceiving, designing, building and evaluating prototypes or versions of the game. Some partial results are the game design document (GDD), low and high fidelity prototypes and the release of two demos – a 2D game with an augmented reality module and a virtual reality module, which can be played with a Google Cardboard. Some improvements are required before conducting an experimental study to evaluate the game.

2.1   X-Dengue: Game Design

The story is centered on the character Pedrinho, who decides to stop dengue because his best friend became ill and could no longer play with him. The game X-Dengue [6] is organized into four modules (Fig. 1(1)). The player's level of

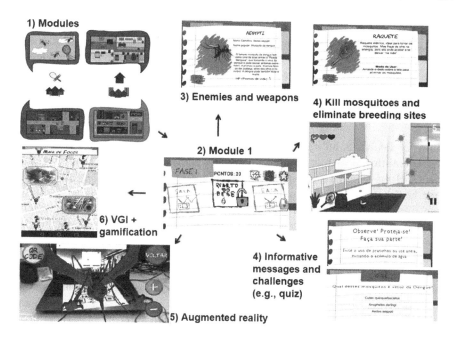

Fig. 1. Overview of the 2D-game modules and main features

comprehension increases with each module. Initially, he will play in his home, directly against adult mosquitoes, using resources such as his hands and electric rackets. Vector breeding sites must also be eliminated to prevent the emergence of new mosquitoes. Over time, the player will realize that actions isolated and restricted to his house are not effective. Thereby, he should extend his activities to the neighborhood (modules 2 and 3), and then to the whole city (module 4).

A demo version (module 1) was developed and tested with some users. In it, each phase consists of a set of rooms (Fig. 1(2)). Some playful (fictitious) and realistic (scientifically grounded) information are available to players, about mosquitoes ("enemies") and weapons (Fig. 1(3)). The player must fight adult mosquitoes and also eliminate breeding sites (Fig. 1(4)). Phases have different types of objectives, such as to kill some mosquitoes, eliminate breeding sites, close windows to avoid entry of mosquitoes, use bed nets or repellents for protection. Messages about preventive actions and challenges (e.g. quiz) (Fig. 1(4)) are also present in the game design. An augmented reality module (Fig. 1(5)) allows interaction with 3D models of the vector in each phase of its life cycle.

An innovative aspect proposed is the interaction between the virtual world (the game) and the real world to promote engagement and support vector surveillance. For instance, players will be invited to perform actions in the real world, such as taking pictures of places that can become mosquito breeding sites and attend educational campaigns. Thereby, the game may be used to support public health as an additional surveillance tool, to the extent that it will allow mapping places that need attention using a crowdsourcing strategy (Fig. 1(6)). Moreover, it can also help with dissemination and monitoring of educative campaigns. A VR module offers an immersive experience, where players may face dengue in a 3D environment and can interact with realistic models of *Ae. aegypti.*

3   Final Remarks

Games for health is an emergent research area. There are many efforts aimed towards training health students and professionals, and at the rehabilitation of patients. However, there is a significant shortage of initiatives that address global public health problems such as mosquito-borne diseases. The costs of mosquito-borne diseases are very high, and considerable resources are used to promote awareness, but usually involve simple advertisements on traditional media. Part of these resources should be used to conduct scientific research aiming to develop and evaluate the application of game-based methods to tackle public health complex problems, such as mosquito-borne diseases. The outcomes could be replicated and scaled to large populations. This study is part of an ongoing project. Future work includes (1) to perform a formal evaluation of the game (gameplay, usability and user experience); (2) to design and conduct an empirical study to assess its effectiveness.

References

1. Claro, L., Barreto, L., Kawa, H., Tricai Cavalini, L., Garcia Rosa, M.L.: Community participation in dengue control in Brazil. Dengue Bulletin 30 (2006)
2. Connolly, T.M., Boyle, E.A., MacArthur, E., Hainey, T., Boyle, J.M.: A systematic literature review of empirical evidence on computer games and serious games. Comput. Educ. **59**(2), 661–686 (2012)
3. Deterding, S., Dixon, D., Khaled, R., Nacke, L.: From game design elements to gamefulness: defining gamification. In: Proceedings of 15th International Academic MindTrek Conference: Envisioning Future Media Environments, pp. 9–15. ACM (2011)
4. Domínguez, A., de Navarrete, J.S., De-Marcos, L., Fernández-Sanz, L., Pagés, C., Martínez-Herráiz, J.J.: Gamifying learning experiences: practical implications and outcomes. Comput. Educ. **63**, 380–392 (2013)
5. Dondlinger, M.J.: Educational video game design: a review of the literature. J. Appl. Educ. Technol. **4**(1), 21–31 (2007)
6. Lima, T., Barbosa, B., Niquini, C., Araújo, C., Lana, R.: Playing against dengue. In: 2017 IEEE 5th International Conference on Serious Games and Applications for Health (SeGAH), pp. 1–8. IEEE (2017)
7. Luna, J., et al.: Social mobilization strategies of education and communication to prevent dengue fever in Bucaramanga. Dengue Bulletin,Colombia (2004)
8. Madeira, N.G., Macharelli, C.A., Pedras, J.F., Delfino, M.C.: Education in primary school as a strategy to control dengue. Revis. Soc. Bras. Med. Trop. **35**(3), 221–226 (2002)
9. Michael, D.R., Chen, S.L.: Serious Games: Games that Educate, Train, and Inform. Muska & Lipman/Premier-Trade, New York (2005)

10. Padmanabha, H., Soto, E., Mosquera, M., Lord, C., Lounibos, L.: Ecological links between water storage behaviors and *Aedes aegypti* production: implications for dengue vector control in variable climates. Ecohealth **7**(1), 78–90 (2010)
11. Pai, H.H., Yu-Jue, H., Hsu, E.L.: Impact of a short-term community-based cleanliness campaign on the sources of dengue vectors: an entomological and human behavior study. J. Environment. Health **68**(6), 35 (2006)
12. Prensky, M.: Don't Bother Me, Mom, I'm learning!. Paragon House, St. Paul (2006)

Converging Data Storytelling and Visualisation

Yangjinbo Zhang[✉]

Visualisation and Interactive Media Lab. (VisLab.), Curtin University,
Perth, WA, Australia
yangjinbo.zhang@postgrad.curtin.edu.au
http://curtin.edu/vismedia

Abstract. The goal of this paper is to discuss and review existing literature in the field of data storytelling and draw the relationship between data storytelling and visualisation. It also associates both domains, as well as it explores pathways how to better present and deliver data driven presentations. To associate data storytelling with visualisation will be a worth-studying and intriguing direction. We summarize in a brief discussion the convergence between visualisation and data storytelling by pinpointing to key theories, illustrating the potentia, and present both concepts as tool in data science, aesthetics and information visualisation.

Keywords: Data storytelling · Serious storytelling · Visualisation
Data visualisation · Narrative structure · Story · Media study · New media
Cognition

1 Introduction

The role of data in today's world is clear. With the increasing amounts of data, it's getting more and more important to find adequate ways to communicate, present, and make data understandable to individuals. Story telling has played a role as "message carrier" in human history for a very long time. In comparison with raw data – a narration is a more natural and smooth-understanding form of message. The convergence of both concepts – storytelling and data science – seems to be the next natural next step forward, in making data easier to comprehend, and to communicate.

Def. Visualization (Tufte 1983): According to (Tufte 1983), visualisation is visually present measured quantities with visual elements such as lines, shapes, colors, words, symbols and so on. It is the art and tool for reasoning data and information (Tufte 1983).

Def. Narrative (Chatman 1978): According to Chatman's idea (Chatman 1978), narrative is a whole with nature of both transformation (deliverable and expressible) and self-regulation (self-maintained and closed structure) and is constructed with discrete events and existents, and with a sequential composition, that function as a whole (Chatman 1978).

Def. Data Storytelling (Knaflic 2015): according to Knafilc's idea (Knaflic 2015), data itself is difficult to understand, but there are stories in data bringing it to life that

E. Clua et al. (Eds.): ICEC 2018, LNCS 11112, pp. 310–316, 2018.
https://doi.org/10.1007/978-3-319-99426-0_36

allow to communicate data in a much more efficient way. Data storytelling transforms data into a better form that can support decision making (Knaflic 2015).

In the way of exploration of how to better present and deliver data, how to make the process more vivid, convenient and plentiful. Within this paper, we discuss the multi-disciplinary facet of data storytelling, and it's basic theories.

2 Review of Basic Theories

A brief review of the relevant topics and literatures are shown as below (see Table 1).

2.1 Visualisation

In recent researches, visualisation as a research domain has considerably developed. There are a lot of important ideas and concepts being provided in many aspects. On visual efficiency, Tufte (1983, 1990) contributed an important concept: data-ink. Data-ink is the cord of an image that cannot be erased. If it is, the message will be incomplete. Maximising data-ink and minimising non-data-ink can dramatically improve efficiency (Tufte 1990). Tufte also cited efficiency as only one of the dimensions of visual design. Other dimensions include complexity, structure, density and beauty (Tufte 2006). So comprehensively consider the various dimensions of visualisation design will be a necessary way to improve the overall quality.

The principles of data analysis and presentation (Tufte 2006), are about the design principles are based on the fundamentals of human cognition and motivation. These are closely related to some basic human activities: decision, purpose, response, consequence, planning, and so on (Tufte 2006). It will be important to further understand and conduct a more comprehensive analysis of what aspects and elements are essential to create human centered visualizations, as e.g. discussed in (Lugmayr et al. 2016, 2017b). Research around visual cognition (Ware 2013), addresses aspects such as the working memory/long-term memory, knowledge formation/transfer, visual cognitive systems and visual thinking processes. Different frameworks have been researched, as well as a concept of sensory versus arbitrary symbols has been provided (Ware 2013). This concept provides a good guide to analyse the relationship between visual cognition and graphic symbolic elements. A important work in visualisation cognition and its information visualization cognition framework has been provided by (Patterson et al. 2014).

2.2 Storytelling and Narrative Structure

The purpose of visualisation is to translate a message into visual form for more convenience understanding. And in order to achieve even better understanding, the massage should be re-organised and re-edited before it is visualised. In the domain of storytelling, there are some theories and researches which can support for this.

According to Chatman's narrative structure research, narratives have two major parts: the story—which is depicted in a narrative—and the discourse—how a narrative is depicted. The story part has two subtopics: events (actions, happenings) and existents

Table 1. Overview of literature resources

Topic	Description	Aspects	Ref.
Visualisation			
Data-ink	Cord of an image that cannot be erased, and Maximizing data-ink, and minimizing non data-ink improves efficiency	Efficiency of visualisation	Tufte (1990)
Analysis and presentation of data	Design principles fundamental to human cognition and motivation, closely related to some basic human activities	Visualisation principles	Tufte (2006)
Visual cognition	Research in aspects such as the working memory/long-term memory, knowledge formation and transfer, visual cognitive system and visual thinking processes	Visualisation and cognition	Ware (2013)
Visualisation design	Ingredients of good visualisation form the perspective of designer, reader and data	Design of visualisation	Iliinsky and Steele (2010, 2011)
Cognitive Big Data	Framework for cognitive understanding of data, and categorizing the traits of Big Data as in	Psychological framework	Lugmayr et al. (2016, 2017b)
Data storytelling			
Storytelling with data	Guidelines for the use of storytelling in data presentation, and support cognition and decision-making	Data presentation	Knaflic (2015)
Serious storytelling	Story for serious purposes. How storytelling can be used for non-entertaining purposes, such as support decision-making and share knowledge	Serious story	Lugmayr et al. (2017c)
Information aesthetics			
Information aesthetics	It provides a unique thread to combine science and art. Research includes studies of sematic and aesthetic information and uncertainties in perceptions of symbols	Information study	Moles (1968)
Aesthetics theory			
Aesthetic response theory	Art can neither be fully identical with the work created by author, nor with the realisation by the viewer. It exists halfway between these two poles	Aesthetic response	Iser (1978)
Layered structure of art	Inner structure of art, phonetic formation, units of meaning, schematized aspects and represented objectives	Structure of art	Ingarden (1973a, 1973b)

(continued)

Table 1. (*continued*)

Topic	Description	Aspects	Ref.
Story narration			
Narrative structure	Narrative parts and subfactors affecting narration: the story (depicted in a narrative); discourse (depiction of narrative)	Structure of story	Chatman (1978)
Characteristics of storytelling	Tell-ability of a story, characteristics of good storytelling and storytelling techniques	Storytelling techniques	Baker and Greene (1977)
Media studies			
Medium's affect to message	Content of a media is always another media, media as translator and carrier of information	Nature of media	McLuhan (1964)
Characteristics of new media	Numerical representation, modularity, automation, viability, and transcoding	Media characteristics	Manovich (2001)

(characters, setting). Many subfactors also affect narration (Chatman 1978). He sees story as a form of sharing massages has been tested by throughout centuries as a way of exchanging information easily to understand, and attractive for people. Therefore, the most obvious step is to link data with storytelling to make data understandable.

How to naturally combine the cord data into story units, meanwhile remain the clarity of the cord data. This is the aim and the direction. About how a story is present in the aspect of visual, Chatman also provided some guide in his research of visual space in cinematic narrative (Chatman 1978) and its digital production (Lugmayr et al. 2008). Visual factors such as scale, density, texture, position, colour, angle, size are the key elements that are presenting and telling the story in the aspect of sense of visual (Chatman 1978). In fact, this is sharing very similar principle with visualisation, and helps it's creation process.

In the research of characteristics of storytelling (Baker and Greene 1977), a central question is discussed: what makes a story tellable? Some of the characteristics are: a single and clear theme, dramatic appeal, characterization (Baker and Greene 1977). This provide a direction which is worth to think, when a message is reorganized and reedited into a story, how this story should like in order to being attractive and can catch people's attention. To explore how these characteristic elements fit in the context of data visualisation, will definitely help to improve the overall quality of cognition and understanding.

In terms of narratives in specific media, research into linguistic structure of comic narratives (Cohn 2014) also provide valuable ideas. In this research, it reveals three structures which are affecting in the visual aspect of comic. They are graphic structure, narrative structure and external composition structure. Through graphic structure, lines and shapes combine into image. Then with narrative structure, a series of images organise into a coherent message. Last with external composition structure, all the organised images fit into a specific media space. We also have to consider the 'medium' carrying the story – which we explore in the next section of the paper.

2.3   Media and Communication Studies

The media is not only the carrier of the information, but also part of the information. It affects how information is presented. "The medium is the message" as stated by McLuhan (1964). McLuhan's research also revealed that the content of a media is always another media. In fact, media plays the role of translator; it carries the information from one form into another form. When discussing the media, some very important parts will be the characteristic of medias, difference between medias, which aspects of message are being affected by the forms of media, and when in the translating form media to another media which parts of message will be changed because of the affection by different media forms. Manovich's research (Manovich 2001) into new media reveals that - compared to former media - new media in the digital age have many new characteristics. These are e.g. (Manovich 2001): numerical representation, modularity, automation, variability and transcoding. These affect how information is presented in new media. Today, media study theories extend towards smart media environments (Pogorelc et al. 2012; Lugmayr et al. 2009) and topics like personalization (Uhlmann and Lugmayr 2008).

2.4   Data Storytelling

In the field of data storytelling, there are many important contributions have been made. Knaflic (2015), provides a method to associate live narration with data figures. This combination provides a good idea to understand the application and context of data story telling. This research also provides a guideline to guide the use of storytelling to better present data and support cognition and decision-making (Knaflic 2015).

Recent research in this domain has produced valuable concepts such as e.g. serious storytelling and cognitive big data (Lugmayr et al. 2017a, 2017c). Questions like the difference between serious storytelling and entertaining storytelling are addressed. It also rethinks, if some methods and theories of traditional storytelling can support serious storytelling; and which domains or disciplines should be considered. These concepts are vital how data storytelling support cognition and human activities.

3   Discussion and Conclusion

Data storytelling and digital visualisation are relatively young concepts. To develop data storytelling, it is essential to intersect theories from multiple domains and disciplines. It is necessary to discuss and analyze which theories in each domains contribute to data storytelling. It will also require creative methods to create these (Lugmayr 2011). It is necessary to essential to explore different characteristics in different aspects and domains and distill the required ones to develop data storytelling as a discipline. In this paper, some key-theories contributing to data storytelling are explored and key-literature described. These need to be applied in concrete application scenarios and application domains to allow new insights into data and decrease the cognitive load of individuals exploring different aspects in data. This research paper is research in progress and is only a starting point for further investigation.

References

Baker, A., Greene, E.: Storytelling: Art and Technique. Bowker, New York (1977)

Chatman, S.B.: Story and Discourse: Narrative Structure in Fiction and Film. Cornell University Press, Ithaca (1978)

Cohn, N.: The architecture of visual narrative comprehension: the interaction of narrative structure and page layout in understanding comics. Front. Psychol. **5**, 680 (2014)

Iliinsky, N., Steele, J.: Designing Data Visualizations: Representing Informational Relationships. O'Reilly Media, Incorporated, Sebastopol (2011)

Iliinsky, N., Steele, J.: Beautiful Visualization: Looking at Data Through the Eyes of Experts. O'Reilly Media, Incorporated, Sebastopol (2010)

Ingarden, R.: The Cognition of the Literary Work of Art. Northwestern University Press, Evanston (1973a)

Ingarden, R.: The Literary Work of Art. Northwestern University Press, Evanston (1973b)

Iser, W.: The Act of Reading: A Theory of Aesthetic Response. Johns Hopkins University Press, Baltimore (1978)

Knaflic, C.N.: Storytelling with Data: A Data Visualization Guide for Business Professionals. Wiley, Hoboken (2015)

Lugmayr, A.: Applying "design thinking" as a method for teaching in media education. In: Proceedings of the 15th International Academic MindTrek Conference: Envisioning Future Media Environments, pp 332–334. ACM, New York (2011). http://doi.acm.org/10.1145/2181037.2181100

Lugmayr, A., Adrian, H., Golebiowski, P., et al.: E = MC2 + 1: a fully digital, collaborative, high-definition (HD) production from scene to screen. Comput. Entertain. **6**, 1–33 (2008)

Lugmayr, A., Risse, T., Stockleben, B., et al.: Special issue on semantic ambient media experiences. Multimed. Tools Appl. **44**, 331–335 (2009)

Lugmayr, A., Stockleben, B., Scheib, C., et al.: A comprehensive survey on big data research and it's implications - what is really 'new' in big data? IT's cognitive big data. In: Liang, T.-P., Chang, S.-I., Hung, S.-Y., Chau, P.Y.K. (ed) Proceedings of the 20th Pacific-Asian Conference on Information Systems (PACIS 2016) (2016). http://www.pacis2016.org/abstract/Index

Lugmayr, A., Stockleben, B., Scheib, C., Mailaparampil, M.: Cognitive big data: survey and review on big data research and its implications. What is really "new" in big data? J. Knowl. Manag. **21**, 197–212 (2017a)

Lugmayr, A., Stockleben, B., Scheib, C., Mailaparampil, M.: Cognitive big data. survey and review on big data research and its implications: what is really "new"? Cognitive big data! J. Knowl. Manag. (JMM) **21** (2017b). http://www.emeraldgrouppublishing.com/products/journals/call_for_papers.htm?id=5855k

Lugmayr, A., Sutinen, E., Suhonen, J., et al.: Serious storytelling - a first definition and review. Multimed. Tools Appl. **76**, 15707–15733 (2017c)

Manovich, L.: The Language of New Media. MIT Press, Cambridge (2001)

McLuhan, M.: Understanding Media: The Extensions of Man. Routledge & Kegan Paul Limited, London (1964)

Moles, A.A.: Information Theory and Esthetic Perception. University of Illinois Press, Urbana (1968)

Patterson, R.E., Blaha, L.M., Grinstein, G.G., et al.: A human cognition framework for information visualization. Comput. Graph. **42**, 42–58 (2014)

Pogorelc, B., Vatavu, R.-D., Lugmayr, A., et al.: Semantic ambient media: from ambient advertising to ambient-assisted living. Multimed. Tools Appl. **58**, 399–425 (2012). https://doi.org/10.1007/s11042-011-0917-8

Tufte, E.R.: The Visual Display of Quantitative Information. Graphics Press, Cheshire (1983)

Tufte, E.R.: Data-ink maximization and graphical design. Oikos **58**, 130–144 (1990)

Tufte, E.R.: Beautiful Evidence. Graphics Press, Cheshire (2006)

Uhlmann, S., Lugmayr, A.: Personalization algorithms for portable personality. In: Proceedings of the 12th International Conference on Entertainment and Media in the Ubiquitous Era. ACM, Tampere (2008)

Ware, C.: Information Visualization: Perception for Design, 3rd edn. Elsevier/MK, Amsterdam/Boston (2013)

A Systematic Mapping of Game-Based Methods to Tackle a Public Health Problem

Tiago França Melo Lima[1,2]([⊠]) [iD] and Clodoveu Augusto Davis Jr.[2] [iD]

[1] Federal University of Ouro Preto (UFOP), João Monlevade, MG, Brazil
tiagolima@decsi.ufop.br
[2] Federal University of Minas Gerais, Belo Horizonte, MG, Brazil
clodoveu@dcc.ufmg.br

Abstract. Mosquito-borne diseases, such as dengue, endanger about half of the world's population. Their spread is affected by individual behavior in our mostly urban society. Public health policies generally include awareness campaigns on the control of the vectors. While game-based initiatives are developed and used to train students and professionals, support patients and educate citizens, public health education remains neglected. In this study, we identify game-based approaches to support education about diseases transmitted by *Aedes* mosquitoes. We carried out a systematic mapping to identify studies which address a proposal, use or contain an evaluation of game-based methods, aiming to raise awareness and promote behavior changes regarding dengue and its prevention. Only 12 papers met the criteria for inclusion and exclusion, and those were selected and categorized. As part of an ongoing project, next steps include adding other databases and other mosquito-borne diseases (e.g., malaria) and drafting guidelines to support the design of games for public health education about mosquito-borne diseases.

Keywords: Systematic mapping · Serious games · Gamification
Public health · Education · Awareness · *Aedes aegypti* · Dengue

1 Introduction

A global public health concern, dengue is a mosquito-borne viral disease. Estimates suggest that about 3.9 billion people are at risk [1]. Its primary vector is the *Aedes aegypti* mosquito, which also transmits chikungunya, yellow fever and zika viruses. Vector population control is an important strategy to face this problem. Humans behavior may contribute to the growth of vector population [22,23], for instance, through the improperly stock of water and inappropriate

The authors acknowledge the support from CNPq and FAPEMIG, Brazilian agencies in charge of fostering research and development, and IFIP Digital Equity Committee.

© IFIP International Federation for Information Processing 2018
Published by Springer Nature Switzerland AG 2018. All Rights Reserved
E. Clua et al. (Eds.): ICEC 2018, LNCS 11112, pp. 317–323, 2018.
https://doi.org/10.1007/978-3-319-99426-0_37

disposal of solid waste which can become vector breeding sites. Thereby, citizens have an important role and must be included in public health policies.

Generally, population awareness is based on traditional media advertisement and educational campaigns (e.g., classes, talks, theater) in schools and public places [4,5,9,17,19]. Game-based approaches are powerful tools to support education, awareness, engagement and behavior changes [2,6,7,20,26,27]. In this context, serious games and gamification can be used to enhance the outcomes of education-based policies for public health. An example is a game which tackles on two related neglected and emerging tropical infectious diseases – Visceral Leishmaniasis and American Cutaneous Leishmaniasis [18].

In this study, we present an overview of game-based methods applied in education about dengue and other diseases transmitted by *Aedes* mosquito.

2   The Systematic Mapping Process

There are some differences between Systematic Mapping (SM) and Systematic Literature Review (SLR) studies. The first may be used as a previous step toward the latter, as it can help to identify areas where is more appropriate to conduct an SLR or a primary study [10,24]. In this study, a systematic mapping was performed. As described by [24], the process steps include: (i) definition of research questions, (ii) conduct search for primary studies (all papers), (iii) screening of papers for inclusion and exclusion (relevant papers), (iv) keywording of abstracts, and (v) data extraction and mapping of studies.

The goal of this study is to identify and analyze game-related methods aiming to understand their application in the context of public health education, in particular, those designed to support awareness and behavior changes for dengue prevention. For such, we established the following research questions:

– RQ1: Which game-based methods were used to raise awareness about *Aedes* mosquito-borne diseases and how to prevent them?
– RQ2: Which types of games have been proposed or used?
– RQ3: In which context and educational levels were they investigated?

The search query used was: *(game OR gamification) AND (dengue OR zika OR chikungunya OR "yellow fever" OR Aedes OR mosquito)*. The electronic databases searched were: ACM Digital Library, IEEE Xplore, PubMed, ScienceDirect, Scopus, Springer Link. The results covered articles, conference papers and book chapters published and indexed until May 10, 2018 (Table 1). Although some databases returned a large number of results, the vast majority of them had no relation to the research objectives. For instance, many papers had as subject the 2014 Olympic Games in Brazil and zika epidemic. Furthermore, there are a reasonable number of apps and games related to the subject available on the web and in app stores. However, the results covered only seven different games (see Table 2). Details about the research such as inclusion/exclusion criteria and protocol are available at www.github.com/ufopleds/publichealthgames.

Table 1. Results summary

	ACM	IEEE	PubMed	ScienceDirect	Scopus	Springer
# papers	3	5	88	1464	143	3877
1st selection	3	3	4	7	19	4
2nd selection (relevant papers)	1	3	1	1	10	3
Total after removing duplicates	12					

Table 2. List of publications grouped by type

Type	References
Journal	[3, 11–14, 29]
Conference	[8, 15, 25, 28]
Book chapter	[16, 21]

3 Results and Discussion

Few studies addressed games-based methods aimed at public health education about diseases transmitted by *Aedes*. In this section, we present some information about them, such as how they were conducted and which were their findings.

Regarding the game-related methods used, RQ1, (Table 3), three of the studies addressed the game design by volunteer participants. Both the design of a game (made by authors) and the evaluation of a game were approached by four studies. Two of them used gamification. None of the studies presented a game from its conception, design and development phases to its systematic evaluation.

Table 3. Game related-methods

Game-related methods	References
Game design (by participants)	[11, 13, 16]
Game design and development (by authors)	[15, 21, 25, 28]
Gamification	[15, 21]
Game evaluation	[3, 12, 14, 29]

Answering RQ2, both digital and analog games were covered (see Table 4). However, the number of different games is even lower, and it is worse if we consider their availability to be used by educators and public health agents. There are two board games - here, the difficulty is having physical access to them. For computers, there are two options, but we found just one available online with the installer – *Pueblo Pitanga: enemigos silenciosos*[1]. Similarly, from the three games for mobile devices, we found only one publicly available – X-Dengue[2]. The context and educational level (RQ3) varies according to the study.

Table 4. Summary of games

Game	Platform	References	Easily acessible
Jugando en salud: dengue	Board	[29]	No
Good-bye to dengue	Board	[12,14]	No
Pueblo Pitanga: enemigos silenciosos	Computer	[8]	Yes
Sherlock Dengue 8	Computer	[3]	No
Hugo against dengue	Mobile	[25]	No
X-Dengue	Mobile	[15]	Yes
AedesBusters	Mobile	[21]	No

Two of the papers reported a study in which authors investigated the ability of a child to create educational games related to dengue using drawings [11,13]. An active role in the creation process was also the subject of another study, in which was used a participatory design to engage a community and students to devise mobile apps.

The board games were the subject of three studies. The game *Jugando en salud: dengue* was evaluated using a pre- and post-test experimental design with 621 students between eight to sixteen-years-old from nine different schools of a Venezuelan city [29]. According to authors, the game had a good acceptance and contributed to improving knowledge about dengue and its prevention. The game *Good-bye to dengue* was used in two studies. In one, the authors conducted a postgame debriefing with 81 Filipino students to explore aspects such as students' feelings, perceptions and information learned [12]. In the other, they evaluated the effectiveness of the game to increase knowledge, positive attitudes-beliefs, and self-efficacy for dengue prevention using an experimental design (pre- and post test) with primary and secondary students from Philippine schools [14].

Design, development and evaluation of digital games were the subjects of the other studies. [25] presented a prototype of a mobile game (*Hugo against dengue*). A simulation game that uses a view from the perspective of a mosquito was described by [28]. The game *Pueblo Pitanga: Enemigos Silenciosos* had its design patterns analyzed by [8]. The design of a mixed-reality game (2D, augmented reality and virtual reality), *X-Dengue*, was presented by [15]. The game *Sherlock Dengue 8* was used in a study-case addressing guidelines for designing and use collaborative-competitive serious games [3]. Moreover, a mobile app used gamification aiming to incentive volunteer contributions of *Aedes aegypti* breeding sites. Although such studies have in some way presented aspects about game

---

[1] http://www.pueblopitanga.com.
[2] https://play.google.com/store/apps/details?id=com.leds.xdengue.

design, development and evaluation, they lack a deeper and systematic evaluation to demonstrate their advantages and limitations to support awareness and behavior change so they can be used as tools for public health policies.

More than half of the world's population live in areas where *Aedes* species are present. There is a consensus about habits to prevent vector breeding sites inside houses, and in many countries, this information is widely disseminated using traditional media and campaigns. However, the exclusive use of these methods demonstrated to be ineffective, since most of vector breeding sites are located inside or around houses. Innovative approaches such as those based on games are needed. Although, there is a lack of games and studies addressing public health education such as mosquito-borne diseases. Primary studies should be systematically undertaken to design and evaluate game-based methods and tools, which could be easily scalable if they prove to be effective and efficient to achieve awareness and behavioral changes.

4   Final Remarks

Games for health is an emergent research area. There are many efforts aimed at training health students and professionals and rehabilitation of patients. However, there is a significant shortage of initiatives addressing global public health problems such as mosquito-borne diseases.

In this study, we performed a systematic mapping of game-based methods aiming to aware and promote behavior changes regarding dengue and its prevention. While some research areas (e.g., software engineering education) have a significant number of studies on games application, we found few studies related to public health education on diseases transmitted by *Aedes*, and fewer were those that did a systematic evaluation of the outcomes. The costs of mosquito-borne diseases are very high, and a significant amount of resources is used to promote awareness, but using advertisement in traditional media. Part of these should be used to conduct scientific research aiming to develop and evaluate the application of game-based methods to tackle public health complex problems, such as mosquito-borne diseases. The outcomes could be replicated and scalable.

As part of an ongoing project, future works include (i) adding other databases and games designed to target other mosquito-borne diseases (e.g., malaria), (ii) elaborate guidelines to support the design of games to promote public health education about mosquito-borne diseases.

References

1. Bhatt, S., et al.: The global distribution and burden of dengue. Nature **496**(7446), 504–507 (2013)
2. Boyle, E.A., Connolly, T.M., Hainey, T., Boyle, J.M.: Engagement in digital entertainment games: a systematic review. Comput. Human Behav. **28**(3), 771–780 (2012)
3. Buchinger, D., Hounsell, M.D.S.: Guidelines for designing and using collaborative-competitive serious games. Comput. Educ. **118**, 133–149 (2018)

4. Chinnakali, P., Gurnani, N., Upadhyay, R.P., Parmar, K., Suri, T.M., Yadav, K.: High level of awareness but poor practices regarding dengue fever control: a cross-sectional study from North India. North Am. J. Med. Sci. **4**(6), 278 (2012)

5. Claro, L., Barreto, L., Kawa, H., Tricai Cavalini, L., Garcia Rosa, M.L.: Community participation in dengue control in Brazil. Dengue Bull. **30**, 214–222 (2006)

6. Connolly, T.M., Boyle, E.A., MacArthur, E., Hainey, T., Boyle, J.M.: A systematic literature review of empirical evidence on computer games and serious games. Comput. Educ. **59**(2), 661–686 (2012)

7. Dondlinger, M.J.: Educational video game design: a review of the literature. J. Appl. Educ. Technol. **4**(1), 21–31 (2007)

8. Ramírez Elizondo, E.: Identification of design patterns for serious games in an educational videogame designed to create awareness on dengue and malaria fever. In: Mata, F.J., Pont, A. (eds.) WITFOR 2016. IAICT, vol. 481, pp. 85–95. Springer, Cham (2016). https://doi.org/10.1007/978-3-319-44447-5_9

9. Khun, S., Manderson, L.: Community and school-based health education for dengue control in rural Cambodia: a process evaluation. PLoS Negl. Trop. Dis. **1**(3), e143 (2007)

10. Kitchenham, B., Charters, S.: Guidelines for performing systematic literature reviews in Software Engineering. Technical report, Keele University and Durham University (2007)

11. Lennon, J.L., Coombs, D.W.: Study of child-invented health educational games on dengue fever. Dengue Bull. **26**, 195–202 (2002)

12. Lennon, J.L., Coombs, D.W.: The good-bye to dengue game: debriefing study. Simul. Gaming **36**(4), 499–517 (2005)

13. Lennon, J.L., Coombs, D.W.: Child-invented health education games: a case study for dengue fever. Simul. Gaming **37**(1), 88–97 (2006)

14. Lennon, J.L., Coombs, D.W.: The utility of a board game for dengue haemorrhagic fever health education. Health Educ. **107**(3), 290–306 (2007)

15. Lima, T., Barbosa, B., Niquini, C., Araújo, C., Lana, R.: Playing against dengue - Design and development of a serious game to help tackling dengue. In: 5th International Conference on Serious Games and Applications for Health, pp. 1–8. IEEE (2017)

16. Lucena, T.F.R., Velho, A.P.M., Dorne, V.D., Domingues, D.M.G.: Devising mobile apps: participatory design for endemic diseases transmitted by the mosquito *Aedes* (dengue, zika and chikungunya). In: Schleser, M., Berry, M. (eds.) Mobile Story Making in an Age of Smartphones, pp. 139–150. Springer, Cham (2018). https://doi.org/10.1007/978-3-319-76795-6_14

17. Luna, J., et al.: Social mobilization using strategies of education and communication to prevent dengue fever in Bucaramanga. Colombia, Dengue Bulletin (2004)

18. Luz, S., Masoodian, M., Cesario, R.R., Cesario, M.: Using a serious game to promote community-based awareness and prevention of neglected tropical diseases. Entertain. Comput. **15**, 43–55 (2016)

19. Madeira, N.G., Macharelli, C.A., Pedras, J.F., Delfino, M.C.: Education in primary school as a strategy to control dengue. Revista da Sociedade Brasileira de Medicina Tropical **35**(3), 221–226 (2002)

20. Michael, D.R., Chen, S.L.: Serious games: games that educate, train, and inform. Muska & Lipman/Premier-Trade, New York (2005)

21. Moura, J.A.B., de Barros, M.A., Oliveira, R.P.: Marketplace-driven, game-changing IT games to address complex, costly community problems. In: Linnhoff-Popien, C., Schneider, R., Zaddach, M. (eds.) Digital Marketplaces Unleashed, pp.

193–204. Springer, Heidelberg (2018). https://doi.org/10.1007/978-3-662-49275-8_21

22. Padmanabha, H., Soto, E., Mosquera, M., Lord, C., Lounibos, L.: Ecological links between water storage behaviors and *Aedes aegypti* production: implications for dengue vector control in variable climates. Ecohealth **7**(1), 78–90 (2010)

23. Pai, H.H., Yu-Jue, H., Hsu, E.L.: Impact of a short-term community-based cleanliness campaign on the sources of dengue vectors: an entomological and human behavior study. J. Environ. Health **68**(6), 35 (2006)

24. Petersen, K., Feldt, R., Mujtaba, S., Mattsson, M.: Systematic mapping studies in software engineering. EASE **8**, 68–77 (2008)

25. Porcino, T.M., Strauss, E., Clua, E.G.: Hugo against dengue: a serious game to educate people about dengue fever prevention. In: 3rd International Conference on Serious Games and Applications for Health, pp. 1–5. IEEE (2014)

26. Prensky, M.: Don't Bother Me, Mom, I'm Learning!. Saint Paul, Paragon House (2006)

27. Squire, K.: Video games in education. Int. J. Intell. Games Simul. **2**(1), 49–62 (2003)

28. Stifter, C., Edenhofer, S., von Mammen, S.: Come Fly with me - perceive the world through a mosquito's senses. In: 8th International Conference on Games and Virtual Worlds for Serious Applications, pp. 1–4. IEEE (2016)

29. Vivas, E., Guevara de Sequeda, M.: Un juego como estrategia educativa para el control de *Aedes aegypti* en escolares venezolanos. Revista Panamericana de Salud Pública **14**, 394–401 (2003)

Workshop on Robot Competitions

David Obdržálek[1], Richard Balogh[2(✉)], and Artur Lugmayr[3]

[1] Charles University, Prague, Czech Republic
david.obdrzalek@mff.cuni.cz
[2] Slovak University of Technology in Bratislava, Bratislava, Slovakia
richard.balogh@stuba.sk
[3] Curtin University, Bentley, Australia
artur.lugmayr@curtin.edu.au

Abstract. Robot competitions are more and more used as a tool for education as well as an entertainment activity. This workshop brings together organizers, participants, teachers, and other people interested to share best practices, discuss issues and possibly improve their work.

Keywords: Robot competition · Entertainment robotics
Educational robotics

1 Introduction

Robot competitions are existing already for more than 40 years [4]. Currently, dozens of competitions are organized every month around the world and are well respected for their help in education and research (see e.g. [1–6]). However, except of a few well-known like RoboCup or FLL, most of them are local and the organizers are not cooperating or exchanging experience.

For more than 40 years [4] to now, dozens of robotics competitions are running each month all around the world.

At the early beginnings, the main task was just to construct a robot. Today, massive data processing from sensors is required and very complex and sophisticated algorithms for robot decisions are involved [2].

Irreplaceable role of the competitions is in promotion and motivation for STEM areas of the study. Student competitions motivate students to produce the best possible design and therefore force them to learn and utilize all the necessary tools and techniques required to achieve a good performance [6]. Students are learning by doing, they immediately see the importance of some theoretical lectures, and can see the results of their effort. Moreover they often work in teams, besides the technical side of the project they learn how to manage resources, time and energy.

To mention both sides of the coin, it is an expensive method of teaching and consumes much more student's, and teacher's time. More consultations are required and the teacher should be gifted by some manager skills. There is also

E. Clua et al. (Eds.): ICEC 2018, LNCS 11112, pp. 324–326, 2018.
https://doi.org/10.1007/978-3-319-99426-0_38

a principal problem of each competition – there is just one winner and several losers. Some education psychologists point out that competitions are therefore harmful to many students' self-esteem [6].

Increasing role of the robot competitions is to support the research and benchmarking. Typically, the research results are reported for a specific robotic system and a self-chosen set of tasks performed in the laboratory of its authors. Quite common technique used is "proof by video", showing the robotic system working once and not showing its problems and alternative scenarios during the less controlled conditions. But when carefully prepared, competitions can also be considered as benchmarks for objective performance assessment [1]. It is possible to make them more scientifically grounded and thus more suitable for the objective benchmarking. To achieve this, standardization is one of the requirements. As one of the successful examples we can mention the AAAI Mobile Robot Competition where the competition platform for the Urban Search and Rescue task was provided by the National Institute of Standards and Technology (NIST) [5].

In order to move the research borders even faster, some competitions organizers require to share the technical information about the winning systems. The teams are required to release a detailed technical description after the competition. It is even more useful, when the competition is accompanied by technical conference, where the underlying methods are discussed [3].

Let us summarize some of the benefits of the robotics competitions [2]:

- they promote interest in robotic studies and research among students,
- they help to compare scientific results, and exchange experiences,
- they establish new contacts between students, schools and industrial companies,
- ideas are often applied also in 'useful' projects,
- they serve as a very good educational tool, widening students' knowledge.
- Last but not least, competitions create media interest and may even generate additional funds from external sources [4].

2   Workshop Description

2.1   Objectives

The main objectives of this workshop are to gather organizers of different robot competition events, competition participants, teachers, and other interested people from various environments to:

- foster establishing of a network of organizers and their events to support participants exchanges and to motivate them to attend also other than local events,
- connect the workshop participants to share best practices, discuss issues and possibly improve their work.

References

1. Amigoni, F., Bonarini, A., Fontana, G., Matteucci, M., Schiaffonati, V.: Benchmarking through competitions. In: European Robotics Forum-Workshop on Robot Competitions: Benchmarking, Technology Transfer, and Education, vol. 604 (2013)
2. Balogh, R.: A survey of robotic competitions. I am a robot - competitor. Int. J. Adv. Robot. Syst. **2**(2), 144–160 (2005). http://intechweb.org/volume.php?issn=1729-8806&v=2&n=2
3. Behnke, S.: Robot competitions-ideal benchmarks for robotics research. In: Proceedings of IROS-2006 Workshop on Benchmarks in Robotics Research. Institute of Electrical and Electronics Engineers (IEEE) (2006)
4. Braunl, T.: Research relevance of mobile robot competitions. IEEE Robot. Autom. Mag. **6**(4), 32–37 (1999)
5. Casper, J., Micire, M., Hyams, J., Murphy, R.: A case study of how mobile robot competitions promote future research. In: Birk, A., Coradeschi, S., Tadokoro, S. (eds.) RoboCup 2001. LNCS (LNAI), vol. 2377, pp. 123–132. Springer, Heidelberg (2002). https://doi.org/10.1007/3-540-45603-1_13
6. Manseur, R.: Hardware competitions in engineering education. In: 30th Annual Frontiers in Education Conference, FIE 2000, vol. 2, pp. F3C-5. IEEE (2000)

Demonstration

NOVELICA: A Visual Novel System to Make People Forget Their Negative Feelings on Mathematics

Nobumitsu Shikine[1]([⊠]), Toshimasa Yamanaka[2], Letizia Jaccheri[4], Javier Gomez[4], and Junichi Hoshino[3]

[1] Graduate School of Integrative and Global Majors, University of Tsukuba, Tsukuba, Japan
shikine-shikine@entcomp.esys.tsukuba.ac.jp

[2] Faculty of Art and Design, University of Tsukuba, Tsukuba, Japan
tyam@geijutsu.tsukuba.ac.jp

[3] Faculty of Engineering, Information and Systems, University of Tsukuba, Tsukuba, Japan
jhoshino@esys.tsukuba.ac.jp

[4] Norwegian University of Science and Technology, Trondheim, Norway
{letizia.jaccheri,javier.escribano}@ntnu.no

Abstract. In this paper we present a new visual novel system "NOVELICA" which employed Japanese anime like character agent and segmented the lesson to conversation size. It is designed to make exciting pace like an entertainment content than ordinary lessons and it is easier to control progression than video learning. We compared with NOVELICA to previous visual novel system and video learning system. And we found that NOVELICA can reduce stress and keeping arousal in learning mathematics, and it makes easier to touch mathematics content.

Keywords: e-Learning · Remedial education · Math anxiety · Video learning
Visual novel · Instructional pacing

1 Introduction

There are many students who are not good at or have anxiety towards math [1]. In many cases, math above the high school level requires cross-referencing of knowledge of various units and, depending on the student, creating the need for instructional pacing that suits the individual.

In recent years, there have been many examples of adaptive learning that introduce an e-Learning system as a follow-up to the one-to-many lecture format. In particular, the self-study system for visual lessons is easy to match to a schedule and is often used in universities and corporate training. However, they do not take into account the pace of students usually, there is no interaction with a teacher and it is difficult to maintain the motivation to study [2], which leads to stress during the learning process. It is known that stress during studying puts pressure on working memory and has a negative effect on learning study contents. Therefore, stress management is becoming a popular

E. Clua et al. (Eds.): ICEC 2018, LNCS 11112, pp. 329–333, 2018.
https://doi.org/10.1007/978-3-319-99426-0_39

matter to work on in schools and at home [3, 4]. Although stress comes from various sources, such as from a dislike of a subject or circumstances at home, either source negatively affects learning.

There are numerous scales when speaking generally about instructional pacing, and we can even consider choosing what to study on a certain day based on a monthly study schedule as instructional pacing. Conventional systems split study into sections such as "trigonometric functions" and "differentials and integrals" according to a learner's comprehension and even use single lessons to keep up pace with the student. However, there has been no consideration made so far for attentive pacing corresponding to motivation and mood for studying in one lesson.

To consider this, it will be necessary to review a new time structure that differs from that held by existing contents such as videos. Therefore, this study focuses on the time structuring of e-Learning systems and developed NOVELICA.

2   NOVELICA

NOVELICA is designed to make exciting pace on visual novel content by segmenting to conversation sized block. The existing self-study e-Learning systems can be split up into the two types of automatic progression and manual progression when classifying them based on the pace of lesson progression, and each has their own issues.

The video learning system (automatic progression) can be watched with comfort, and since the visual novel system (manual progression) has the time structural advantage of being able to carefully read content, we examined a time segmenting method that allows us to incorporate both of these.

NOVELICA is a visual novel system which splits lessons into time segments of single response prompts of conversations in order to solve the aforementioned issues [5]. These are referred to as "blocks". One block consists of a single voice file, and text and images are displayed in sync with the conversation from that voice file. One block therefore maintains prosodic information intended by the teacher (Figs. 1 and 2).

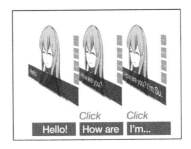

Fig. 1. Time structure of visual novel

Because one conversation's asking and replying takes 5 to 10 s, the recommended length of a block is 5 to 10 s. There is also no essential need for clicks in between each block, and a video experience is made possible by having the game automatically

Fig. 2. Time structure of NOVELICA

progress. A big difference when compared to video is that the producer can insert click prompts (response prompts) in between blocks anywhere they choose. In other words, they can basically progress it automatically, like a video, while leaving it to the student to progress in situations where they want to put emphasis on speech or give the student time for deliberation. In addition, it is a semi-automatic type system that allows the user to stop at the current block or jump to a block of her choice in the middle of automatic progression. Since speech can be cued for each block, listening back to topics can be carried out smoothly. And inserting click prompts (response prompts) makes the learner keep suitable arousal level. This is because learner does not know where the prompts are and they have to be awake to respond. Teacher can design pace of the lesson and learner can control its progress adjusting to individual motivation and feeling.

We developed the first NOVELICA content named "AKAHONe! Prototype A" (Fig. 3). This content is designed to reduce the negative feeling on mathematics by putting exciting conversation like an entertainment video. And it focused its speedy progress pace. The content consists of two characters' conversation. The first one is a high school girl character, Su, and she acts as a teacher. The second one is a high school boy, Shikine, and he acts as a learner. Both characters are drew like a Japanese anime style and in comical way because it is popular among young people. Learners can superimpose themselves on Shikine and watch content of Su's lesson.

Fig. 3. NOVELICA content "AKAHONe! Prototype A"

3   Evaluation

Two evaluation were conducted for NOVELICA. The first one was conducted to compare NOVELICA to other type of e-learning system [5]. 21 Japanese men and women who had graduated high school and reported to have weak interests at math cooperated as participants for the experiment. We used Two-Dimensional Mood Scale [6] and POMS [7] as evaluation indicators. The results indicated that NOVELICA's segmentation makes it possible to create individually suited lesson paces and acts as a time structure that reduces stress during learning and assists with comprehension. The second one was held during the workshop "Games, culture and science for boys and girls". This event took place at the Gunnerus Library (Trondheim, Norway) (Fig. 4). Participants were 10 Norwegian men and women aged 13 to 70 years old. After playing NOVELICA, participants answered mathematical questions and feeling questions about NOVELICA. And we measured how long participant takes for each block and whole lesson time they took. Among the impressions of the participants, there were things that "I liked that it taught a lot of information in such a short time" and "I like the way it kind a looked like anime". This is thought that our content was effective for touching mathematics. But some participants said "It was too fast to understand" and we found they tend to take a longtime (more than 1 min) for thinking to respond to a prompt in playing NOVELICA. It will be our next task to clarify the relationship between thinking time and whether or not leaner can enjoy lesson content.

Fig. 4. The workshop "Games, culture and science for boys and girls"

4   Conclusion

NOVELICA is a visual novel system which segment the lesson to conversation size and make progress automatic. Developer can design exciting paced lesson on NOVELICA to make people forget their negative feelings on mathematics with Japanese anime like characters. For the future work, clarify the relationship between thinking time and whether or not leaner can enjoy lesson content and we will develop other subjects of NOVELICA content.

Acknowledgements. This work has been partially supported by NTNU ARTEC and carried out during the tenure of an ERCIM "Alain Bensoussan" fellowship. The authors would like to thank Alexandra Angeletaki for organizing the international experiment workshop at the Gunnerus library of NTNU. We also give deep gratitude to the staff of indie game developer team Chloro and the translator David Evelyn.

References

1. Stoet, G., Bailey, D.H., Moore, A.M., Geary, D.C.: Countries with higher levels of gender equality show larger national sex differences in mathematics anxiety and relatively lower parental mathematics valuation for girls. PLoS ONE **11**(4), e0153857 (2016). https://doi.org/10.1371/journal.pone.0153857. Accessed 21 Apr 2016
2. Nakamura, R., Inoue, A., Ichimura, S., Okada, K., Matsushita, Y.: "Ghost-Tutor": a learning support system suggesting learning pace for on-demand learning. IPSJ **47**(7), 2099–2106 (2006)
3. Vukovic, R.K., Kieffer, M.J., Bailey, S.P., Harari, R.R.: Mathematics anxiety in young children: concurrent and longitudinal associations with mathematical performance. Contemp. Educ. Psychol. **38**(1), 1–10 (2013)
4. Berkowitz, T., et al.: Math at home adds up to achievement in school. Science **350**, 196 (2015)
5. Shikine, N., Yamanaka, T., Hoshino, J.: A game system for learning mathematics with pacing considering individual motivation and feeling. In: ICEC 2017, pp. 169–176 (2017)
6. Sakairi, Y., Nakatsuka, K., Shimizu, T.: Development of the two-dimensional mood scale for self-monitoring and self-regulation of momentary mood states. Jpn. Psychol. Res. **55**(4), 338–349 (2013)
7. Yokoyama, K.: POMS tanshukuban tebiki to jirei kaisetsu (in Japanese), KANEKOSHOBO (2005): ISBN 9784760840144

Art Exhibition

Imperceptible Art

Aleksandra Vasovic[(✉)]

Alekse Nenadovica 5, 11000 Belgrade, Serbia
a.s.vasovic@gmail.com

Abstract. The paper is text based artwork, a part of the ongoing project, work in progress, contemporary digital art live performance and it is contemplating about the idea to what extent could the process of employment of the instruments (which are assisting the visualization procedures within the field of visual and contemporary art, like augmented reality or virtual reality tools) – evolve.

Keywords: Augmented reality · Virtual reality · Artificial intelligence
Digital live performance · Contemporary art · Text based artwork
Philosophy · Spirituality

1 Introduction

1.1 The Context – in the Art. The Objectives – in the Art

The text-based artwork, situated within the practice of contemporary art and media art, is contemplating and thinking artistically in which ways is possible to expand, refer to and explore, via the mechanisms of art, the philosophical and spiritual approach - that the visible or perceptual reality does not exist and is merely an abstract concept.

The goal is to be comprehended inside the context of art – because of the specific nature of the "goal" when applied to the art and artistic activities. It is not mandatory and generally not possible to propose the goals when attempting to undertake or be involved in the artistic process, or to actualize the final artistic outcome or product. Accordingly, the artistic process and action itself is a goal, and it coincides with the spiritual thesis, which is also included in the artistic project: the witnessing or observing the unfolding of some process is some kind of a goal. Even though in transcendental terms, any goal can be defined as abstract concept, beyond any practical potential and implementation, it is exciting to examine what would visualization instruments, like augmented reality or virtual reality devices, in fact visualize, in the situations when there is nothing at all to be visualized. Or more precisely, when there is nothing more left except for the unadulterated substance within the contexts of art, philosophy or spirituality (Fig. 1).

© IFIP International Federation for Information Processing 2018
Published by Springer Nature Switzerland AG 2018. All Rights Reserved
E. Clua et al. (Eds.): ICEC 2018, LNCS 11112, pp. 337–339, 2018.
https://doi.org/10.1007/978-3-319-99426-0_40

Fig. 1. Imperceptible art – drafts. Video: https://youtu.be/AIcaOGzb1I4

2   Description

2.1   A Prefered Methodology and Potential Outcome

The artwork, a part of the artistic installation, consists of several variations, which not only are the constitutive elements of the artistic process, but also are independent, autonomous, and sustainable to maintain as separate individual artworks.

The initial part of the artwork is text-based; there would be other stages, e.g. art installations and performances.

In a suitable exhibiting space, maybe at the conference venue, some augmented reality (AR) or virtual reality (VR) tools and technology, would be applied.

Art installation or artwork consists of:

- VR headset, EEG neuroheadset and custom made software (running on PC). Brain activity is presented by computer generated virtual environment that responds to brain activity in real time. Hardware integration, software development (and implementation directly at the exhibiting space/conference venue) is provided by a team of developers specializing in virtual reality applications.
- The public, which interacts with the technology and continues to co-create artwork, which is in this way expanding by creating random outcome which is to be documented and evaluated – both from the artistic (and perhaps) scientific aspect in consequent stages of the ongoing project.
- The interaction between the technology and the public is generating the live performance, which is then developing further when shared via social networks and the internet, in which way the live performance alters from the on the spot event to the ongoing ubiquitous ever-expanding situation and experience, which absorbs certain characteristics existing within the context of the theater.

The procedure: the public, the audience, would apply the tool and create whatever is the product of their mental content, thoughts, imagination, emotions, whatever illustrates the mental and cognitive process.

As the project evolves, the meditations and prayers, or other applicable techniques will be introduced to the process and the VR tools would be used for creating the visualizations of the altered process. However, it is crucial that the art audience also consists of some individuals who perform meditation techniques, or prayers, or any other advanced spiritual methods and practice. It would be desirable, in subsequent stages, if the machines, which are creating artistic works using artificial intelligence, were also be incorporated in both personifications - as art public and as co-authors within this project. The results or visualizations would also be recorded.

The next phase is to use the VR tool to attempt to visualize or bring to life the content which is thought-less, and which is gained in the most advanced phases of spiritual practice – or even better, spontaneously, without the spiritual practice, which is in this case the preferred alternation compared to implementation of any proscribed technique or method, spiritual or not spiritual. When there are no thoughts, ideas and concepts to be seen or observed, detected, what is the resultant - would be interesting to record.

This final and most advanced phase for some participants will be reached and executed within nanoseconds, for some within years, for most within decades and even longer… it is a regular routine, as this live performance is ongoing, work in progress [1].

The other part of this artistic experiment would be recording activity and defining what is the significance of the recording and documenting when there is no detectable essence to document.

3 Conclusions

3.1 Art, Life, Entertainment

In such an extensive and dispersed territory like contemporary art, the safe conclusion is that the consistent artistic practice to never stop arising questions remains the very foundation of the discipline [2].

If art live performance succeeds to record that there is nothing to be recorded in the final phases of the live performance, then it is obvious to point to whom and why will it be relevant to evaluate the recordings? Is the artist, the author, authorized to evaluate them more than the artwork's co-creators; or is some distant observer, who is observing the progress of the performance, accredited to do so - is yet to be defined, if possible [3].

Another conclusion might be that (although there is no perceivable substance to be recorded and there is no one, no real person, as metaphysics or some branches of philosophy indicate, who could take the documentation into consideration), the process in its entirety and complexity was entertaining, that art is entertaining discipline and this is the sufficient and valuable reason for the procedure to be performed.

Maybe the entertainment is also the reason valid enough for the entire idea perceived as reality (in spiritual and philosophical context) to occur [4].

References

1. Swami, V.: The Concise Yoga Vasistha. In: Page 5 Hinduism, Philosophical Script, Advaita Vedanta. State University of New York, Albany (1984)
2. Smith, T.: What is Contemporary Art? Chicago: University of Chicago Press (2009)
3. Chandler, L.: Science and Buddhism agree: there is no "you" there. In: bigthink.com (2016). http://bigthink.com/ideafeed/good-news-science-buddha-agree-theres-no-you?utm_campaign =Echobox&utm_medium=Social&utm_source=Facebook#link_time=1495747728K
4. Vedral, V.: Decoding Reality. Oxford University Press, Oxford (2012)

Tappetina: An Ecosystem of Art, Software, and Research

Letizia Jaccheri[✉], Javier Gomez, and Sindre B. Skaraas

Department of Computer Science,
Norwegian University of Science and Technology, Trondheim, Norway
{letizia.jaccheri,javier.escribano}@ntnu.no,
sibsen@live.com

Abstract. Tappetina is a fairy tale about mentoring, social innovation and technology. A set of projects have been developed around the Tappetina concept. These include science workshops for teenagers and the associated material created by the participants, illustrations, a website, a video, a story telling game. These projects are all connected in an ecosystem of art, science, and research expressions.

Participants are supposed to experience the works sequentially. Participants will be invited into the projects and encouraged to give feedback about how they perceive the experience. Sessions for playing the collaborative story telling game will be organized.

Keywords: Fairy tales · Serious games · Affective learning · Empathy
Collaborative storytelling

1 Introduction

We offer an as an artistic experience around an ecosystem of works. This ecosystem is formed under the novel of "The Little Doormaid: Tappetina", authored by Letizia Jaccheri. When asked why she wrote this story, Letizia answered that she hoped it could inspire girls who read it to be more interested in technology. The story would not only try to combat stereotypes of girls in tech, but also create an emotional impact that creates interest in and even romanticizes technological concepts. In essence, it aims to build enthusiasm in kids to tech, and is thus used in IT workshops for learning IT and programming. The ecosystem that came out of this is an initiative to encourage nuanced views of people. It is formed under to combat the stigma surround women entering male-associated fields such as technology.

The novel has inspired several actors who have cooperated to produce workshops, a video, and a story telling game. This work, when exhibited will offer an experience of at least 20 min if one chooses to participate to a gaming session.

All the materials related to the project and events can be found at Tappetina's webpage: www.tappetina.com.

The video is available at https://tinyurl.com/ybksf6dm. It has been developed by a group of students and aims to encourage teenagers to study computer science and

E. Clua et al. (Eds.): ICEC 2018, LNCS 11112, pp. 340–342, 2018.
https://doi.org/10.1007/978-3-319-99426-0_41

promote the contribution of women in computer science by advertising the female character "Tappetina".

2 About the Authors

Letizia Jaccheri (Ph.D. from Politecnico di Torino, Italy) is Professor at the Depart- of Computer and Information Science. Jaccheri's research is on: software engineering; entertainment computing; computational creativity; ICT-enabled social innovation.

Javier Gomez (PhD. from Universidad Autónoma de Madrid, Spain) is an ERCIM "Alain Bensoussan" fellow at Department of Computer and Information Science, NTNU. His research interests include human-computer interaction, assistive technologies and serious games.

Sindre B. Skaraas graduated from NTNU in 2018 with a Master thesis titled Tappetina's Empathy A Study of Serious Games Facilitating Empathy with Storytelling.

Acknowledgements. This work has been partially supported by NTNU ARTEC and by the ERCIM fellowship program. The authors would like to thank Alexandra Angeletaki for organizing the international experiment workshop at the Gunnerus library of NTNU and all the participants to the Tappetina workshops. We thank the students who developed the video: Biljana Arsenic, Farzana Quayyum, Kshitiz Adhikari, Letizia Balzi, Md Shah Newaz, Nazli Sila Kara, and master student Uyen Dan Nguyen (Mimi) and PhD student Sofia Papavlasopoulou for workshop design and evaluation.

For the development of the game, the Unity Engine and editor was utilized, as developed by Unity Technologies.

Workshops

Designing Entertainment for the Aging Population

Paula Alexandra Silva[1] and Masood Masoodian[2(✉)]

[1] DigiMedia Research Center, University of Aveiro, Aveiro, Portugal
palexa@gmail.com
[2] School of Arts, Design and Architecture, Aalto University, Espoo, Finland
masood.masoodian@aalto.fi

Abstract. Despite the ever-increasing aging world population, most interactive entertainment and fun technologies are not specifically being designed for older adults. However, this trend is starting to change, particularly in the area of entertainment for health and wel-being. Therefore, this workshop aims to bring together researchers, designers, developers and entrepreneurs interested in the design, development, evaluation, commercialization and deployment of entertainment technologies for the aging population, targeting their needs and promoting their health and well-being.

Keywords: Aging population · Older adults
Entertainment for aging · Design for aging · Health · Well-being

1 Background

The world population is aging [1]. It is estimated that by 2040, 21.7% of the population of the United States [2], and by 2070, 42% of the population of the European Union [3] will be over 65 years old. It is, therefore, becoming ever more important to design products and services to better accommodate for the needs, requirements, expectations and characteristics of older adults.

Health and healthy living is clearly important to us humans, and we all want to have healthy and active lives which we can enjoy for as long as possible. In this context, it is not surprising that an increasing number of interactive tools and technologies are being developed to support us in this regard. Many of these interactive tools and technologies also tend to rely on our desire to have fun and be entertained, while working towards achieving a longer, active, and healthy life, in which we meet our goals, needs and desires.

Unfortunately, most such interactive entertainment and fun tools for health and well-being have not been designed specifically for an aging population. This is perhaps due to a misperception that older adults are not, or have not been in the past, very technologically able. In reality, however, analysts point out that it is indeed a misperception that "the 50+ are technologically challenged and

E. Clua et al. (Eds.): ICEC 2018, LNCS 11112, pp. 345–348, 2018.
https://doi.org/10.1007/978-3-319-99426-0_42

unplugged. In fact, aging consumers are tech savvy and eager for more." [4]. This myth is slowly being demystified with innovative, multidisciplinary, collaborative, and user-led approaches becoming more and more common. Arguably, by following such interdisciplinary approaches, we will better design for fun, engaging, inclusive, and entertaining technologies that reward the longevity that us humans have conquered.

Despite the importance of research into design of entertainment technology targeting older adults, there are not many opportunities for researchers and practitioners to meet and discuss their interests and ideas. This workshop aims to provide such a forum, enabling researchers and practitioners to share learnings and experiences related to design, development, evaluation, and deployment of entertainment tools and technologies for the ageing population.

2   Objectives

The main objective of this workshop is to bring together researchers, designers, developers and entrepreneurs interested in the design, development, evaluation, commercialization and deployment of entertainment tools and technologies for the aging population, targeting their needs and desire, and promoting their health and well-being.

Further to this, the workshop aims to create links between interested parties, and to encourage them to collaborate across disciplines and professional boundaries. We also hope that this workshop will be the first in a series of future workshops, which will become a forum for gathering of participants interested in entertainment technologies of the aging population.

3   Contributions

To achieve the above objectives, we invited researchers and practitioners from related backgrounds to submit their papers reporting their contributions to the topics of the workshop. Topics of interest included: healthy living, rehabilitation, prevention, active aging, independent living, person-centred approaches, connected health, quality of life and well-being. We sought submissions related to the following areas:

- Design, development, and evaluation of fun and entertainment technologies for the aging population.
- Acceptability and adoption of fun and entertainment technologies by the aging population.
- Examples and case studies of fun and entertainment technologies for the aging population.
- Innovative approaches to the design, development, evaluation, and commercialization of fun and entertainment technologies for the aging population.
- Community- and user-led innovations in fun and entertainment technologies for the aging population.
- Participatory and co–design methodologies and approaches for smart, active, and healthy aging.

4   Expected Outcomes

In addition to sharing and generating ideas amongst its participants, through a planned discussion session, this workshop will investigate potential future outcomes. These may include a special issue of an international journal and/or a co-authored report for dissemination of the workshop findings.

Furthermore, the accepted workshop papers have been published in this conference proceedings. We will also make the accepted papers and presentations available on the workshop website[1], which has been created for publicizing its aims and objectives, and disseminating its outcomes.

5   Workshop Programme

Our aim is to make this workshop as engaging and participatory as possible by including plenty of time for discussions and exchange of ideas. The workshop will achieve this aim through the inclusion of:

- Short presentations of the accepted papers.
- A follow-up interactive session to allow further discussions.
- A collaborative design activity.
- Concluding discussions and planning of future directions and outcomes.

6   Workshop Organizers

Dr. Paula Alexandra Silva is a Human-Computer Interaction (HCI) researcher and practitioner whose passion is to understand how to leverage technology to create a better future for us all. She has earned her Ph.D. in Computer Science from the University of Lancaster, United Kingdom. Since finishing her Ph.D. she focuses on designing applications for older adults with a view to improve their overall health and well-being and enable their active participation in society. She is also a passionate teacher who strives to create exceptional learning experiences for her students. She is currently a Research Fellow in the University of Aveiro. Before she held appointments as lecturer at a number of universities, as Postdoc Fellow at the University of Hawai'i and as Senior Scientist at Fraunhofer Portugal, where she managed the Human-Computer Interaction area and group.

Prof. Masood Masoodian leads the Aalto Visual Communication Design (AVCD) research group at Aalto University, Finland. He has a Ph.D. from the University of Waikato, New Zealand. His research interests include visualization, interactive media, and interaction design, with particular interest in designing interactive visualizations to provide effective means of understating information by ordinary people in areas such as health, energy, and sustainability. He is also

---

[1] http://avcd.aalto.fi/deap2018/.

actively involved in research related to different aspect of designing for older adults, including emotional design for entertainment, health and well-being. Prof. Masoodian has served as the programme chair, programme committee member, and reviewer for many international conferences and scientific journals. He has also been a co-organizer of several international conferences and workshops.

7   Programme Committee

Sergi Bermúdez i Badia *(Universidade da Madeira, Portugal)*, Leah Burns *(Aalto University, Finland)*, Masood Masoodian *(Aalto University, Finland)*, Francisco Nunes *(Fraunhofer - AICOS, Portugal)*, Thomas Rist *(University of Applied Sciences Augsburg, Germany)*, Rita Santos *(Universidade de Aveiro, Portugal)*, Paula Alexandra Silva *(Universidade de Aveiro, Portugal)*, Ana Veloso *(Universidade de Aveiro, Portugal)*.

References

1. United Nations Department of Economic and Social Affairs Population Division: World population ageing (2015). http://www.un.org/en/development/desa/population/publications/pdf/ageing/WPA2015_Report.pdf. Accessed July 2018
2. United States Department of Health and Human Services: 2017 profile of older Americans (2018). https://www.acl.gov/aging-and-disability-in-america/data-and-research/profile-older-americans. Accessed July 2018
3. European Union: The 2018 ageing report (2017). https://ec.europa.eu/info/sites/info/files/economy-finance/ip065_en.pdf. Accessed July 2018
4. Irving, P., Chatterjee, A.: The longevity economy: from the elderly, a new source of economic growth (2013). http://www.milkeninstitute.org/publications/view/687. Accessed July 2018

Storytelling: A Medium for Co-design of Health and Well-Being Services for Seniors

Leah Burns and Masood Masoodian[✉]

Department of Media School of Arts, Design and Architecture, Aalto University,
Helsinki, Finland
{leah.burns,masood.masoodian}@aalto.fi

Abstract. Much of the current research on ageing-related technologies, tools, and services has focused on issues related to supporting mainly the physical health and well-being of seniors. There is, however, a growing need for better support for other needs of ageing populations, including their entertainment, recreation and social connectedness. The success of future solutions for these needs requires active participation of senior users in their co-design. In this paper, we investigate the potential of storytelling as a practical medium for supporting this co-design process.

Keywords: Storytelling · Health · Well-being · Seniors · Older adults
Ageing population · Entertainment

1 Introduction

The world population is ageing rapidly, mainly as a result of longer life expectancies and lower birth rates. This phenomenon provides many benefits but also many challenges. Globally, economic and social practices tend to be based on the needs and interests of the highest income earners and those representing the full-time workforce—generally people aged 19–65 years. Service sectors, for instance, focus the majority of their efforts on addressing the necessities and desires of the generations that constitute this large group, including Millennials (19–34), Generation X (35–47) and Baby Boomers (48–67) [1]. However, as the Baby Boomer generation begins to leave the workforce and transition into retirement, the balance of the population of workforce age shifts dramatically. This shift brings with it a new emphasis on addressing the needs of senior populations.

Much of the current research on how to better support the well-being of the growing senior population has so far focused on health, housing, and financial welfare. Much less attention has been given to the support of meaningful social activities and pursuits for seniors that are not tied directly to subsistence-based concerns—such as ignoring the fact that seniors also seek support for meaningful engagement in terms of entertainment, recreation and social connectedness.

In fact, positive physical health outcomes are frequently linked to other well-being factors such as positive social relationships; a sense of personal autonomy,

E. Clua et al. (Eds.): ICEC 2018, LNCS 11112, pp. 349–354, 2018.
https://doi.org/10.1007/978-3-319-99426-0_43

agency, and purpose; self-acceptance, and personal growth [2–4]. The World Health Organization (WHO) describes health as being socially determined by "the conditions in which people are born, grow, work, live, and age, and the wider set of forces and systems shaping the conditions of daily life. . . " [5]. The WHO recommends taking an approach to promoting health that requires cross-sectoral collaboration and recognition that all aspects of health are interconnected.

How to design and integrate health and well-being services for ageing populations with creative forms of social engagement is a growing field of research, needing further investigation and cross-disciplinary collaboration [6]. Here, we examine the potential of storytelling as a medium for collaborative inquiry into, and co-design of, well-being technologies, tools, and services for seniors. We discuss the relevance of storytelling as a medium for well-being research, and provide a demonstrative example of such current research. We then review the methodological principles for an ethical approach to using storytelling in the design and evaluation of health and well-being technologies, tools, and services.

2   Potential of Storytelling

Experiences of ageing in contemporary contexts, and research on how to design better support for healthy ageing has been greatly impacted not only by socio-political and demographic changes but also by rapid changes in technology. The "digital age" has influenced how communications and social services are being conceived and provided for seniors. Mobile medical alert devices with GPS tracking and fall detection, virtual reality programs that allow users to experience and interact with other people, and tools for remote consultation with doctors, are just a few examples of tools and services that aim to support seniors.

How such tools and services get taken up by seniors themselves, however, frequently draws attention to a disconnect between what the technology affords in theory and what users desire and do in practice [7,8]. The types of entertainment and communications technology that are favoured in contemporary contexts and how these types of technology are used often echo social practices from the past. In addition, despite the affordances many new technologies offer in terms of spanning vast geographic distances instantaneously or creating spaces where information is perpetually available, many people of all ages still benefit greatly from in-person social and environmental encounters, especially when it comes to supporting well-being and social inclusion. Research has also shown that methods which may see success amongst younger populations for the purpose of education, provision of health and well-being services, or as a source of social connectedness, may be less effective in the case of seniors [9].

There is some evidence from recent research, showing the potential of storytelling as a medium which could improve the uptake of technology by senior users. Chu et al. [10] report a study comparing the use of gaming and storytelling to promote social connectedness with seniors. The study found that "[g]aming as a means of social interaction was seen [by seniors] as just a way to socially interact in the sense that it is an activity to do with other people. . . whereas storytelling as a means of social interaction was seen as a way to create human connections and relationships, to enable one to feel useful, and to bring attention to oneself among others" (p. 31). Chu et al. examined both games and storytelling systems as motivators for engaging seniors in the use of technologies for social and cognitive support and found that seniors were more interested and motivated by storytelling frameworks. They recommend that an understanding of "the needs, wants and desires of older adults" must be sought to support "truly useful and effective" design (p. 32). Numerous studies and reports regarding design for health and well-being confirm this supposition [11] and further, recommend processes of co-design [12] where seniors themselves are part of the design process from conception to implementation and evaluation. Chu et al., as well as others [13–15], also advocate the use of storytelling with older adults as a design framework or medium for design related to health and well-being.

3   An Example of Storytelling-Based Research

Stories, as mediums of social engagement, are extremely malleable and diverse and at the same time very familiar. Taking these qualities into consideration, various forms of storytelling have begun to gain popularity as methods for working with seniors to address issues of health and well-being. In this section, we describe a demonstrative example of storytelling with seniors, which has been used to improve their well-being in ways that move beyond oversimplified notions of healthy or successful ageing.

3.1   Narrative Gerontology

In *Beyond healthy aging: The practice of narrative care in gerontology* [13], Randall examines the role of narratives in shaping perceptions of ageing. He explores how the provision of medical and long-term care services for seniors may improve when service providers and health practitioners seek out the life stories of the seniors that they are working with. He refers to this practice as "narrative care", where care providers embody "sensitivity to [individuals] not as a 'patient' or a 'case', but as a person, with a lifetime of experiences and stories" (p. 178). Randall cites gerontologist Gene Cohen's critique of dominant representations of "successful ageing" which focus primarily on minimizing physical, social and cognitive decline "rather than recognizing the huge potential for positive growth in later life" [16] (quoted in [13], p. 179). Randall and other critical gerontologists claim that the overwhelming focus on maintenance of fitness and avoidance of decline medicalizes and pathologizes both the ageing process and "the elderly themselves" (p. 180). This dominant perspective limits how we approach the design and provision of services for seniors' health and well-being; how seniors are perceived and engaged with, and how seniors' may perceive themselves. There is an underlying assumption that as a senior "the story of one's life has effectively ended" [17] (quoted in [13], p. 184).

Randall proposes shifting this paradigm by promoting a *biographical* approach to understanding ageing, in addition to the *biological* approach which tends to dominate. Biographical ageing emphasizes on-going development—self-understanding, self-reflection, meaning-making—rather than mere maintenance or subsistence. Randall suggests that seniors may experience a kind of push and pull in terms of their sense of identity and life stories. They may feel a push to advancing self-knowledge by sharing their experiences, further reflecting on what they have learned and exploring what it might mean. At the same time, they may feel deflated and pulled toward a sense of irrelevance if they have no opportunities or encouragement to engage in and impart the value of their self-expressions and self-reflections.

Narrative care, as described by Randall, trains healthcare providers to develop a more holistic understanding of ageing persons' health needs by seeking out biographical encounters. Narrative care includes creating opportunities and allocating time to elicit life stories through conversations and shared activities between patients and caregivers. It requires listening with the whole body, being patient, attentive and fully present "conveying the impression [to seniors] that they are not just another patient but a unique individual with a unique story that extends beyond their circumstances here and now" [13] (p. 187). Narrative care also requires caregivers to participate in their own processes of self-reflection and examination of their own stories and how this may impact their interactions and assumptions.

Randall cites the example of one nursing home that uses a method of *Narrative Biography*, where storytelling is used to improve resident and staff relations and services. The home uses "reminiscence groups, storytelling circles, conversation corners, scrapbooking parties... [and a] biography program involv[ing] extensive interviews with selected residents by specially trained staff, volunteers, family members, or even local high school students" [13] (pp. 188–189) to create books and videos about residents' lives which are presented back to residents and to the larger nursing home community. Narrative care is described by Randall as a method of storytelling that serves as a means of individual and interpersonal exploration, and as a resource for identifying alternative approaches to designing and implementing health and well-being support services for seniors.

4   Methodological Principles of Storytelling

When proposing storytelling as a method for collaborative research or co-design it is important to take into consideration a few principles regarding how the method addresses the needs, desires and goals of the community or project for which it will be used. Chu et al. [10] have identified seven factors to account for in the design of storytelling systems for working with seniors:

"Designing around storytelling requires a focus on (1) audience or listeners. Support structures in the system design have to be provided for (2) content (older adults having too much to tell, or too little), (3) process (cognitive processes that are being supported), and (4) intention (the older adult's purpose in telling a story). A system design may not necessarily have to provide explicit support structures, but may need to account for storytelling (5) triggers (planned or instantaneous), (6) the medium of storytelling (face-to-face or mediated), and (7) the context of the story itself or how it is presented and shared (fluid, peripheral or fixed)" [10] (p. 32).

The factors that Chu et al. identify align closely with principles for equitable community arts collaboration [18] or co-design processes which emphasize the *relevance*, *accessibility* and *evaluation* of collaborative methods.

4.1   Relevance

The principle of relevance ensures that who participants are, as well as their interests and capacities, is understood and taken into consideration before choosing a particular storytelling method. Choosing a specific storytelling method in advance based on researchers/designers' own interests or based on assumptions of what a community may need or want can result in fitting the community into the method rather than creating a method that emerges in response to particular people and a particular context. Relevance also considers how the chosen storytelling medium serves community and project goals.

4.2   Accessibility

The principle of accessibility considers to what extent a particular storytelling method is accessible both to participants (those engaging in the production of stories) and to other stakeholders (those with whom participants seek to share their stories). For example, is digitally-based on-line storytelling suitable for participants (or intended audiences) with limited access to, or experience with, such technologies? Accessibility is also linked to feasibility, accounting for the resources required to facilitate the use of a particular method. For example, how much production time does a particular method require? Do participants or facilitators require a certain level of expertise to use a specific method?

4.3   Evaluation

The principle of evaluation in storytelling as a method of co-design incorporates opportunities for evaluation throughout the co-design process rather than only assessing an end-product after a project is completed. Storytelling for co-design also includes participants and, where possible, other stakeholders in determining what the criteria and processes of evaluation should be.

5   Conclusions

Recent research suggests that embracing more holistic conceptions of health and well-being is necessary if we seek to support seniors as valued individuals and community members rather than generic patients. The success of future solutions for improving support for seniors' biographical and biological well-being requires active participation of senior users in their co-design. With critical attention to methodological principles, storytelling as a medium, method and motivator for the development of such tools, services, and interventions shows some potential.

References

1. Financial Post: Which generations dominate the workforce now? (2014). https://business.financialpost.com/executive/management-hr/which-generations-dominate-the-workforce-now. Accessed July 2018
2. Ryff, C.D., Keyes, C.L.M.: The structure of psychological well-being revisited. J. Personal. Soc. Psychol. **69**(4), 719–727 (1995)
3. Diener, E., Chan, M.Y.: Happy people live longer: subjective well-being contributes to health and longevity. Appl. Psychol.: Health Well-Being **3**(1), 1–43 (2011)
4. Ryff, C.D.: Psychological well-being revisited: advances in the science and practice of eudaimonia. Psychother. Psychosom. **83**(1), 10–28 (2014)
5. World Health Organization: Social determinants of health (2018). http://www.who.int/social_determinants/tools/en/. Accessed July 2018
6. Swinnen, A., Port, C.: Aging, narrative, and performance: essays from the humanities. Int. J. Ageing Later Life **7**(2), 9–15 (2012)
7. Heinz, M., et al.: Perceptions of technology among older adults. J. Gerontol. Nurs. **39**(1), 42–51 (2013)
8. Vaportzis, E., Giatsi Clausen, M., Gow, A.J.: Older adults perceptions of technology and barriers to interacting with tablet computers: a focus group study. Front. Psychol. **8**, 1687 (2017)
9. Koivisto, J., Hamari, J.: Demographic differences in perceived benefits from gamification. Comput. Hum. Behav. **35**, 179–188 (2014)
10. Chu, S.L., Garcia, B., Quance, T., Geraci, L., Woltering, S., Quek, F.: Understanding storytelling as a design framework for cognitive support technologies for older adults. In: Proceedings of the International Symposium on Interactive Technology and Ageing Populations, ITAP 2016, pp. 24–33. ACM, New York (2016)
11. Hassenzahl, M., Eckoldt, K., Diefenbach, S., Laschke, M., Lenz, E., Kim, J.: Designing moments of meaning and pleasure. Int. J. Des. Exp. Des. Happiness. **7**(3), 21–31 (2013)
12. Botero, A., Hyysalo, S.: Ageing together: steps towards evolutionary co-design in everyday practices. CoDesign **9**(1), 37–54 (2013)
13. Randall, W.: Beyond healthy aging: the practice of narrative care in gerontology. In: English, L. (ed.) Adult Education and Health, pp. 178–192. University of Toronto Press (2012)
14. Sarvimäki, A.: Healthy ageing, narrative method and research ethics. Scand. J. Public Health **43**(16), 57–60 (2015)
15. de Medeiros, K.: Narrative gerontology: countering the master narratives of aging (invited). Narrat. Works **6**(1), 63–81 (2016)
16. Cohen, G.D.: The Mature Mind: The Positive Power of the Aging Brain. Basic Books, New York (2005)
17. Freeman, M.P.: Hindsight: The Promise and Peril of Looking Backward, 1st edn. Oxford University Press, New York (2010)
18. Louis, S., Burns, L.: Arts & Equity Toolkit. Toronto Arts Foundation and the Neighbourhood Arts Network, Toronto (2012)

User-Centered Design of an Online Mobile Game Suite to Affect Well-Being of Older Adults

Isabelle Kniestedt[(✉)], Stephan Lukosch, and Frances Brazier

Delft University of Technology, Delft, The Netherlands
i.kniestedt@tudelft.nl

Abstract. This paper describes the ongoing design process of *Pocket Odyssey*, an online multi-player game suite designed for mobile phones that supports older adults in maintaining their physical, social, and mental well-being. It has been designed to provide engaging gameplay that supports positive emotion, fosters online social connections between players, enables play with others in a player's physical surroundings, and integrates tasks that exercise physical and cognitive skills. This paper discusses the user-centered design approach that takes entertainment preferences, views on technology, and aspects of life that older adults consider meaningful as a basis. Based on the results of an exploratory survey and a series of workshops with the user group, this paper presents the initial game concept and the rationale behind its design. Finally, it describes early prototyping efforts and future activities.

Keywords: User-centered design · Game · Well-being · Older adults

1 Introduction

Understanding how to enable, acquire and maintain a feeling of well-being is a challenge. As life expectancy increases, the aging process comes with a variety of more specific challenges that influence a person's autonomy, social network, and the ability to act and enjoy [1]. This paper explores the potential of technological innovation, in particular of digital games, to tackle this challenge.

The effects of digital games have been studied ever since they became mainstream media [2]. With their ever increasing ubiquity, in part due to their availability on mobile devices, this field of study has only grown. Although a growing body of work points towards the short-term positive effects that games can have on players [3,4], little is known about long-term effects. Whether games can contribute to well-being over time, and how designers should approach such a task, requires more study.

This project has received funding from the European Union's Horizon 2020 research and innovation program under grant agreement No. 769643.

E. Clua et al. (Eds.): ICEC 2018, LNCS 11112, pp. 355–361, 2018.
https://doi.org/10.1007/978-3-319-99426-0_44

This paper describes the early design of *Pocket Odyssey*, a mobile game suite for players over 55 years of age. This mobile game suite has been designed to (1) foster social contact both online and between players in the same physical space, (2) stimulate cognitive functioning through knowledge and reasoning-based game mechanics, and (3) encourage light physical activity by utilizing the sensors of a mobile phone. By combining these different types of play, *Pocket Odyssey* aims to provide positive playful experiences over an extended period of time that contribute to a player's overall well-being.

An iterative, user-centered approach has been followed, based on requirements gathered from an initial survey on leisure and entertainment preferences, including device preferences, and from four workshops that focused on factors that influence user well-being and use of technology. This paper presents the first game concept, the rationale behind the design, experience with initial prototypes, and future plans.

2   Related Work

Well-being is a construct that consists of multiple measurable dimensions. The main dimensions considered in the literature are: emotional well-being, that describes positive emotion or affect [5–7] and life satisfaction [7]; psychological well-being, that addresses factors such as autonomy [7,8], accomplishment [6], and engagement [5,6]; social well-being, that focuses on positive relationships [6–8] and factors such as social acceptance, coherence, and integration [7]; and physical well-being [9]. A person's resources determine whether a stable equilibrium between these dimensions of well-being can be maintained given the challenges with which an individual is faced [10]. When challenges outweigh resources, well-being is affected negatively. In turn, when resources outweigh challenge, stagnation can occur. Therefore, maintaining a sense of equilibrium can be achieved by teaching individuals to increase their resources or the number and types of challenges with which they are faced [10].

Digital games have become both widespread entertainment media and an object of academic study. They are a dynamic, interactive medium that enables a unique form of player engagement [11]. Games often take the form of challenges to be overcome and therefore, together with other elements such as pleasing aesthetics and story, provide short-term impact on psychological and emotional well-being [3]. Another potential positive effect of games is in fostering social connections, be it through online or co-located multi-player games with friends or strangers [12].

3   Context

The H2020 project NESTORE, provides the context for acquisition of initial design *requirements* (annotated in this paper with 'RX', see Table 1), such as the ability to affect well-being in the various domains (R1), and engage players over time (R2).

To contribute to well-being over time, target users need to engage with the game over an extended period of time. To this purpose, an iterative development cycle is followed that involves testing and adapting the game in interaction with its target users at various stages of development [13]. Specific usability needs of older audiences have been identified on the basis of the literature (R3) [1], as well as the need for an appropriate game experience (R4) [13] based on age related interests, such as entertainment preferences [14] and factors that influence motivation [15]). Building on this existing work, direct feedback was sought from the target audience through an *exploratory survey* and a *series of workshops* in order to further inform the early stages of the design process.

4   Interests and Technology Survey

A survey was designed and conducted to determine the leisure and entertainment preferences of, and the types of technology used by the target audience. 30 Dutch participants participated in the survey, with ages ranging from 55 to 69 (M = 60.8, SD = 3.95) and 67% female. Participants were asked to rate 17 leisure activities (e.g. sports, gardening, travel) and 23 entertainment genres (e.g. fantasy, action, drama), having the choice between 'Dislike', 'Neutral', 'Like', and 'I don't know' for each item. Finally, the survey contained questions relating to technology use.

The results show a variety of activities that are enjoyed by the target audience. The top five consists of travel (83%), spending time with friends and family (80%), reading (73%), watching movies/tv (70%), and listening to the radio (70%). Regarding games in particular, 47% reported enjoying board or card games, 53% liked word or number puzzles, and 33% liked digital games. Similarly, with respect to genres of entertainment the top five consisted of adventure, history, crime/detective, tension/thriller, and comedy.

All participants reported owning and using a smart-phone with a data connection (R5). Less frequent were the use of laptops and tablets (80% and 67% respectively). The dominant operating system was Android for smart-phones (60%). A minority of participants reported playing digital games on a tablet (30%), smart-phone (27%), or laptop/computer (7%).

5   Exhibition-in-a-Box Workshops

After the survey, a total of 17 participants took part in four workshops organized to increase understanding of factors that influence well-being and the influence of technology. Each workshop lasted approximately two hours and deployed the Exhibition-in-a-Box [16] method, which utilizes objects as associative prompts for conversation. Participants took an object from the box at random, after which they were asked to discuss what they find meaningful or technology using the object as a guide. Results from the workshops show the importance of staying active, physically and mentally, as well as maintaining social contacts as one gets older. Participants took part in many activities, for which social contact was often named as a motivator. Those who live alone mentioned relying on group activities in community centers, as opposed to those who live with a partner or who have family close by. Regarding technology, the participants indicated that systems should be easy to use (relating to R3), fit into their routine (R6), be designed with the user in mind (relating to R3/R4), and provide enough support as they are introduced (R7). Finally, while participants were positive about the fact that technology enables social contact with those who are further away, face-to-face contact was perceived to be very valuable (R8). Participants showed a general concern for how digital technology is changing patterns of communication.

When asked about games, participants generally expressed positive views. Opinions on digital games were mixed; particularly the level of violence and its potential effect on younger people was a cause for concern. Board games were generally seen to be a positive activity (R9), and several participants mentioned playing digital games as well, e.g. *Pokemon Go*[1], *Farm Heroes Saga*[2], and *Words with Friends*[3]. Games and puzzles were considered to be good for 'keeping the brain active' and an enjoyable social activity.

6   Pocket Odyssey: Game Concept

This section briefly describes the initial design of *Pocket Odyssey*. Design choices are based on identified requirements (see Table 1). Note that in time, as requirements change, decisions are necessarily going to change over the course of iterative development. However, the desired gaming experience remains intact.

Table 1. Identified design requirements

R1	Affect well-being in the emotional, psychological, social, and physical domain
R2	Engage players over time
R3	Adhere to usability needs for older audiences
R4	Provide a suitable game experience for the audience
R5	Utilise platform widely used by target audience (smartphone)
R6	Easily fit into existing routines
R7	Provide support during introduction
R8	Enable face-to-face contact
R9	Provide experience reminiscent of board games

In accordance with R5, the game suite has been designed to play solely on mobile phones, as this is a device that participants already own and is part of their routine (R6). In the game, a player takes on the role of an explorer

[1] Niantic, 2016.

[2] King, 2016.

[3] Zynga, 2009.

uncovering mysteries as he/she travels through the world. This theme is based on themes distinguished in existing literature [15] and the exploratory survey (described above), in which the themes of travel, history, adventure, and mystery were reported, indicating alignment with user interests (R4). The game suite's main screen shows a player's *personal ship*. This provides the first distinct gameplay component, namely a customizable environment that requires periodic interaction with the player (R2). The other main component is that of *expeditions*: turn-based, online mystery-solving game sessions between 2 players (R1). As part of expeditions, players engage in *mini-games*, each of which tackles various aspects of well-being (R1). These games, in turn, can be used to host a *local multi-player game session* (R8), or be played on their own.

As stated above, a player's ship provides a customizable environment that develops over time. Its design is inspired by casual simulation games such as *Animal Crossing*[4] and *Farmville*[5]. In these games, players perform short, repeating tasks to collect items and develop a virtual space (e.g. a house, town, or farm). This requires a player to leave the game temporarily and return at a later time. Therefore, regular interactions that can easily be slotted into 'idle' time are rewarded, addressing R2 and R7. Additionally, this particular type of game adheres to suggested aesthetics for older people (R4) [15]: 'nurturing', by building and customizing a personal space over time; 'curiosity', through unexpected items and effects; and 'nostalgia', through implementing recognizable objects from the past and the ability to add personal content. The option to add personal content (e.g. descriptions and photos), makes it possible to personalize a multi-player experience, even though interaction with the ship is mainly a single player activity. Players can view the decoration of the ships of others, and their personal content. This has been designed to make the game experience less impersonal and to promote social activity between players (R1).

Expeditions is a turn-based online game between 2 players, in which a virtual environment of a fictional society is explored. Players take turns in solving a mystery, based on questions about the fictional society. A randomized environment is revealed to players throughout the game as they uncover clues, on the basis of which a solution to the mystery can be devised. Players are encouraged to communicate with each other about clues they have found via a chat interface. The goal of this design is to integrate both collaborative and competitive elements and simulate a board game-like experience (R9).

Some clues in *Expeditions* require the completion of a randomized mini-game designed to stimulate light physical activity, cognitive training, or emotional training (R1). These mini-games may also be played individually or in a local multi-player session. Here, a random sequence of mini-games is assigned to individual players and projected on a larger shared screen. This last option changes the game experience to that of a shared, social, co-located group experience (R8) [17], with players competing to get the highest score. While mini-games

---

[4] Nintendo, 2001.

[5] Zynga, 2009.

have yet to be designed and implemented, each will be based on research and expert input related to the desired activity.

Pocket Odyssey will be further developed using an iterative user-centered design approach [13]. Initial paper prototypes have been tested with a small group of people with game design experience. The next phase includes involvement of the target audience with a focus on usability (R3). Once the game has been 'finalized', training and support will be arranged (R7) for a one-year study in the three pilot countries involved in this project to examine user engagement and effects on well-being. The ultimate goal of this project is to identify game requirements and design guidelines for games designed to increase well-being over time through engagement.

References

1. Gerling, K.M., Schulte, F.P., Smeddinck, J., Masuch, M.: Game design for older adults: effects of age-related changes on structural elements of digital games. In: Herrlich, M., Malaka, R., Masuch, M. (eds.) ICEC 2012. LNCS, vol. 7522, pp. 235–242. Springer, Heidelberg (2012). https://doi.org/10.1007/978-3-642-33542-6_20
2. Barlett, C.P., Anderson, C.A., Swing, E.L.: Video game effects - confirmed, suspected, and speculative: a review of the evidence. Simul. Gaming **40**(3), 377–403 (2009)
3. Ryan, R.M., Rigby, C.S., Przybylski, A.: The motivational pull of video games: a self-determination theory approach. Motiv. Emot. **30**(4), 344–360 (2006)
4. Johnson, D., Jones, C., Scholes, L., Carras, M.C.: Videogames and Wellbeing: A Comprehensive Review. Young and Well Cooperative Research Centre (2013)
5. Huppert, F.A., So, T.T.: Flourishing across Europe: application of a new conceptual framework for defining well-being. Soc. Indic. Res. **110**(3), 837–861 (2013)
6. Seligman, M.E.: Flourish: A Visionary New Understanding of Happiness and Well-Being. Simon and Schuster, New York (2012)
7. Keyes, C.L.: Promoting and protecting mental health as flourishing: a complementary strategy for improving national mental health. Am. Psychol. **62**(2), 95 (2007)
8. Ryff, C.D.: Beyond Ponce de Leon and life satisfaction: new directions in quest of successful ageing. Int. J. Behav. Dev. **12**(1), 35–55 (1989)
9. Butler, J., Kern, M.L.: The PERMA-Profiler: a brief multidimensional measure of flourishing. Int. J. Wellbeing **6**(3) (2016)
10. Dodge, R., Daly, A.P., Huyton, J., Sanders, L.D.: The challenge of defining well-being. Int. J. Wellbeing **2**(3) (2012)
11. Calleja, G.: In-Game: From Immersion to Incorporation. MIT Press, Cambridge (2011)
12. Vella, K.: The social context of video game play: relationships with the player experience and wellbeing. Ph.D. thesis, Queensland University of Technology (2016)
13. Fullerton, T.: Game Design Workshop: A Playcentric Approach to Creating Innovative Games. CRC Press, Boca Raton (2014)
14. Brown, J.A.S.: Let's play: Understanding the role and significance of digital gaming in old age. University of Kentucky (2014)

15. De Schutter, B.: Gerontoludic design: extending the mda framework to facilitate meaningful play for older adults. Int. J. Gaming Comput.-Mediat. Simul. (IJGCMS) **9**(1), 45–60 (2017)
16. Chamberlain, P., Craig, C.: Engagingdesign – methods for collective creativity. In: Kurosu, M. (ed.) HCI 2013. LNCS, vol. 8004, pp. 22–31. Springer, Heidelberg (2013). https://doi.org/10.1007/978-3-642-39232-0_3
17. Bianchi-Berthouze, N., Isbister, K.: Emotion and body-based games: overview and opportunities. In: Karpouzis, K., Yannakakis, G. (eds.) Emotion in Games. Socio-Affective Computing, pp. 235–255. Springer, Cham (2016). https://doi.org/10.1007/978-3-319-41316-7_14

Providing Life-Style-Intervention to Improve Well-Being of Elderly People

Thomas Rist[1(✉)], Andreas Seiderer[2], and Elisabeth André[2]

[1] Hochschule Augsburg, Augsburg, Germany
Thomas.Rist@hs-augsburg.de
[2] Universität Augsburg, Augsburg, Germany

Abstract. We report on a user-centered approach towards the development of an augmented digital picture frame - called "CARE" - for senior users with the aim to improve their general well-being. The central idea is to interleave the display of pictures with the provision of recommendations of activities that seniors may perform in addition to their ordinary daily routines. We also report on our attempt to encourage durable use of the CARE system by introducing reward schemes for recommended activities. Feedback from users suggests that reward schemes should be made individually configurable.

Keywords: Ambient Assisted Living · Gamification · Senior-centered design

1 Introduction

Aging - sooner or later - goes hand in hand with a decline in physical performance and intellectual functions. Many elderly people suffer from various kinds of diseases, some of which can be chronic. Physical impairments definitely have an impact on their everyday life and also their psychological state. Therefore, lifestyle choices are among the most important factors that determine a person's well-being and quality of life. Studies have shown that regular physical activities can help mitigate many age-related diseases. Furthermore, creative activities, such as painting, have a positive influence on well-being. Studies conducted in a senior citizen's apartment building have shown that interventions that encourage the elderly to participate in activities, such as taking over responsibility for household chores, have been effective means to prevent social isolation and loneliness.

We report on the CARE project (a sentient Context-Aware Recommender system for the Elderly) which makes use of a digital picture frame as display device for providing recommendations [1]. Recommendations are chosen on the basis of data acquired by sensors embedded in the user's environment and possibly body-worn sensors as well as a user model, a discourse model, and a model of well-being factors to carefully decide on at which point in time what kind of activity will be most suitable to suggest in order to increase the user's well-being.

Whether a system like CARE can reach its aims essentially depends on whether the given recommendations are actually followed in general and - depending on the kind of recommendation - how accurately they are followed. Also as CARE has been designed

E. Clua et al. (Eds.): ICEC 2018, LNCS 11112, pp. 362–367, 2018.
https://doi.org/10.1007/978-3-319-99426-0_45

for long term usage, users need to be encouraged to follow repeatedly recommended activities. With the ambition to increase the effectiveness of CARE, it was questioned, in what way well-known computer game elements and principles, such as live feedback and especially rewards, may be used to enhance the user's overall appreciation of the CARE system. To find out which activities recommended by CARE should get rewarded and what kind of rewards would be appropriate, we prepared and ran a co-design workshop with a peer group of senior citizens.

2   Requirements Gathering

To inform the design of the envisioned system, we recruited a peer group of potential users, 27 German seniors (aged 59–92, 12 male, 15 female), and conducted structured interviews which were focused on the seniors' life-style, medical needs, attitude towards so-called Ambient Assisted Living technologies, and, more specifically, on desired functions of a CARE system (reminders, recommendations etc.) and preferences for a certain configuration (display type, presentation media and interaction modalities) system configurations of a system that gives them recommendations.

The most frequently desired functions were: (a) services that would remind them of intaking medicine, regular drinking and important dates, (b) sending emergency calls to family members and medical staff in case of accidents and illness, (c) warnings concerning not-switched-off electrical appliances, lights or open windows when leaving the house or going to bed. In addition, seniors saw a benefit in getting recommendations for healthy nutrition, physical activity and mental training. Regarding system configuration there was no clear winner among the presented interaction devices (tablet, picture frame, smartphone, smartwatch, humanoid robot) although the smartwatch was slightly preferred over the other devices. Regarding interaction modalities, some of the interviewees mentioned speech-based interaction as desirable, in particular for the smartwatches due to their small displays and for the robots.

3   CARE Prototypes

After requirement gathering we decided to deploy a digital picture frame as display device for providing recommendations. However, CARE makes a substantial extension to the classical concept of a digital picture frame. It interleaves the display of photos with physical exercises, brain-twisters and situation-specific life style recommendations, i.e. it switches between a picture frame mode and a recommender mode.

In Picture frame mode, CARE appears to the user like an ordinary picture frame that displays photos that are either taken from local repository, or which are remotely uploaded by family members via an internet connection (Fig. 1 left). The Picture frame mode is usually active when the user is further away from the display.

In recommender mode users receive context-specific recommendations (Fig. 1 right) chosen on the basis of: (a) data acquired by sensors embedded in the user's environment and possibly body-worn sensors, (b) a user model, (c) a discourse model, and (d) a model of well-being factors to carefully decide on at which point in time what

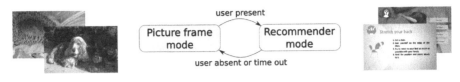

Fig. 1. Digital picture frame augmented by a recommender mode

kind of activity will be most suitable to suggest in order to increase the user's well-being.

For the sake of simplicity, CARE switches to recommender mode every time a user is detected in front of the display for a minimum of two seconds.

During the project, several versions of CARE prototypes have been developed and tested in living environments of pilot users. A first proof-of-concept version was based on a tablet PC cased in a wooden frame so that it appeared as an ordinary digital picture frame (Fig. 2a). It turned out that the readability of presented recommendations would benefit if the display screen was mounted at the user's eye level. This leads to a CARE version that was mounted on a rack rail (Fig. 2b). In addition, this version featured a magnetic pin board which allowed users to stick notes on it, and also to store some items such as a stretch band, needed for certain physical exercises (Fig. 2c). A revised version of CARE has been integrated in a shelf (Fig. 2d). This version features both soft buttons as well as external hardware buttons to ease interaction in case a person feels more comfortable pressing hardware buttons than soft-buttons on the screen. In addition, this version can be connected with an ambient light to indicate that the user may have a look at CARE as there are new recommendations.

Fig. 2. Different versions of CARE prototypes

4   Rewarding Schemes for Recommended Activities

With the ambition to increase the effectiveness of CARE, it was questioned, in what way well-known computer game elements and principles, such as live feedback and especially rewards, may be used to enhance the user's overall appreciation of the CARE system. The idea is to link given recommendations with some measurable indicators of whether or not recommendations have been followed. For instance, if the recommender system suggests a physical exercise, a possible indicator is the number of repetitions or just elapsed exercising time.

Initially, we speculated that a uniform rewarding scheme across all kinds of recommended activities would increase the users' perception of CARE as a coherent recommendation system. Following this approach, measured indicators for different recommendations are mapped onto abstract points, which in turn are mapped to a rewarding scheme of choice, such as score boards, badges or virtual currencies. Scores encompass rewarding in form of comparison with oneself, like a high-score in speed races, and with other players in a leaderboard. Badges are a means to represent the status of each player (CARE user) by providing him or her with awards or the recognition by others. The virtual currency category stands for all kind of rewards which can be exchanged with virtual or real goods. For instance, virtual coins may be used to purchase yet needed pieces of a jigsaw puzzle on screen or to have a virtual plant grow and prosper. Another option would be to use the coins for purchasing real-world goods, such as a cup of coffee.

However, there was uncertainty which recommended activities should get rewarded at all, and what kind of rewards users would find appropriate. To shed light on these questions we arranged two user workshops (W1, W2) with elderly people, having in mind the following objectives (1) to learn about the daily routines of the participants and their engagement in activities that promote a healthy lifestyle, (2) to elicit feedback on technology that actively gives recommendations and suggests activities, and (3) to gather opinions on meaningful rewarding schemes for recommended activities and (4) to learn about contextual factors, such different living environments.

For workshop W1 we established contact with a local seniors' association and recruited a group of seniors (aged 60–70, 11 female, 1 male). All seniors are retired, live independently, and maintain their own households. In contrast, for the second workshop (W2) we recruited nine residents (aged 80+, 8 female, 1 male). Compared to W1 participants, members of this age group were notably suffering more strongly from age-related impairments, such as limited mobility and lower levels of cognitive performance.

To elicit information about the participants' daily routines and activities, and to reveal their attitudes towards rewarding schemes, a working sheet with a timeline and three piles of cards have been prepared. The first pile consisted of cards depicting daily routines. Cards of the second pile showed activities that CARE would recommend for promoting a healthier lifestyle, e.g. physical or mental exercises. By means of cards from the third pile, participants could allocate different kinds of reward to activities. While there is a huge variety of possible rewards, we focused on three types of reward, which we found suitable for CARE: scores, badges and virtual currencies. Finally, several blank cards were included so that participants could use them to write down additional activities or rewards for which no cards had been prepared. With exception of blank cards, the visual appearance of all cards resembled the graphical style used for screen content displayed by the CARE system.

Workshop W1 took place at a senior meeting center, while W2 was held in an assembly room of the retirement home. Both workshops were administered by one female and two male experimenters. In the workshops, participants:

- received an introduction to CARE including the opportunity to practice instructed and monitored by the system,

- got an explanation of their role in helping us extend and improve CARE,
- took part in three card-laying tasks to inform us about daily routines and activities, and to reveal their attitudes towards rewarding schemes,
- were asked to provide verbal feedback on a number of predefined questions which are to be prompted by the experimenters during the workshop.

Throughout the workshops three experimenters took notes on verbal responses and comments, and took pictures of the outcomes of the card-laying tasks. Grouping and analysis of the recorded material took place after each workshop.

Participants first laid out their typical daily schedule (Task 1), then indicated preferences for potential recommendations (Task 2), and indicated for which of the recommended activities they would appreciate receiving rewards (Task 3) (Fig. 3).

Fig. 3. Two samples of finished worksheets.

Examining W1 and W2 worksheets to see which activities got associated with rewards (scores, badges, or virtual currency) revealed a quite heterogeneous picture. Only 4 out of 9 W2 participants wanted to receive rewards at all. In contrast, W1 participants were more open towards the idea of receiving rewards. Only one W1 participant did not assign any reward arguing that having accomplished an activity is enough rewarding itself and doesn't need an extra reward on top of it. Three W1 participants rewarded only activities which were already part of their agendas (such as cleaning, gardening, or surfing the Internet as this was considered a challenging activity), but not to recommended activities. In contrast, 7 W1 participants only rewarded recommended activities; and only one participant rewarded both routine activities as well as recommended activities.

With regard to reward types we observed among W1 participants a strong preference (21 cases) for virtual currencies that could be used to purchase real or virtual goods. Several suggestions were given for potential exchanges, such as using collected virtual currency for sports equipment. Badges were assigned in 6 cases, and scores in another 5 cases. Only 3 W1 participants rewarded activities consistently with the same type of reward, while all others suggested different reward types for different activities. We did not observe dominant occurrences of activity/reward associations among all W1 and W2 participants, but a variety of individual preferences. There was common agreement among the participants of both workshops that it is often the activity itself or its outcome that constitutes a tangible reward to them.

5   Related Work

The concept of a digital picture frame has also been researched by Rowan and Mynatt [2] to enhance awareness within a family of a senior's daily life by augmenting a portrait of the elderly person with data related to health and well-being. Lumsden et al. [3] reviewed 33 studies of gamified applications for cognitive training and identified a number of different reasons for deploying game elements in cognitive training and testing, including the aim to increase the users' motivation and long-term engagement, as well as usability, intuitiveness and appeal of an application. Johnson et al. [4] revisited 19 papers that report empirical evidence on the effect of gamified physical as well as mental exercises on health and wellbeing. While the majority of studies suggest that gamification has worked in many cases, it still remains a challenge for application designers to decide on which gamifying elements should be added because they are likely to add value to an application, and which ones should be neglected since they may even cause opposite effects. Suggestions for application design can be extracted from works compiling gamification guidelines based on interviews with seniors [5].

6   Conclusions

In this paper, we described work towards a recommender system for elderly people with the ultimate objective to contribute positively to a senior person's well-being through little interventions provided during the day in the form of contextualized recommendations which are related to factors that determine well-being. After first user studies, we feel encouraged to incorporate a reward mechanism into CARE. However, we no longer think that a uniform rewarding scheme across all recommendation types is the approach of choice. Therefore, we will give users the opportunity to configure the rewarding schemes individually.

References

1. Rist, T., Seiderer, A., Hammer, S., Mayr, M., André, E.: CARE: extending a digital picture frame with a recommender mode to enhance well-being of elderly people. In: Pervasive Health 2015, pp. 112–120 (2015)
2. Rowan, J., Mynatt, E.D.: Digital family portrait field trial: support for aging in place. In: Proceedings of CHI 2005, pp. 521–530. ACM, New York (2005)
3. Lumsden, J., Edwards, E.A., Lawrence, N.S., Coyle, D., Munò, M.R.: Gamification of cognitive assessment and cognitive training: a systematic review of applications and efficacy. JMIR Serious Games 4(2) (2016)
4. Johnson, D., Deterding, S., Kuhn, K.-A., Staneva, A., Stoyanov, S., Hides, L.: Gamification for health and wellbeing: a systematic review of the literature. Internet Interv. 6, 89–106 (2016)
5. De Schutter, B., VanDen Abeele, V.: Designing meaningful play within the psycho-social context of older adults. In: Fun and Games 2010, pp. 84–93. ACM, New York (2010)

Intergenerational Joint Media Engagement

Pre-testing Interviews, Activities and Tablet's Applications

Ana Carla Amaro$^{(\boxtimes)}$ ⓘ, Lidia Oliveira ⓘ, and Vania Baldi ⓘ

Digimedia - Digital Media and Interaction (CIC.Digital), University of Aveiro, Aveiro, Portugal
{aamaro,lidia,vbaldi}@ua.pt

Abstract. This paper presents the results of a preliminary study, in which grandchildren/children and grandparents/middle aged to older adults were observed while interacting with each other and with an App, on a tablet, to develop a proposed activity. Before and after these Joint Media Engagement (JME) sessions, participants were also interviewed, in order to collect data and to assess the perceived impact of the JME sessions in the quality of the intergenerational relationship, on the attitude towards each other and on children and older adults' digital literacy. The main goals of this preliminary study were to validate data collection instruments and techniques, namely the JME sessions activities, Apps and protocols and the pre- and post-JME session interviews' scripts. This preliminary study is part of a research that aims to understand the interactions and communication processes taking place during JME sessions involving grandparents/older adults (over 55 years old) and grandchildren/children (5 to 10 years old) in collaborative usage of tablets and tablets' Apps, in order to develop guidelines for designing mobile contents and Apps to support and promote intergenerational interactions.

Keywords: Intergenerational · Older adults · Grandparents · Children
Mobile · Tablets · Communication · Interaction

1 Introduction

The World is getting old: that's a fact. As reported by [1–3], population aging is a worldwide phenomenon, resulting from decreasing mortality and declining fertility, that will continue to grow. In this way, coexistence between generations, namely between grandparents and grandchildren, is becoming more common and lasting for longer periods of time. The age gap between generations often leads to: (i) age-segregated beliefs, behaviors and communication practices; (ii) the discrediting and waste of each generation knowledge and experiences; and (iii) the lack of reciprocal learning and mutual understanding [4, 5].

Research has shown that the promotion of intergenerational relations and contact is crucial, as a way of countering those age gap's issues and ensure the cognitive, emotional and social wellbeing of both children and older adults [4, 6–8]. Quality

E. Clua et al. (Eds.): ICEC 2018, LNCS 11112, pp. 368–373, 2018.
https://doi.org/10.1007/978-3-319-99426-0_46

intergenerational relations and contact between grandparents and grandchildren, particularly, are of extreme importance, being related with more positive behaviors towards older adults and a more effective transition to adulthood (for grandchildren) and a higher social interaction, satisfaction and mental and physical health (for grandparents) [4, 8, 9].

Studies also suggest that mobile devices and applications (Apps) are particularly appropriated tools to foster intergenerational engagement in playful and educational activities, providing opportunity and facilitating collaboration and cooperation between generations in a range of settings and contexts [10, 11]. By using touch screens and enabling gesture-based interaction, these devices allow to overcome interaction barriers and seem to be best suited for supporting intergenerational engagement that goes beyond the technology, happening in the physical environment [10, 12, 13].

Most research on intergenerational joint media consuming and technology usage has been focused on TV co-viewing by children and parents. More recently, the term Joint Media Engagement (JME) has been coined, extending the concept beyond TV and referring "to spontaneous and designed experiences of people using media together, that can happen anywhere and at any time when there are multiple people interacting together with digital or traditional media" [13]. JME research, however, remains mainly focused on parents and children, rather than on grandparents and grandchildren. In fact, grandparents and grandchildren's intergenerational interactions, generally speaking, are acknowledged as being poorly studied, making informed development of technologies to support them much difficult [14]. We have been conducting research that aims to understand the interactions and communication processes taking place during JME sessions involving grandparents/middle aged (over 55 years old) to older adults, and grandchildren/children (from 5 to 10 years old), in collaborative usage of tablets and tablets' Apps, in order to develop guidelines for designing mobile contents and apps to support and promote intergenerational interactions. This paper, particularly, describes the results of a preliminary study, in which JME sessions between grandchildren/children and grandparents/middle aged to older adults were conducted, along with pre- and post-JME session interviews.

2 Method

The preliminary study was exploratory and non-experimental, aiming to validate data collection instruments and techniques. During the study, two pairs of participants, selected through criterion sampling procedures and by convenience, were interviewed and observed in JME sessions, in which they used a particular tablet App to develop a specific activity proposed by the researcher.

In this way, the session with parental related participants involved a 58 years old grandmother and her 5-year's old granddaughter, building their family tree using the App Notes HD on an iPad Mini. The session with the non-parental participants involved a 65 years old lady and an 8-year-old boy, jointly drawing the older adult as a child and the child as an older adult, using the App NOTEPAD+ on an iPad Mini.

The proposed activities were thought to be potentially promoters of reciprocal learning and enjoyable by both (grand)children and grandparents/older adults.

A total of two interviews were performed to each element of the pairs, one before and the other after JME sessions, in order to collect data from participants, such as demographic data, level of digital literacy, quality of the intergenerational relationship and attitude towards each other. In the post-JME sessions' interviews, questions were introduced to assess the perceived impact of JME sessions in the quality of the intergenerational relationship, on the attitude towards each other and on children and older adults' digital literacy.

The areas of competence and levels of proficiency proposed by DIGCOMP project [15, 16] were used to assess digital literacy of the older participants, understood as the ability to mobilize knowledge, skills and attitudes to critically identify, access, manage, assess and integrate digital resources to build new knowledge and communicate with others, in an effective way and through different formats [15–18]. However, some indicators were added, in order to integrate important skills that were not originally foreseen (e.g., the use of instant messaging services), as well as to incorporate mobile-specific skills (e.g., search for and installing Apps or using geo-location services). In this way, digital literacy indicators were assessed from a set of questions that were gradually and contextually introduced during the pre-JME sessions' interviews, after a brief conversation concerning access to tablets, smartphones and computers. As far as 5 to 10 years old children is concerned, no fully appropriate set of digital literacy's indicators and scales have been found. Therefore, interviews were used to collect as many information as possible concerning what children are able and used to do with mobile devices and computers, considering the same 4 areas of competence used for older adults, and scales are to be deductively developed.

Concerning the quality of intergenerational relationship, indicators were developed based on what the literature suggests to be a well-succeeded relationship: people spend time together; communicate and engage in meaningful and enjoyable activities; participate in each other's life; and, learn reciprocally [4, 5]. All these indicators were surveyed through a set of questions integrated into the pre-JME session' interview script and the definitive scales for the quality of intergenerational relationship are to be deducted from results.

Most of the questions in both interviews' scrips were initiation questions, designed to introduce the topics, trigger the very first ideas about them and that could be posed without any specific order, for example: "Did you enjoy the activity? Did you learn/teach anything? What do you think of grandparents and grandchildren using technology together?". These questions were complemented with development and contextual ones, intended to expand or supplement the initially introduced ideas. Regarding the interviews' scripts, the study aimed to verify the adequacy of initiation questions to trigger the collection of the needed data and the duration of the interviews.

The JME sessions took place in the living rooms of the older participants' homes. Participants were seated in the couch and the researcher was seated near them. Sessions were recorded using a GoPro HERO4. Both sessions began with a description of the activities by the researcher and a brief introduction to the Apps and their main features. During each session, data collection was performed by direct and participant observation, and, whenever possible and/or desirable, participants were questioned in order to build a shared interpretation of the activities and processes taking place. In what concerns this JME sessions, the study aimed to obtain children and older adults' feedback regarding the proposed activities, as well as the assessment of the adequacy of the selected Apps.

3   Results

All the initiation questions posed during the pre-JME session interviews, both to children and older participants proved to be effective in triggering the conversation around the indicators of digital literacy and the quality of intergenerational relationship and attitude toward each other. In the same way, no problems were identified in the post-JME session interviews made to the older participants. Concerning the (grand) children post-JME session interviews, however, some worrying issues were observed. In fact, even though children have demonstrated an understanding of the questions posed, they mostly provided "yes" or "no" answers, or short and poorly elaborated ones. Although it was explained to them that there were no right or wrong answers and that the important thing was to know their opinion, children were reluctant to answer the development questions requesting argumentation.

Regarding the Grandmother/Grandchild JME session, and after the initial introduction by the researcher, grandmother handed the tablet to the granddaughter, who controlled the interaction with it for most of the time, showing reluctance in letting the tablet go or sometimes moving the tablet away, when grandmother tried to interact. In this way, grandmother's role was more related to the management of tasks, suggesting how the activity should progress, helping with the writing and the positioning of elements on the screen. The version of the App NOTE HD used in this session (free version), proved to be extremely unstable. The App crashed a few times, some of which while undoing inadvertent actions and trying to incorporate a child's photo. Other main problems aroused from the fact that, after inserted into the canvas, elements merge with the background and can no longer be individually manipulated. When not overlapping, elements could be resized and repositioned through pinching, spreading, rotating and dragging that slice of the canvas. Also, the App's drawer menu often interfered with content creation process, leading to inadvertent selection of tools.

In the Boy/Older Lady JME session, the researcher's explanation of the activity immediately triggered a conversation about how old the boy thought the Lady was and how he thought he was going to be when he was her age. In this way, the Lady was the first to draw: they went talking, and the lady went drawing, with the tablet resting on her lap. No signs of impatience were observed; on the contrary, the boy watched closely and helped whenever he thought it was necessary. When they both agreed that the drawing of the boy when he was old was finished, they switched roles. The older Lady handed the tablet to the boy and began to tell him what she looked like when she was his age. The Lady told the boy that she could only wear dresses, because, at that time, girls could not wear pants and that led to more talk on the subject and to the exchange of historical knowledge. Throughout the session, they talked about which tools and sub-tools were most appropriate for drawing what they intended and the interaction with the device was often shared. Regarding the App, and although NOTEPAD+ shares with NOTE HD some problems (such as elements merging with background), it proved to be much more stable. The interaction is intuitive, as the interface is very simple. Although some options are hidden, the access is relatively easy and cannot be made inadvertently, as it demands a long-press. The only problem concerned the touch target area, which was too small for the older Lady fingertips.

4 Conclusions

The preliminary study was very important for the validation of data collection protocols and instruments. It was possible to conclude that there is a need to rethink the development questions to ask kids in post JME interviews, since younger children may have difficulties in deepening the introduced themes. Some strategies can include decreasing the child defensiveness by, for example, avoiding open-ended questions beginning with "why" [19], introduce the themes with more age-appropriate vocabulary and sentence structure, use references from the child's personal field of experience, among others.

In what concerns the JME session, the activity proposed to the non-parental related participants proved to be much more interesting than the construction of the family tree, resulting in a more shared content creation process, with more effective collaboration and balanced roles and in a final product that was actually built by the child and the older adult. In this way, and in the main study, the collaborative drawing activity will be proposed to both parental and non-parental related participants and the construction of the family tree will be eliminated.

Regarding the Apps, NOTEPAD+ has proved to be more stable, having a simpler interface and a more intuitive interaction paradigm. Although some of the problems observed during the study could eventually be solved by selecting an App that allow for the use of layers, those are a high-difficulty feature considering the research participants. Therefore, NOTEPAD+ will be the App used in the research future empirical studies. It is expected that these studies' results will allow the outline of a set of recommendations for designing tablets' contents, intended to mediate and support intergenerational interactions.

References

1. World Health Organization: Ageing and Life Course. Facts About Aging (2014). http://goo.gl/hzrQlV
2. United Nations: World Population Ageing 2013. United Nations, Department of Economic and Social Affairs, Population Division. ST/ESA/SER.A/348 (2013). http://goo.gl/wOFHdc
3. European Union: Population Structure and Ageing. Eurostat, Statistics Explained (2014) http://goo.gl/hgbtSw
4. Strom, R.D., Strom, P.S.: Assessment of intergenerational communication and relationships. Educ. Gerontol. 41(1), 41–52 (2014)
5. Harwood, J.: Understanding Communication and Aging: Developing Knowledge and Awareness. SAGE Publications, Inc., Thousand Oaks (2007)
6. Christian, J., Turner, R., Holt, N., Larkin, M., Cotler, J.H.: Does intergenerational contact reduce ageism? When and how contact interventions actually work? J. Arts Humanit. (JAH) 3(1), 1–15 (2014)

7. Pieri, M., Diamantinir, D.: Young people, elderly and ICT. Procedia – Soc. Behav. Sci. **2**(2), 2422–2426 (2010)
8. Soliz, J., Harwood, J.: Perceptions of communication in a family relationship and the reduction of intergroup prejudice. J. Appl. Commun. Res. **31**(4), 320–345 (2003)
9. Hurme, H., Westerback, S., Quadrello, T.: Traditional and new forms of contact between grandparents and grandchildren. J. Intergener. Relat. **8**(3), 264–280 (2010). https://doi.org/10.1080/15350770.2010.498739
10. Gutnick, A., Robb, M., Takeuchi, L., Kotler, J.: Always connected: the new digital media habits of young children. In: The Joan Ganz Cooney Center at Sesame Workshop, New York (2011). http://goo.gl/s4K009
11. Kaplan, M., Sanchez, M., Shelton, C., Bradley, L.: Using technology to connect generations. Penn State University and Generations United, Washington D.C (2013). http://goo.gl/8UzB6g
12. de Castro, M., Ruiz, B., Sánchez-Pena, J., Crespo, A., Iglesias, A., Pajares, J.: Tablets helping elderly and disabled people. In: Bierhoff, I., Nap, H., Rijnen, W., Wichert R. (eds.) Partnerships for Social Innovation in Europe. Proceedings of the AAL Forum 2011, Lecce, pp. 237–244. Drukkerij Coppelmans, Eersel (2011) http://goo.gl/GnRnHm
13. Takeuchi, L., Stevens, R.: The new coviewing: designing for learning through joint media engagement. In: The Joan Ganz Cooney Center at Sesame Workshop, New York (2011) http://goo.gl/cNM74T
14. Davis, H., Vetere, F., Gibbs, M., Francis, P.: Come play with me: designing technologies for intergenerational play. Univ. Access Inf. Soc. **11**(1), 17–29 (2012)
15. Measuring Digital Skills Across the EU: EU Wide Indicators of Digital Competence. European Commission (2014). https://goo.gl/ZZZg4d
16. The Digital Skills Indicator 2015 - Methodological Update Note. European Commission (2015). https://goo.gl/cr2Dlh
17. Borges, J., Oliveira, L.: Competências infocomunicacionais em ambientes digitais. Observatorio **5**(4), 291–326 (2011)
18. Green Paper: Digital Literacy. 21st Century Competencies for Our Age: The Digital Age. The Fundamental Building Blocks of Digital Literacy: From Enhancement to Transformation. UK Government (2015). http://dge.mec.pt/estudos-sobre-tecnologiaseducativas
19. Kanfer, R., Eyberg, S.M., Krahn, G.L.: Interviewing strategies in child assessment. In: Walker, C.E., Roberts, M.C. (eds.) Handbook of Clinical Child Psychology, pp. 95–108. Wiley, New York (1983)

Physical Activity Among Older Adults: A Meta-review of EU-Funded Research Projects

Paula Alexandra Silva[✉]

DigiMedia Research Center, University of Aveiro, Aveiro, Portugal
palexa@gmail.com

Abstract. To keep physically active is key to live a long and healthy life. It is therefore important to invest in research targeting the uptake of physical activity by the ageing population. This paper presents an overview of concluded EU-funded research projects which address the subject of physical activity among older adults. From an initial set of 330 projects, 29 are analyzed in this meta-review that describes the projects, its goals, types of physical activity promoted, and technologies used. Entertainment technologies, in particular exergames, emerge as a frequent approach.

Keywords: Older adults · Physical activity · Entertainment · Active ageing
AAL · CORDIS

1 Introduction

Since the 1960's that global average life expectancy had not had such a fast increase as it did between 2000 and 2016 and, after an increased by 5.5 years, global life expectancy at birth in 2016 was 72.0 years [1]. While the evidence of people living longer marks a significant achievement for humankind, it also poses societies with the challenge of supporting citizens to live a healthier life, if they are to experience both a longer and satisfying extended life spam. Partaking in physical activity and/or exercise training programs can reduce the impacts of aging and contribute to improvements in health and well-being [2, 3]. The importance and benefits of engaging in physical activity for health promotion are numerous and range from improvements in depression [4] to preventing or slowing down disablement due to chronic diseases [5].

International organizations have been working with researchers, governments, and decision makers to ensure that physical activity becomes an important component of the daily life of each citizen. The World Health Organization (WHO) offers global recommendations on physical activity for health [6], where different levels of physical activity are recommended for different age groups. The specific guidelines for people aged 65+ recommend aerobic physical activity, muscle strengthening activities, as well as balance training activities [7]. In particular, per week, older adults should engage in 150 min of moderate-intensity aerobic physical activity or in at least 75 min of vigorous-intensity aerobic physical activity (or equivalent combinations). Aerobic physical activity should be complemented with muscle-strengthening activities,

E. Clua et al. (Eds.): ICEC 2018, LNCS 11112, pp. 374–387, 2018.
https://doi.org/10.1007/978-3-319-99426-0_47

involving major muscle groups, two or more days a week. In addition, it is suggested that older adults engage in physical activity that promotes balance three or more days per week, with this recommendation particularly applying to older adults with poor mobility. Recognizing the limitations imposed by specific health conditions, the WHO underlines that, if under limiting circumstances, older adults should be as physically active as their abilities and conditions allow.

All Europe Union (EU) member states are advised to implement the WHO guidance documents [8]. However, not all EU member states follow those recommendations, with some using instead similar guidelines from the United States Centers for Disease Control and Prevention, or from the Canadian Society for Exercise Physiology, and the American College of Sports Medicine [9].

During the last decade, aging has been part of the priorities in the agenda of the European Commission, with several initiatives targeting active aging and healthy aging. Several research projects have been funded addressing the ageing challenge. This paper presents a review and comparison of projects concerning physical activity and older adults, aiming to understand how the EU has been prioritizing the area and how projects have been addressing the subject. Two main sources of information are used to retrieve relevant projects: (i) The Community Research and Development Information Service (CORDIS) database [5], the primary public repository and portal to disseminate information on all EU-funded research projects, and (ii) The Active and Assistive Living (AAL) Programme Website [6], a funding activity which specifically targets the improvement of life conditions of older adults.

2   Method

The goal of this research was to identify completed EU-funded collaborative research projects, which had encouraged the uptake of physical activity among older adults and aimed at promoting health and well-being, to then determine their characteristics and investigate the approaches taken by such projects to achieve their goals. Besides understanding the extent of the EU efforts in this area, this research wanted to understand if physical activity was an important goal in those projects and if/what specific technologies were being utilized to support physical activity.

In order to identify EU-funded collaborative research projects, this study reviewed two online resources: the CORDIS database [10] and the AAL Website [11]. To determine relevant projects to include in this meta-review, i.e.: projects targeting the uptake of physical activity among older adults with a view promote their health and well-being, inclusion and exclusion criteria were defined. Projects targeting older adults, involving some sort of exercise and/or physical activity, aiming at health and well-being, and which had been concluded would be included. Projects involving only one single European country, or focusing solely on health monitoring aspects, biology studies, or on developing aids (e.g. walking aids) would be excluded.

Building upon these resources and criteria, this research then followed a number of steps (see Fig. 1 for an overview). First, it was necessary to retrieve all potentially interesting projects from the CORDIS database, for which five search strings[1] were used. All projects funded by the AAL programme were deemed interesting, thus no specific search was needed to retrieve relevant projects from this source. Once a pool of projects was created, each project was screened, initially based on its title and short description, and then again, considering the full descriptions available online. In cases where information was insufficient to determine the relevance of the project, a quick search through the project website (if available) was made. Finally, projects, which remained in the data set, were analyzed with a view to addressing the research questions.

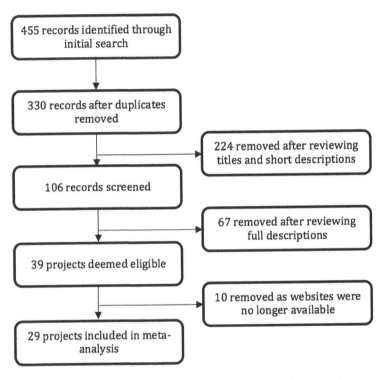

Fig. 1. Overview of the process followed to retrieve relevant projects.

---

[1] Five searches made: 'active' AND 'ageing' AND 'physical' AND 'health' AND 'activity' AND contenttype='project'; 'senior' AND 'exercise' AND contenttype='project'; 'ageing' AND 'health' AND 'exercise' AND contenttype='project'; 'active' AND 'ageing' AND 'exercise' AND contenttype='project'; 'old' AND 'exercise' AND contenttype='project'.

3 Results and Analysis

The initial set of results included 455 records: 170 consisting of all concluded projects listed in the AAL website and 285 retrieved from the CORDIS database. Once repeated records were removed, 160 individual projects remained from the CORDIS database, which resulted in a pool of 330 eligible projects. After reviewing the project's titles and short descriptions, 106 projects remained in the dataset and were further analyzed based on their full descriptions and, whenever needed, also based on their websites. 67 results were excluded at this stage, two of them because they referred to Strategic Research Agendas, and the remaining because they did not meet the inclusion criteria. An extra ten projects were removed because their websites were no longer available and the information displayed in the CORDIS and AAL websites was rendered insufficient to make a proper assessment of the project's approach and activities. Figure 1 presents an overview of the process followed to retrieve the 29 projects identified as relevant and that form the basis for this research. The table in Appendix 1 shortly describes the 29 projects included in this meta-review.

3.1 Characteristics of the Projects Included in the Meta-review

The 29 projects analyzed represent €101 millions of investment, from which €65 millions came from public/EU contribution. Nine different funding programs have funded these projects: seven by FP7-ICT, five by AAL-Call4, three by AAL-Call1, three by AAL-Call2, three by AAL-Call5, three by AAL-Call6, two by FP7-Health, two by CIP, and one by H2020-EU.3.1. On average each of those projects lasted for 35.17 months (Max. 42, Min. 24) and cost an average of €3.5 millions (Max. €7.4 millions, Min €1.4 millions), with and average of €2.2 millions (Max. €5.7 millions, Min. €33.7 thousands) of public contribution. Those projects were more often coordinated by Germany (seven projects), followed by Spain (four projects), the Netherlands (four projects), France (three projects), Italy (three projects), and Switzerland (two projects). Countries such as Austria, Finland, Poland, Denmark, Greece, and Israel coordinated one project each. The remaining countries involved were diverse, often including the participation of more than one partner from the same country. The size of the consortia was also diverse involving on average 8.3 partners (Max. 14, Min. 5).

3.2 Goals, Approaches, and Strategies

All 29 projects included in this meta-review foster the uptake of physical activity among older adults to some extent. The table in Appendix 2 captures the most important aspects analyzed in each of the projects included for review, such as: the goals, types of physical activity, and approaches followed by the projects, namely in terms of technology used and evidence of entertainment-related attributes. These aspects are detailed in the following subsections.

Main Goals of Projects. Into what concerns to the main goals of the projects, from the 29 projects analyzed, 25 have physical activity and/or its promotion as its main goal. However, five of these projects have parallel goals, such as: providing dietary/nutrition advice, promoting cognitive training, and promoting stress management at work. For the remaining four projects, physical activity was a side goal. Projects claimed broader health improvements, from physical to cognitive and social, with most projects aiming to improve more than one of these areas. While nine projects had physical health in the outlook, seven aimed at physical and social health, six at physical and cognitive health, and another seven aimed to improve all three areas. Another aspect investigated was whether the projects were aiming at specific health conditions, for which the analysis concluded that most projects (19) did not aim at any specific condition. The remaining projects were looking into fall prevention (four projects), stress (two projects), chronic conditions, stroke, rehabilitation, loneliness and also malnutrition and cognitive decline.

Type of Physical Activity Encouraged by Projects. When it comes to the type of physical activity promoted, the majority of the projects (20) provided no specific details about the kind of physical activity targeted. The remaining nine projects resorted to different types of activities, with two projects resorting to all three main types of activities listed in the WHO recommendations, as described in Sect. 1. The exercises included ranged from simple chair-based exercises and walking to biking, hiking, gardening and the use of treadmills.

Nature of Technology Used. When analyzing the projects concerning the nature of the solutions they propose to address their goals, it is noteworthy that a significant number (19 out of 29) of the projects resorts to digital technology to achieve their objectives and that those same projects employ some sort of entertainment technology to do so[2]. The most popular approach, employed by 12 projects, is to use games, namely exergames and serious games, to motivate to exercise. Another tendency, although less prevalent, is the use of virtual coaches which is observed in six projects. Several projects offer the possibility of defining personalized programs and of facilitating the exercise to take place in the home of the older person. Yet another commonality among projects is the monitoring of both physical activity and health conditions, as well as the use of both sensor technology and approaches to behavior change.

4 Discussion and Concluding Remarks

The analysis of the projects included in this meta-review shows that entertainment technologies, in particular games in the form of serious games and exergames, are indeed a popular approach among EU-funded collaborative research projects to address physical activity targeting older adults. From the 29 projects analyzed, 19 use some sort of entertainment technology to achieve their goals. It is important to note that this study

---

[2] Appendix 2 presents an overview of the projects included in this meta-review, where the projects that clearly resort to entertainment technologies are indicated in Bold Underline; projects in which this connection is not so clear are indicated in Underline, and projects where this link is not apparent are in plain text. The same table also displays information regarding the goals, types of physical activities, and approaches followed by the projects.

looked only at projects, which have already been concluded. Given the rising interest in games, serious games, exergames, and gamification in recent years, it is likely that the number of projects using technology and entertainment would be even higher in the near future, when ongoing projects would have been completed and thus included in the research.

To correctly interpret the results presented in this study it is important to highlight that conclusions were solely drawn upon the analysis of information which is publicly available online, therefore interpretations may be based on incomplete descriptions. To this adds the fact that a single researcher performed the research and some level of subjectivity should be expected. Furthermore, projects were retrieved from only two sources, so an additional more exhaustive search and inclusive study warrants further investigation and fully fledged conclusions and findings. In the future, it would be interesting to extend the research to the study of the specific characteristics of the entertainment approaches employed and the understanding of the most effective ones.

Appendix 1: Projects Descriptions

Acronym	Project description
GameUP	Sustain mobility of older adults through exergames that include exercises defined by physiotherapists. The system developed by the project has a coach who advises and sets goals for the older person
AIB	Create a process and technologies to covering the full chain of fall risk management, from assessment, to preventive recommendations, care plan, and interventions for fall prevention
FARSEEING	Develop and test a falls management service (for prevention and prediction), together with assessment of exergames to improve strength and balance, thus reducing risk of falls
IS-ACTIVE	To devise a person-centric healthcare solution for older adults with chronic conditions based on miniaturized wireless inertial sensors, which provide distributed motion capture and intelligent recognition of activities
A2E2	A^{2}E^2 aims at breaking sedentary life styles though ambient virtual coaching motivating elderly before, during and after daily activities. A^{2}E^2 allows for systematic interaction and adaptive feedback and selection of tasks
Join-In	Develop a social networking platform for elderly citizens to encourage and support communication and socializing. Solution includes computer game to enhance cognitive abilities, biking exergames, and other video exercises
V2me	Increase integration of older people in the society through the provision of advanced social connectedness and social network services and activities

(continued)

(continued)

Acronym	Project description
iStoppFalls	Develop technologies which can be integrated in daily life practices of older people living at home, and allow for continuous exercise training, reliable fall risk assessment, and appropriate feed-back mechanisms
Long-Lasting Memories	The LLM platform that targets mind, body and fitness through three components: the Physical Training, the Cognitive Training and the Independent Living Component
MOB MOTIVATOR	Motivate older adults to increase physical activity and exercise cognitive skills through an at-home system based on gaming environment that provides a truly innovative and enjoyable approach to healthy living and ageing
PAMAP	PAMAP helps patients at home to perform their rehabilitation exercises by monitoring and providing feedback to patients and their caregivers about level of activity
Rehab@Home	Rehabilitation after stroke at home with serious games in order to create the necessary motivation to continue at home rehabilitation after stroke
SAFEMOVE	The project aims to increase the mobility of the elderly, both at home and on journeys, through encouraging self-confidence in own abilities
V-TIME	V-TIME proposes a unique rehabilitation-like training program that simultaneously targets multiple elements of fall risk and teaches individuals new strategies for fall prevention and maintenance of a healthy lifestyle in a safe and enjoyable manner
DOREMI	To develop a solution for older people to prolong their functional and cognitive capacity by empowering, stimulating and unobtrusively monitoring their daily activities; these are monitored by professionals
BeatHealth	Exploit the link between music and movement for boosting individual performance and enhancing health and wellness
Inspiration	Help older adults live a healthier life and to stay mentally and physically fit. Besides a digital coach, system provides health tips and a daily planner. Recorded activities can be accessed by relatives, friends and caregivers
PERSSILAA	Innovates the way care services are organized. From fragmented, reactive disease management into preventive, personalized services that are offered through local community services and telemedicine technology
Wellbeing	Wellbeing offers a holistic platform, combining physical exercises, workplace ergonomics, nutritional balance, and stress management in order to ensure a healthy life at the workplace
TRAINUTRI	To raise consciousness about self wellness, by developing healthy habits and enabling exchange of knowledge on physical and nutritional healthy habits
ACANTO	To spur older adults into a sustainable and regular level of physical exercise under the guidance and the supervision of their carers
MOTION	Develop an ICT-based service for remote multi-user physical training of seniors at home by specialized coaches

(*continued*)

Acronym	Project description
Fit4Work	A system for self-management (detecting, monitoring and countering) of physical and mental fitness of older workers
ELF@Home	Elderly self-care based on self-check of health conditions and self-fitness at home (∼ personal trainer at home)
Alfred	Develop a mobile, personalized assistant for the elderly, which helps them stay independent, coordinate with carers and foster their social contacts
PhysioDom-HDIM	To guide elder people in their health well-being and independence, providing physical activity and dietary coaching in their own home
Florence	Improve the well-being of elderly (and their caregivers) and efficiency in care through AAL services supported by a general-purpose robot platform
DOSSY	Develop an intelligent outdoors navigation app with high quality route information and basic safety system
Give&Take	Strengthen the quality of life of senior citizens through occupation and social engagement as a key to mental, social and physical fitness. Also, support civic engagement and ability to live independently

Note: The use of entertainment is clear for the project in bold underline, unclear for the projects in bold, and not used by the remaining projects.

Appendix 2: Projects Characteristics

Project acronym	Specific condition?	PA main goal?	Health Improvement	Type of physical activity and specific exercises	Technology use and evidence of entertainment-related attributes
GameUP	No	Yes	Physical	Type of PA: Aerobic, Muscle strengthening and Balance. Walking and exergames for balance, strength, and endurance that track user's progression	System uses games. These link to stepcounter, motion sensors, camera
AIB	Falls prevention	No	Unspecified, general health	Type of PA not specified Games using Kinect with coach who offers exercise guidance and monitors progression of the older person	Games and persuasive technologies build upon the use of Kinect. Solution is tailored to each individual and targets motivation and behavior change

(*continued*)

(*continued*)

Project acronym	Specific condition?	PA main goal?	Health Improvement	Type of physical activity and specific exercises	Technology use and evidence of entertainment-related attributes
FARSEEING	Falls prevention	No	Physical	Type of PA: Muscle strengthening, Balance. Exercises in chairs, knee strengthened shoulder mobility exercise, side hip strengthened etc.	Exergames offer muscle and balance training and are used to motivate older adults to take-up and maintain exercise. Technologies used include: wearable sensors, depth camera, accelerometer, Kinect, GAITRite walkway
IS-ACTIVE	Chronic conditions	Yes	Physical, Social	Type of PA: Aerobic, Muscle strengthening Coaching through games displayed on the TV, prepared with physical therapists collaboration	Persuasive technologies and serious games used to improve feedback and motivation, in combination with wireless sensing, pulse oximeter, tablet, smartphone
A2E2	No	Yes	Physical	Type of PA not specified Not specified. From descriptions seems personalised	3D digital coach with bio-sensors including activity sensors, blood pressure and weight sensors for interaction and adaptive feedback
Join-In	No	Yes	Physical, Social	Type of PA: Aerobic, Muscle strengthening Biking indoor exergame, walking game, video exercises	Exergames used to persuade seniors to increase physical activity through a social and gaming platform accessible via PC, TV and set-top box, or tablet. Walking exergame "AntiqueHunt" uses motion sensors
V2me	Loneliness	Yes	Physical, Cognitive, Social	Not specified	Virtual coach

(*continued*)

(*continued*)

Project acronym	Specific condition?	PA main goal?	Health Improvement	Type of physical activity and specific exercises	Technology use and evidence of entertainment-related attributes
iStoppFalls	Falls prevention	Yes	Physical	Type of PA: Balance. Stepping games, balance	TV and Kinect games with TV
Lona-Lastina Memories	No	Yes	Physical, Cognitive	Type of PA not specified Various games, some of which using a Wii balance board	Exergaming platform to help elderly exercise and maintain physical status and well being via innovative, low-cost ICT platform, e.g. Wii Balance Board
MOB MOTIVATOR	No	Yes	Physical, Cognitive, Social	Not specified	Tablet, multiplayer gaming environment, to increase mobility, cognitive skills, gender equality, and autonomy among older adults, both indoor and outdoor, under supervision of health professionals
PAMAP	No	Yes	Physical	Type of PA: Aerobic, Muscle strengthening and Balance. Walking, hiking, cycling, housework, gardening	Captures almost any type of movement/ activity/ exercise and has a avatar showing how to do exercises that are linked to wearable sensor network, smartphone, kinematics, repetitive limb movements
Rehab@Home	Stroke rehabilitation	Yes	Physical, Social	Type of PA not specified Rehabilitation exercises after stroke with serious games	Smartphones in cameras and control unit to track movement during game to collect data, online feedback from doctors, feedback, goals, achievements, sharing achievements with friends and challenging friends; Kinect

(*continued*)

(continued)

Project acronym	Specific condition?	PA main goal?	Health Improvement	Type of physical activity and specific exercises	Technology use and evidence of entertainment-related attributes
SAFEMOVE	No	Yes	Physical, Cognitive, Social	Type of PA not specified. Seems to include all. Various serious games and monitoring activities	Serious games at home, e.g. golf, games outside, management of health by doctors, engagement, quests, personalised games
V-T1ME	Fall prevention, Parkinson's	Yes	Physical, Cognitive	Type of PA not specified. Treadmill	Virtual Reality treadmill and tracking with Kinect
DOREMI	Nutrition, sedentarism, Cognitive decline	Yes -i-Nutrition, cog training	Physical, Cognitive, Social	Type of PA: Aerobic, Balance. App with serious games and exergames for daily physical activity.	Smart bracelet, smart carpet, tablet, smartphone, stepcounter, social networking, wireless sensor network, activity recognition and contextualization, behavioural pattern analysis
BeatHealth	No	Yes	Physical	Type of PA: Aerobic. Walking and running	App leverages on entrapment and uses music and movement rhythms to promote exercise. Solution uses wearable technologies and sensors
Inspiration	No	Yes	Physical, Cognitive	Type of PA not specified. Seems to include all. Not specified	Digital coach will motivate them to be active every day
PERSSILAA	No	Yes. +Cognition and Nutrition, workplace ergonomics, and stress management	Physical, Cognitive	Not specified	Activity videos and game displayed through a TV. Also offers efficient, reliable, and easy to use services that make use of gamification, and

(continued)

(*continued*)

Project acronym	Specific condition?	PA main goal?	Health Improvement	Type of physical activity and specific exercises	Technology use and evidence of entertainment-related attributes
Wellbeing	Stress	Yes +Nutrition	Physical, Cognitive	Not specified	3D sensor, suggestions for exercises shown as exercises videos or as mini games, combining physical exercise with gaming elements. Games which are able to tackle health related problems in entertaining way
TRAINUTRI	No	Yes +Nutrition	Physical, Social	Type of PA not specified Not specified. There are indications that is personalised	Web and smartphone apps with monitoring of activity, feedback, summaries, setup of objectives, groups, social platform
ACANTO	No	Yes	Physical	Not specified	Robotic walking assistant with brakes that supports in execution of daily activities and require and recommends PA in compelling and rewarding way
MOTION	No	Yes	Physical	Type of PA not specified. Seems to include all Not specified. Coach seems to design personalised activities	The service uses a high level video system allowing four simultaneous training sessions by a coach. When a user subscribes, he receives an all in one PC remotely controlled and sessions can immediately started
Fit4Work	Stress	Yes	Physical, Cognitive	Type of PA not specified. Training participation scheme with exercises	Smartphone and watch like with sensors forming core of personal wellness network, ambient sensors, AAL middleware and cloud services

(*continued*)

(continued)

Project acronym	Specific condition?	PA main goal?	Health Improvement	Type of physical activity and specific exercises	Technology use and evidence of entertainment-related attributes
ELF@Home	No	Yes	Physical	Type of PA not specified Personalized fitness plan offered according to health status and life style. Fitness exercises at home using a TV interface	Wearable activity sensor, biomedical sensors, personalization
Alfred	No	No	Physical, Cognitive, Social	Type of PA not specified Walking, swimming, and app for back pain rehab and serious games to improve physical and cognitive conditions	Robot (virtual butler) used for back pain rehabilitation
PhysioDom-HDIM	No.	Yes +Dietary advice	Physical, Social	Type of PA not specified. Possibly aerobic Not specified but use of pedometer indicates walking	Telemonitoring through medical sensors and TV, podometer, blood pressure sensors
Florence	No	Yes	Physical, Social	Not specified	Robot with wheels, 1.5 m height, screen-based, with no arms. Sensor input based on 2D laser scanner, 3D structured light (Kinect) and camera
DOSSY	No	Yes	Physical, Social.	Type of PA: Aerobic. Hiking.	Localization, navigation and geo-tracking
Give&Take	No	No	Physical, Cognitive, Social	Not specified	Webpage for senior citizens to connect through to local communities and organisations for conversations, sharing, event coordination, etc.

Note: The use of entertainment is clear for the project in bold underline, unclear for the projects in bold, and not used by the remaining projects. PA: physical activity

References

1. WHO—Life expectancy, WHO. http://www.who.int/gho/mortality_burden_disease/life_tables/situation_trends_text/en/. Accessed 07 July 2018
2. Ciolac, E.: Exercise training as a preventive tool for age-related disorders: a brief review. Clinics **68**(5), 710–717 (2013)
3. Chodzko-Zajko, W.J., et al.: Exercise and physical activity for older adults. Med. Sci. Sports Exerc. **41**(7), 1510–1530 (2009)
4. Silveira, H., Moraes, H., Oliveira, N., Coutinho, E.S.F., Laks, J., Deslandes, A.: Physical exercise and clinically depressed patients: a systematic review and meta-analysis. Neuropsychobiology **67**(2), 61–68 (2013)
5. Tak, E., Kuiper, R., Chorus, A., Hopman-Rock, M.: Prevention of onset and progression of basic ADL disability by physical activity in community dwelling older adults: a meta-analysis. Ageing Res. Rev. **12**(1), 329–338 (2013)
6. WHO—Global recommendations on physical activity for health, WHO. http://www.who.int/dietphysicalactivity/factsheet_recommendations/en/. Accessed 05 July 2018
7. WHO—Physical activity and older adults, WHO. http://www.who.int/dietphysicalactivity/factsheet_olderadults/en/. Accessed 10 Apr 2016
8. EU Working Group "Sport and Health": EU Physical Activity Guidelines: Recommended Policy Actions in Support of Health-Enhancing Physical Activity (2008)
9. WHO Regional Office for Europe: Factsheets on Health-enhancing Physical Activity in the 28 European Union Member States of the WHO European Region (2015). http://ec.europa.eu/sport/library/factsheets/eu-wide-overview-methods.pdf. Accessed 11 Apr 2016
10. CORDIS—European Commission. https://cordis.europa.eu/home_en.html. Accessed 05 July 2018
11. Active and Assisted Living Programme—ICT for ageing well. http://www.aal-europe.eu/. Accessed 05 July 2018

Entertainment Computing - A Key for Improving Inclusion and Reducing Gender Gap?

Javier Gomez[1], Letizia Jaccheri[1(✉)], and Jannicke Baalsrud Hauge[2,3]

[1] Department of Computer Science,
Norwegian University of Science and Technology (NTNU), Trondheim, Norway
{javier.escribano,letizia.jaccheri}@ntnu.no
[2] Bremen Institute for Production and Logistics (BIBA), Bremen, Germany
baa@biba.uni-bremen.de
[3] Royal Institute of Technology (KTH), Stockholm, Sweden
jmbh@kth.se

Abstract. Entertainment Computing application areas are increasing day after day. The same way serious games become part of the teaching materials as schools, they can be useful tools to improve inclusion of people with special needs and reduce the gender gap. With this workshop we want to set a discussion space for researchers, designers and practitioners on Entertainment Computing interesting in its application to solve social issues, such as reducing the gender gap, preventing social exclusion of people in risk and promoting the inclusion of people with special needs.

Keywords: Inclusion · Entertainment computing · Gender · Diversity

1 Workshop Objective

In this workshop, we want to invite researchers, designers and practitioners in Entertainment Computing (EC) to discuss why and how the community should improve inclusion of people who do not participate or participate less than mainstream user groups to entertainment computing activities, such as video-games, digital arts or serious games for health or education. These user groups include people with special needs (i.e. people with disabilities or people in risk of social exclusion). Female gamers are a concrete example of people at risk of social exclusion. We want to share best-practice experience of successful initiatives, discuss empirical outcomes and novel designs to build up and strengthen the community of interest in gender and inclusion in EC. Besides building an international community, the workshop aims to identify challenges and opportunities related to gender and inclusion based on presented research and experiences and related to the following questions:

- How can we improve the inclusion of people with special needs by Entertainment Computing? This is, how can we make EC so flexible and adaptable so that it can be used by people with special needs?

© IFIP International Federation for Information Processing 2018
Published by Springer Nature Switzerland AG 2018. All Rights Reserved
E. Clua et al. (Eds.): ICEC 2018, LNCS 11112, pp. 388–391, 2018.
https://doi.org/10.1007/978-3-319-99426-0_48

- How can we arise the position of women in this topic? Traditionally, software is designed by men to men. But female contributions, preferences and approaches should be included, shared and promoted as well.

2 Background

The use of Information and Communication Technologies for promoting involvement of minority group (gender, race…) in specific working fields as well as for inclusion of people with special needs (i.e. people with disabilities, people in risk of social exclusion, elderly people) is growing year after year. According to recent studies, by 2024 the assistive technologies market will surpass $24 billion [1].

Particularly, if we focus on the entertainment computing area, the use of these technologies as tools to promote inclusion are also popular. Examples of that are [2–6], in these studies researchers introduced different video games (Nintendo Wii devices and computer based) to work on different skills and therapies, such as music, sciences, verbal communication and motor abilities.

This process, the inclusion of people with special needs, can be understood as a sequence of stages: diagnosis, education and self-achievement. Many professionals are involved in this process, such as psychologists, teachers or occupational therapists. In the recent years, technologies of support are becoming more and more popular, and results and approaches from fields such as EC can be applied at the different stages.

From a demographic point of view, there is a huge difference in gender between the professionals involved in the process and researchers/developers involved in the design and development of technologies of support. Historically, the professions involved are related to knowledge areas where women have had a dominant position [7–9], while technology has been historically a men dominated area. This arises the motivation of promoting women participation in EC for inclusion. Even though women make up half of the total gaming population, their place and role in gaming culture and industry is not well understood. Research on gender and computer games has been going on since the 1990s [10, 11] and it is still a relevant topic [12, 13].

3 Expected Outcomes

The topics for discussions include, but are not limited to:

1. Theoretical contribution.
2. Pedagogical frameworks for teaching and learning computer game design related to inclusion and gender issues.
3. Specific aspects of play.
4. Examples of games for learning, designed and developed by women.
5. Examples of inclusive game design or processes of inclusive design.

Authors will be asked to submit a 4 pages extended abstract to present their work and they will be invited to present an extended version of their research in a special issue of a journal. As follow up, the workshop organizers will summarize outcomes in a paper, preferably to be published at ICEC 2019 or Entertainment Computing Journal. Through the workshop, we also want to collect a list of relevant literature and successful initiatives to be shared on the workshop's website.

4 Expected Number of Participants

A minimum number of 8 participants and maximum of 20 will be expected.

5 Due Dates

Submission deadline: 24th June
Notifications of acceptance: 6th July
Workshop will be organized as a half day session.

6 Organizers

Javier Gomez is an ERCIM postdoctoral fellow at IDI, NTNU. He obtained his Ph.D. in Computer Science and Telecommunications at the Universidad Autónoma de Madrid, where he held a lecturer position at the Computer Engineering Department. His research interests include mobile assistive technologies for people with cognitive disabilities, inclusive design and technologies for education. As a result of his work, he had published articles in relevant conferences and journals. He had also participated in different projects in collaboration with the public and private sector.

Letizia Jaccheri is Professor of software engineering at IDI and Department Head from 2013 to 2017. Her research interests are in software engineering, computing education, and entertainment computing. Jaccheri has worked in the Italian IT industry for several years, and in academic institutions covering different positions for 25 years, in collaboration with industry and public sector. She is independent director of "Reply S.p.A. She has published over 100 refereed papers in journals, books and archival proceedings. Jaccheri's ongoing research projects include: (a) H2020 SOCRATIC (b) H2020 UMI-Sci-Ed, (c) H2020 Initiate (2018–2019). She has supervised and/or evaluated over 40 young researchers (Ph.D./Postdoc). She has been the general chair of the IFIP International Conference of Entertainment Computing in 2015. She will be co-chair of IDC 2018 and program chair of the European Computer Science Summit of Informatics Europe in 2018. Letizia has worked for many years to recruit and retain female talents in Computer Science from students, to researchers.

Jannicke Baalsrud Hauge is head of the BIBA GamingLAB and works as a senior researcher at Bremer Institut für Produktion und Logistik (BIBA) Bremen, Germany. She is also co-director of GaPSLabs at KTH (Royal institute of Technology); Stockholm, Sweden. She holds a Ph.D. in Engineering from the University of Bremen. In 2015 she also joined KTH (Kungliga Tekniska Högskolan), where she is managing EIT Digital projects (industry driven projects) and research projects funded by the EU.

Besides supervising BSc, Master and Ph.D. students, she is teaching SG application development, re-engineering, decision making and supply chain risk management. Her main topics are on development of SG and simulation applications, development of GBL concepts, Requirements engineering (IT solutions for logistics, CPS and SG), process analysis and business modelling. Jannicke is member of several boards and has authored 200+ papers.

References

1. Coherent Market Insights: Global elderly and disabled assistive devices market, by end user (hospital, home care settings), by device type (medical mobility aids and ambulatory devices, medical furniture and bathroom safety products, hearing aids, vision and reading aids), and by geography - trends and forecast 2014–2024 (2017)
2. Benveniste, S., Jouvelot, P., Pin, B., Péquignot, R.: The MINWii project: renarcissization of patients suffering from Alzheimer's disease through video game-based music therapy. Entertain. Comput. **3**, 111–120 (2012)
3. Marino, M., Gotch, C., Israel, M., Vasquez, E., Basham, J., Becht, K.: UDL in the middle school science classroom: can video games and alternative text heighten engagement and learning for students with learning disabilities? Learn. Disabil. Q. **37**, 87–99 (2013)
4. Navarro-Newball, A., et al.: Talking to Teo: video game supported speech therapy. Entertain. Comput. **5**, 401–412 (2014)
5. Israel, M., Wang, S., Marino, M.: A multilevel analysis of diverse learners playing life science video games: interactions between game content, learning disability status, reading proficiency, and gender. J. Res. Sci. Teach. **53**, 324–345 (2015)
6. Tarakci, D., Ersoz Huseyinsinoglu, B., Tarakci, E., Razak Ozdincler, A.: Effects of Nintendo Wii-Fit®video games on balance in children with mild cerebral palsy. Pediatr. Int. **58**, 1042–1050 (2016)
7. Olos, L., Hoff, E.: Gender ratios in European psychology. Eur. Psychol. **11**, 1–11 (2006)
8. American Psychological Association: Demographics of the US psychology workforce: findings from the American Community Survey (2015)
9. US Bureau of Labor Statistics: Women in the labor force: a databook. US Department of Labor (2017)
10. Jenson, J., Castell, S.: Online games, gender and feminism. In: The International Encyclopedia of Digital Communication and Society (2015)
11. Cassell, J., Jenkins, H.: From Barbie to Mortal Kombat: Gender and Computer Games. MIT Press, Cambridge (2000)
12. Kafai, Y.B., Richard, G.T., Tynes, B.M.: Diversifying Barbie and Mortal Kombat: Intersectional Perspectives and Inclusive Designs in Gaming. ETC Press, Pittsburgh (2016)
13. Giannakos, M.N., Chorianopoulos, K., Jaccheri, L., Chrisochoides, N.: "This game is girly!" Perceived enjoyment and student acceptance of edutainment. In: Göbel, S., Müller, W., Urban, B., Wiemeyer, J. (eds.) Edutainment/GameDays 2012. LNCS, vol. 7516, pp. 89–98. Springer, Heidelberg (2012). https://doi.org/10.1007/978-3-642-33466-5_10

Who Will Be the Leaders in Top Academic Positions in Entertainment Computing?

Letizia Jaccheri[1]([✉]), Soudabeh Khodambashi[1], Katrien De Moor[2], Özlem Özgöbek[1], and Katina Kralevska[2]

[1] Department of Computer Science, NTNU, Trondheim, Norway
[2] Department of Information Security and Communication Technology, NTNU, Trondheim, Norway
{letizia.jaccheri,soudabeh,katrien.demoor,ozlem.ozgobek,katinak}@ntnu.no

Abstract. To address the issue of under-represented women in Entertainment Computing (EC), this paper builds on a set of theoretical references and ongoing projects to propose a set of guidelines that can be used to set up projects to improve inclusion of female and other people at risk of exclusion in top academic positions in STEM and in Entertainment Computing. This set is fourfold, including: 1. Knowledge development phase; 2. A strategy development and implementation process; 3. A push for strategic international networking, deploying mentors closely aligned to the aforementioned strategy; and 4. Sharing the project's findings with the community.

Keywords: Gender equality · Gender balance · Gender imbalance
STEM · Entertainment computing · Mentoring · Internationalization

1 Introduction

Gender balance within STEM (Science, Technology, Engineering and Mathematics) education and research is a well established scientific field [8–11]. Moreover, more women than men drop out of academic STEM careers. This does not only contribute to gender bias in research (sex differences in study design and analysis), but also results in an under-representation of women in leading positions, a loss of talent for society and a lack of diversity in the workplace, each of which presents a potential threat to the search for excellence in research [4,5].

In particular, gender issues in EC have been a hot topic in the last few years. Theoretical references and concrete suggestions have been addressed in [2,3]. For instance, of the twenty-eighth IFIP Technical Committee 14 (Entertainment Computing) National representatives only three are women. This under-representation of women also has implications for research in the field of Entertainment Computing and for the too limited inclusion of a more diverse set of perspectives and approaches, which would allow to reflect the diversity in the society in a better way.

E. Clua et al. (Eds.): ICEC 2018, LNCS 11112, pp. 392–396, 2018.
https://doi.org/10.1007/978-3-319-99426-0_49

Furthermore, even though we here predominantly focus on gender, gender is not the only aspect impacting diversity that needs to be considered. European STEM departments in the broad sense exhibit a strong predominance of men, but also of a strong international profile. This introduces another diversity dimension with both potential gains and challenges in terms of cultural differences. Significant portions of women who study and work in STEM at European universities are international. However, women's social capital is hampered by the fact that women are often excluded from influential international networks [8] (for instance, the earlier example of the IFIP Technical Committee), and that women seem to use the networks in a different way than men - to fulfill social objectives rather than career objectives [10].

Several previous research projects [2,3,10] have - often individually - approached issues of gender bias in STEM employment at different academic and industry levels, but rarely within a comprehensive framework or from a more holistic view (e.g., considering not only gender but also origins and cultural background jointly). Integrating these lessons could create a renewed push for gender equality in STEM and its sub-fields and may potentially be transferable to other diversity traits and characteristics. On the one hand, although improvements have been and continue to be made, there remains a long way to go with regards to increasing the share of top positions occupied by women. The persisting low percentage of women at the student level must be scrutinized in connection to gender imbalance at the professor level. Is a lack of role models at the highest level a contributing factor to women being less likely to be recruited to entry-level research positions and more likely to drop out of academic career pathways? Several studies have looked at the inter-sectional experiences of being a female and a foreigner in an academic context, each reaching conclusions useful to this study but demanding more emphasis on the individual's own perspective [1,7]. The need for more in-depth knowledge of the interaction between international mobility and gender equality in academia is thus great. STEM departments' tendency toward excellent international profiles could be used as a resource for better national and international recruitment of female academics, and better networking between recruits to support each other as they continue their academic journeys.

With the increasing awareness of the gender imbalance, many national and international gender balance projects have started. The international projects and networks, such as ACM Council on Women in Computing[1], IEEE Women in Engineering[2], Grace Hopper Celebration[3], European Center for Women and Technology[4] and European Women in Mathematics[5], provide us a wide perspective on the necessity, sustainability and broad dissemination opportunities of gender balance projects.

---

[1] https://women.acm.org.
[2] http://wie.ieee.org.
[3] http://gracehopper.org.
[4] http://www.ecwt.eu/en/home.
[5] www.europeanwomeninmaths.org.

Our work is guided by two objectives: sustain participation of girls of diverse backgrounds and raising awareness for intersectionality of gender with other dimensions such as race and class among researchers).

2   Guidelines

Based on these local initiatives, best practices and related work, we propose a framework consisting of four main guidelines that can be integrated into projects or initiatives aimed at improving the gender balance in top academic positions in STEM. We advocate a holistic view of gender representation in STEM all the way from the level of student to that of professor, and one in which internationalization is used consistently as both a lens through which to view participant's experiences and as a resource to help overcome the disadvantages of gender bias and working abroad. These four pillars (knowledge, a strategy development process, international networking and mentoring and knowledge sharing) can be considered as essential elements to incorporate in strategic initiatives that aim to foster a better gender balance and that may be transferable/applicable to imbalance and threats to diversity linked to other variables (e.g., class, ethnicity, social-cultural background).

Guideline 1 - Knowledge Integration. Many projects, local initiatives and measures exist to overcome the gender inequality in academia, but their impact may remain limited if not integrated into a more holistic knowledge base. In an initial phase it is therefore of crucial importance to gather and integrate insights from previous and ongoing projects: what can we learn from these (e.g., (un)successful measures)? What are main challenges and how/at which level should they be addressed? Developing such a knowledge base - as an essential foundation for strategy development - thus means gaining a more thorough understanding of relevant broad issues and theories, gathering ideas for action, evaluating experiences with the implementation of different types of measures.

Guideline 2 - Strategy Development (Targeting Cultural and Structural Management Changes). This activity involves initiating and building up a long-term strategic process to develop good measures to improve equality and diversity as represented by academic recruitment and appointment. A potential approach to this strategic development process is that two groups across departments work together in a common strategy-development process. One strategy process research group consists of men and women in academic positions. The second group consists of faculty management. Diversification issues and internationalization are important for both groups, but may be managed in different ways. An essential question here is therefore how to manage processes in academia with a focus on gender balance? Strategy process research group should run throughout the project period, in a participant-centered and iterative way. By implementing a strategy to gather and share knowledge, applied reflections and practical measures over time, there is a potential to affect cultural conditions - not just for those who are directly involved, but at the level of institutions as a whole.

Guideline 3 - International Networking and Mentoring. A large proportion of female STEM students and employees at European institutions have a foreign background, and many institutional activities are internationally directed, with international partners and the possibility of international recruitment. A third guideline is therefore to set up a dedicated networking and mentoring program to recruit, retain and lift up female (inter)national employees to the next level. Several international studies have shown that academic mentoring is experienced as beneficial for both mentors and mentees and that it can be an important career development instrument [6].

Senior faculty members and a pool of adjunct professors from Industry and from International Universities could be assigned to assist with mentoring, career guidance and international networking for employees in the various categories. The institution as a whole can play an important role here by encouraging and incentivizing the development of a mentoring culture. It can also contribute with the development of a set of best practices for academic mentoring, with for instance clear descriptions on the roles and responsibilities of mentor and mentee, organization of networking events for mentors and mentees, sharing of experiences and best practices with academic mentoring, etc.

Guideline 4 - Sharing. An important target group for the dissemination of the results will be the faculty staff of departments directly involved in the investigation. More broadly, the resulting findings and suggestions may be adapted for audiences at STEM departments that exhibit a similarly skewed diversity balance in occupation of top-level positions. Finally, the findings and recommendations of the project will be conveyed nationally (through blog, social media, articles and other dissemination activities) and internationally (through participation in international conferences and networking activities, especially those with a front-and-centre focus on gender).

3   Conclusions and Future Work

In order to improve balance of gender and other dimensions such as race and class among researchers in STEM fields in general and EC in particular, it is important to increase the percentage of women and people with diverse race and class background in academic positions. We have proposed a set of guidelines based on a four pillars cycle. We have started to implemented these guidelines in the WeLead project at NTNU and we are in the process of establishing a follow up project which will systematically implement them. Further, monitoring and evaluation of implementation can provide more insights about the four pillars which can benefit researchers for reusing the results. Our future work can benefit from creating a clear connection between the local, National, and International networks (with focus on the the EC community) and will explore in more detail how the general guidelines and their results could be transferred and applied to imbalance linked to other diversity dimensions.

Acknowledgements. This work was partially supported by the WeLead program at NTNU.

References

1. Acker, J.: Helpful men and feminist support: more than double strangeness. Gender, Work Organ. **15**(3), 288–293 (2008)
2. Jaccheri, L., Wang, A.I., Ask, K., Petersen, S.A., Brend, K.: Women and Computer Games (Workshops and Tutorials). In: Munekata, N., Kunita, I., Hoshino, J. (eds.) Entertainment Computing - ICEC 2017 Part 9, vol. 10507, pp. 507–509. Springer, Heidelberg (2017)
3. Katterfeldt, E.S., Dittert, N., Schelhowe, H., Kafai, Y.B., Jaccheri, L., Escribano, J.G.: Sustaining girls' participation in stem, gaming and making. In: Proceedings of the 17th ACM Conference on Interaction Design and Children, IDC 2018, pp. 713–719 (2018)
4. Lagesen, V.A.: The woman problem in computer science. In: Encyclopedia of Gender and Information Technology, pp. 1216–1222. IGI Global (2006)
5. Lagesen, V.A.: The strength of numbers: strategies to include women into computer science. Soc. Stud. Sci. **37**(1), 67–92 (2007)
6. Mathews, P.: Academic mentoring: enhancing the use of scarce resources. Educ. Manag. Adm. **31**(3), 313–334 (2003)
7. Maximova-Mentzoni, T., Egeland, C., Askvik, T., Drange, I., Støren, L.A.: Being a foreigner is no advantage (2016)
8. Metz, I., Tharenou, P.: Women's career advancement: the relative contribution of human and social capital. Group Organ. Manag. **26**(3), 312–342 (2001)
9. Pappas, I.O., Aalberg, T., Giannakos, M.N., Jaccheri, L., Mikalef, P., Sindre, G.: Gender differences in computer science education: lessons learnt from an empirical study at NTNU. In: NIK (2016)
10. Terjesen, S.: Senior women managers' transition to entrepreneurship: leveraging embedded career capital. Career Dev. Int. **10**(3), 246–259 (2005)
11. Zuckerman, H.E., Cole, J.R., Bruer, J.T.: The outer circle: women in the scientific community. In: This Volume is Based on Papers from Four Symposia Held at Stanford University, CA, from 1983 to 1986. WW Norton & Co. (1991)

Serious Games in Special Education.
A Practitioner's Experience Review

Guadalupe Montero[1] and Javier Gomez[2(✉)]

[1] C.E.E. Alenta, new social way, Madrid, Spain
lupemontero@alenta.org
[2] Norwegian University of Science and Technology, Trondheim, Norway
javier.escribano@ntnu.no

Abstract. In this paper we present the experiences with serious games used in a special education school. Particularly, these games provides a engagement context to motivate students with special needs and introduce them basic instrumental skills. The paper summarises the intervention blocks and the games used for each. Finally, an outline of the key ideas to do a successful intervention are presented.

Keywords: Special education · Serious games · Edutainment

1 Introduction

The inclusion of technologies in the classroom is becoming a popular practice in both mainstream and special education [1]. The adapted learning features and the use of playful or fun resources make these technologies very attractive for students, increasing acceptance rates [3].

In order to provide an effective learning experience in the special education context, accessibility and simple interfaces are critical aspects for practitioners to decide whether to use a technology approach with children and teenagers with different capabilities. Moreover, in order to be successful, technologies should be included as routines and be arranged as the rest of activities in the class: setup times and spaces, select the most appropriate applications and customised them according to the intervention objectives for each student.

Another factor that may determine the selection of any software or hardware is based on the methodology employed in the educational intervention. For example, in the case of people with autism spectrum disorders (ASD), it is mandatory that the applications or games follow a learning without error approach, have a clear start and end and fit to the interests of the user.

These pre-requisites may help to a successful intervention. However not all the applications or games need to be specifically designed for people with disabilities, but they need to be customised enough to fit them.

© IFIP International Federation for Information Processing 2018
Published by Springer Nature Switzerland AG 2018. All Rights Reserved
E. Clua et al. (Eds.): ICEC 2018, LNCS 11112, pp. 397–401, 2018.
https://doi.org/10.1007/978-3-319-99426-0_50

In this paper we present the experience of including serious games in a special education school. Particularly, we present the set of most used applications in the school to help in the development of instrumental skills, such as reading, writing and calculus.

2   Experiences in the Classroom

Alenta is a special education school located in Madrid (Spain)[1]. In this school they teach students with cognitive disabilities and/or Autism Spectrum Disorders during the whole education process, as they are from 6 to 21 years old. Regarding the academic curriculum, they address all the necessary skills to provide an independent and autonomous life, raging from reading, behaviour control and motor skills for the youngest students, to job-related and social skills for the adults.

For the last 5 years the school staff have been including iPads as part of their in-class materials. These devices are very motivating for the students and, thanks to the increasing number of applications available, they open new possibilities to work on many specific areas. These technological resources are widely used in the classes in the following three intervention blocks:

1. Augmentative and Alternative Communication (AAC).
2. Support to improve personal autonomy.
3. Resources for school learning.

Serious games are more present in the third block, as they support and contribute to different class activities. Particularly, they are used in the development of instrumental abilities, cognitive competences as well as other academic abilities related to the curriculum.

Basic instrumental skills are related to the acquisition of reading and writing skills as well as calculus. These areas have a great impact on people's lives and therefore, they are included as mandatory contents in the curriculum. The set of serious games that are actually in use in the Alenta is summarise in Tables 1 (reading), 2 (writing) and 3 (calculus).

In general, all the games used in class share a set of features: they focus clearly in an area to work, provide a wide variety of customisation options and adapt to user progress. Regarding the price, some of them are free but they usually include in-app purchases or ads. This last option is the worst in terms of design, as these ads are very flashy and animated, and may distract the user.

---

[1] https://www.alenta.org/.

Table 1. Summary of reading games

Name	Description	Suitability
Leo con Lula [2]	Based on global reading methods. The player has to connect words (and syllables in higher levels) to words	Full configuration options and adaptation. Personalised vocabulary
Leo con Grin	Focus on reading and writing (including motricity). Look and feel like game and based on levels	Two levels of difficulty. Very motivating thanks to the prizes and diplomas reward system
Ya leo	A reading comprehension game. Starts at the sentence level, moving on to short texts. Includes linking activities and short questions about the texts	The difficult increases as the player advances. Caregiver portal to manage users, etc.

Table 2. Summary of writing games

Name	Description	Suitability
Dexteria Jr.	A game to stimulate fine psychomotor abilities. It trains movements such as press or drag and drop	Includes different levels to train the different movements, by means of attractive and animated interfaces
See me draw	A digital version of the "link the dots" game. The user has to draw the connections between the different numbers in order to reveal the hidden figure. Visual - motor abilities are deeply trained	Very simple and attractive, with a visual support to guide the user
Trazos y letras	Game that improves manual dexterity by a set of activities (increasing difficulty) with strong visual and audio motivational feedback	It includes different levels of assistance and feedback. Player can draw with a finger or a stylus

Table 3. Summary of calculus games

Name	Description	Suitability
Cuenta con tus dedos	The game makes use of the multitouch capabilities of the device to "count with the fingers"	Provides visual support (hands drawings) and a natural way to learn
Números especiales	A set of six activities to work with the numbers (1 to 20) in different ways	It is highly customizable to fit users' needs, either in terms of interface and gameplay (rewards)
Math Fight	Multiplayer game in which the two players compete to solve the operation as fast as possible	Contextualises mental calculus and social interaction

3   Conclusions

Applications and serious games are becoming a powerful tools in schools. Many students, and particularly those with special needs, benefit from their interactive and multimedia capabilities that current developments offer, as well as the motivational effect and ease of use.

XXI century teachers must know the different resources available and value their suitability regarding the special needs of the students. This way, the learning process could be more functional and the inclusion of technology in class may be successful. Thus, the student should be the main point of focus. Her objectives and needs should be defined in order to select the most appropriate games. However, the teacher support should be also present, providing any additional resource and valuations to guarantee the comprehension and proper use of the resources.

From Alenta teaching staff's experience, this is the only way for serious games to success, teaching abilities (in an engagement way) that will allow students to keep on building and acquire knowledge at a higher level.

Besides the review and the experience summarised in this paper, a systematic review of the applications in the market should be carried out, in order to extract the most common features as guidelines to design new serious games for special education students.

Acknowledgements. This work has been carried out during the ternue of an ERCIM "Alain Bensoussan" fellow.

References

1. Dicheva, D., Dichev, C., Agre, G., Angelova, G.: Gamification in education: a systematic mapping study. J. Educ. Technol. Soc. **18**(3), 75 (2015)
2. Gomez, J., Jaccheri, L., Torrado, J.C., Montoro, G.: Leo con lula, introducing global reading methods to children with ASD. In: Proceedings of the 17th ACM Conference on Interaction Design and Children, pp. 420–426. ACM (2018)
3. Korn, O., Funk, M., Schmidt, A.: Design approaches for the gamification of production environments: a study focusing on acceptance. In: Proceedings of the 8th ACM International Conference on PErvasive Technologies Related to Assistive Environments, p. 6. ACM (2015)

Perspectives on Accessibility in Digital Games

Jannicke Baalsrud Hauge[1,2(✉)], Neil Judd[3], Ioana Andreea Stefan[4],
and Antoniu Stefan[4]

[1] BIBA – Bremer Institut für Produktion und Logistik GmbH,
Hochschulring 20, 28359 Bremen, Germany
baa@biba.uni-bremen.de
[2] Royal Institute of Technology, Kvarnbergagatan 12, 15136 Södertälje, Sweden
jmbh@kth.se
[3] Hands Free Computing Ltd, The Courtyard, Holmsted Farm, Staplefield Road,
Cuckfield, West Sussex RH17 5JF, UK
Neil.judd@hands-free.co.uk
[4] Advanced Technology Systems,
Str. Tineretului Nr 1., 130029 Targoviste, Romania
{ioana.stefan,antoniu.stefan}@ats.com.ro

Abstract. Gaming technologies provides new ways of learning, but even though the new technologies have unique opportunities to support different individual needs, most games are not designed for people with impairments. This is specifically a problem in a learning context in mixed groups as well as for teachers with impairments who have to use the technology for preparing their classes. This paper focuses on how to make games for learning more accessible for students and teachers with different impairments.

Keywords: Accessibility · Educational serious games · Serious game design
Customisation · Choices · Alternatives

1 Introduction

Gaming technologies enable the construction of new learning environments that foster collaboration skills and creativity [1]. Pervasive Learning represents such new way of learning and it is defined as "learning at the speed of need through formal, informal and social learning modalities" [2]. The BEACONING project builds upon playful pervasive experiences and provides game-based, personalized learning paths. The focus is on STEM and on problem-based learning [3]. The BEACONING platform will provide the users (teachers, students) a set of applications that enable teachers to author gamified, customized lesson paths and students to play them. It is a clear goal of the project to make the Beaconing platform more accessible for people (students, teachers) with special needs, so that all students and teachers can use the same applications in a classroom setting. In general, the project looks at the following categories of impairment: (a) visual impairment (b) hear impairment (c) mobility impairment and (d) cognitive impairment.

In this workshop paper, due to limited space, we have focussed on explaining how we can achieve better accessibility for visual impairments of games used for STEM education. The solution will be shown and discussed during the workshop.

E. Clua et al. (Eds.): ICEC 2018, LNCS 11112, pp. 402–406, 2018.
https://doi.org/10.1007/978-3-319-99426-0_51

2   Accessibility and the Beaconing Project

Digital accessibility implies making an application or a website, with all of its data and functions, available for all users, regardless of how they interact with it, or what difficulties they might have (e.g. visual, hearing, or physical impairments; cognitive disabilities) [4]. Since the digital world is a visual medium, most of the efforts of making digital tools and websites accessible fall under visual accessibility. For example, for those with visual impairments there are a variety of alternate ways to access websites: use a screen reader that reads the content of a page back to them; override the default styling on a website, allowing individuals to use colours that are higher contracts or fonts that are easier to read; or increase the font size until it is legible. There are, however, several common issues that can occur when implementing such solutions: poorly structured html; images with no meaningful alt text; features that require vision; repetitive items that cannot be skipped; poorly structured forms.

Unlike websites and applications, digital games represent very dynamic environments, with specific gameplay, which make it difficult to implement such generic accessibility solutions, even in the case of basic HTLM-based games. In digital games, whether entertainment or educational ones, since the gameplay usually unfolds at a fast pace, it is difficult or even impossible to use a screen reader. Therefore, customized solutions are required. To fundament such customized solutions, it has become critical to identify best practices and provide recommendations, in order to support the large-scale implementation of accessibility features in digital educational games. There are many studies that discuss the pros and cons of using gaming as a mean of rehabilitation [5–8]. However, they focus mostly on the potential that gaming systems to support rehabilitation (e.g. enable personalized treatment recommendations) and less on the accessibility features that these games provide.

The BEACONING platform will enable the personalization of the learning units to the specific student's needs, including adaption for impairment. A gamificd lesson path has in addition to a normal lesson plan several gamified elements, called minigames. Currently we have different forms of geo-location games, quests and quizzes as an integrated part of the lessons path. These minigames needs to be adapted and changed for the different students, and for this a authoring tool has been developed [5]. Also the graphical user interfaces for students and teachers need to be adaptable to sight impaired users. A more detailed description of the gamified lesson plan as well as different types of mini-games that are integrated can be found in [9, 10]. How this is realized is described in the next section.

3   Making Games Accessible

The focus in this paper is on visual impairment. In addition to dyslexia, it is a common impairment also for teachers, which is quite easy to address, if thought of at an early stage [11].

The core features in Fig. 1 and their implications for the accessibility are described below [11].

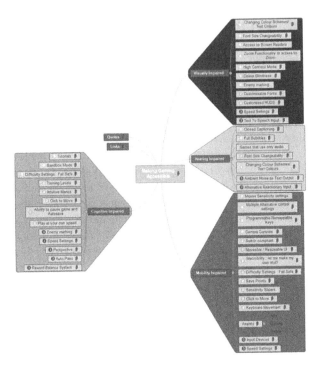

Fig. 1. How to make games accessible

- **Changing Colour Schemes/Text Colours** ❶

  For those that have difficulty distinguishing between colors, often referred to as color deficiency, the ability to change the color of text associated with a particular function improves overall gameplay. Note that color deficiency differs from color blindness. Color-deficient people can still see a certain color, but they cannot distinguish shades of the color, red vs maroon, or lime green vs dark green.

- **Font Size Changeability** ❶

  Gamers with visual difficulties including those that are legally or almost totally blind can still participate in many games, but reading text in the subtitles, directions/instructions and chats can be frustrating if the size of the text is just barely too small to read.

- **High Contrast Mode** ❶

  For First Person Shooters, it is extremely important that the target reticle uses colors that are easy to distinguish from the other environmental elements in the game. In situations where both the enemy and reticle are red, the user is unable to identify between the target and the sight, leaving no way to tell where the actual target is aiming.

- **Colour Blindness** ❶

  Ideally all games should have colorblind options that can be enabled to compensate for a variety of color deficiency issues. The most prevalent of these disorders is the inability to tell the difference between the colors green and red. This is most often avoided by providing a way to change the color green to blue when indicating friendly information such as group mates or health bars.

- **Text To Speech Input** ❸

  Another top rated accessibility option would be to include the ability of the game to read the text on the screen and repeat it in audio form. Many programs now do this for users on the web, but it has not yet made its way into the game universe. The successful implementation of this feature would be to offer text-to-speech on user created text, like guild chat, or other chats created by end users.

4   Implementation of These Features in the BEACONING Platform

Beaconing draws upon this research to provide an experience not like any other with innovative tools for users with disabilities. These include a fully interactive toolbar interface called Accessabar which makes content accessible to users of all differing disabilities. A unique Accessibility Profile Wizard compliments this tool. Built into the account set up interfaces, the user will perform several simple exercises to determine whether certain accessibility features are needed in the main interface. Settings can be saved for individual user profiles. There will be differentiation but continuity in design between different user type portals, and the ability to switch in and out of roles within a single sign in account. For example, this allows a teacher to not only view and assign lesson plans within the Beaconing portal but also edit and configure them within the Authoring tool itself. Bring in the gamification, immersive gaming environment, compelling mini games and learning content of the highest quality and this is what sets Beaconing apart from the rest [12].

The figure below shows the some of the features already implemented in the Beaconing platform in order to increase the accessibility for sight impaired. Much more information is to be found in [6] which is the public deliverable. The toolbar is discreet and is accessed via the Accessibility link in the main navigation panel. A series of tools are presented in the toolbar all with their unique features which can manipulate text and objects on the screen making them accessible to all (Fig. 2).

Fig. 2. Accessabar

5   Conclusions and Next Steps

This article has reported on work carried out on doing educational games and learning platforms used for STEM education more accessible for students and teachers with sight impairments. It has presented design considerations for improving the accessibility and introduced the concept of Accessabar as a suitable solution. The platform is under evaluation before large scale pilots will start in autumn 2018.

Acknowledgement. The work presented herein is partially funded under the Horizon 2020 Framework Program of the European Union, BEACONING – Grant Agreement 68676.

References

1. Ştefan, A., et al.: Approaches to reengineering digital games. In: Proceedings of the ASME 2016, IDETC/CIE 2016 (2016)
2. Pontefract, D.: Learning by Osmosis (2013). http://www.danpontefract.com/learning-by-osmosis/
3. BEACONING Cons: D3.3 Learning Environment System Specification (2017)
4. Cunningham, K.: Accessibility Handbook. O'Reilly Media Inc., Newton (2012)
5. Gauthier, L.V., Richter, T.A., George, L.C., Schubauer, K.M.: Gaming for the brain: video gaming to rehabilitate the upper extremity after stroke. In: Krames, E.S., Peckham, P.H., Rezai, A.R. (eds.) Neuromodulation, 2nd edn, pp. 465–476. Academic Press, Cambridge (2018)
6. Jurdi, S., Montaner, J., Garcia-Sanjuan, F., Jaen, J., Nacher, V.: A systematic review of game technologies for pediatric patients. Comput. Biol. Med. **97**, 89–112 (2018). ISSN 0010-4825
7. Lv, Z., Esteve, C., Chirivella, J., Gagliardo, P.: Serious game based personalized healthcare system for dysphonia rehabilitation. Pervasive Mob. Comput. **41**, 504–519 (2017). ISSN 1574-1192
8. Tannous, H., Istrate, D., Tho, M.H.B., Dao, T.T.: Serious game and functional rehabilitation for the lower limbs. Eur. Res. Telemed./La Recherche Européenne en Télémédecine **5**(2), 65–69 (2016)
9. Hauge, J.M.B., Stefan, I.A., Stefan, A.: Exploring pervasive entertainment games to construct learning paths. In: Munekata, N., Kunita, I., Hoshino, J. (eds.) ICEC 2017. LNCS, vol. 10507, pp. 196–201. Springer, Cham (2017). https://doi.org/10.1007/978-3-319-66715-7_21
10. Hauge, J.B., et al.: Exploring context-aware activities to enhance the learning experience. In: Dias, J., Santos, Pedro A., Veltkamp, Remco C. (eds.) GALA 2017. LNCS, vol. 10653, pp. 238–247. Springer, Cham (2017). https://doi.org/10.1007/978-3-319-71940-5_22
11. Barlet, M.C., Spohn, S.D., Drumgoole, A., Mason, J.T.: A practical guide to game accessibility, vol. 1.4 (2012)
12. Judd, N., et al.: D4.5 Beaconing Platform GUI (2018). https://zenodo.org/record/1256522#.WzlP3tUzapo

Adult Perception of Gender-Based Toys and Their Influence on Girls' Careers in STEM

Serena Lee-Cultura$^{(\boxtimes)}$, Katerina Mangaroska$^{(\boxtimes)}$, and Kshitij Sharma$^{(\boxtimes)}$

Norwegian University of Science and Technology, 7034 Trondheim, Norway
{serena.leecultura,katerina.mangaroska,kshitij.sharma}@ntnu.no

Abstract. STEM and Computer Science (CS) in general, are perceived as masculine disciplines; a dangerous fallacy that discourages girls to show interest in the domain. However, companies are moving towards designing toys to attract and educate girls about science. Consequently, this study tries to explore adults perception of gender packaged toys (e.g. Barbie) and their intervention potential for engaging more girls in CS. Results show that old Barbie used to convey shallow ideals to young girls, placing emphasis on fashion and appearance. On the other hand, the new Barbie themed programming course has the power to attract more girls into CS.

Keywords: Gender · Toys · Computer Science · STEM

1 Introduction

The perception of Computer Science (CS) as an inherently masculine discipline is a dangerously ubiquitous fallacy that discourages female's sense of ambient belonging and subsequent interest in the domain [2,3]. From an early age, the majority of girls are diverted from STEM associated disciplines and future careers [4]. One such example can be found in implicit messages delivered by gender stereotyped toys [12]. Moreover, Barbie is of notable concern as her negative ability to promote self objectification and sexualization of self, reduces the breadth of future career options a young girl can envision for herself [12].

However, there have been societal protest over toys like Teen Talk Barbie, who enthusiastically claims that "math is tough", and the more recent "I can be a computer engineer" Barbie book, in which she infects her laptop with a virus, and laughs at her lack of ability to find quick and clever ways to overcome difficulties. This same Barbie depends on her male friends to program a game on her behalf, underlining the societal stereotype about female lack in ingenious ways to handle science [7]. Cheryan et al. argue that to strengthen female interest in CS and engineering, the focus should be to diversify the existing stereotypes to be more representative of an inclusive culture [2]. In an effort to synchronize with the changing academic and societal mindset, companies are moving towards designing toys to attract and educate girls about science.

E. Clua et al. (Eds.): ICEC 2018, LNCS 11112, pp. 407–410, 2018.
https://doi.org/10.1007/978-3-319-99426-0_52

Consequently, the aim of this study is to examine the perceptions of gender packaged toys and their intervention potential for increasing female engagement in STEM, in particular CS education, perceived from an adult frame of reference. Participants consisted of 12 adults, 6 females and 6 males, who watched a video from Barbie's vlog. In the vlog, Barbie encourages viewers to follow their dreams and pursue education and professions in science by discussing a highly accomplished female scientist and engineer. Results showed that although Barbie's vlog was positively accepted by all participants, female and male perspectives regarding a Barbie themed programming curriculum as tool to attract young girls into CS professions differed largely; women supported the idea (5/6), while male opinions were split (3/6).

2   Background

Past research has emphasized the role of early childhood education (ECE) in building the foundation for gender-based behavior and academic preferences that encourage children to undertake a particular learning path [13]. As mentioned in Sherman and Zurbrigge's work, "children build cognitive schemas for understanding their world and learn early that gender is a critically important lens for organizing information and influencing behaviour" [12]. Moreover, the process of gender role socialization through which children learn to abide by culturally prescribed norms, is stimulated by playing with gender-oriented toys. As a result, children learn about "gender differences" and "gender-appropriate" behaviors, which collectively represent a serious issue by increasing the gender gap in future education and professions [4,9]. For example, studies show that while girls are often given toys associated with domestic or mothering activities, boys are typically provided toys that encourage exploration, invention, or assembly behaviors [1,6]. Consequently, these studies observed differences among genders in cognitive processing and problem-solving strategies [11].

Broadly speaking, toy differentiation with respect to gender, reinforces the cultural ideals demonstrated via media; in particular, a girl's role in society and societal expectations of her appearance and behaviour [12]. One such example is Barbie. According to McKnight, Barbie sends cultural messages and defines expectations that are potentially damaging for girls developing self-concepts [8]. Furthermore, results from one study indicated that the girls who played with Barbie identified a significantly reduced number of future career opportunities for themselves relative to the occupation possibilities they considered for boys when compared to the Mrs Potato Head control group [12]. In contrast to aforementioned studies, recent years have birthed a new era of toys and technologies purposed to interest young girls in STEM related concepts. One such example is GoldieBlox; a doll exclusively marketed to young girls, purposed to promote female engagement with engineering concepts [5,10]. Consequently, the main objective of our study is to develop a deeper understanding how adults perceive gender packaged toys and to consider the use of gender packaged toys as a successful intervention technique for attracting more girls into STEM related fields over time.

3   Case Study Set up

During spring 2018, an experiment was performed at a contrived computer lab setting at Anonymous University with 12 CS PhD students (6 females and 6 males). The mean age of the participants was 31 years (Std. Dev. = 4.96 years). Upon arrival in the laboratory, the participants signed an informed consent form and filled in a pre-questionnaire regarding their attitudes towards gender-based toys. Then, the participants were required to watch a 2 min Barbie vlog video, titled "You Can Be Anything or Everything!". After watching the video, the participants were asked to complete a post-questionnaire about their attitudes towards gender-based toys. As previously mentioned, the aim of the study was to examine adults perceptions of gender packaged toys and their intervention potential for engaging more girls in STEM education, in particular, CS education.

4   Discussion and Future Directions

The pre-questionnaire revealed that initially none of the participants viewed Barbie to be a good female role model. However, during the 80s and 90s, the Barbie franchise was primarily focused on the doll itself and lacked motivational online content. Considering this precursory image of Barbie, female participants described Barbie as conveying shallow ideals to young girls, placing emphasis on fashion and appearance (specifically being "slim" and "beautiful"), and defining female success through attainment of men. Male participants supported the same perspective, underlining that Barbie teaches girls to be pretty, stylish, wear make-up and be constantly happy. In addition, both male and female participants agreed that Barbie also teaches young boys that girls should dress nicely, be clean, and beautiful. However, despite initial attitudes opposing Barbie as a female role model, the "You Can Be Anything or Everything!" video was positively accepted by all participants, especially females, who described it as "inspiring", "impressive and useful". Half of the female and male participants improved their attitude towards Barbie's impact as a female role model (this includes going from negative to positive, neutral to positive, or negative to neutral).

Building upon this, another interesting finding showed that although prior to watching the video only a third of the female participants (and none of the male participants) indicated that Barbie demonstrated the potential to encourage girls into CS through positive gender association, after watching the video, 80% of female participants (and 50% of the male participants) agreed that a Barbie themed programming course had the power to attract more girls into CS. This demonstrates that participants support Cheryan et al. recommendation to diversify the perception of computer scientist to attract more girls into CS [2]. Moreover, it shows support extending on research claiming that toys can be used to influence career choice [4] and that children program and create games based on their favorite toys, stories or movies characters. Finally, it is worth mentioning that two of the male participants said that to get girls into CS we need societal transformation that will bring children and adults together into making change that will have a positive and long-term impact.

In summary, the study demonstrates potential for further exploration of adults attitudes towards gender-based toys and technique for attracting more girls into STEM related fields, specifically CS. In future studies, we plan to use EEG, eye-tracking and wristbands to gather insights into the emotional state of the participants. Furthermore, we also plan to repeat the study on children to investigate their attitudes towards gender-based toys and the new incarnation of Barbie.

References

1. Bradbard, M.R.: Sex differences in adults' gifts and children's toy requests at christmas. Psychol. Rep. **56**(3), 969–970 (1985)
2. Cheryan, S., Master, A., Meltzoff, A.N.: Cultural stereotypes as gatekeepers: increasing girls' interest in computer science and engineering by diversifying stereotypes. Front. Psychol. **6**, 49 (2015)
3. Cheryan, S., Plaut, V.C., Davies, P.G., Steele, C.M.: Ambient belonging: how stereotypical cues impact gender participation in computer science. J. Personal. Soc. Psychol. **97**(6), 1045 (2009)
4. Cooper, S.E., Robinson, D.A.: Childhood play activities of women and men entering engineering and science careers. Sch. Couns. **36**(5), 338–342 (1989)
5. Coyle, E.: Influences on children's play with a STEM toy: interactions among children, parents, and gender-based marketing. Ph.D. thesis, Pennsylvania State University (2015)
6. Fagot, B.I.: Sex differences in toddlers' behavior and parental reaction. Dev. Psychol. **10**(4), 554 (1974)
7. Godwin-Jones, R.: Emerging technologies the evolving roles of language teachers: trained coders, local researchers, global citizens. Lang. Learn. Technol. **19**(1), 10–22 (2015)
8. McKnight, L.: Still in the LEGO (LEGOS) room: female teachers designing curriculum around girls' popular culture for the coeducational classroom in Australia. Gend. Educ. **27**(7), 909–927 (2015)
9. Miller, C.L.: Qualitative differences among gender-stereotyped toys: implications for cognitive and social development in girls and boys. Sex Roles **16**(9–10), 473–487 (1987)
10. Mueller, U.: Advancing Developmental Science: Philosophy, Theory, and Method. Taylor & Francis, Abingdon (2017)
11. Rubin, K.H.: The social and cognitive value of preschool toys and activities. Can. J. Behav. Sci./Revue Canadienne des Sciences du Comportement **9**(4), 382 (1977)
12. Sherman, A.M., Zurbriggen, E.L.: "Boys can be anything": effect of Barbie play on girls' career cognitions. Sex Roles **70**(5–6), 195–208 (2014)
13. Welsh, M.E., Miller, F.G., Kooken, J., Chafouleas, S.M., McCoach, D.B.: The kindergarten transition: behavioral trajectories in the first formal year of school. J. Res. Child. Educ. **30**(4), 456–473 (2016)

Author Index

Printed in the United States
By Bookmasters